Lecture Notes in Computer Sci

Commenced Publication in 1973
Founding and Former Series Editors:
Gerhard Goos, Juris Hartmanis, and Jan van Leeuwen.

Ingemar J. Cox   Ton Kalker
Heung-Kyu Lee (Eds.)

Digital
Watermarking

Third International Workshop, IWDW 2004
Seoul, South Korea, October 30 - November 1, 2004
Revised Selected Papers

 Springer

Volume Editors

Ingemar J. Cox
University College London
Department of Computer Science &
Department of Electronic and Electrical Engineering, UK
E-mail: ingemar@ieee.org

Ton Kalker
Hewlett-Packard Lab.
Multimedia Communications & Networking Department
1501 Page Mill Road, Palo Alto, CA 94305, USA
E-mail: Ton.Kalker@hp.com

Heung-Kyu Lee
KAIST, Department of EECS
373-1 Gusong-Dong, Yusong-Gu, Daejon, South Korea, 305-701
E-mail: hklee@mmc.kaist.ac.kr

Library of Congress Control Number: 2005921087

CR Subject Classification (1998): K.4.1, K.6.5, H.5.1, D.4.6, E.3, E.4, F.2.2, H.3, I.4

ISSN 0302-9743
ISBN 3-540-24839-0 Springer Berlin Heidelberg New York

Springer is a part of Springer Science+Business Media

springeronline.com

© Springer-Verlag Berlin Heidelberg 2005
Printed in Germany

Typesetting: Camera-ready by author, data conversion by Scientific Publishing Services, Chennai, India
Printed on acid-free paper   SPIN: 11392385   06/3142   5 4 3 2 1 0

Preface

We are happy to present to you the proceedings of the 3rd International Workshop on Digital Watermarking, IWDW 2004. Since its modern reappearance in the academic community in the early 1990s, great progress has been made in understanding both the capabilities and the weaknesses of digital watermarking.

On the theoretical side, we all are now well aware of the fact that digital watermarking is best viewed as a form of communication using side information. In the case of digital watermarking the side information in question is the document to be watermarked. This insight has led to a better understanding of the limits of the capacity and robustness of digital watermarking algorithms. It has also led to new and improved watermarking algorithms, both in terms of capacity and imperceptibility. Similarly, the role of human perception, and models thereof, has been greatly enhanced in the study and design of digital watermarking algorithms and systems.

On the practical side, applications of watermarking are not yet abundant. The original euphoria on the role of digital watermarking in copy protection and copyright protection has not resulted in widespread use in practical systems. With hindsight, a number of reasons can be given for this lack of practical applications.

We now know that watermark imperceptibility cannot be equated to watermark security. An information signal that cannot be perceived by the human sensory system is not necessarily undetectable to well-designed software and hardware systems. The existence of watermark readers bears proof of this observation. Designing watermarking methods that are robust to intentional and targeted attacks has turned out to be an extremely difficult task. Improved watermarking methods face more intelligent attacks. More intelligent attacks face improved watermarking methods. This cycle of improved attacks and counterattacks is still ongoing, and we do not foresee it ending soon.

It was the goal of IWDW 2004 to update the scientific and content-owner communities on the state of the art in digital watermarking. To that end, more than 60 submissions to IWDW 2004 were carefully reviewed, with at least three reviewers each. Emphasizing high quality and the state of the art, fewer than 50% of the submitted papers were selected for oral presentation. The topics that were addressed in the accepted papers cover all the relevant aspects of digital watermarking: theoreticals modeling, robustness, capacity, imperceptibility and the human perceptual system, security and attacks, steganography, methods, and watermarking systems. Every effort was made to give the authors the best possible podium to present their findings.

We hope that you enjoy the workshop proceedings and find it an inspiration for your future research.

October 2004

Ingemar J. Cox
Ton Kalker
Heung Kyu Lee

Organization

General Chair

P.J. Lee (POSTECH, South Korea)

Program Committee Co-chairs

Ingemar J. Cox (UCL, UK)
Ton Kalker (Philips, The Netherlands)
Heung-Kyu Lee (KAIST, South Korea)

Program Committee

Mauro Barni (U. of Florence, Italy)
Jana Dittman (Otto-von-Guericke U., Germany)
Jean-Luc Dugelay (Eurecom, France)
Jessica Friedrich (SUNY Binghamton, USA)
Teddy Furon (UCL, UK)
Stefan Katzenbeiser (Vienna U. of Tech., Austria)
Inald Lagendijk (Delft U. of Tech., Netherlands)
Benoit Macq (UCL, UK)
Nasir Memon (Polytechnic U., NY, USA)
Matt Miller (NEC, USA)
Pierre Moulin (U. of Illinois, USA)
Fernando Perez (U. of Vigo, Spain)
Ioannis Pitas (U. of Thessaloniki, Greece)
Sviatoslav Voloshynovsky (U. of Geneva, Switzerland)
Min Wu (U. of Maryland, USA)
Jiwu Huang (Zhongshan U., China)
Mohan Kankanhalli (NUS, Singapore)
K. Sakurai (Kyushu U., Japan)
Yun-Qing Shi (New Jersey Inst. of Tech., USA)
Yong-Man Ro (ICU, South Korea)
Hyung-Joong Kim (KangWon National University, South Korea)
Kivanc Mihcak (Microsoft, USA)

Organizing Committee Chair

Choong-Hoon Lee (KAIST, South Korea)

Table of Contents

Session III: Authentication and Stego

Session IV: Cryptography

Session V: Methods

Reversible Data Hiding

Yun Q. Shi

Department of Electrical and Computer Engineering,
New Jersey Institute of Technology,
Newark, NJ 07102, USA
shi@njit.edu

Abstract. Reversible data hiding, in which the stago-media can be reversed to the original cover media exactly, has attracted increasing interests from the data hiding community. In this study, the existing reversible data hiding algorithms, including some newest schemes, have been classified into three categories: 1) Those developed for fragile authentication; 2) Those developed for achieving high data embedding capacity; 3) Those developed for semi-fragile authentication. In each category, some prominent representatives are selected. The principles, merits, drawbacks and applications of these algorithms are analyzed and addressed.

1 Introduction

Digital watermarking, often referred to as data hiding, has recently been proposed as a promising technique for information assurance. Owing to data hiding, however, some permanent distortion may occur and hence the original cover medium may not be able to be reversed exactly even after the hidden data have been extracted out. Following the classification of data compression algorithms, this type of data hiding algorithms can be referred to as *lossy* data hiding. It can be shown that most of the data hiding algorithms reported in the literature are lossy. Here, let us examine three major classes of data hiding algorithm. With the most popularly utilized spread-spectrum watermarking techniques, either in DCT domain [1] or block 8x8 DCT domain [2], *round-off* error and/or *truncation* error may take place during data embedding. As a result, there is no way to reverse the stago-media back to the original without distortion. For the least significant bit-plane (LSB) embedding methods, the bits in the LSB are substituted by the data to be embedded and the bit-replacement is *not memorized*. Consequently, the LSB method is not reversible. With the third group of frequently used watermarking techniques, called quantization index modulation (QIM) [3], *quantization* error renders lossy data hiding.

In applications, such as in law enforcement, medical image systems, it is desired to be bale to reverse the stego-media back to the original cover media for legal consideration. In remote sensing and military imaging, high accuracy is required. In some scientific research, experimental data are expensive to be achieved. Under these circumstances, the reversibility of the original media is desired. The data hiding schemes satisfying this requirement can be referred to as *lossless*. The terms of *reversible*, or *invertible* also used frequently. We choose to use reversible in this paper.

I.J. Cox et al. (Eds.): IWDW 2004, LNCS 3304, pp. 1–12, 2005.

In Section 2, we classify the reversible data hiding techniques that have appeared in the literature over the past several years into three different categories. In each category, the most prominent representatives are selected and the principles, merits, drawbacks and applications of these algorithms are analyzed in Sections 3, 4, and 5, respectively. Conclusions are drawn in Section 6.

2 Classification of Reversible Data Hiding Algorithms

The following list contains, to our knowledge, most of reversible data hiding algorithms published in the literature. The list is not expected to be completed as the research in this area continues to make vigorous progress. These algorithms can be classified into three categories: 1st, those for fragile authentication, 2nd, those for high embedding capacity, and 3rd, those for semi-fragile authentication. Among each category, one or two prominent algorithms are selected as representative. Their fundamental idea and scheme to achieve reversibility, and their performance are discussed in the following sections.

1. Barton's U.S. Patent 5,646,997 (97)   (1st)

2. Honsinger et al.'s US Patent 6,278,791 B1 (01)   (1st)

3. Fridrich et al.'s method (SPIE01)   (1st)

4. de Vleeschouwer et al.'s method (MMSP01)   (3rd)

5. Goljan et al.'s method (IHW01)   (2nd)

6. Xuan et al.'s method (MMSP02)   (2nd)

7. Ni et al.'s method (ISCAS03)   (2nd)

8. Celik et al.'s method (ICIP02)   (2nd)

9. Tian's method (CSVT03)   (2nd)

10. Yang et al.'s method (SPIE04)   (2nd)

11. Thodi & Rodríguez's method (SWSIAI04)   (2nd)

12. Ni et al.'s method (ICME04)   (3rd)

13. Zou et al.'s method (MMSP04)   (3rd)

14. Xuan et al.'s method (MMSP04)   (2nd)

15. Xuan et al.'s method (IWDW04)   (2nd)

3 Those for Fragile Authentication

The first several reversible data hiding algorithms developed at the early stage belong to this category. Since fragile authentication does not need much data to be embedded in a cover medium, the embedding capacity in this category is not large, normally between 1k to 2k bits. For a typical 512×512 gray scale image, this capacity is equivalent to a data hiding rate from 0.0038 bits per pixel (bpp) to 0.0076 bpp.

In this category, we choose Honsinger et al.'s patent in 2001 [5] as its representative. It describes in detail a reversible data hiding technique used for fragile authentication. Their method is carried out in the image spatial domain by using modulo-256 addition. In the embedding, $Iw = (I + W)$ mod 256, where Iw denotes the marked image, I an original image, W is the payload derived from the hash function of the original image. In the authentication side, the payload W can be extracted from the marked image by subtracting the payload from the marked image, thus reversibly recovering the original image. By using modulo-256 addition, the issue of over/underflow is avoided. Here, by over/underflow, it is meant that grayscale values either exceeding its upper bound (*overflow*) or its lower bound (*underflow*). For instance, for an 8-bit gray image, its gray scale ranges from 0 to 255. The overflow refers to grayscale exceeds 255, while the underflow refers to below 0. It is clear that either case will destroy reversibility. Therefore this issue is often a critical issue in reversible data hiding. Using modulo-256 addition can avoid over/underflow on the one hand. On the other hand, however, the stego-image may suffer from the salt-and-pepper noise during possible grayscale flipping over between 0 and 255 in either direction due to the operation of modulo-256 addition. The effect caused by salt-and-pepper noise will become clear when we discuss an algorithm also using modulo-256 addition in the third category.

4 Those for High Data Embedding Capacity

All the reversible data hiding techniques in the first category aim at fragile authentication, instead of hiding large amount data. As a result, the amount of hidden data is rather limited and may not be suitable for applications such as covert communications and medical data systems. Hence, Goljan et al. [10] presented a first reversible data hiding technique, referred to as R-S scheme, which is suitable for the purpose of having high data embedding capacity. Later, a difference expansion scheme was developed by Tian [15], which has greatly advanced the performance of reversible data hiding in terms of data embedding capacity versus PSNR of marked images with respect to original images. Recently, some integer wavelet transform based reversible data hiding schemes have been developed by Xuan et al. [16,17], which have demonstrated superior performance over that reported in [15]. These representative schemes are presented in this section.

4.1 R-S Scheme

The mechanism of this scheme is described as follows. The pixels in an image are grouped into non-overlapped blocks, each consisting of a number of adjacent pixels. For instance, it could be a horizontal block consisting of four consecutive pixels. A discrimination function that can capture the smoothness of the groups is established to classify the blocks into three different categories, Regular, Singular and Unusable. An invertible operation F can be applied to groups. That is, it can map a block from one category to another as $F(R)=S$, $F(S)=R$, and $F(U)=U$. It is invertible since applying it to a block twice produces the original block. This invertible operation is hence called *flipping F*. An example of the invertible operation *F* can be the permutation between 0 and 1, 2 and 3, 3 and 4, and so on. This is equivalent to flipping the least significant bit (LSB). Another example is the permutation between 0 and 2, 1 and 3, 4 and 6, and so on, i.e., flipping the second LSB. Apparently, the *strength* of the latter flipping is stronger than the former. The principle to achieve reversible data embedding lies in that there is a bias between the number of regular blocks and that of singular blocks for most of images. This is equivalent to say that there is a redundancy and some space can be created by lossless compression. Together with some proper bookkeeping scheme, one can achieve reversibility.

The proposed algorithm first scan a cover image block-by-block, resulting in a so-called *RS*-vector formed by representing, say, an *R*-block by binary 1 and an *S*-block by binary 0 with the *U* groups simply skipped. Then the algorithm losslessly compresses this *RS*-vector – as an overhead for bookkeeping usage in reconstruction of the original image late. By assigning binary 1 and 0 to *R* and *S* blocks, respectively, one bit can be embedded into each *R* or *S* block. If the bit to-be-embedded does match the type of a block under consideration, the flipping operation *F* is applied to the block to obtain a match. The actual embedded data consist of the overhead and the watermark signal (pure payload). In data extraction, the algorithm scans the marked image in the same manner as in the data embedding. From the resultant *RS*-vector, the embedded data can be extracted. The overhead portion will be used to reconstruct the original image, while the remaining portion is the payload.

While it is novel and successful in reversible data hiding with a large embedding capacity, the amount of data that can be hidden by this technique is still not large enough for some applications such as covert communications. From what is reported in [10], the estimated embedding capacity ranges from 0.022 bpp to 0.17 bpp when the embedding strength is six and the PSNR of the marked image versus the original image is about 36.06 dB. Note that the embedding strength six is rather high and there are some block artifacts in the marked image generated with this embedding strength. On the one hand, this embedding capacity is much higher than that in the first category discussed in the previous subsection. On the other hand, however, it may be not high enough for some applications. This limited embedding capacity is expected because each block can at most embed one bit, *U* blocks cannot accommodate data, and the overhead is necessary for reconstruction of the original image. Another problem with this method is that when the embedding strength increases, the embedding capacity will increase, at the same time the visual quality will drop. Often, block artifacts will take place at this circumstance, thus causing visual quality of marked image to decrease.

4.2 Difference Expansion Scheme

Tian presented a promising high capacity reversible data embedding algorithm in [15]. In the algorithm, two techniques are employed, i.e., difference expansion and generalized least significant bit embedding, to achieve a very high embedding capacity, while keep the distortion low. The main idea of this technique is described below. For a pair of pixel values x and y, the algorithm first computes the integer average l

and difference h of x and y, where $h = x - y$. Then h is shifted to the left-hand size by one bit and the to-be-embedded bit b is appended into the LSB. This is equivalent to $h' = 2 \times h + b$, where h' denotes the expanded difference, which explains the term of Difference Expansion. Finally the new x and y, denoted by x' and y', respectively, are calculated based on the new difference values h' and the original integer average value l. In this way, the stego-image is obtained. To avoid over/underflow, the algorithm only embeds data into the pixel pairs that shall not lead to over/underflow. Therefore, a two-dimensional binary bookkeeping image is losslessly compressed and embedded as overhead.

Note that the above-mentioned relationship between the pair of integers x and y versus the pair of integers l and h is implemented in the following manner.

$$l = \lfloor 0.5 \times (x + y) \rfloor \qquad x = l + \lfloor 0.5 \times (h + 1) \rfloor$$
$$h = x - y \qquad y = l - \lfloor 0.5 \times h \rfloor \qquad (1)$$

where the floor operation is utilized. According to integer Haar transform, it is reversible between these two integer pairs. Apparently, the reversible transformation between integers avoids round-off error. This together with the bookkeeping data mentioned above guaranteed reversibility.

It has been reported in [15] that the embedding capacity achieved by the difference expansion method is much higher than that achieved by [10]. This does not come with surprise since intuitively each pair of pixels can possibly embed one bit, while only each block of pixels can possibly embed one bit.

4.3 Integer Wavelet Transform Based Schemes

Xuan et al. proposed three high capacity reversible data hiding algorithms based on integer wavelet transform (IWT) [11, 16, 18]. These three algorithms have three features in common. The first is that they are all implemented in the IWT domain. Consideration is as follows. IWT as a WT is known to be able to decorrelate signal well in the transformation domain. Its feature consists with that of our human vision system (HVS). WT can be implemented efficiently by using lifting scheme. IWT can further ensure the reversible forward wavelet transform and inverse wavelet transform. For these reasons, IWT have been used in JPEG2000 for lossless compression. It is shown in Xuan et al.'s algorithms that IWT plays an important role in reversible data hiding. The second feature is that these algorithms all contain a preprocessing stage, histogram modification, in order to prevent overflow and underflow. That is, an efficient scheme has been developed to shrink the histogram towards the center, leaving two ends empty. Consequently, the perturbation caused by modification of selected IWT coefficients will not cause overflow and underflow. For reversibility, the histogram modification parameters need to be embedded as overhead. Because of the efficiency of the modification scheme [12], the overhead is not heavy. The third feature is that all of three algorithms embed data in IWT coefficients of high frequency subbands. This is because the modification of coefficients in these subbands will be imperceptible if the magnitude of the modification is not large.

The first algorithm [11, 12] losslessly compresses some selected middle bit-planes of IWT coefficients in high frequency subbands to create space to hide data. Since the bias between binary 1 and 0 in the bit-planes of IWT high frequency coefficients becomes much larger than that in the spatial domain, this method achieves rather higher embedding capacity than [7], that is the counterpart of this algorithm in spatial domain.

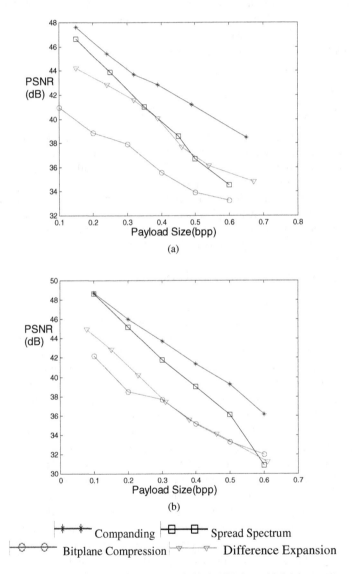

(a)

(b)

Fig. 1. Comparison results on Lena (left) and Barbara (right) images

The second algorithm [16] uses spread spectrum method to hide data in IWT coefficients in high frequency subbands. Pseudo bits are used to indicate those coefficients that are not selected for data embedding, thus saving overhead data. As a result, this method is more efficient than the bit-plane compression scheme, described above.

The third method [18] uses companding technique for data embedding, which was inspired by [17]. Based on the study of statistical distribution of IWT coefficients in high frequency subbands, a piecewise linear companding function is designed.

The performance of these three algorithms, applied to two typical test images: Lena and Baboon, are shown in Figure 1 in terms of data embedding capacity versus PSNR. It is clear that the IWT-based companding algorithm performs best. This can be explained from an investigation on the amount of magnitude that the selected IWT high frequency coefficients have been changed and how many coefficients are required to embed one bit during the data embedding by these three algorithms. It can be shown that the companding algorithm causes the least amount of changes in the selected IWT coefficients among the three algorithms, followed by the spread-spectrum algorithm, while both the spread-spectrum and companding algorithms can embed almost one bit into one IWT high frequency coefficient. Note that both IWT-based companding and spread-spectrum algorithms have outperformed the difference expansion algorithm, discussed above in this section.

It is noticed that more and more advanced algorithms in this category are being and to be developed. One recent example is shown in [24]

5 Those for Semi-fragile Authentication

For multimedia, content-based authentication makes more sense than representation-based authentication. This is because the former, often called semi-fragile authentication, allows some incidental modification, say, compression within a reasonable extent, while the latter, called fragile authentication, does not allow any alteration occurred to stego-media, including compression. For instance, when an image goes through JPEG compression with a high quality factor, the content of this image is considered unchanged from the common sense. Hence, it makes sense to claim this compressed image as authentic. For the purpose of semi-fragile authentication, we need reversible data hiding algorithms that are robust to compression, maybe called semi-fragile reversible data hiding or robust reversible data hiding. This can be further illustrated by the following scenario. In a newly proposed JPEG2000 image authentication framework [19], both fragile and semi-fragile authentications are included. Within the semi-fragile authentication, both cases of lossy and lossless compressions are considered. In this framework, some features corresponding to an image below a pre-specified compression ratio are first identified. By "corresponding" it is meant that these features will remain as long as the compression applied to the image is below this pre-specified compression ratio. The digital signature of these features is reversibly embedded into the image. Then in the verification stage, if the marked image has not been changed at all, the hidden signature can be extracted and the original image can be recovered. The matching between the extracted signature and the signature generated from the reconstructed (*left-over*) image renders the image authentic. If the marked image has been compressed with a compression ratio below the pre-specified one, the original image cannot be recovered due to the lossy compression applied, but the hidden signature can still be recovered without error and verify the compressed image as authentic. Obviously, if the marked image goes through a compression with the compression ratio higher than the pre-specified ratio will render the image un-authentic. Any malicious attack will render the attacked image non-authentic owing to the resultant dismatch between the extracted signature and the signature generated from the received image after the hidden data extraction. A robust lossless data hiding algorithm is indeed necessary for this framework. In general, robust lossless data hiding can be utilized in lossy environment.

5.1 Patchwork-Based Scheme Using Modulo-256 Addition

De Vleeschouwer et al. [20] proposed a reversible data hiding algorithm based on patchwork theory [21], which has certain robustness against JPEG lossy compression. This is the only existing robust reversible data hiding algorithm against JPEG compression. In this algorithm, each hidden bit is associated with a group of pixels, e.g., a block in an image. Each group is pseudo-randomly divided into two subsets of equal number of pixels, let's call them Zones A and B. The histogram of each zone is mapped into a circle in the following way. That is, each point on the circle is indexed by the corresponding luminance, and the number of pixels assuming the luminance will be the weight of the point. One can then determine the *mass* center of each zone. It is observed that in the most cases the vectors pointing from the circle center to the mass center of Zones A and B are *close* (almost equal) to each other because the pixels of Zone A and Zone B are highly correlated for most of images. Considering a group, rotating these two vectors in two opposite directions by a small quantity, say, rotating the vector of Zone A counter-clockwise and rotating the vector of Zone B clockwise allows for embedding binary 1, while rotating the vector of Zone A clockwise, and the vector of Zone B counter-clockwise embeds a binary 0. As to the pixel values, rotation of the vector corresponds to a shift in luminance. In data extraction, the angles of the mass center vectors of both Zone A and Zone B versus the horizontal direction are first calculated, and the difference between these two angles are then determined. A positive difference represents a binary 1, while the negative a binary 0.

One major element of this algorithm is that that it is based on the patchwork theory. That is, within each zone, the mass center vector's orientation is determined by all the pixels within this zone. Consequently, the algorithm is robust to image compression to certain extent. Another major element of this algorithm lies in that it uses modulo-256 addition to avoid overflow and underflow, thus achieving reversibility. Consequently, however, as pointed out in Section 3, this algorithm will suffer from the salt-and-pepper noise. One example from our extensive investigation is presented in Figures 2. In the stego-medical image, the severe salt-and-pepper noise is clear. The PSNR of stego-image versus the original image is below 10 dB when 476 information bits are embedded into this 512x512 image. Not only for medical image, the salt-and-pepper noise may be severe for color images as well. We have applied this algorithm to eight JPEG2000 test color images. There are four among the eight images that suffer from severe salt-and-pepper noise, while the other four some less severe salt-and-pepper noise. The PSNR can be as low as less than 20 dB when severe noise exists when 1412 information bits are embedded into a color image of 1536x1920x24.

From the above investigation, it can be concluded that all reversible data hiding algorithms based on modulo-256 addition to avoid overflow and underflow, say, in [5] and [20] cannot be applied to many real applications, and hence should be avoided.

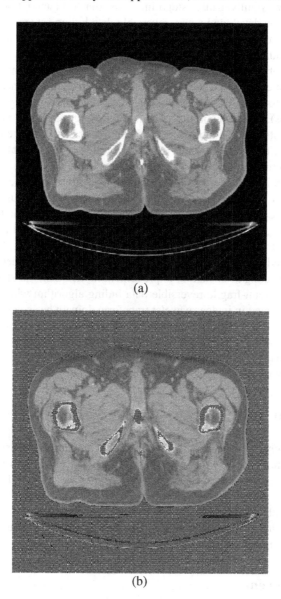

(a)

(b)

Fig. 2. (a) Original medical image, (b) Stego-image with severe salt-and-pepper noise. 746 information bits are embedded into the image of 512x512 with a PSNR of the stego-image versus the original image lower than 10 dB

5.2 Patchwork-Based Scheme Without Using Modulo-256 Addition

Realizing that modulo-256 addition, though can prevent overflow and underflow and hence achieve reversibility, causes stego-images suffer from annoying salt-and-pepper noise, Ni et al. have developed a new reversible data hiding scheme that does not use modulo-256 addition [22]. It is based on the patchwork theory to achieve the semi-fragility in data hiding. Specifically, it identifies a statistical quantity within a block of pixels which is robust to minor alteration of pixel values within the block, and manipulates it to embed a bit into the block. Together with additional measures including error correction coding and permutation, it thus achieves semi-fragility (or in other words, robustness). The reversibility is gained by using a novel strategy in data embedding. That is, it classifies a block of pixels into four different categories according to the distribution of pixel grayscale values within the block. For blocks in different categories, a different embedding strategy is used.

This novel semi-fragile reversible data hiding algorithm has achieved superior performance over the semi-fragile reversible data hiding algorithm using modulo-256 addition. It was reported in [22] that their method has been applied to all of eight medical test images, including that shown in Figure 2 (a), to embed the same amount of data (746 information bits in the images of 512x512). In all of eight stego-images, there is no salt-and-pepper noise at all. The PSNR of all of eight medical images are above 40 dB, indicating a substantial improvement in the quality of stego-images.

Another novel semi-fragile reversible data hiding algorithm with the similar idea as in [22] implemented in integer wavelet transform domain has been reported in [23]. Some special measures have been taken to avoid overflow and underflow.

These two algorithms have been utilized in a unified framework of authentication of JPEG2000 images. The framework has been included into the Security Part of JPEG2000 (known as JPSEC), CD 1.0 in April 2004 [19].

6 Conclusion

This article presents an investigation on the development of the existing reversible data hiding techniques. These techniques are classified into three different categories. The principles, merits and drawbacks of each category are discussed. It is shown that the reversible data hiding opens a new door to link two groups of data: cover media data and to-be-embedded data. This will find wide applications in information assurance such as authentication, secure medical data system, and intellectual property protection to name a few.

Acknowledgement

The work has been supported in part by the Digital Data Embedding Technologies group of the Air Force Research Laboratory, Rome Research Site, Information Directorate, Rome NY, under contract F30602-03-1-0264. The U.S. Government is authorized to reproduce and distribute reprints for Governmental purposes notwithstanding any copyright notation there on. The views and conclusions contained herein are those of the authors and should not be interpreted as necessarily representing the official policies, either expressed or implied, of Air Force Research Laboratory, or the·U.S. Government. It has also been supported in part by New Jersey Commission of Science and Technology via New Jersey Center of Wireless Network and Internet Security (NJWINS).

References

1. I. J. Cox, J. Kilian, T. Leighton, and T. Shamoon, "Secure spread spectrum watermarking for multimedia," in *IEEE Trans. on Image Processing*, vol. 6. No. 12, pp. 1673-1687, Dec. 1997.
2. J. Huang and Y. Q. Shi, "An adaptive image watermarking scheme based on   visual masking," *Electronics Letters*, 34 (8), pp. 748-750, 1998.
3. B. Chen, G. W. Wornell, "Quantization index modulation: a class of provably good methods for digital watermarking and information embedding," *IEEE Transaction on Information Theory*, vol. 47, no. 4, pp. 1423-1443, May 2001.
4. J. M. Barton, "Method and apparatus for embedding authentication information within digital data," U.S. Patent 5,646,997, 1997.
5. C. W. Honsinger, P. Jones, M. Rabbani, and J. C. Stoffel, "Lossless recovery of an original image containing embedded data," US Patent: 6,278,791, 2001.
6. R. C. Gonzalez and R. E. Woods, *Digital Image Processing*, Upper Saddle River, NJ: Prentice Hall, 2001.
7. J. Fridrich, M. Goljan and R. Du, "Invertible authentication," *Proc. SPIE, Security and Watermarking of Multimedia Contents*, pp. 197-208, San Jose, CA, January 2001.
8. J. Fridrich, M. Goljan and R. Du, "Invertible Authentication Watermark for JPEG Images," *Proc. IEEE ITCC 2001,* Las Vegas, Nevada, pp. 223-27, April 2001.
9. J. Fridrich, Rui Du, Lossless "Authentication of MPEG-2 Video," *Proc. IEEE ICIP 2002,* Rochester, NY.
10. M. Goljan, J. Fridrich, and R. Du, "Distortion-free data embedding," *Proceedings   of 4th Information Hiding Workshop*, pp. 27-41, Pittsburgh, PA, April 2001.
11. G. Xuan, J. Zhu, J. Chen, Y. Q. Shi, Z. Ni, W. Su "Distortionless Data Hiding Based on Integer Wavelet Transform," *IEE journal, ELECTRONICS LETTERS,* Volume 38, No 25, pp.1646-1648, Dec.2002.
12. G. Xuan, Y. Q. Shi, Z. C. Ni, J. Chen, C. Yang, Y. Zhen, J. Zhen, "High capacity lossless data hiding based on integer wavelet transform," *IEEE International Symposium on Circuits and Systems*, Vancouver, Canada, May 2004.
13. M. Celik, G. Sharma, A.M. Tekalp, E. Saber, "Reversible data hiding," in *Proceedings of the International Conference on Image Processing 2002*, Rochester, NY, September 2002.
14. Z. Ni, Y. Q. Shi, N. Ansari and W. Su, "Reversible data hiding," *IEEE International Symposium on Circuits and Systems,* Bangkok, Thailand, May 2003.
15. J. Tian, "Reversible data embedding using a difference expansion," *IEEE Transaction on Circuits and Systems for Video Technology*, Vol. 13, No. 8, August 2003.
16. G. Xuan, Y. Q. Shi, Z. Ni, "Lossless data hiding using integer wavelet transform and spread spectrum," *IEEE International Workshop on Multimedia Signal Processing*, Siena, Italy, September 2004.

17. B. Yang, M. Schmucker, W. Funk, C. Busch, S. Sun, "Integer DCT-based reversible watermarking for images using companding technique," *Proceedings of SPIE Vol. #5306*, January 2004.

18. G. Xuan, Y. Q. Shi, Z. Ni, "Reversible data hiding using integer wavelet transform and companding technique," *Proc. IWDW04*, Korea, October 2004.

19. Z. Zhang, Q. Sun, X. Lin, Y. Q. Shi and Z. Ni, "A unified authentication framework for JPEG2000 images," *IEEE International Conference and Expo*, Taipei, Taiwan, June 2004.

20. C. De Vleeschouwer, J. F. Delaigle and B. Macq, "Circular interpretation of bijective transformations in lossless watermarking for media asset management," *IEEE Tran. Multimedia*, vol. 5, pp. 97-105, March 2003.

21. W. Bender, D. Gruhl, N. Mprimoto and A. Lu, "Techniques for data hiding," *IBM Systems Journal*, pp. 313-336, vol. 35, Nos. 3&4, 1996.

22. Z. Ni, Y. Q. Shi, N. Ansari, W. Su, Q. Sun and X. Lin, "Robust lossless data hiding," *IEEE International Conference and Expo*, Taipei, Taiwan, June 2004.

23. D. Zou, Y. Q. Shi, Z. Ni, "lossless data hiding," *IEEE International Workshop on Multimedia Signal Processing*, Siena, Italy, September 2004.

24. M. Thodi and J. J. Rodríguez, "Reversible watermarking by prediction-error expansion," *Proceedings of 6th IEEE Southwest Symposium on Image Analysis and Interpretation*, pp. 21-25, Lake Tahoe, CA,USA, March 28-30, 2004.

Fingerprinting Curves

Hongmei Gou and Min Wu

University of Maryland, College Park, U.S.A.*

Abstract. This paper presents a new method for robust data hiding in curves and highlights potential applications including digital fingerprinting of map document for trace and track purposes. We parameterize a curve using the B-spline model and add a spread spectrum sequence to the coordinates of the B-spline control points. In order to achieve robust fingerprint detection, we propose an iterative alignment-minimization algorithm to perform curve registration and deal with the non-uniqueness of B-spline control points. We show through experiments the robustness of our method against various attacks such as collusion, geometric transformations and perturbation, printing-and-scanning, and some of their combinations. We demonstrate the feasibility of our method for fingerprinting topographic maps as well as writings and drawings. The extension from hiding data in 2D topographic maps to 3D elevation data sets is also discussed.

1 Introduction

Map represents geospatial information ubiquitous in government, military, intelligence, and commercial operations. The traditional way to protecting map from unauthorized copying and distribution is to place deliberate errors in the map, such as spelling "Nelson Road" as "Nelsen Road", bending a road in a wrong way, and/or placing a non-existing pond. If an unauthorized user has a map containing basically the same set of errors, this is a strong piece of evidence on piracy that can be presented in court. However, the traditional protection methods alter the geospatial meanings conveyed by a map, which can cause serious problems in critical government, military, intelligence, and commercial operations where highly precise geospatial information is needed. Further, in the situations where the distinct errors serve as fingerprints to trace individual copies, such intentional errors can be rather easily identified and removed by computer algorithms after multiple copies of a map are brought to the digital domain. All these limitations of the traditional methods prompt for a modern way to map protection that can be more effective and less intrusive.

Curve is one of the major components appearing in maps as well as other documents such as drawings and signatures. A huge amount of curve-based documents are being brought to the digital domain owing to the popularity of scanning devices and pen-based devices (such as TabletPC). Digital maps

---

* The authors can be contacted via email at {hmgou, minwu}@eng.umd.edu.

I.J. Cox et al. (Eds.): IWDW 2004, LNCS 3304, pp. 13–28, 2005.

and drawings are also generated directly by various computer programs such as map-making software and CAD systems. Having the capability of hiding digital watermarks or other secondary data in curves can facilitate digital rights management of important documents in government, military, intelligence, and commercial operations. For example, trace-and-track capabilities can be provided through invisibly embedding a unique ID, referred to as a *digital fingerprint*, to each copy of a document before distributing to users [1]. In this paper, we present a new, robust data hiding technique for curves and investigate its feasibility for fingerprinting maps.

As a forensic mechanism to deter information leak and to trace traitors, digital fingerprint must be difficult to remove. For maps and other visual documents, the fingerprint has to be embedded in a robust way against common processing and malicious attacks. Some examples include collusion, where several users combine information from different copies to generate a new copy in which the original fingerprints are removed or attenuated [1]; various geometric transformations such as rotation, scaling, and translation (RST); and D/A-A/D conversions such as printing-and-scanning. On the other hand, the fingerprint must be embedded in a visually non-intrusive way without changing the geographical and/or visual meanings conveyed by the document. Such changes may have serious consequences in critical military and commercial operations, for example, when inaccurate data are given to troops or fed into navigation systems.

There is a very limited amount of existing work on watermarking maps [2], and few exploits curve features or addresses fingerprinting issues. A text-based geometric normalization method was proposed in [3], whereby text labels are used to normalize the orientation and scale of the map image and conventional robust watermarking algorithms for grayscale images are then applied. As maps can be represented as a set of vectors, two related works on watermarking vector graphics perturb vertices through Fourier descriptors of polygonal lines [4] or spectral analysis of mesh models [5] to embed copyright marks. The embedding in [4] introduces visible distortions, as shown in their experimental results. The watermarking approach in [5] has high complexity resulting from the mesh spectral analysis. Besides, it cannot be easily applied to maps beyond urban areas, where curves serve as an essential component in mapping a vast amount of land and underwater terrains. Since curve-based documents can also be represented as binary bitmap images (known as the raster representation), we expand the literature survey to data embedding works for general binary images. The data hiding algorithm in [6] enforces the ratio of black versus white pixels in a block to be larger or smaller than 1, and the "flippable" pixels are defined and used to enforce specific block-based relationship to embed data in [7][8]. The fragility of the embedding and the reliance on precise sampling of pixels for correct decoding pose challenges in surviving geometric transformations, printing-and-scanning, and malicious removal in fingerprinting applications.

There are several watermarking algorithms for graphic data employing parametric features, such as representing 3D surfaces by the non-uniform rational B-spline (NURBS) model and changing the NURBS knots or control points to embed data [9][10]. While these works provide enlightening analogy for watermarking the 2D counterpart (i.e. curves) in the B-spline feature domain, most of the existing explorations and results are for fragile embedding in 3D surfaces and have limited robustness. There has been few discussion on robust watermarking of curves, and to our knowledge, no existing work has demonstrated the robustness against curve format conversion and D/A-A/D conversion.

In this paper, we propose a robust curve watermarking method and apply it to fingerprinting maps without interfering with the geospatial meanings conveyed by the map. We select B-spline control points of curves as the feature domain and add mutually orthogonal, noise-like sequences as digital fingerprints to the coordinates of the control points. A proper set of B-spline control points forms a compact collection of salient features representing the shape of the curve, which is analogous to the perceptually significant spectral components in the continuous-tone images [11]. The shape of curves is also invariant to such challenging attacks as printing-and-scanning and the vector/raster-raster/vector conversion. The additive spread spectrum embedding and the corresponding correlation based detection generally provide a good tradeoff between imperceptibility and robustness [11]. To determine which fingerprint sequence(s) are present in a test curve, registration with the original unmarked curve is an indispensable preprocessing step. B-splines have invariance to affine transformation in that the affine transformation of a curve is equivalent to the affine transformation of its control points. This affine invariance property of B-splines can facilitate automatic curve registration. Meanwhile, as a curve can be approximated by different sets of B-spline control points, we propose an iterative alignment-minimization (IAM) algorithm to simultaneously align the curves and identify the corresponding control points. Through the B-spline based data hiding plus the IAM algorithm for robust fingerprint detection, our curve watermarking technique can sustain a number of challenging attacks such as collusion, geometric transformations, vector/raster-raster/vector conversions, and printing-and-scanning, and is therefore capable of building collusion-resistant fingerprinting for maps and other curve-based documents.

The paper is organized as follows. Section 2 discusses the feature domain in which data hiding is performed and presents the basic embedding and detection algorithms with experimental results on marking simple curves. Section 3 details the proposed iterative alignment-minimization algorithm for the fingerprint detection and analyzes its robustness. Experimental results on fingerprinting topographic maps are presented in Section 4 to demonstrate the robustness of our method against a number of processing and attacks. Section 5 extends our curve watermarking method to protecting 3D geospatial data set. Finally conclusions are drawn in Section 6.

2   Basic Embedding and Detection

We first present the basic embedding and detection scheme on curves. We employ the coordinates of B-spline control points as the embedding feature domain, and adopt spread spectrum embedding [11] and correlation-based detection for watermarking curves.

2.1   Feature Extraction

A number of approaches have been proposed for curve modelling, including using the chain codes, the Fourier descriptors, the autoregressive models, and the B-splines [12]. Among them, the B-splines are particularly attractive and have been extensively used in computer-aided design and computer graphics. This is mainly because the B-spline model provides a bounded and continuous approximation of a curve with excellent local shape control and is invariant to affine transformations [13]. These advantages also lead to our choosing B-splines as the feature domain for data embedding in curves.

B-splines are piecewise polynomial functions that provide local approximations of curves using a small number of parameters known as the *control points* [12]. Let $\{\mathbf{p}(t)\}$ denote a curve, where $\mathbf{p}(t) = (p_x(t), p_y(t))$ and t is a continuous time variable. Its B-spline approximation $\{\mathbf{p}^{[B]}(t)\}$ can be written as

$$\mathbf{p}^{[B]}(t) = \sum_{i=0}^{n} \mathbf{c}_i B_{i,k}(t), \qquad (1)$$

where $\mathbf{c}_i = (c_{x_i}, c_{y_i})$ is the ith control point $(i = 0, 1, \ldots, n)$, t ranges from 0 to $n-1$, and $B_{i,k}(t)$, the weight of the ith control point for the point $\mathbf{p}^{[B]}(t)$, is a corresponding k^{th} order B-spline blending function recursively defined as

$$B_{i,1}(t) = \begin{cases} 1 & t_i \leq t < t_{i+1} \\ 0 & \text{otherwise,} \end{cases}$$

$$B_{i,k}(t) = \frac{(t - t_i)B_{i,k-1}(t)}{t_{i+k-1} - t_i} + \frac{(t_{i+k} - t)B_{i+1,k-1}(t)}{t_{i+k} - t_{i+1}} \qquad k = 2, 3, \ldots \quad (2)$$

where $\{t_i\}$ are parameters known as *knots* and represent locations where the B-spline functions are tied together [12]. The placement of knots controls the form of B-spline functions and in turn the control points.

As a compact representation, the number of B-spline control points necessary to represent the curve at a desired precision can be much smaller than the number of sample points from the curve typically obtained through uniform sampling. Thus, given a set of samples on the curve, finding a smaller set of control points for its B-spline approximation that minimizes the approximation error to the original curve can be formulated as a least-squares problem. Coordinates of the $m+1$ samples on the curve can be represented as an $(m+1) \times 2$ matrix of $\mathbf{P} \triangleq (\mathbf{p}_x, \mathbf{p}_y)$. The time variables of the B-spline blending functions corresponding to these $m+1$ samples are $t = s_0, s_1, s_2, \ldots, s_m$, where $s_0 < s_1 < s_2 < \ldots < s_m$. Further, let $\mathbf{C} \triangleq (\mathbf{c}_x, \mathbf{c}_y)$ represent the coordinates of $n+1$ control points. Then we can write the least-squares problem with its solution as

$$\mathbf{BC} \approx \mathbf{P} \quad \Longrightarrow \quad \mathbf{C} = \left(\mathbf{B}^\mathbf{T}\mathbf{B}\right)^{-1}\mathbf{B}^\mathbf{T}\mathbf{P} = \mathbf{B}^\dagger\mathbf{P}, \qquad (3)$$

where $\{\mathbf{B}\}_{ji}$ is the value of the kth-order B-spline blending function $B_{i,k}(t)$ in (2) evaluated at $t = s_j$ and † denotes the pseudo inverse of a matrix. Due to the natural decoupling of the x and y coordinates in the B-spline representation, we can solve the problem separately along each of the two coordinates as

$$\begin{cases} \mathbf{Bc}_x \approx \mathbf{p}_x \\ \mathbf{Bc}_y \approx \mathbf{p}_y \end{cases} \implies \begin{cases} \mathbf{c}_x = \mathbf{B}^\dagger \mathbf{p}_x \\ \mathbf{c}_y = \mathbf{B}^\dagger \mathbf{p}_y \end{cases}. \tag{4}$$

2.2   Data Embedding and Detection in Control Points

The control points of a curve are analogous to the perceptually significant spectral components of a continuous-tone image [11] in that they form a compact set of salient features for curve. In such a feature domain, we apply spread spectrum embedding and correlation based detection.

The spread spectrum embedding generally offers a good tradeoff between imperceptibility and robustness, especially when the original host signal is available to the detector as in most of the fingerprinting applications [1]. In the embedding, we use mutually orthogonal, noise-like sequences as digital fingerprints to represent different users/IDs for trace and track purposes. As each of the $n + 1$ control points has two coordinate values x and y, the overall length of the fingerprint sequence is $2(n + 1)$. To apply spread spectrum embedding on a curve, we add a scaled version of the fingerprint sequence $(\mathbf{w}_x, \mathbf{w}_y)$ to the coordinates of a set of control points obtained from the previous subsection. This results in a set of watermarked control points $(\mathbf{c}'_x, \mathbf{c}'_y)$ with

$$\begin{cases} \mathbf{c}'_x = \mathbf{c}_x + \alpha \mathbf{w}_x \\ \mathbf{c}'_y = \mathbf{c}_y + \alpha \mathbf{w}_y \end{cases}, \tag{5}$$

where α is a scaling factor adjusting the fingerprint strength. A watermarked curve can then be constructed by the B-spline synthesis equation (1) using these watermarked control points.

To determine which fingerprint sequence(s) are present in a test curve, we first need to perform registration using the original unmarked curve that is commonly available to a detector in fingerprinting applications. After registration, control points $(\tilde{\mathbf{c}}_x, \tilde{\mathbf{c}}_y)$ are extracted from the test curve. The accurate registration and correct extraction of control points are crucial to the accurate detection of fingerprints, which will be detailed in Section 3. Assuming we have the set of sample points given by $(\tilde{\mathbf{p}}_x, \tilde{\mathbf{p}}_y) = (\mathbf{B}(\mathbf{c}_x + \alpha \mathbf{w}_x), \mathbf{B}(\mathbf{c}_y + \alpha \mathbf{w}_y))$, we can extract the test control points $(\tilde{\mathbf{c}}_x, \tilde{\mathbf{c}}_y)$ from $(\tilde{\mathbf{p}}_x, \tilde{\mathbf{p}}_y)$ using (4). After getting $(\tilde{\mathbf{c}}_x, \tilde{\mathbf{c}}_y)$, we compute the difference between the coordinates of the test and the original control points to arrive at an estimated fingerprint sequence

$$\begin{cases} \tilde{\mathbf{w}}_x = \frac{\tilde{\mathbf{c}}_x - \mathbf{c}_x}{\alpha} \\ \tilde{\mathbf{w}}_y = \frac{\tilde{\mathbf{c}}_y - \mathbf{c}_y}{\alpha} \end{cases}. \tag{6}$$

We then evaluate the similarity between this estimated fingerprint sequence and each fingerprint sequence in our database through a correlation-based statistic.

In our work, we compute the correlation coefficient ρ and convert it to a Z-statistic by

$$Z = \log\left(\frac{1+\rho}{1-\rho}\right)\frac{\sqrt{2(n+1)-3}}{2}. \tag{7}$$

The Z-statistic has been shown to follow an approximate unit-variance Gaussian distribution with a large positive mean under the presence of a fingerprint, and a zero mean under the absence [14][15]. Thus, if the similarity is higher than a threshold (usually set between 3 to 6 for Z statistics), with high probability the corresponding fingerprint sequence in the database is present in the test curve, allowing us to trace the test curve to a specific user.

2.3   Fidelity and Robustness Considerations

Estimating the control points requires a set of properly chosen sample points from the curve. Uniform sampling can be used when there are no abrupt changes in a curve segment, while nonuniform sampling is desirable for curve segments that exhibit substantial variations in curvature.

The number of control points is an important parameter for tuning. Depending on the shape of the curve, using too few control points could cause the details of the curve be lost, while using too many control points may lead to over fitting and bring artifacts even before data embedding. The number of control points not only affects the distortion introduced by the embedding, but also determines the fingerprint's robustness against noise and attacks. The more the control points, the longer the fingerprint sequence, and in turn the more robust the fingerprint against noise and attacks. In our tests, the number of control points is about 5-8% of the total number of curve pixels and the specific numbers will be provided with the experimental results.

The scaling factor α also affects the invisibility and robustness of the fingerprint. The larger the scaling factor, the more robust the fingerprint, but the larger the distortion resulted in. For cartographic applications, industrial standards provide guidelines on the maximum allowable changes [5]. Perturbation of 2 to 3 pixels is usually considered acceptable. We use random number sequences with unit variance as fingerprints and set α to 0.5 in our tests.

2.4   Experimental Results of Fingerprinting Simple Curves

We first present the fingerprinting results on a simple "Swan" curve in Figure 1(a) to demonstrate our basic embedding and detection algorithms. The curve was hand-drawn on a TabletPC and stored as a binary image of size 392×329. We use the contour following algorithm in [16] to traverse the curve and obtain its vector representation. Then uniform sampling of a total of 1484 curve points and the quadratic B-spline blending function (order $k = 3$) are employed to estimate 100 control points. Then we mark these control points and construct a fingerprinted "Swan" curve as shown in Figure 1(b). By comparing it with the original curve in Figure 1(a), we can see that they are visually identical.

Based on the assumption and the detection method discussed in Section 2.2, we obtain the detection statistic of *12.75* when correlating the fingerprinted "Swan" curve with the true user's fingerprint sequence and very small statistic values when with innocent users, as shown in Figure 1(c). This suggests that the embedded fingerprint is identified with high confidence.

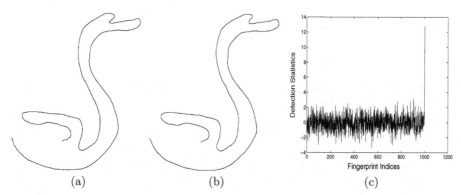

(a)   (b)   (c)

Fig. 1. Fingerprinting a hand-drawn *"Swan"* curve: (a) the original curve, (b) the fingerprinted curve, (c) Z statistics

3   Robust Fingerprint Detection

The set of test sample points $(\tilde{\mathbf{p}}_x, \tilde{\mathbf{p}}_y)$ assumed in Section 2.2 is not always available to a detector, especially when a test curve undergoes geometric transformations (such as rotation, translation, and scaling), vector/raster conversion, and/or is scanned from a printed hard copy. There must be a pre-processing registration step preceding the basic fingerprint detection module to align the test curve with the original one. In order to improve the accuracy and efficiency of the registration, an automated registration is desirable over a manual registration. With the affine invariance property, B-splines have been utilized in a few existing curve alignment works. In a recent method employing a *super-curve* [17], two affine-related curves are superimposed with each other in a single frame and then this combined *super-curve* is fitted by a single B-spline. Through minimizing the B-spline fitting error, both transform parameters and control points of the fitting B-spline can be estimated simultaneously. Since neither integration nor differentiation is needed, this method is robust to noise and will serve as a building block in our work.

Another problem related to the previous assumption is the inherent non-uniqueness of B-spline control points, which refers to the fact that a curve can be well approximated by different sets of B-spline control points. With a different time assignment or a different set of sample points, we may induce a quite different set of control points that can still accurately describe the same curve. It is possible for the differences between two sets of unmarked control points to be much larger than the embedded fingerprint sequence. Therefore, if we cannot find from a test curve a set of control points corresponding to the one used in the embedding, we may not be able to detect the fingerprint sequence. Considering the one-to-one relationship between sample points (including their time assignments $\{s_j\}$) and control points, we try to find the set of sample points on a test curve that corresponds to the set of sample points used in the embedding. We shall refer to this problem as the *point correspondence problem*. As we shall see, the non-uniqueness issue of B-spline control points can be addressed through finding the point correspondence.

3.1   Problem Formulation

We now formulate the curve registration and point correspondence problem in the context of fingerprint detection.

We use "View-I" to refer to the geometric setup of the original unmarked curve and "View-II" the setup of the test curve. Thus we can register the two curves by transforming the test curve from "View-II" to "View-I", or transforming the original curve from "View-I" to "View-II". We focus on registration under the affine transformations, which can represent combinations of scaling, rotation, translation, and shearing. These are common geometric transformations and can well model common scenarios in printing-and-scanning.

We call two points (x, y) and $(\tilde{x}, \tilde{y})$ *affine related* if

$$\begin{bmatrix} \tilde{x} \\ \tilde{y} \\ 1 \end{bmatrix} = \begin{bmatrix} a_{11} \ a_{12} \ a_{13} \\ a_{21} \ a_{22} \ a_{23} \\ 0 \ \ 0 \ \ 1 \end{bmatrix} \begin{bmatrix} x \\ y \\ 1 \end{bmatrix} = \begin{bmatrix} \mathbf{a}_x^T \\ \mathbf{a}_y^T \\ 0 \ 0 \ 1 \end{bmatrix} \begin{bmatrix} x \\ y \\ 1 \end{bmatrix} = \mathbf{A} \begin{bmatrix} x \\ y \\ 1 \end{bmatrix}, \qquad (8)$$

where $\{a_{ij}\}$ are parameters representing the collective effect of scaling, rotation, translation, and shearing. These transform parameters can be represented by two column vectors $\mathbf{a}_x = [a_{11} \ a_{12} \ a_{13}]^T$ and $\mathbf{a}_y = [a_{21} \ a_{22} \ a_{23}]^T$ or by a single matrix $\mathbf{A}$. Similarly, the inverse transformation can be represented by

$$\begin{bmatrix} x \\ y \\ 1 \end{bmatrix} = \mathbf{A}^{-1} \begin{bmatrix} \tilde{x} \\ \tilde{y} \\ 1 \end{bmatrix} \triangleq \begin{bmatrix} \mathbf{g}_x^T \\ \mathbf{g}_y^T \\ 0 \ 0 \ 1 \end{bmatrix} \begin{bmatrix} \tilde{x} \\ \tilde{y} \\ 1 \end{bmatrix} \qquad (9)$$

The original curve available to the detector in fingerprinting applications can be a raster curve or a vector curve. The detector also knows the original set of sample points $(\mathbf{p}_x, \mathbf{p}_y)$ that is used for estimating the set of control points upon which spread spectrum embedding is to be applied. In addition to possible affine transformations between the original and the test curve, the correct point correspondence information may not always be available, i.e., the set of test sample points $(\tilde{\mathbf{p}}_x, \tilde{\mathbf{p}}_y)$ assumed in Section 2.2 is absent. This is especially the case after a fingerprinted curve goes through vector-raster conversions and/or printing-and-scanning. Under this situation, not only transform parameters for the curve alignment but also the point correspondence must be estimated in order to locate the fingerprinted control points successfully. The test curve can be a vector curve with sampled curve points $(\tilde{\mathbf{v}}_x, \tilde{\mathbf{v}}_y)$ or a raster curve with pixel coordinates $(\tilde{\mathbf{r}}_x, \tilde{\mathbf{r}}_y)$. As a vector curve can be rendered as a raster curve through interpolation, we consider that the original and the test curve are represented in raster format and formulate the problem as:

Given an original raster curve with a set of sample points $(\mathbf{p}_x, \mathbf{p}_y)$ and a test raster curve $(\tilde{\mathbf{r}}_x, \tilde{\mathbf{r}}_y)$, we register the test curve with the original curve and extract the control points of the test curve. Both transform parameters $(\mathbf{a}_x, \mathbf{a}_y)$ (or equivalently $(\mathbf{g}_x, \mathbf{g}_y)$) and a set of sample points on the test curve $(\tilde{\mathbf{p}}_x, \tilde{\mathbf{p}}_y)$ corresponding to the one used in the fingerprint embedding must be found from the test raster curve.

3.2 Iterative Alignment-Minimization (IAM) Algorithm

To align the test curve with the original curve and in the mean time identify the point correspondence of the sample points, we develop an Iterative Alignment-Minimization (IAM) algorithm. The IAM algorithm is an iterative algorithm consisting of three main steps. We first obtain an initial estimation of the test sample points. With the estimated point correspondence, we then perform "super" curve alignment to estimate both the transform parameters and the control points of the test curve. With the estimated transform parameters, we refine the estimation of point correspondence through a nearest-neighbor rule.

Step-1 Initial Estimation of Sample Points on the Test Curve: We initialize the sample points $(\tilde{\mathbf{p}}_x^{(1)}, \tilde{\mathbf{p}}_y^{(1)})$ on the test curve using the following simple estimator. Let N and $\tilde{N}$ be the number of points on the original raster curve and on the test raster curve, respectively. From the known indices of the original curve's $m+1$ sample points $\mathbf{J} = [j_0, j_1, j_2, \ldots, j_m]$, where $j_0 < j_1 < j_2 < \ldots < j_m$ are integers ranging from 0 to $N-1$, we can estimate indices of the test curve's $m+1$ sample points by $\tilde{\mathbf{J}} = round\left(\frac{\tilde{N}-1}{N-1} \cdot \mathbf{J}\right)$. Using this estimated index vector $\tilde{\mathbf{J}}$, we can identify the corresponding sample points from the test curve and take them as the initial estimate.

Step-2 Curve Alignment with the Estimated Sample Points: Given the estimated point correspondence and the corresponding sample points $(\tilde{\mathbf{p}}_x^{(i)}, \tilde{\mathbf{p}}_y^{(i)})$ for the test curve in the ith iteration, we apply the curve alignment method in [17] to estimate the transform parameters and the control points of the test curve. More specifically, let the transform parameters from View-I (the original curve) to View-II (the test curve) be $(\mathbf{a}_x^{(i)}, \mathbf{a}_y^{(i)})$. The sample points on the test curve can be transformed back to View-I by $(\mathbf{g}_x^{(i)}, \mathbf{g}_y^{(i)})$. We then fit these transformed test sample points as well as the original sample points with a single B-spline curve (referred to as a "super-curve" in [17]) and search for both the transform parameters $(\hat{\mathbf{g}}_x^{(i)}, \hat{\mathbf{g}}_y^{(i)})$ and the B-spline control points $(\hat{\mathbf{c}}_x^{(i)}, \hat{\mathbf{c}}_y^{(i)})$ to minimize the fitting error

$$f(\hat{\mathbf{c}}_x^{(i)}, \hat{\mathbf{c}}_y^{(i)}, \hat{\mathbf{g}}_x^{(i)}, \hat{\mathbf{g}}_y^{(i)}) = \left\|\begin{bmatrix}\mathbf{B}\\\mathbf{B}\end{bmatrix}\hat{\mathbf{c}}_x^{(i)} - \begin{bmatrix}\mathbf{p}_x\\\tilde{\mathbf{P}}^{(i)}\hat{\mathbf{g}}_x^{(i)}\end{bmatrix}\right\|^2 + \left\|\begin{bmatrix}\mathbf{B}\\\mathbf{B}\end{bmatrix}\hat{\mathbf{c}}_y^{(i)} - \begin{bmatrix}\mathbf{p}_y\\\tilde{\mathbf{P}}^{(i)}\hat{\mathbf{g}}_y^{(i)}\end{bmatrix}\right\|^2, (10)$$

where $\tilde{\mathbf{P}}^{(i)} \triangleq [\tilde{\mathbf{p}}_x^{(i)} \quad \tilde{\mathbf{p}}_y^{(i)} \quad \mathbf{1}]$ and $\mathbf{1}$ is a column vector with all $1's$. The partial derivatives of the fitting error function with respect to $\hat{\mathbf{g}}_x^{(i)}, \hat{\mathbf{g}}_y^{(i)}, \hat{\mathbf{c}}_x^{(i)}$, and $\hat{\mathbf{c}}_y^{(i)}$ being zero is the necessary condition for the solution to this optimization problem. Thus we obtain an estimate of the transform parameters and the B-spline control points as:

$$
\begin{cases}
\hat{\mathbf{g}}_x^{(i)} = \mathbf{C}^{(i)}\mathbf{D}^{(i)}\mathbf{p}_x, \quad \hat{\mathbf{g}}_y^{(i)} = \mathbf{C}^{(i)}\mathbf{D}^{(i)}\mathbf{p}_y, \\
\hat{\mathbf{c}}_x^{(i)} = \mathbf{D}^{(i)}\mathbf{p}_x, \quad \hat{\mathbf{c}}_y^{(i)} = \mathbf{D}^{(i)}\mathbf{p}_y
\end{cases},
$$

$$
\text{where} \quad
\begin{cases}
\mathbf{C}^{(i)} \triangleq \left(\tilde{\mathbf{P}}^{(i)T}\tilde{\mathbf{P}}^{(i)}\right)^{\dagger} \tilde{\mathbf{P}}^{(i)T}\mathbf{B} \\
\mathbf{D}^{(i)} \triangleq \left(2\mathbf{B}^T\mathbf{B} - \mathbf{B}^T\tilde{\mathbf{P}}^{(i)}\mathbf{C}^{(i)}\right)^{\dagger} \mathbf{B}_0^T
\end{cases}. \tag{11}
$$

The estimated control points $(\hat{\mathbf{c}}_x^{(i)}, \hat{\mathbf{c}}_y^{(i)})$ can then be used to estimate the embedded fingerprint sequence and further compute the detection statistic $Z^{(i)}$, as described in Section 2.2.

Step-3 Refinement of Sample Point Estimation on the Test Curve: Given the estimated transform parameters $(\hat{\mathbf{g}}_x^{(i)}, \hat{\mathbf{g}}_y^{(i)})$, we align the test raster curve $(\tilde{\mathbf{r}}_x, \tilde{\mathbf{r}}_y)$ with the original curve by transforming it to View-I. As the fingerprinted sample points $(\mathbf{B}(\mathbf{c}_x + \alpha\mathbf{w}_x), \mathbf{B}(\mathbf{c}_y + \alpha\mathbf{w}_y))$ are located at the neighborhood of their corresponding unmarked version $(\mathbf{B}\mathbf{c}_x, \mathbf{B}\mathbf{c}_y)$, we apply a *nearest neighbor* rule to get a refined estimation of the test curve's sample points. More specifically, for each point of $(\mathbf{B}\mathbf{c}_x, \mathbf{B}\mathbf{c}_y)$, we find its closest point from the aligned test raster curve and then denote the collection of these closest points as $(\tilde{\mathbf{p}}_{x,I}^{(i+1)}, \tilde{\mathbf{p}}_{y,I}^{(i+1)})$. These nearest neighbors form refined estimates of the test sample points in View-I and are then transformed with parameters $(\hat{\mathbf{a}}_x^{(i)}, \hat{\mathbf{a}}_y^{(i)})$ back to View-II as new estimates of the test sample points:

$$
\begin{cases}
\tilde{\mathbf{p}}_x^{(i+1)} = \begin{bmatrix} \tilde{\mathbf{p}}_{x,I}^{(i+1)} & \tilde{\mathbf{p}}_{y,I}^{(i+1)} & \mathbf{1} \end{bmatrix} \hat{\mathbf{a}}_x^{(i)} \\
\tilde{\mathbf{p}}_y^{(i+1)} = \begin{bmatrix} \tilde{\mathbf{p}}_{x,I}^{(i+1)} & \tilde{\mathbf{p}}_{y,I}^{(i+1)} & \mathbf{1} \end{bmatrix} \hat{\mathbf{a}}_y^{(i)}
\end{cases}. \tag{12}
$$

After this update, we increase i and go back to Step-2. The iteration will continue until convergence or for an empirically determined number of times. A total of 15 rounds of iterations are used in our experiments.

3.3 Detection Example and Robustness Analysis

We present a detection example employing the proposed IAM algorithm on a curve taken from a topographic map. Shown in Figure 2(a) are the original curve and a fingerprinted curve undergone vector-raster conversion and some geometric transformations. After the vector-raster conversion, the point correspondence is no longer directly available from the curve representation and therefore our proposed IAM algorithm is desirable. The estimated sample points for the test curve after one iteration and 15 iterations are shown in Figure 2(b) and

Figure 2(c), respectively. We can see that the initial estimates deviate from the true values by a non-trivial amount, while after 15 iterations the estimated values converge to the true values. We plot the six estimated transform parameters for each iteration in Figure 2(d), which shows an accurate registration by the proposed IAM algorithm. Upon convergence, we utilize the estimated control points $(\hat{\mathbf{c}}_x^{(i)}, \hat{\mathbf{c}}_y^{(i)})$ and arrive at a high fingerprint detection statistic value as shown in Figure 2(e). This suggests the positive identification of the correct fingerprint by using the proposed IAM algorithm.

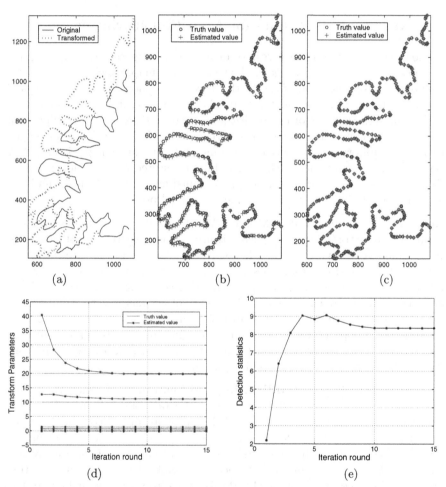

Fig. 2. Detection example using the IAM algorithm: a) the original and the test raster curve; b) estimated sample points after 1 iteration; c) estimated sample points after 15 iterations; d) estimated transform parameters; e) fingerprint detection statistic

The above example shows that through the IAM algorithm, we can register the test curve with the original unmarked curve and extract the fingerprinted control points with high accuracy. With good estimation of affine transform parameters, our data embedding method for curves is resilient to combinations of scaling, rotation, translation, and shearing. The explicit estimation of point correspondence also provides resilience against the vector-raster conversion. With the robustness resulting from spread spectrum embedding in B-spline control points and the IAM algorithm, our curve fingerprinting approach can resist a number of challenging attacks and distortions. The next section will provide further demonstration.

4   Experimental Results for Map Fingerprinting

We now present experimental results of our curve fingerprinting approach in the context of tracing and tracking the topographic map, which provides a two-dimensional representation of the earth's three-dimensional surface. Vertical elevation is shown with contour lines (also known as level lines) to represent the earth's surfaces that are of equal altitude. Contour lines in topographic maps often exhibit a considerable amount of variations and irregularity, prompting the need of non-uniform sampling of curve points in the parametric modelling of the contours. In our experiments, the original map is stored in vector format. A set of discrete, non-uniformly vector points is defined for each contour line and used as sample points in our tests for estimating control points.

Fingerprinted Topographic Maps.   A 1100×1100 topographic vector map obtained from http://www.ablesw.com is used in our experiment. Starting with the original map shown in Figure 3(a), we mark nine curves that are sufficiently long. A total of 1331 control points are used to carry the fingerprint. We overlay in Figure 3(b) these nine original and marked curves using solid lines and dotted lines, respectively. To help illustrate the fidelity of our method, we enlarge a portion of the overlaid image in Figure 3(c). We can see that the fingerprinted map preserves the geospatial information in the original map up to a high precision. The perturbation can be adapted to be compliant with cartographic industry standards and/or the need of specific applications.

Resilience to Collusion and Printing-and-Scanning.   To show the robustness of our approach against the combinational attack of collusion and printing-and-scanning, we first generate a colluded map by averaging coordinates of the control points from four users' fingerprinted maps, then render it and print it out using a HP laser printer, and finally scan back as a binary image by a Canon scanner with 360dpi resolution. Preprocessing before detection includes a thinning operation to extract one-pixel wide skeletons from the scanned curves that are usually several-pixel wide after high resolution scanning. By using the proposed IAM algorithm, we get Z statistics of *7.27, 8.91, 6.15, 8.12* for the four colluders, indicating that the embedded fingerprints from all the four colluders survive this combinational attack thus the sources of leak for this map can be identified. This combinational attack also involves vector-raster conversion and affine transformations, and the result shows the resilience of our method to them.

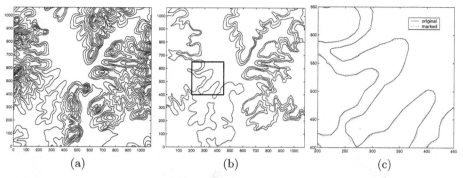

Fig. 3. Fingerprinting topographic maps: (a) original map, (b) original and finger-printed curves overlaid with each other; (c) a zoomed-in view of (b)

Resilience to Point Deletion in Vector and Raster Maps. As traitor tracing applications usually involve adversaries who have strong incentives to remove the fingerprints, attackers may delete a certain number of points from a fingerprinted vector/raster map while keeping similar shapes of its contour lines. For a fingerprinted vector map, 20% points are randomly chosen and removed from each fingerprinted curve, while in a fingerprinted raster map 70% points are randomly chosen and removed. As the point correspondence is corrupted by the point deletion, we first construct a raster map from the remaining points by linear interpolation and then apply our IAM algorithm. The detection statistics for these two cases are *11.40* and *15.61*, respectively. Thus the embedded fingerprints survive point deletion applied to both vector maps and raster maps.

5   Extension to Fingerprinting 3D Geospatial Data

In addition to 2D topographic maps, geospatial data are often acquired and archived as a 3D data set, which includes a set of spatial locations and their height information. The 3D geospatial data can be represented both as 3D surface and as 2D contours. An example of Monterey Bay region is shown in Figure 4, where the 3D oceanfloor depth data obtained from the U.S. National Geophysical Data Center (NGDC) [18] are rendered in Figure 4(a), and the corresponding 2D topographic map is shown in Figure 4(b). Since the same geospatial data set can be represented using different dimensionalities, we explore in this section such fingerprinting method that can allow the fingerprints to be detected from both the 3D data set and the 2D representation, whichever readily available to the detector. This can be achieved by extending our proposed fingerprinting method for curves.

Our basic idea of fingerprinting 3D elevation data is as follows. Given a set of 3D elevation data, we first extract its 2D contours and then embed a watermark into these contour curves using the method presented earlier in this paper. From the original 3D elevation data set and the marked 2D contours, we construct a marked 3D elevation data set. The new issues to be addressed here are how

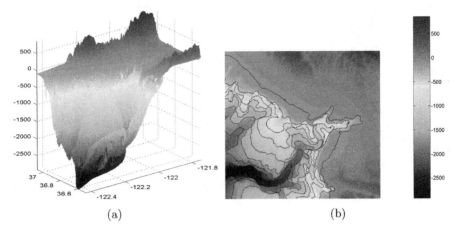

Fig. 4. Elevation map: (a) a 3D geospatial data set, (b) the corresponding 2D contours

to perform 2D contour extraction from a 3D data set and how to construct a marked 3D elevation data set from marked 2D contours.

The 2D contour extraction starts from performing a planar cut of the elevation data set at a selected height and then a binary map can be generated by assigning $1's$ to locations of height greater than the given height and $0's$ to the other locations. We apply a robust edge detector, such as the Canny method, to the binary map to obtain a raster representation of the contour of the given height. Using the contour following algorithm in [16], we traverse this raster contour and obtain a vector representation. Non-uniform sampling is employed to acquire more samples for segments with substantial variations in curvature and fewer in flat areas. Finally, we use the least-squares approach to estimate the B-spline control points of the contour.

When constructing a marked 3D data set, we need to generate a set of 3D elevation data under application-specific constraints, including preserving the geospatial meanings and ensuring the marked 2D contours can be estimated from the marked 3D data set with high accuracy. We recall that in the embedding stage, each original 2D contour is generated from a binary image with $1's$ in locations of height greater than the contour height and $0's$ in other locations. As the marked 2D contour represents a slightly different partition, we need to modify the height values of the 3D data set for locations around the marked contour so that the 2D contour generated from this new 3D data set is the same as the marked 2D contour. To accomplish this, we search for the locations that have higher elevation in the marked 2D contour map than in the original one, and modify their height in the 3D data set to be slightly higher. Similar adjustment is made to the locations with lower elevation in the marked 2D contour map than before.

To extract fingerprint from a 3D elevation data set, we perform some basic alignment if necessary. Using the same contour extraction approach as in the embedding, we then extract from the 3D data set the 2D contours for the same elevations as selected in the embedding. Since the extracted contours are in raster format, we can apply the IAM algorithm as discussed earlier in Section 3 to extract the embedded fingerprint.

We apply the proposed fingerprinting method to the Monterey Bay data set of Figure 4(a). We hide a fingerprint sequence in three 2D contours of height -100, -400, and -700, respectively. A total of 484 control points are used for carrying the fingerprint. To detect fingerprint, we extract the three 2D contours for the above heights from the fingerprinted 3D data set and obtain a Z detection statistic of *8.02* through the proposed IAM algorithm. This suggests a successful fingerprint detection from these three elevation levels.

6   Conclusions

In this paper, we have presented a new data hiding algorithm for curves by parameterizing a curve using the B-spline model and adding spread spectrum sequences to curve parameters. In conjunction with the basic embedding and detection techniques, we have proposed an iterative alignment-minimization algorithm to allow for robust fingerprint detection under unknown geometric transformations and in absence of explicit point correspondence. We have demonstrated the fidelity of our method as well as its robustness against collusion, affine transformations, vector-raster conversion, printing-and-scanning, and their combinations. Our work has shown the feasibility of the proposed algorithm in fingerprinting applications for tracing and tracking topographic maps as well as writings/drawings from pen-based inputs. We have also extended our curve watermarking method from protecting 2D topographic maps to 3D elevation data sets. The protection of all of these documents has increasing importance to the emerging digital operations in government, military, intelligence, and commerce.

References

1. Wu, M., Trappe, W., Wang, Z., Liu, K.J.R.: Collusion resistant fingerprinting for multimedia. IEEE Signal Processing Magazine **21** (2004) 15–27.
2. Chang, H., Chen T., Kan K.: Watermarking 2D/3D graphics for copyright protection. Proc. of IEEE ICASSP (2003) 720–723.
3. Barni, M., Bartolini, F., Piva, A., Salucco, F.: Robust watermarking of cartographic images. EURASIP Journal on Applied Signal Processing **2** (2002) 197–208.
4. Solachidis, V., Pitas, I.: Watermarking polygonal lines using fourier descriptors. IEEE Computer Graphics and Applications **24** (2004) 44–51.
5. Ohbuchi, R., Ueda, H., Endoh, S.: Watermarking 2D vector maps in the mesh-spectral domain. Proc. of the Shape Modeling International (SMI) (2003).
6. Koch, E., Zhao, J.: Embedding robust labels into images for copyright protection. Proc. Int. Congr. Intellectual Property Rights for Specialized Information, Knowledge and New Technologies (1995).
7. Wu, M., Tang, E., Liu, B.: Data hiding in digital binary image. Proc. of IEEE ICME (2000) 393–396.

8. Wu, M., Liu, B.: Data hiding in binary image for authentication and annotation. IEEE Trans. on Multimedia Vol.**6** (2004) 528–538.
9. Ohbuchi, R, Masuda, H., Aono, M.: A Shape-Preserving Data Embedding Algorithm for NURBS Curves and Surfaces. Proc. of CGI (1999) 180–187.
10. Lee, J. J., Cho, N. I., Kim, J. W.: Watermarking for 3D NURBS graphic data. Proc. of IEEE MMSP (2002) 304–307.
11. Cox, I., Killian, J., Leighton, F., Shamoon, T.: Secure spread spectrum watermarking for multimedia. IEEE Transcations on Image Processing **6** (1997) 1673–1687.
12. Jain, A.K.: Fundamentals of Digital Image Processing. Prentice Hall (1989).
13. Farin, G.E.: Curves and surfaces for computer-aided geometric design: a practical guide. 4th edn. Academic Press (1997).
14. Stone, H.: Analysis of attacks on image watermarks with randomized coefficients. Technical Report 96-045, NEC Research Institute (1996).
15. Zhao, H., Wu, M., Wang, Z., Liu, K.J.R.: Nonlinear collusion attacks on independent multimedia fingerprints. accepted by IEEE Trans. on Image Proc (2004).
16. Cabrelli, C., Molter, U.: Automatic representation of binary images. IEEE Trans. on Pattern Analysis and Machine Intelligence **12** (1990) 1190–1196.
17. Xia, M., Liu, B.: Image registration by 'super-curves'. IEEE Trans. on Image Processing **13** (2004) 720–732.
18. National Geophysical Data Center (NGDC): http://www.ngdc.noaa.gov, U.S. Oceanic and Atomospheric Administration.

Informed Detection Revisited

Jeffrey A. Bloom[1] and Matt L. Miller[2]

[1] Sarnoff Corporation, Princeton NJ 08540, USA
[2] NEC Labs America, Princeton NJ 08540, USA

Abstract. Watermarking systems can employ either *informed detection*, where the original cover work is required, or *blind detection*, where it is not required. While early systems used informed detection, recent work has focused on blind detection, because it is considered more challenging and general. Further, recent work on "dirty-paper watermarking" has suggested that informed detection provides no benefits over blind detection.

This paper discusses the dirty-paper assumptions and questions whether they apply to real-world watermarking. We discuss three basic ways in which an informed video-watermark detector, developed at Sarnoff, uses the original work: canceling interference between the cover work and the watermark, canceling subsequent distortions, and tailoring the watermark to the perceptual characteristics of the source. Of these, only the first is addressed by theoretical work on dirty-paper watermarking. Whether the other two can be accomplished equally well with blind watermarking is an open question.

1 Introduction

A watermarking system embeds a message into a cover work, such as an image, video clip, or audio stream, without perceptibly changing that work. Systems can be divided into two major categories according to whether detecting and decoding the message requires knowledge of the original, unwatermarked cover work. In a system that employs *blind detection*, only the watermarked work is required during the detection process, while in *informed detection*, the detection process requires both the watermarked work and the unwatermarked original.

At first glance, it may appear that informed detection should yield better performance than blind detection. An informed watermark detector can subtract the unwatermarked work from the watermarked one, easily canceling out any interference in the message that results from the cover work. Nevertheless, the past decade of watermarking research has seen a steady decline in interest in informed-detection systems, culminating in a belief that informed detection should *not* offer any fundamental advantage over blind detection. The main purpose of the present paper is to discuss whether that belief is justified.

Judging from our experience, the declining interest in informed watermarking can be attributed to several causes. From the point of view of watermark researchers, blind detection is attractive because it is more generally applicable

I.J. Cox et al. (Eds.): IWDW 2004, LNCS 3304, pp. 29–41, 2005.

than informed detection. An informed detector can only be used in applications, such as traitor tracing or proof of ownership (see [9]), where those who need to detect the watermark have access to the original. In other applications, such as copyright notification and copy prevention (again, see [9]), the general public must be able to detect watermarks, so we cannot employ informed detection without publicly distributing the unmarked originals (which, presumably, would defeat the purpose of the watermark). On the other hand, a blind system can be used for any application, provided its performance is sufficiently good.

Furthermore, there is a consensus that developing blind watermarking systems is more challenging, and therefore more interesting, than developing informed systems. The problem of canceling out interference from the cover work without knowledge of the original at the detector cannot be solved without inventing clever ideas that make for good research publications and patents. Informed detection, by contrast, seems like a solved problem.

At the same time, from the point of view of watermark users, the possible applications of informed detection were not as attractive as applications requiring blind detection. A few companies tested the market for proof-of-ownership systems (e.g., [20]), but found that market to be weak. Other potential applications of informed detection, such as traitor tracing, were overshadowed by a quest for a silver bullet: a system that could *prevent* illegal copying. It was the quest for such copy prevention systems that led to projects like SDMI [14] and watermarking for DVD [1], which inspired much watermarking research in the late 90's.

Finally, in 2000, Chen & Wornell [2] introduced Costa's *dirty paper* result [8] into watermarking research. This result strongly suggests that, in theory, the performance of a properly designed blind-detection system should be just as good as any informed-detection system. Application of Costa's basic principles led directly to dramatic improvements in the performance of blind-detection watermarking systems [3, 11, 6, 17, 18], and it appeared that there should no longer be any reason to work on informed detection.

However, the quest for a silver bullet against illegal copying became bogged down in real-world problems. For a variety of reasons – mostly non-technical – no watermarking system has yet been deployed for DVD, and SDMI-compliant devices have yet to find a market. There is, therefore, a growing interest in less-complete aids to copyright enforcement, most notably the application of watermarks for traitor tracing. This interest has been encouraged by the recent success of a video watermark in identifying two men responsible for a substantial movie-pirating operation [13]. With rising interest in a potential application of informed detection, it is worth revisiting the question of whether blind and informed systems are, in fact, equally capable.

Our discussion of this question begins by describing, in Section 2, a watermark developed at Sarnoff Corporation between 2001 and 2003. This system is designed for traitor tracing in digital cinema, and employs informed detection. Though the ways its detector uses the unwatermarked original are not unique, some of them exploit aspects of real-world watermarking that differ dramatically from Costa's theoretical formulation, and thus call into question the applicability of his result to watermarking. That is, we believe Costa's result *does not* indicate that watermarking with blind detection is necessarily equivalent to watermarking with informed detection. This point is argued and elaborated in Section 3. Finally, Section 4 concludes the paper with a summary of our argument and the challenges it poses.

2   Sarnoff's Video Watermark

Sarnoff's video watermark [16] was developed to help identify the source of unauthorized distributions of movies exhibited in digital cinemas[1]. Each authorized copy of a motion picture, including those distributed prior to the theatrical release, is watermarked with a unique serial number. In addition, each projector will embed a watermark indicating the identity of the screen onto which it is projecting, the show time, and perhaps some additional information about the operator or the showing. Insiders with direct access to the movie who make unauthorized copies can then be identified. Theaters that allow audience members to videotape the movie with a camcorder can be identified if a copy of that tape is distributed. Such a watermark provides the motion picture studies with a tool to help them understand and manage the piracy problem.

The requirements for such a watermark are quite strict. Though the data payload can be fairly small (about 0.5 bits per second is sufficient), the fidelity and robustness must be extremely high. Part of the point of digital cinema is to improve picture quality, so any degradation caused by watermarking will be unacceptable. For example, the watermark must be completely invisible in images with the quality shown in Figure 1 (a). At the same time, pirated copies can have very poor quality, so the watermark must be detectable in severely degraded video, such as that shown in Figure 1 (b).

To meet these requirements, the Sarnoff watermark uses very low frequency spatio-temporal patterns referred to as *carriers*. Each carrier is a spatially-limited pattern, one third to two thirds of the screen height in size, that appears and disappears slowly over time. Carriers are modulated (e.g., by sign or phase) to encode 1's and 0's and added to the frame sequence. This design takes advantage of the human visual system's low sensitivity to extremely low frequencies. At the same time, it makes for extremely robust watermarks, because virtually all processing to which pirated video might be subjected preserves the low frequencies.

Unfortunately, in spite of the eye's insensitivity to low frequencies, randomly-placed carriers are occasionally visible. To counter this problem, the embedder employs some automated perceptual analysis to identify locations where carriers

---

[1] Original work was funded in part under the U.S. Department of Commerce, National Institute of Standards and Technology, Advanced Technology Program, Cooperative Agreement Number 70NANB1H3036.

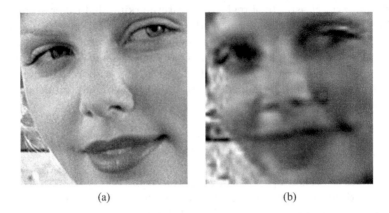

(a)   (b)

Fig. 1. A digital cinema application places extreme requirements on fidelity and robustness. The images shown are close-ups of a small region of a movie frame (courtesy of Miramax Film Corporation). The fidelity of the high resolution detail of the original content, shown in (a), must be maintained while the watermark must be detectable in video with quality like that in (b)

can be invisibly placed. The watermark is then embedded at a subset of these locations only.

The detector receives the suspect video (i.e. the pirated copy) along with two pieces of side information: the original unwatermarked video and a description of the carrier locations used by the embedder, as determined by perceptual analysis. Note that this second piece of side information could just as well be obtained by re-running the perceptual analysis on the original video, so, in principle, only the first piece of side information is truly needed.

The detector first adjusts the original video's geometry, timing, and color histogram so that it matches the suspect video (see [4, 5] for details on how this is done) and subtracts the two, obtaining a difference video. It then adjusts the pattern of carriers the same way that it adjusted the original video, and correlates it with the difference video. This yields either a positive or negative correlation for each carrier, which is then decoded to obtain the watermark information.

The embedding and detection processes are described in more detail in [16]. For our purposes here, however, we need only focus on the three basic ways in which the original video is used in the detector:

1. The original is subtracted from the suspect video to cancel out interference between the video and the watermark.
2. The pattern of carriers is adjusted according to the registration of the original and suspect videos, thus canceling out the effects of temporal, geometric, and histogram distortions.
3. The pattern of carriers that the detector looks for, and thus the appearance of the watermark, depends on the perceptual properties of the original video.

The question we face is whether these functions – canceling interference, canceling distortions, and perceptual shaping – could, in theory, be performed equally well with a blind detector. To answer this question, we must take a closer look at the theoretical reasons for believing that they might be.

3   Informed Detection Versus Blind Detection

The reason for believing that blind and informed detection are equivalent comes from Costa's dirty-paper result of 1983 [8]. This says that the two *are* equivalent, for a specific type of channel that is highly analogous to watermarking. After briefly reviewing the result here, we go on to discuss the differences between Costa's channel and the reality of watermarking, and how those differences are exploited in Sarnoff's watermark.

3.1   Costa's Dirty-Paper Result

The channels Costa discussed are illustrated in Figure 2 and Figure 3. A message, m, is mapped to a signal vector, x, by the encoder. This signal is limited by a power constraint:

$$\frac{1}{n}\sum_i x_i^2 \leq P \tag{1}$$

where n is the number of elements in the vector. x is then corrupted by two additive, Gaussian noise vectors, s and z. s is drawn from the *first noise source*, and z is drawn from the *second noise source*. We refer here to $x + s$ as w, and to $w + z$ as y. y is received by the decoder, and decoded to the received message, $\hat{m}$. Figure 2 shows the case of *informed decoding*, in which s is provided to the decoder as side information. Figure 3 shows the case of *informed encoding*, in which s is provided to the encoder, before it must select x. The question is what are the capacities of these two channels?

Clearly, in the case of informed decoding (Figure 2), the capacity can be computed as if the first noise source does not exist. The decoder can simply subtract s from y, obtaining $x + z$. Thus, the capacity is given by the standard formula for capacity of an additive Gaussian channel:

$$C = \frac{1}{2}\log\left(1 + \frac{P}{\sigma_z}\right) \tag{2}$$

where C is the capacity, and σ_z is the standard deviation of the second noise source.

In the case of informed encoding (Figure 3), it is tempting to try a similar approach, by encoding the message with some vector, u, and letting $x = u - s$. This would mean that $w = u$ and $y = u + z$, so the resulting channel looks like one that has a single noise source. The problem is that $\sum(u_i - s_i)^2$ will generally be larger than $\sum u_i^2$, so u is more limited by the power constraint than x. In general, u must be limited by $\sum u_i^2 \leq P - \sigma_s^2$, where σ_s is the standard deviation of the first noise source. Thus, the code rate achieved by this approach must be lower than the capacity of Equation 2.

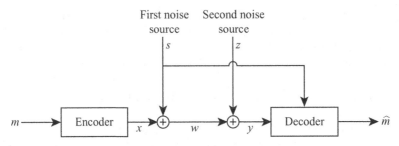

Fig. 2. Channel with informed decoding

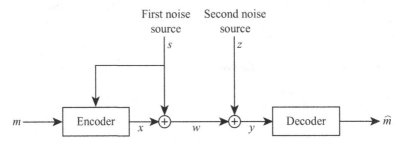

Fig. 3. Channel with informed encoding

Costa showed, however, that higher code rates can be achieved using

$$x = u - \alpha s \tag{3}$$

where α is a carefully chosen constant. When α is computed as

$$\alpha = \frac{P}{P + \sigma_z} \tag{4}$$

the highest possible code rate is actually *equal* to the capacity of Equation 2. Thus, knowledge of the first noise source at *either* the encoder or the decoder allows its complete cancellation for purposes of computing channel capacity.

The implications of this for watermarking become clear when we see that the channels of Figures 2 and 3 are essentially the same as informed and blind watermarking, respectively. The first noise source is analogous to the original cover work. w is analogous to the watermarked work. The second noise source is analogous to subsequent distortions applied to the watermarked work. And the power constraint is analogous to a limit on perceptibility of the watermark.

If these analogies are perfect, then Costa's result means that the cover works have no effect on watermark capacity, and blind and informed watermarking should have equivalent performance. We now, therefore, examine each of these analogies in turn.

3.2   First Noise Versus Cover Works

Is Costa's first noise source a good analogy for the original cover work? In general, no. The problem is that most types of media are not Gaussian distributed.

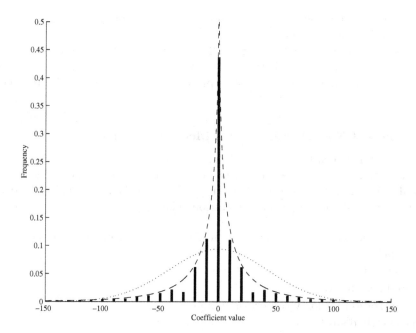

Fig. 4. Example of the distribution of values for an image transform coefficient. The bars show the distribution of one coefficient in the 8x8 block DCT of 100 images. The dotted line shows the best approximation of this distribution as a Gaussian. The dashed line shows the best approximation of the distribution as a generalized Gaussian, with a shape parameter of 0.5

The simplest models that provide reasonable matches to real distributions of images and audio clips are generalized Gaussians in transform domains. For example, Figure 4 shows the distribution of values for one block DCT coefficient in a corpus of 100 images. The dotted line shows the best fit obtainable with a normal Gaussian. The dashed line shows a fit obtainable with a generalized Gaussian, computed as

$$P(x) = \frac{\lambda\beta}{2\Gamma\left(\frac{1}{\beta}\right)}e^{-|\lambda x|^{\beta}} \tag{5}$$

with the *shape parameter*, β, equal to 0.5, and the scaling constant, λ, equal to 0.2583.

In truth, the distribution of cover works is more complex than that shown in Figure 4. Different image textures, different musical instruments, different voices, etc. all have different statistical characteristics, and real works of media are drawn from a complex mixture of these distributions.

Fortunately, it has been shown that none of this matters. Cohen & Lapidoth [7], and Erez, Shamai & Zamir [12] have proven independently (and in different ways) that Costa's result holds regardless of the distribution of the first noise source. As long as this noise is additive, its effect on channel capacity can be cancelled at the encoder.

This means that, in principle, Sarnoff's watermark detector should not need to subtract the original from the suspect video. Instead, the embedder could use coding techniques based on Costa's proof (*dirty paper* coding [17]) to cancel interference from the cover work.

3.3   Second Noise Versus Digital Media Distortions

The analogy between Costa's second noise source and actual media distortions is weaker than that between the first noise source and original cover works. Digital media is rarely corrupted by the addition of Gaussian noise. Instead, more common distortions include operations like

- valumetric scaling (multiplying each pixel or audio sample by some scaling factor),
- spectral filtering,
- non-linear filtering,
- quantization for lossy compression, and
- geometric distortions.

This distortions are completely different from additive noise.

Unlike the first noise source, furthermore, deviation from a Gaussian distribution in the second noise source is likely to invalidate Costa's result. In the same paper where they proved that the first noise source can be arbitrary, Cohen & Lapidoth put forth a conjecture that Costa's result holds *only* if the second noise is additive Gaussian. Though they did not quite prove this conjecture, their argument for its validity is very strong.

One possible escape from Cohen & Lapidoth's conjecture is that it only holds for systems that compute x in the manner of Equation 3. It is likely that, with different equations for x, Costa's result can be obtained for some larger class of second noise sources. However, it is far from clear that this should include every conceivable noise source, or even the common types of distortion listed above.

A major issue with digital media distortions is that they are *not* additive. The change made in a work by each of the distortions listed above is highly dependent on the work itself. That is, there is significant mutual information between w and z. This is a complete departure from Costa's basic dirty-paper channel, and allows an informed detector to do something Costa's decoder has no opportunity to do: obtain information about the distortion by looking at the cover work.

In Sarnoff's system, the detector obtains information about geometric and histogram distortions by comparing the unmarked original with the suspect video. It uses this information to cancel out the effect of these distortions, thus effectively increasing the channel capacity beyond what could be acheived in a channel that had no first noise source. There is, as yet, no reason to believe that a similar increase in channel capacity can be obtained with a blind detector.

Fig. 5. Effect of adding two different patterns, x_0 and x_1, to the same image with the same power

3.4   Power Constraint Versus Fidelity Limit

The third part of the analogy between Costa's channel and watermarking is the mapping of watermarking's fidelity constraint with the channel's power constraint. This, too, is not a perfect analogy.

In the analogy, the vector x is the pattern added to the cover work s. By limiting the magnitude of x with a power constraint, we hope to limit the perceptibility of the change caused by adding it to s. In reality, however, the perceptibility of changes in a work is highly dependent on that work. For example, an audio signal of pure white noise can be dramatically changed without changing its perceptual effect, while a recording of a single, clear musical note is much less forgiving. This means that, at a minimum, the power limit P should be viewed as dependent on s.

Furthermore, the limit should also depend on x itself. Figure 5 shows an example. This shows two different patterns for x, x_0 and x_1, and the perceptual effect of adding each pattern, with the same power, to the same image. Because x_1 is shaped to have energy only in areas where the image has texture, its impact is much less perceptible than the impact of x_0. Thus, the power constraint for x_0 should be tighter than for x_1. Clearly, however, this is image-dependant, so to capture the true fidelity limit, we would need a power constraint based on both s and x.

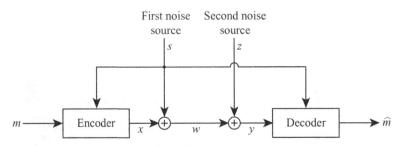

Fig. 6. Channel with both encoding and decoding informed

It is not clear what effect this complication has on channel capacity. Certainly, an informed embedder can shape x to take advantage of perceptual phenomena, improving the performance of a system with blind detection. This has been demonstrated in numerous practical watermarking systems. The question, however, is whether better performance can be obtained when the detector is informed.

In the Sarnoff watermark, both the embedder and detector are informed, so the channel matches that shown in Figure 6. This allows the embedder and the detector to agree on the placement of the carriers, effectively designing a unique code for each cover video, according to that video's perceptual characteristics. Whether this yields a fundamental improvement in channel capacity is an open question – a question that is not addressed by the analogy with Costa's channel.

3.5   A Possible Solution: Perceptually-Uniform Space

One possible way to make the analogy between Costa's channel and watermarking exact would be to use a perceptually-uniform space. In principle, we could define some non-linear transform that, when applied to an image, maps it into a space where Euclidian distance corresponds to perceptual distance. This should simplify the two main areas where actual watermarking is more complex than Costa's channel.

Clearly, in a perceptually-uniform space, the power constraint will be a good analogy for watermarking's fidelity limit, because the perceptual difference between two images is, by definition, indicated entirely by the Euclidian distance between them. Perceptual distortion does not vary with location in the space, nor does it vary with direction of the distortion vector.

Less clearly, a perceptually-uniform space might also simplify the distribution of subsequent distortions, making it more analogous to the second noise source in Costa's channel. The reason for this is that all the distortions to which media will be subject are intended to preserve (to some degree) the perceptual quality of that media. Thus, if we are in a space where the perceptibility of a distortion is dependent only on the length of the distortion vector, and independent of the starting point, then we might be justified in assuming that the distribution of subsequent distortions is likewise independent of the work being distorted.

Basically, the dependancy between the distortion and the work is subsumed in the non-linearities of the transform into perceptually-uniform space. Under such an assumption, we should be able to represent distortions with a simple, additive noise source.

Unfortunately, defining a perceptually-uniform space is extremely difficult, and may never be possible in practice. There exist several perceptual models for judging small differences between images [10, 15, 19], and these might serve as starting points for developing such a transform, but there are, as yet, no good models for measuring larger perceptual differences. A space that's uniform over small changes should typically be sufficient to make the fidelity limit analogous to a power constraint, because the fidelity limits typically only allow small changes. But subsequent distortions, especially if introduced by a pirate, can be much larger (see Figure 1 again). We have little hope, at present, of making a space that is uniform over a large enough area to allow such distortions to be modelled as simple additive noise.

Thus, even if a perceptually-uniform space is theoretically possible, it is likely to be impractical. In the absence of such a space, informed detection will probably provide additional channel capacity.

4   Conclusion

The application of dirty-paper coding to the watermarking channel has suggested that blind detection with side information available at the encoder is equivalent to informed detection, in which side information is made available to the detector. This extension relies on the validity of three important assumptions: the distribution of cover works can be modelled as an additve Gaussian noise source, the distribution of noise applied to a watermarked work prior to detection can be modelled as an additive Gaussian noise source, and the maximum allowable watermark power is independent of the cover work.

While the first of these assumptions does not directly hold, there is research that shows that Costa's result applies regardless of the distribution of cover works. The other two assumptions are not so easily reconciled. The distortions applied to watermarked works are highly dependent on the cover work and are neither additive nor Gaussian. The fidelity limit places restrictions on the shape of the watermark as well as on it's power. Further, that shape is dependent on the cover work. Thus, it appears that Costa's result *does not* indicate that watermarking with blind detection is necessarily equivalent to watermarking with informed detection.

Sarnoff's watermarking system for traitor tracing in digital cinema represents an example of informed detection in which the detector can infer information about the second noise source and the fidelity constraint applied during embedding. Costa's framework does not address such systems.

If the watermarking community is to continue to rely on Costa's dirty paper model to assess the capacity of the watermarking channel, there are a number of questions that must be addressed.

1. We need to better understand the role of the second noise source. It appears that providing the detector with information about real distortions, those that are non-additive and highly dependent on the cover work, can improve the channel capacity. Can we prove that such knowledge does not improve capacity?

2. We need to better understand the role of the fidelity constraint. Can we design a perceptually uniform space in which the fidelity constraint becomes a Euclidean power constraint? Or can we extend Costa's model to address content-dependent fidelity constraints rather than power?

3. An issue that has not been addressed here is the challange of distinguishing between distortions that are introduced by the second noise source and the watermark pattern itself. Given the original content, how can a detector infer and compensate for distortions without damaging the watermark pattern?

References

1. J. A. Bloom, I. J. Cox, T. Kalker, J-P Linnartz, M. L. Miller, and B. Traw. Copy protection for DVD video. *Proc. IEEE*, 87(7):1267–1276, 1999.

2. B. Chen and G. W. Wornell. An information-theoretic approach to the design of robust digital watermarking systems. *IEEE Transactions on Acoustics, Speech, and Signal Processing*, 1999.

3. B. Chen and G. W. Wornell. Quantization index modulation: A class of provably good methods for digital watermarking and information embedding. In *Proc. Int. Symp. Inform. Theory (ISIT-2000)*, 2000.

4. H. Cheng. Temporal video registration. In *Proc. of IEEE Int'l Conf. on Acoustics, Speech and Signal Processing (ICASSP'03)*, volume 3, pages 489–92, Hong Kong, China, April 2003.

5. H. Cheng and M. Isnardi. Spatial, temporal and histogram video registration for digital watermark detection. In *Proc. of IEEE Int'l Conf. on Image Processing (ICIP'03)*, volume 2, pages 735–8, Barcelona, Spain, Sept. 2003.

6. Jim Chou, S. Sandeep Pradhan, and Kannan Ramchandran. On the duality between distributed source coding and data hiding. *Thirty-third Asilomar conference on signals, systems, and computers*, 2:1503–1507, 1999.

7. A. S. Cohen and A. Lapidoth. Generalized writing on dirty paper. In *International Symposium on Information Theory (ISIT)*, 2002.

8. M. Costa. Writing on dirty paper. *IEEE Trans. Inform. Theory*, 29:439–441, 1983.

9. I. J. Cox, M. L. Miller, and J. A. Bloom. *Digital Watermarking*. Morgan Kaufmann, 2001.

10. Scott Daly. The Visible Difference Predictor: An algorithm for the assessment of image fidelity. In A. B. Watson, editor, *Digital Images and Human Vision*, chapter 14, pages 179–206. MIT Press, 1993.

11. J. J. Eggers, J. K. Su, and B. Girod. A blind watermarking scheme based on structured codebooks. In *IEE Seminar on Secure Images and Image Authetication*, pages 4/1–4/21, 2000.

12. U. Erez, S. Shamai, and R. Zamir. Capacity and lattice-strategies for cancelling known interferance. In *Proc. of the Cornell Summer Workshop on Inform. Theory*, Aug. 2000.

13. B. Fritz and T. M. Gray. Acad member tied to piracy bust. *Variety*, Jan. 23, 2004.

14. Secure Digital Music Initiative. SDMI portable device specification, 1999. Available at http://www.sdmi.org.
15. J. Lubin. The use of psychophysical data and models in the analylsis of display system performance. In A. B. Watson, editor, *Digital Images and Human Vision*, chapter 14, pages 163–178. MIT Press, 1993.
16. J. Lubin, J. A. Bloom, and H. Cheng. Robust, content-dependent, high-fidelity watermark for tracking in digital cinema. *Security and Watermarking of Multimedia Contents V*, SPIE-5020:536–45, 2003.
17. M. L. Miller. Watermarking with dirty-paper codes. In *IEEE International Conference on Image Processing*, September 2001.
18. M. L. Miller, G. J. Doërr, and I. J. Cox. Applying informed coding and embedding to design a robust, high capacity watermark. *IEEE Transactions on Image Processing*, 13(6):792–807, 2004.
19. Christian J. van den Branden Lambrecht and Joyce E. Farrell. Perceptual quality metric for digitally coded color images. *Proc. EUSIPCO*, pages 1175–1178, 1996.
20. G. Voyatzis and I. Pitas. The use of watermark in the protection of digital multimedia products. *Proceedings of the IEEE, Special Issue on Identication and Protection of Multimedia Information*, 87(7):1197–1207, 1999.

A Counter-Geometric Distortions Data Hiding Scheme Using Double Channels in Color Images*

Gang Xue, Peizhong Lu, and Jinlian Wang

Fudan University, Shanghai 200433, P.R.China
{012021194, pzlu, 012018046}@fudan.edu.cn

Abstract. This paper presents a new approach for data hiding with robustness to global geometric distortions. The global geometric distortions can be described by a 6-parameters affine transformation. Our scheme is designed for color images, which is combined with error-correcting code, double-channels steganography, feature point extraction, and triangle warping. Two color spaces of RGB images are considered two independent channels, one for synchronization information, and the other for a large amount of hiding data. The synchronization information consists of the coordinates of triangles' centers, cyclic redundancy check bits, and parity check bits of convolutional codes. Global geometric distortions can be estimated successfully by least square method and K-means method. Then a large amount of data with low bit-error rate can be decoded by SOVA algorithm of Turbo coding after the geometric adjustment. We also improve the method for feature point extraction. Simulation results show that our scheme is robust to rotation, scaling, translation, cropping, shearing, and so on.

1   Introduction

Data hiding has an inevitable problem of synchronization. Geometric distortions can induce synchronization errors during the detection process. Hence, the robustness to geometric distortions is very important for data hiding.

We focus our work on the problem of geometric synchronization in data hiding scheme, which is very difficult to tackle. Existing data hiding schemes have realized a few part of the robustness to noise-like signal processing, such as JPEG compression, Gaussian noise, and so on. So far, we have not found any existing data hiding scheme with satisfying robustness to geometric distortions, although several watermarking approaches, which counterattack geometric distortions, have been reported.

Patrick Bas et al. [1] proposed a feature-based watermarking scheme employing feature points extraction. The mark is embedded by using a classical additive

* This work was supported by National Natural Science of China(10171017, 90204013), Special Funds of Authors of Excellent Doctoral Dissertation in China, and Shanghai Science and Technology Funds(035115019)

I.J. Cox et al. (Eds.): IWDW 2004, LNCS 3304, pp. 42–54, 2005.

Table 1. The differences between our scheme and the work of P. Bas [1]

	Our Scheme	P. Bas [1]
Purpose	Watermarking or data hiding	Only Watermarking
Number of channels	Two. One for digital synchronization information, the other for hiding data.	One. Only for watermark.
Digital Synchronization Information	Coordinates of centers of triangles. Embedded in each triangle of one color space	None.
Hiding data	In another color space with full size	In each triangle of one color space
Effective volume of embedded content	More than 500 bits	Less than 50 bits
Using ECC	Convolutional codes, Turbo codes	No
Estimation of distortions	Yes	No

scheme inside each triangle of the Delaunay tessellation which is obtained by feature points extraction and Delaunay tessellations on the set of feature points. The detection is realized by using properties of correlation on different triangles. Simulation results show that the watermarking scheme is robust to some geometric distortions. But the capacity of channel, which is an important target in the data hiding, is not considered in his scheme.

This paper is inspired by the work of [1]. We propose a data hiding scheme which can counterattack global geometric distortions. The synchronization problem of data hiding is more difficult than that of watermarking, because the volume of data hiding is much larger than that of watermarking. The differences between our scheme and the work of [1] are shown in Table 1.

1.1   Global Geometric Distortions

Global geometric distortions, such as cropping, scaling, and rotation, can be considered 6-parameters affine transformations. Let (x, y) and (x', y') denote the coordinates of the original point and the affine point, respectively. We have

$$A(x,y) = \begin{pmatrix} a & b \\ d & e \end{pmatrix} \begin{pmatrix} x \\ y \end{pmatrix} + \begin{pmatrix} c \\ f \end{pmatrix} = \begin{pmatrix} x' \\ y' \end{pmatrix}. \tag{1}$$

1.2   Main Ideas

A color image can be considered two independent channels. One, named as the Synchronization Channel(SC), transmits the synchronization information. The other, named as the Communication Channel(CC), carries the hiding data. The SC is composed of triangles of the Delaunay tessellation which are based on the image content. And the CC spreads to the whole image. For example, we can choose blue space of RGB as the CC, and red tone of embedded triangles as the SC. Only 2 color spaces are modified in our scheme. After the image undergoes a geometric distortion, the six parameters of the global geometric distortion can be estimated by extracting a part of these synchronization information. Finally, the hiding data are extracted from the recovered CC. The synchronization problem is reduced by estimation of global geometric distortions.

1.) The Synchronization Channel: The purpose of SC is to re-synchronize the CC during the detection. We embed some information of synchronization, whose length is short, in some special triangles. The location of these triangles can be obtained by performing a Delaunay tessellation on a set of feature points in the image. These feature points can resist various types of geometric distortions. The synchronization information are the coordinates of the centers of these triangles where the information are embedded. During the detection, part of embedded triangles can be re-detected. Warping these triangles into the standard triangles, the receiver can extract original coordinates of the center in each triangle. According to the relationship of original centers and current centers, we can estimate the global geometric distortion.

2.) The Communication Channel: The purpose of this channel is to transmit a large amount of hiding data using the algorithm of [7]. Because the image can be recovered by the estimation of the global geometric distortion in the SC, the scheme is robust to geometric distortions.

This paper is organized as follows. Section 2 presents the embedded triangle detector. Synchronization information and ECC are discussed in Section 3. The triangle normalization process and its inverse is described in Section 4. Section 5 and Section 6 detail the embedding scheme and detection scheme. Simulation results in Section 7 will show the robustness to geometric distortions. Finally, Section 8 concludes our presentation.

2   Embedded Triangle Detector

In this section, we present our embedded triangle detector(ETD) used in the SC. The ETD is used to find some geometry-invariant triangles, so that the synchronization information can be embedded in them. Our ETD is based on the Harris corner detector and Delaunay tessellation.

2.1   Harris Corner Detector

Corners and vertices are strong and useful features in Computer Vision [3, 4]. We extract the feature points by Harris corner detector.

Harris and Stephens [2] proposed a corner detector, which works directly at grey scale level. It is used to compute locally a measure of *cornerness* C defined as the product of gradient magnitude and the rate of gradient direction. Let I denote the intensity of the image.

$$C = \begin{pmatrix} \hat{I_x^2} & \hat{I_x I_y} \\ \hat{I_x I_y} & \hat{I_x^2} \end{pmatrix}, \quad R(x,y) = Det(C) - kTrace^2(C), \tag{2}$$

where $\hat{I}$ denotes the smoothing operation on I, I_x and I_y represent the gradient magnitude. Harris gave a value of k (0.04) for providing discrimination against high contrast pixel step edges.

The output $R(x, y)$ is thresholded for the corner detection. A set of corners, eg. feature points, can be obtained by searching for local maxima.

$$S = \{(x, y) | R(x, y) > \eta, \forall (u, v) \in V_{x,y}, R(x, y) \geq R(u, v)\}, \tag{3}$$

where $V_{x,y}$ represents the neighborhood of (x, y).

To attain a homogeneous distribution of feature points, P. Bas et al. [1] suggest searching local maxima in a circular neighborhood, whose diameter depends on the image dimensions. In an image $(width \times height)$, let λ be a quantizer, and the diameter D of the neighborhood can be calculated by $D = \frac{\sqrt{width^2 + height^2}}{\lambda}$.

2.2   Embedded Triangle Detector

Some measurements must be applied to improve the robustness of the ETD. In our experiments, when running Harris corner detector directly on the image data, it is easy to find that feature points are lost significantly when the image undergoes strong geometric distortions, such as rotation and scaling. It results in more Delaunay triangles lost. We develop a method to tackle that problem. Firstly, the Harris corner detector is performed on the image, and the feature points are registered. Secondly, the Harris corner detector is applied on the distorted image, after the image undergoes a geometric distortion, such as rotation and scaling. The feature points are registered, too. Finally, comparing these two sets of feature points, we can obtain a set of feature points existing in both images. These feature points, more geometry-invariant than either of two cases, are chosen for our next triangulation.

The set of feature points permits image partition using a Delaunay tessellation. The Delaunay tessellation, for a set of vertices S, is a tessellation such that for each circumscribing circle of triangle formed by three vertices in S, no vertex of S is in the interior of the circle. The key advantage of using Delaunay tessellation is that the tessellation has stable local properties [6]. Furthermore, for a given set of points, the result of Delaunay tessellation are independent of scaling and rotation.

2.3   Evaluation

We define a parameter m in (4) to evaluate the capability to preserve the embedded triangles for our ETD when the image undergoes geometric distortions.

$$m = N_{pre}/N_{ini}, \tag{4}$$

where N_{ini} denotes the number of embedded triangles presented in the initial image, and N_{pre} represents the number of preserved embedded triangles after the process. When m is equal to 1, all of the embedded triangles are preserved. m directly affects the number of extracted synchronization information in the

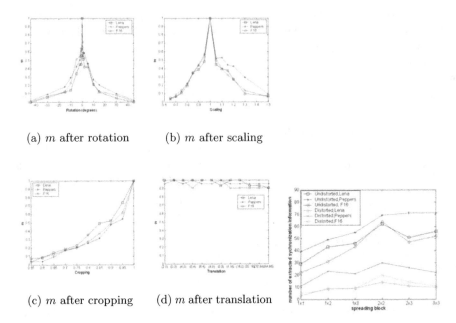

(a) m after rotation   (b) m after scaling

(c) m after cropping   (d) m after translation

Fig. 1. m— the ratio of preserved embedded triangles

Fig. 2. The performance of spreading blocks

SC, which have significant effect on the accuracy of estimation of geometric distortions.

We calculate m to evaluate our ETD by applying different geometric distortions on three popular standard pictures: Lena, Peppers, and F16, whose dimensions are 512×512.

16 rotations	$\pm45°$, $\pm30°$, $\pm15°$, $\pm10°$, $\pm5°$, $\pm2°$, $\pm1°$, $\pm0.5°$
10 scaling operations	0.7, 0.8, 0.85, 0.9, 0.95, 1.05, 1.1, 1.15, 1.2, 1.5
9 cropping operations	0.55, 0.60, 0.65, 0.7, 0.75, 0.8, 0.85, 0.9, 0.95
12 translations	$(2,0)$, $(0,2)$, $(4,0)$, $(0,4)$, $(6,4)$, $(8,0)$, $(0,8)$, $(8,16)$, $(16,0)$, $(32,16)$, $(32,64)$, $(64,96)$

where (x, y) ,in translation, denotes the new coordinates of the origin.

Simulation results are illustrated by Fig.1. If we threshold the parameter m by 0.15, there will be enough preserved embedded triangles when rotation angles are in -15° and 15°, scaling factors are in 0.8 and 1.2, and cropping factors are larger than 0.7. The ETD is strongly robust to translations.

3   Synchronization Information

In this section, we discuss the synchronization information and the ECC technology used in the SC. The synchronization information is composed of the

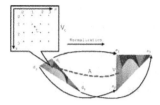

Fig. 3. Triangle normalization

Table 2. No. of extracted synchronization information before(B) and after(A) an 8° rotation

constraint	Lena B	Lena A	Peppers B	Peppers A	F16 B	F16 A
3	56	13	72	34	57	17
5	62	17	69	30	64	20
7	54	9	67	25	48	12

coordinates of centers of embedded triangles, cyclic redundancy check (CRC) bits, and parity check bits of convolutional codes.

3.1 Choosing Synchronization Information

The coordinates of embedded triangles' centers are considered as synchronization information for several reasons. Firstly, as far as a 6-parameters affine transformation is concerned, at least three pairs of corresponding points are required to estimate the six parameters. Let $v_i \in \mathbb{R}^2 (i = 1, 2, 3)$ be vertices of a triangle, the center of the triangle (v_1, v_2, v_3) is v. Applying an affine transform A on the triangle, it is true that

$$v = \frac{v_1 + v_2 + v_3}{3} \Rightarrow A(v) = \frac{A(v_1) + A(v_2) + A(v_3)}{3}. \tag{5}$$

Secondly, we can ensure that synchronization information are different from each other, since the location of Delaunay triangles' centers are different. Thirdly, the coordinates of a center can be represented by a twenty-bits sequence, when assuming the maximum dimensions of the image is 1024×1024. Each information has short length and can be felicitously embedded in the 96×96 standard triangles.

Further more, in order to exclude the great mass of wrong decoded synchronization information during detection, cyclic redundancy check bits accompany each synchronization information.

3.2 Using Error-Correcting Code for Synchronization Information

The SC, with low signal-to-noise ratio(SNR), is viewed as a noisy channel which transmits synchronization information. The pixels in the SC can be considered as additive white gaussian noise(AWGN). In our scheme, convolutional codes [8] are employed, and soft-decision Viterbi decoding algorithm is adopted to achieve a lower bit error rate (BER). Convolutional encoding with Viterbi decoding is a forward error correction (FEC) technique that is particularly suitable to a channel in which the transmitted signal is corrupted mainly by AWGN.

We compare the performance of convolutional codes with different constraint values. We extract synchronization information in the SC before and after an

$8°$ rotation. The correct extracted synchronization information are registered. According to experiments in Table 2, the best performance is achieved when the constraint value is 5.

4   Triangle Normalization and Its Inversion

Warping a triangle into another triangle can be done via affine transformation and spline-cubic interpolation. In our scheme, the standard triangle T_S is define as a 96×96 isosceles right-triangle. The procedure of warping a Delaunay triangle into a standard triangle is triangle normalization, while the triangle inversion is the inverse of the triangle normalization.

Fig.3 illustrates the process of the triangle normalization. Let $T(v_1, v_2, v_3)$ be a triangle with three vertices $v_1, v_2, v_3 \in \mathbb{Z}^2$, whose angles are descending. While warping a Delaunay triangle $T_D(d_1, d_2, d_3)$ into a standard triangle $T_S(s_1, s_2, s_3)$, we can calculate an affine transformation A satisfying $A(s_i) = d_i$, for $i = 1, 2, 3$. Let $s_1 = (0,0), s_2 = (0, q), s_3 = (q, 0)$ and $q = 96$, we have

$$A(v) = \frac{1}{q} \left(d_3^T - d_1^T \ d_2^T - d_1^T \right) v^T + d_1^T = t^T, \quad v, t \in \mathbb{R}^2. \tag{6}$$

Every point v in T_S can be mapped into its corresponding affine point t in T_D. A spline-cubic interpolation process [5] is applied on the neighborhood of the affine point to obtain the pixel value. The dimensions of its neighborhood, illustrated in Fig.3, are 4×4.

Inversely, a standard triangle can also be transformed into a Delaunay triangle with A^{-1}.

5   Embedding Scheme

Our scheme is designed for data hiding. The insertion and extraction are based on the pseudo-random spread spectrum technique, which provide robustness and imperceptibility via models of human visual system(HVS). The embedding scheme is divided into two parts detailed as follows.

5.1   Embedding in the CC

We embed hiding data in the CC using a spatial embedding algorithm[7]. We adopt Turbo codes instead of convolutional codes, since turbo codes provide better error-rate performance for long blocks than convolutional codes. Turbo codes [9] are a class of near channel capacity ECC, and they can transmit across the channel with arbitrary low BER. There are two primary decoding strategies for turbo code: one based on the maximum a posteriori(MAP) algorithm, the other based on the soft output Viterbi algorithm(SOVA). In our scheme, we adopt turbo codes with SOVA decoder and the code rate is equal to $\frac{1}{3}$.

5.2   Embedding in the SC

In the SC, all embedded triangles are considered independent sub-channels which carry different synchronization information. We input the original image and a secret key K.

1) The embedded triangles are obtained applying the ETD to the input image. $T = \{T_i\}, 0 \leq i < N_T$, where N_T denotes the number of triangles.

2) The pseudo-random sequence generator initialized by a secret key K generates pseudo-random sequences $P = \{p_k\}, p_k \in \{-1, +1\}$.

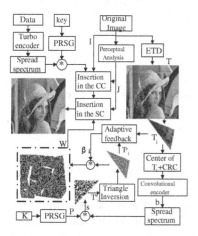

Fig. 4. Double-channels embedding scheme

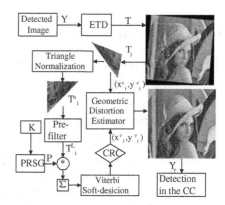

Fig. 5.   Double-channels   detection scheme

3) Obtain mark triangle blocks. Calculate coordinates of the center in T_i, add CRC bits, and perform a convolutional encoding process on the codes. After the process of a classical pseudo-random spread spectrum, we obtain modulated signals s. The 1-D sequence s is arranged in the shape of the standard triangle by the zigzag scanning mode.

$$s[k] = b[\lfloor \frac{k}{N_l} \rfloor] \cdot p_k, \tag{7}$$

where b denotes the output bits of convolutional encoder, and N_l represents the spreading length of every bit.

4) Warp T_i^w into T_i^e in the same shape as T_i by the inversion of triangle normalization.

5) An adaptive embedding strength β_i is estimated for T_i^e. T_i^e is embedded in the T_i by $T_i' = T_i + \beta_i \cdot T_i^e$. A detection process is performed on the T_i'. We search a minimal value $\beta_i \in [1, 4]$ without error. We call it adaptive feedback.

6) When all signal triangles are done, we can embed these signal by

$$I_r' = I_r + J \cdot W, \quad W = \cup\{(\beta_i \cdot T_i^e)\}, \tag{8}$$

where W denotes the mark signal in the SC, I_r and I_r' denote color components of the SC in the original image and the marked image, and J presents the spatial perceptual mask [7] considering the HVS .

In order to avoid the superposition of signals between adjacent triangles, we shouldn't arrange modulated signals near the border of the standard triangle in step 3). The modulated signals are spread on 2×2 pixel blocks, which allows improving the signature detection after affine transformations. The performance of different shapes of spreading blocks is illustrated in Fig.2. We compare 6 kinds of spreading blocks: 1×1, 1×2, 1×3, 2×2, 2×3 and 3×3, before and after an $8°$ rotation. Simulation results show that the best performance is achieved when the shape of the spreading block is 2×2.

6 Detection Scheme

The detection scheme, illustrated in Fig.5, is mainly divided into three procedures detailed as follows. The detection does not need original image.

6.1 Detection in the SC

Given a detected image Y and the secret key K, the detection procedure in the SC obtains a set of synchronization information.

Step 1) and 2) are identical to the step 1) and 2) in the subsection 5.2.

3) $T_i \in T$ is warped into a standard triangle T_i^n by triangle normalization.

4) Immediately, a pre-filter is applied on the normalized triangle T_i^n. A majority of image's energy, which is considered AWGN, is eliminated.

$$
\begin{aligned}
T_i^L &= T_i^n * \tfrac{1}{16}\mathbf{L}, \\
\mathbf{L} &= (L_{i,j}), 0 \leqslant x,y \leqslant 8,
\end{aligned}
\qquad
L_{x,y} =
\begin{cases}
-1 & x = 4 \ \ or \ \ y = 4 \ \ and \ \ x \neq y; \\
16 & x = y = 4; \\
0 & others.
\end{cases}
\qquad (9)
$$

5) The synchronization codes are extracted from each T_i^L by Viterbi soft-decision. By cyclic redundancy checking process, we obtain $\{(x_k^e, y_k^e)\}$, $0 \leq k < N_e$, where N_e denotes the number of extracted synchronization information (NESI).

6) Let (x_k^c, y_k^c) be the current center of the corresponding triangle where (x_k^e, y_k^e) is extracted. We collect a set of pairs of corresponding points:

$$
\chi = \{((x_k^e, y_k^e), (x_k^c, y_k^c))\}, 0 \leq k < N_e. \qquad (10)
$$

6.2 Estimation of Geometric Distortion and Image Recovery

According to the set χ, our algorithm, combined with K-means algorithm and least square method (LSM), can estimate geometric distortion accurately, even if there are a few incorrect pairs in χ.

Estimation algorithm of geometric distortion:

```
MaxCluster = 0;
for all {k₁, k₂, k₃} ∈ C³_Ne  {
    Q = {k₁, k₂, k₃};
    do{  F = LSM(Q);    Q = Φ;
        for all i ∈ [0, Ne − 1]  {
            (xᵃᵢ, yᵃᵢ) = F • (xᵉᵢ, yᵉᵢ);
            dᵢ = √((xᶜᵢ − xᵃᵢ)² + (yᶜᵢ − yᵃᵢ)²);
            if (dᵢ < ε) then    Q = Q∪{i};
        }
    }while ‖Q‖ increasing;
    if (MaxCluster < ‖Q‖)  {
        MaxCluster=‖Q‖;    A = LSM(Q);
    }
}.
```

where ε represents a threshold of distance d_i, $\boldsymbol{F} \bullet$ is the operation of an affine transform using $\boldsymbol{F}$, and $\|Q\|$ denotes the size of the set Q. The $LSM(\cdot)$ is a function used to calculate $\boldsymbol{A}$ by LSM algorithm described below.

For more pairs of corresponding points, the linear relationship in Equation (1) can be expressed more compactly in a matrix form as:

$$
\begin{aligned}
\boldsymbol{Z} &= H\boldsymbol{A}, \\
\boldsymbol{Z} &= (x_0', y_0', x_1', y_1', ...)^T, \quad H = \begin{pmatrix} x_0 & y_0 & 1 & 0 & 0 & 0 \\ 0 & 0 & 0 & x_0 & y_0 & 1 \\ x_1 & y_1 & 1 & 0 & 0 & 0 \\ 0 & 0 & 0 & x_1 & y_1 & 1 \\ \vdots & \vdots & \vdots & \vdots & \vdots & \vdots \end{pmatrix}, \\
\boldsymbol{A} &= (a, b, c, d, e, f)^T,
\end{aligned} \tag{11}
$$

where column vector $\boldsymbol{A}$ represents the parameters of affine transform, vector $\boldsymbol{Z}$ contains the coordinates of affine points (x_i', y_i') stung out into a column vector, and the rows of matrix H contain the coordinates of original points (x_i, y_i) stung out into row vectors. At least three pairs of corresponding points are required to estimate the 6 parameters. The estimation of affine transformation can be done by minimizing the square difference, e.g. the Least Square Method.

$$
\boldsymbol{A} = (H^T H)^{-1} H^T \boldsymbol{Z}. \tag{12}
$$

According to the parameters $\boldsymbol{A}$, the CC can be re-synchronized by image reconstruction using the affine transformation and spline-cubic interpolation.

6.3   Detection in the CC

We extract the hiding data from the re-synchronized CC by the detector of [7].

7   Simulation Results

We test our proposed data hiding scheme on the popular test images 512×512 Lena, Peppers and F16. We define a 512-bits sequence as the hiding data. We

Table 3. Simulation results of our data hiding scheme. BER denotes the Bit-Error Rate of the extracted hiding data in the CC. NESI represents the Number of Extracted Synchronization Information in the SC

attacks		Y-shearing		X-shearing		Translation		General		Cropping		
		A_1	A_2	A_3	A_4	A_5	A_6	A_7	A_8	0.75	0.85	0.95
Lena	BER%	0	0.39	0	0	0	0	1.95	0	6.44	4.10	2.34
	NESI	22	19	24	17	51	50	13	14	14	20	25
Peppers	BER%	0	0.20	0	0.59	0	0	0	1.17	2.54	1.17	1.17
	NESI	38	30	40	28	62	62	25	29	4	21	33
F16	BER%	0	0.78	0	0	0	0	1.17	1.75	3.51	1.75	0.98
	NESI	23	21	30	32	56	53	19	15	9	19	30

attacks		Removing lines							Scaling						
		10	20	30	40	50	60	70	0.75	0.85	0.95	1.10	1.20	1.30	1.50
Lena	BER%	9.77	0.78	0	0.78	0.78	0.78	0	37.9	0	0	0	6.45	9.38	29.9
	NESI	7	16	25	13	25	33	24	5	12	15	17	10	8	6
Peppers	BER%	6.05	0.78	1.95	0	0.59	0	0	20.7	0.98	0.98	0	1.37	7.42	14.3
	NESI	19	23	21	31	33	29	37	6	16	25	33	21	11	8
F16	BER%	12.1	5.66	5.01	0	2.34	0	0	23.0	1.37	0	0.39	5.27	6.64	23.8
	NESI	5	13	12	18	27	25	32	4	13	17	22	15	10	8

attacks		Rotation														
		-15	-10	-5	-2	-1	-0.5	-0.25	0.25	0.5	1	2	5	10	15	30
Lena	BER%	7.62	5.66	0	1.17	0.98	1.17	0	0.20	0	0	0	1.17	3.71	5.27	20.3
	NESI	9	11	18	16	21	22	30	25	23	20	22	20	13	10	6
Peppers	BER%	0.98	0.78	0.78	1.17	0	0.59	0	0	0.20	0.59	0	0	1.17	1.17	1.17
	NESI	19	26	34	38	39	40	51	49	39	35	37	38	24	18	11
F16	BER%	6.45	4.10	0	0.78	0.78	1.17	0.39	0.20	0.20	1.56	0.39	1.95	2.53	6.45	19.9
	NESI	11	16	20	23	26	20	27	26	22	25	26	21	15	12	7

choose blue space for the CC, and red space for the SC. The $PSNR$ values between the original and the marked images are 45.31dB, 47.44dB, and 46.60dB for Lena, Pepper, and F16, respectively.

Stirmark4.0 [10] is employed to evaluate the robustness to geometric distortions. The simulation results for geometric distortions are shown in Table 3.

- Affine transformations.
  Y-shearing $A_1 = (1, 0, 0, 0.02, 1, 0)$ $A_2 = (1, 0, 0, 0.05, 1, 0)$
  X-shearing $A_3 = (1, 0.02, 0, 0, 1, 0)$ $A_4 = (1, 0.05, 0, 0, 1, 0)$
  Translation $A_5 = (1, 0, 4, 0, 1, 16)$ $A_6 = (1, 0, 32, 0, 1, 64)$
  General $A_7 = (1.015, 0.013, 0, 0.02, 1.011, 0)$ $A_8 = (1.025, 0.01, 0, 0.04, 1.012, 0)$
- Cropping: Crop image at different ratio. ratio = 0.75, 0.85, 0.95. The cropping below 0.75 will lose too much image content, which results in high BER;
- Scaling: Scale image at different scale: 0.75, 0.85, 0.95, 1.1, 1.2, 1.3, 1.5;
- Removing Lines: Remove one line at different frequency of row and column: $10, 20, \cdots 70$;
- Rotation: Rotate image at different angles: $30°, \pm 15°, \pm 10°, \pm 5°, \pm 2°, \pm 1°$, $\pm 0.5°, \pm 0.25°$.

Our scheme is robust to affine transformation, centered cropping, removing lines, rotation, scaling, and translation. When geometric distortions get stronger, NESI decreases rapidly and BER of the hiding data in the CC ascends sharply. This is caused by significant loss of the embedded triangles. For instance, cropping attacks change the size of image, but not the size of the image content. As a result, the diameter of searching neighborhood is changed and some feature points are lost. So the embedded triangles can not be identified correctly and completely. The BER is above 20% because of too many pixel information being lost when the factor of cropping is below 0.75 or the factor of scaling is outside [0.85,1.3]. Our scheme shows strong robustness to removing lines process which is similar to scaling process. Because signal are embedded in spatial domain, our scheme can counterattack a very slight noise or high quality jpeg processing.

8   Conclusions

In this paper, we propose a new approach for data hiding that counterattack global geometric distortions. We emphasize our key elements as follows. The synchronization information and estimation of geometric distortions in the SC guarantee the re-synchronization of the CC. Channels are separated for synchronization and communication. Although it may reduce the channel capacity, the robustness to geometric distortions is improved greatly. Convolutional codes in the SC and Turbo codes in the CC provide a satisfying performance.

One immediate extension of our scheme is the video data-hiding that counterattack geometric distortions. Another extension is the robustness to the global geometric distortion with 8-parameters. The future line of research consists of designing a more stable ETD to improve the m, and modifying the scheme in frequency domain to improve the robustness to signal processing.

References

1. P. Bas, J.-M. Chassery, and B. Macq, "Geometrically invariant watermarking using feature points," *IEEE Trans. Image Processing*, Vol. 11, No. 9, pp. 1014-1028, Sept. 2002.
2. C. Harris and M. Stephen, "A combined corner and edge detector," in *Proc. of the 4th Alvey Vision Conf.*, pp. 147-151, 1988.
3. G. Giraudon and R. Deriche, "A computational approach for corner and vertex detection," *International Journal of Computer Vision*, vol.10, no.2, pp. 101-124, 1993.
4. N. Gracias and J. Santos-Victor, "Underwater video mosaics as visual navigation maps," *Computer Vision and Image Understanding*, Vol. 79, No. 1, pp. 66-91, July 2000.
5. D.P. Mitchell and A.N.Netravali, "Reconstruction filters in computer graphics," *Computer Graphics (Proc. of ACM SIGGRAPH 88)*, Vol. 22, No. 4, pp. 221-228, Aug. 1988.
6. M. de Berg, M. van Kreveld, M. Overmars, and O.Schwarzkopf, *Computational Geometry: Algorithms and Applications*, Springer-Verlag, 2nd edition, 2000.

7. Zhiyan Du, Yan Zou, Peizhong Lu, "An optimized spatial data hiding scheme combined with convolutional codes and hilbert scan," *Lecture Notes in Computer Science*, Vol. 2532, pp. 97-104, Jan. 2002.

8. G.C. Clark and J.B. Cain, *Error-Correction Coding for Digital Communications*, Plenum Press, New York, 1981.

9. C. Heegard, S.B. Wicker, *Turbo Coding*, Kluwer Academic Publishers, Boston, 1999.

10. F.A.P. Petitcolas, StirMark Benchmark 4.0, [Online].
    Available: http://www.petitcolas.net/fabien/watermarking/stirmark/, 2003.

A Secure Internet-Based Personal Identity Verification System Using Lossless Watermarking and Fingerprint Recognition

Guorong Xuan[1], Junxiang Zheng[1], Chengyun Yang[1],
Yun Q. Shi[2], Dekun Zou[2], Liu Liansheng[3], and Bai Weichao[3]

[1] Tongji University, Shanghai, China
[2] New Jersey Institute of Technology, New Jersey, USA
[3] Baojia Electronic Equipments, Co. Ltd, Shenzhen, China

Abstract. This paper proposes an internet-based personal identity verification system using lossless data hiding and fingerprint recognition technologies. At the client side, the SHA-256 hash of the original fingerprint image and sensitive personal information are encrypted and embedded into the fingerprint image using an advanced lossless data hiding scheme. At the service provider side, after the hidden data are extracted out, the fingerprint image can be recovered without any distortion due to the usage of the lossless data hiding scheme. Hence, the originality of the fingerprint image can be ensured via hash check. The extracted personal information can be used to obtain the correct fingerprint feature from the database. The fingerprint matching can finally verify the client's identity. The experimental results demonstrate that our proposed system is effective. It can find wide applications in e-banking and e-government systems to name a few.

1   Introduction

As more and more activities are being conducted through Internet, people are more willing to use this convenient way to handle personal business including financial activities. Some of them involve large amount of money. However, Internet by itself is not a safe place. Criminals prefer to rob banks by using advanced technology rather than by using gun nowadays. Most of the online crimes rely on feigning the identity of other people. Thus, personal identity verification has emerged as a crucial issue for the safety of online activities.

In this paper, we proposed a smart internet-based personal identity verification system using lossless digital image watermarking and fingerprint recognition. On the one hand, our system utilizes the fingerprint to identify person. We use one way hash SHA256 to ensure the originality of the fingerprint image. On the other hand, personal information is embedded into the fingerprint

I.J. Cox et al. (Eds.): IWDW 2004, LNCS 3304, pp. 55–65, 2005.

image losslessly and imperceptibly so that it can be transmitted through the Internet covertly. At the client side, fingerprint and encrypted user information serve as input of the identity verification. At the service provider side such as banks verify the fingerprint by using the hash value and the encrypted data to authorize the remote client. We claim that the combination of fingerprint and encryption can achieve better security than either of them alone. Firstly, secure messages are embedded into the fingerprint images. As a result, the data amount needed to transmit will not increase. Secondly, since the secure message cannot be seen directly by human eyes, it is safer than encryption alone in which the malicious attackers will easily know that there exist secret messages. Thirdly, the fingerprint is hashed and the hash value is embedded into the fingerprint image itself. As a result, the originality of the fingerprint can be guaranteed via authentication.

To the best knowledge of the authors of this paper, there is no prior art concerning embedding information into fingerprint images in the literature. Our proposed system can be applied to various applications such as e-banking, e-trading and e-government systems. In fact, it has been applied into an online pension distribution system in China.

2   Invertible Data Hiding

The invertible data hiding scheme adopted in this paper is to embed watermark into middle bit-planes of the image wavelet coefficients of the highest frequency sub-bands. We apply histogram modification before embedding to ensure that no over/under-flow will occur after data hiding. The watermark scheme we used has very high capacity and low visual artifact. In addition, the computational complexity of the proposed algorithm is low. In this section, we present a brief introduction of the basic idea of the scheme. The new improvements of the scheme [1], that has made the scheme much more efficient, and the application of the updated scheme to the verification system are described.

2.1   Selection of Wavelet Family

Although our invertible watermarking scheme can be applied to various wavelet families, after experimental comparison, we have discovered that CDF(2,2) is better than other wavelet families in terms of embedding capacity and visual quality of watermarked image in general.

2.2   Selection of Embedding Sub-band and Bit-Plane

Manipulating on sub-band HL, LH and HH of the highest resolution level will cause the least visual artifact because they contain only the highest frequency components. In these sub-bands, we embed data into a particular bit-plane. For a coefficient, if a flip occurs in the nth bit-plane, its value will change by amount of 2^{n-1}. For example, a flip on 4th bit-plane will either increase or decrease the coefficient value by 8. The higher the bit-plane is, the larger the change is and the lower the marked image quality will be. However, usually, the higher the bit-plane is, the shorter bit stream it can be compressed into. As a result, higher embedding capacity can be achieved. Hence, there is a trade-off between image quality and embedding capacity. Instead of only embedding data in one bit-plane as in [1], we propose here to use multiple bit-planes for data hiding if the capacity provided by one bit-plane is not enough. We define the bit-plane(s) used to embed data as *Embedding Bit-plane(s)* , and the remaining as *Untouched Bit-planes*.

2.3   Histogram Modification

The purpose of histogram modification is to compress the histogram range of the original fingerprint image so that, after data hiding, the pixel value of the marked image will not exceed the permitted value range which is (0,255) usually. If over/under-flow occurs, the lossless property of the watermarking scheme will be lost and the original fingerprint image cannot be recovered.

We select G grey levels, G/2 on both borders, which need to be merged as illustrated in Fig. 1 After modification, the histogram range is reduced to [G/2, (255-G/2)]. In order to recover the original fingerprint losslessly, the information about how to recover the original histogram will be embedded into the fingerprint as well as overhead. The parameter G is related to which wavelet family we choose and which sub-band we choose as the embedding carrier. An analysis is provided as follows:

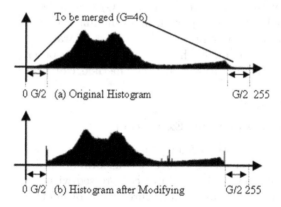

Fig. 1. Histogram modification

If CDF(2,2) is selected and the data are to be embedded into the fourth bit-plane of HH, HL, LH sub-bands of the highest resolution level, according to integer lifting scheme formula,

$$d_i \Leftarrow d_i - \left[\frac{1}{2} \left(s_i + s_{i+1} \right) + \frac{1}{2} \right] \tag{1}$$

$$s_i \Leftarrow s_i - \left[\frac{1}{2} \left(d_{i-1} + d_i \right) + \frac{1}{2} \right] \tag{2}$$

We can estimate pixel value change. If a flip on the 4th bit-plane occurs, the coefficients will change by amount of 8. We can find out that the pixel value will change by amount of M=42 in the worst case. Thus, the histogram adjusting value G should be 84.

The estimation of M considers only the worst case in all steps. In reality, the probability that this result occurs is very small. According to our experiments, when moderate watermarking capacity is required, it is enough for G to be 30 to avoid over/under-flow for most natural images [1].

Although the histogram modification is to prevent over/under-flow, it will degrade the visual quality of the marked image. Two problems are brought out by big G. One is that the number of pixels needed to be changed increases. As a result, visual quality degrades. The other problem is the information for recovering original histogram increases. Thus, the effective capacity will decrease. In conclusion, the value G should be as small as possible.

Obviously, we need to embed the data representing the bookkeeping information in histogram modification in order to late recover the original image. In [1] a coordinate-based bookkeeping is used, in which the coordinates of pixels moved towards the middle and their gray levels are recorded. This results in a large amount of bookkeeping data when either the image size is large or the number of pixels assuming two end levels is large. Here, we propose to use the merge-and-shift based bookkeeping method. That is, to empty G/2 gray levels at one side of the histogram, we choose G/2 suitable gray level pairs (two neighboring gray levels form a pair) from examining the histogram. We merge a pair of levels and leave an empty level. The rest of gray levels are shifted from the end towards the middle of the gray levels. For the other side of histogram, we do the similar modification. This new method can save bookkeeping data effectively.

2.4   Data Embedding and Extraction

As illustrated in Fig. 2, the original fingerprint image is subject to histogram modification first. After forward wavelet transform applied to the modified image, the embedding bit-plane(s) is(are) compressed with JBIG algorithm. The left-over part is used to embed data. Three kinds of information are needed to be embedded. They are the hash value of the fingerprint image, the information about recovering the original histogram and the user's personal information. All of them are combined together and encrypted with an encryption key. The encrypted bit-stream is embedded into the left-over part of the embedding bit-plane(s). Then, the embedding bit-plane(s) and the untouched bit-planes are

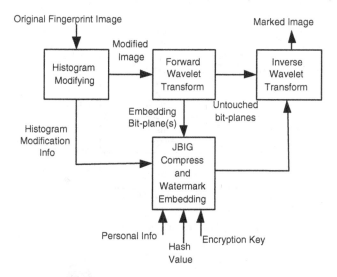

Fig. 2. Watermark embedding

combined together for inverse wavelet transform. Finally, we have the marked fingerprint image which is ready for transmission. Watermark extraction procedure is the reverse of the embedding part which is illustrated by Fig. 3. After the embedded data is extracted, it is decrypted with a decryption key. Two encryption/decryption schemes can be applied in our system. One is symmetric scheme in which both keys are the same and the key is needed to be transmitted. The other is non-symmetric scheme which is known as public/private key pair. The recovered fingerprint image will be subject to hash verification to determine its originality.

2.5 Performance Analysis

We have applied our algorithm to two fingerprint libraries. Library A is FVC2000 fingerprint database[3]. Image size is 300x300. Library B is generated in our work using Verdicom's fingerprint mouse[4]. The image size is 256x300. Our experiments show that for Library A, the embedding capacity can be as large as 0.6bpp. For Library B, the capacity is 0.11bpp. Both are enough for our system requirement. In terms of image quality, for A, if watermark is embedded at the rate of 0.4bpp, the PSNR of the marked image vs. the original image is over 30dB. For B, if the embedding data rate is 0.07bpp, the PSNR is over 24dB. All of marked images have no visual artifact. It is noted that the result of Library A is better than that of Library B.

Fig. 4 and Fig. 5 are the testing results of a fingerprint, named A1, in Library A. The histogram is low on borders. The pixel grey values range from 101 to 250. Hence the histogram modification will not change the image much. In the test, the amount of 0.11bpp data is losslessly embedded in the 4th bit-plane of HH subband of the highest resolution. G is set to be 12 so that the modified histogram

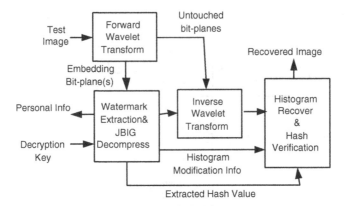

Fig. 3. Watermark extraction

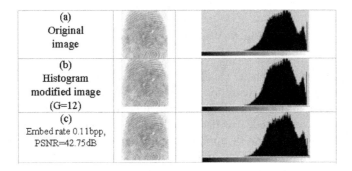

Fig. 4. Fingerprint A1 and its histogram before and after modification and embedding

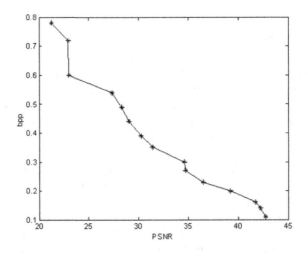

Fig. 5. Relationship between PSNR and payload for A1

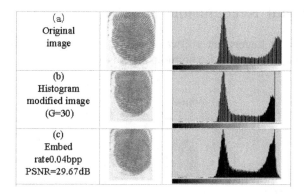

Fig. 6. Fingerprint B1 and its histogram before and after modification and embedding

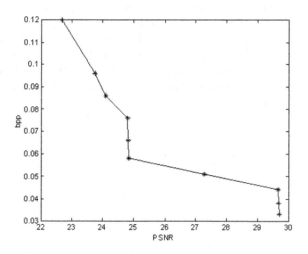

Fig. 7. Relationship between PSNR and payload for B1

ranges from 101 to 249. Only 1 grey level, 250, is needed to be merged. PSNR of marked image is 42.75dB. Library B is generated by Veridicom's fingerprint mouse[4]. All fingerprints in it are different from those in Library A in some aspects such as histogram structure. Although the result of Library B is not as good as that of Library A, both watermarking capacity and visual quality meet our system's need.

Fig. 6 and Fig. 7 are the testing results of a finger B1, in Library B. The histogram ranges from 0 to 255 and is high on both borders but low on center. 0.04bpp data is embedded in the 5th bit-plane of the HH sub-band of the highest resolution. G is set to be 30, so that after modification, the histogram range will be compressed to [15, 240]. 30 grey levels are to be merged. The PSNR of the marked B1 is 29.67dB.

3   Fingerprint Recognition

We use Veridicom's fingerprint software and fingerprint mouse to capture the fingerprint image[2][4]. Fig. 8 is the mouse we used.

Fig. 8. Veridicom's fingerprint mouse

Because the watermarking scheme used in this paper is invertible, watermarking itself will not affect the fingerprint recognition process at all. Thus, the performance of recognition will be influenced by the fingerprint software and hardware. To test the performance, we apply the recognition to FVC2000 fingerprint database[3]. In this database, we select 8 categories of fingerprints and for each category, we choose 10 fingerprints. The total number is 8x10=80 fingerprints. Fig. 9 contains eight fingerprints in one category.

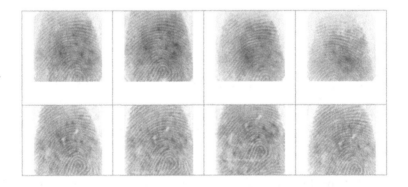

Fig. 9. Eight fingerprints in one category

Then, we select 8 fingerprints in each category to train the recognition software. Finally, we match all the 80 fingerprints to the training results. Table 1 is the matching results. If two fingerprints have the number of matched features great than the *Threshold Value*, we consider them belonging to the same person. The *Correct Matching Rate* is the rate by which the system can successfully identify a person. The *Error Rate* is the rate by which the system wrongly identify person Y in the database as person X. It is noted that the lower the Threshold Value is, the higher the matching rate will be. In addition, the error rate is zero

Table 1. Matching Results

Threshold Value	Correct Matching Rate	Error Rate
15	72.5%	0%
13	77.5%	0%
11	82.5%	0%
10	85%	0%
8	87.5%	0%
5	90%	0%
3	90%	0%
1	90%	0%

for all the threshold values listed. In order to increase the matching rate, the user can input their fingerprint by three times. Assuming they are independent event, the final matching rate will be 97.2% if we set the threshold to be 5 for all three matches.

4   Personal Identity Verification

Our proposed system can be used to verify a person's identity through Internet.

4.1   System Architecture

Fig. 10 is the proposed system architecture. Central Database stores the features of the registered users' fingerprints and their other personal information. The Server receives marked fingerprints transmitted from registered users and extracts personal information. If the identity is verified, the user will be authorized for further transaction.

Fig. 10. System architecture

4.2   Software Module

Identity Registration. Before identity verification, user must register their fingerprint and other personal information in the central database. Specifically, fingerprint capture device will capture three fingerprint images of the same finger and extract the features of them. Finally, the features and user's personal information are stored in the central database.

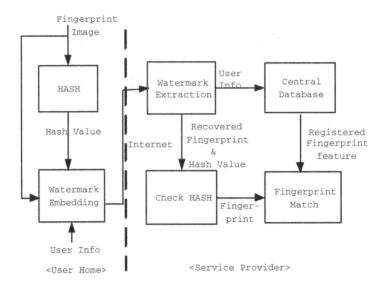

Fig. 11. Identity verification

Identity Verification. Identity verification procedure is depicted in Fig. 11. The fingerprint is compared with the registered fingerprint feature. If a match achieves, the user is authorized. It can be seen that two level of security is provided here. One is the hash check, the other is fingerprint match. The former authenticates the originality of the fingerprint, while the latter recognizes the registered person's identity. Failure of either one will cause the failure of the authentication.

5   Summary

In our proposed system, messages are embedded into the fingerprint image itself. No visible artifact can be detected. It is more secure than encryption protection method alone. The invertible feature of the adopted watermarking scheme combines with the feature of SHA, the originality of the fingerprint image is guaranteed.

Acknowledgement

This project is supported by China NSFC: The Research of Theory and Key Technology of Lossless Data Hiding (90304017), and NJCST via NJWINS.

References

1. G. Xuan, J. Chen, J. Zhu, Y. Q. Shi, Z. Ni, W. Su : Distortionless data hiding based on integer wavelet transform. Proceedings of IEEE Workshop on Multimedia Signal Processing (MMSP'02). US Virgin Islands, Dec. 2002; IEE Electronics Letters, vol. 38, no. 25, pp. 1646-1648, Dec.2002.
2. Veridicom Authentication Software Development Kit: Users Manual (For Evaluation) Version 3.0.0
3. http://bias.csr.unibo.it/fvc2000/
4. http://www.veridicom.com

Better Use of Human Visual Model in Watermarking Based on Linear Prediction Synthesis Filter

Xinshan Zhu and Yangsheng Wang

Institute of Automation, Chinese Academy of Sciences,
Beijing 100080, China
{xszhu, wys}@nlpr.ia.ac.cn

Abstract. This paper presents a new approach on utilizing human visual model (HVM) for watermarking. The approach introduces the linear prediction synthesis filter, whose parameters are derived from a set of just noticeable differences estimated by HVM. After being filtered by such a filter, the watermark can be adapted to characteristics of human visual system. As a result, the watermark visibility is noticeably decreased, while at the same time enhancing its energy. The theoretic analysis of the detector is done to illustrate the affect of the filter on detection value. And the experimental results prove the effectiveness of the new approach.

1   Introduction

Image watermarking [1], is finding more and more support as a possible solution for the protection of intellectual property rights. To this aim, the most important features a watermarking technique should exhibit are unobtrusiveness and robustness. However, there exists mutual contradiction between them during watermark embedding. For obtaining the robust watermark, the cover data are modified largely which degrades their quality and fidelity. Presently it is widely accepted that robust image watermarking techniques should largely exploit the characteristics of the human visual system (HVS) [1], [2], [3].

The response of HVS varies with the spatial frequency, brightness, and color of its input. Many perceptual models of HVS have been constructed in spatial domain [4], frequency domain [5, 6] and wavelet domain [7, 8]. Generally the just noticeable differences (JND) can be derived in a HVM, which prescribe the smallest amount of change to be discernible in local image. And a perceptual distance is introduced to estimate the overall change in a work.

There has been much research over the years in applying HVS to image watermarking. In [9], each component of a watermarking signal is first weighted using the JND and then embedded into an original image. Many other algorithms follow the scheme [4,10-15]. Obviously, such perceptually shaped (linear scaling) watermark signal can not reflect the local image characteristics very well. If the watermark signal is generated independently by a Gaussian random number generator, most components are near zeros and some ones are beyond

I.J. Cox et al. (Eds.): IWDW 2004, LNCS 3304, pp. 66–76, 2005.

one. As a result, most local image characteristics are not used sufficiently, while at some locations, embedding may lead to visible artifacts. In [14], the optimal use of perceptual models is proposed. Two alternative optimal behaviors for the embedder are specified: 1) maximizing the robustness of an embedded mark, while maintaining a constant perceptual distance. 2) minimizing perceptual distance while maintaining a constant robustness. The optimality disregards the considerations of the local image characteristics. The above problems still exist. In addition, JND is used to derive perceptually based quantizer and to determine perceptually based bit allocation in some algorithms [16, 17].

In this paper, a linear prediction (LP) synthesis filter is introduced to shape the watermarking signal. Section 2 describes the construction and property of the filter. Based on these, it is applied to adapt the spectral structure of the watermark to the JND obtained from the adopted HVM in Section 3. And the model of watermark embedding is also presented. Section 4 theoretically analyzes the performance of the modified linear correlation detector. A specific watermarking is designed according to the proposed scheme and a serial of tests are done to evaluate it in Section 5. Finally, we conclude the paper.

2   Linear Prediction Synthesis Filter

One of the classical results of science of speech coding theory has been the development of the LP synthesis filter [18]. Recently, some work is done to extend it from 1-D to 2-D in theory and application [19, 20]. In this section, the 2-D model and properties of it are described concisely.

Suppose that $x(n_1, n_2)$ represents a 2-D discrete spatial signal. Applying optimum linear prediction theory (i.e. forming and solving 2-D Yule-Walker normal equations) to $x(n_1, n_2)$, the linear prediction coefficients (LPC), $A = \{a(m_1, m_2) \in R | 0 \leq m_1 \leq m_2, 0 \leq m_2 \leq p_2\}$ can be obtained, where p_1 and p_2 represent the row order and column order respectively [18, 19]. And the linear prediction error $e(n_1, n_2)$ with variance $G^2 = \varepsilon\{|e(n_1, n_2)|^2\}$ has the form

$$e(n_1, n_2) = x(n_1, n_2) - \sum_{\substack{m_1=0 \\ m_2 \neq 0}}^{p_1} \sum_{\substack{m_2=0 \\ m_1 \neq 0}}^{p_2} a(m_1, m_2) x(n_1 - m_1, n_2 - m_2) \qquad (1)$$

The LP synthesis filter is defined as an IIR filter using the LPC array A as the filter taps. Therefore, it is expressed in the form of I/O difference equation as

$$y(n_1, n_2) = \sum_{\substack{m_1=0 \\ m_2 \neq 0}}^{p_1} \sum_{\substack{m_2=0 \\ m_1 \neq 0}}^{p_2} a(m_1, m_2) y(n_1 - m_1, n_2 - m_2) + G\nu(n_1, n_2) \qquad (2)$$

It has been shown in [20] that a nice property of this filter is that it can adapt the spectral structure of the processing noise, $\nu(n_1, n_2)$ to that of the host signal $x(n_1, n_2)$, which is illustrated in 1-D in the bottom of Fig. 1. According to the conclusion, this filter is also able to adapt the spectral structure of the processing

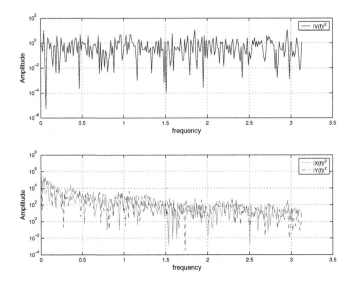

Fig. 1. The spatial domain LP synthesis filter adapts the structure of the noise spectrum to that of the signal spectrum

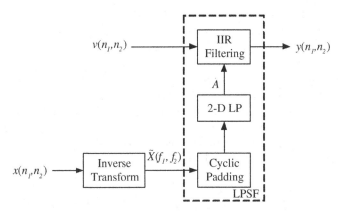

Fig. 2. Basic design of LP synthesis filter to adapt the spectral structure of the processing noise to the signal $x(n_1, n_2)$ itself

noise to the signal $x(n_1, n_2)$ itself, as long as A is derived by applying optimum linear prediction theory to the 2-D inverse Fourier transform of $x(n_1, n_2)$, which is denoted with $\widetilde{X}(f_1, f_2)$. In fact, $x(n_1, n_2)$ is viewed as the spectrum to be simulated. The design of LP synthesis filters for the latter purpose is depicted in Fig. 2.

In the practical application of such a filter, the main difficulty is to calculate the LPC. The problem has been investigated adequately in [19]. Real filterbanks, such as discrete cosine transform (DCT) or modified DCT (MDCT), are best used for spectral transform. Additionally, unlike 1-D LP synthesis filter, 2-D LP synthesis filter cannot be guaranteed to be stable. One solution is to cyclically pad the host signal before calculating the LPC. Another one is to weight the calculated LPC. More detail can be found in [20].

3 Watermark Embedding

LP synthesis filter is applied broadly to speech coding, image coding and compression. In this section, it is adopted to adapt the spectral structure of watermark signal to the JND obtained from some HVM, which allows more efficient use of HVM.

In most of watermarking algorithms, the watermark, w_m to express a specific message is a set of random numbers of independently Normal distribution with zero mean. Therefore

$$w_m(i,j) \sim N(0, \sigma_{wm}^2) \tag{3}$$

It is embedded into the target image I_o using the linear modulation as

$$c_{wm}(i,j) = c_o(i,j) + \alpha_m w_m(i,j) \tag{4}$$

where c_o, c_{wm} denote the cover data and the covered data respectively and α_m is a global embedding strength. Assume that c_o is drawn from I_o in the spatial domain and a JND array, s is estimated using some proposed HVM in frequency domain. Intuitively, a stronger watermark can be embedded if w_m is reshaped as w_s, the spectral coefficients of which, W_S is near to s. Based on this idea, LP synthesis filter can be applied to obtain w_s according to the property of it. Since the simulated signal s is in frequency domain, the operation of filtering should be performed in spatial domain and the filter is implemented as shown in Fig. 2. Therefore, the reshaped watermark signal w_s has the form

$$w_s(n_1, n_2) = \sum_{\substack{m_1=0 \\ m_2 \neq 0}}^{p_1} \sum_{\substack{m_2=0 \\ m_1 \neq 0}}^{p_2} a(m_1, m_2) w_s(n_1 - m_1, n_2 - m_2) + G w_m(n_1, n_2) \tag{5}$$

where $a(m_1, m_2)$ is the LPC of s in spatial domain. So Equation (4) is modified as

$$c_{ws}(i,j) = c_o(i,j) + \alpha_s w_s(i,j) \tag{6}$$

When s is estimated in spatial domain, all the operations are similar except that it is in the inverse spectral domain that the filter is constructed and c_o is extracted from I_o. We observe that in both cases, watermark embedding and filtering are both carry out in the same domain, i.e. the inverse spectral domain of the signal s. Such choice is to ensure that the perceptually shaped watermark w_s and w_m has the linear relationship represented by Equation (5), which is convenient for the analysis of detector in the next section. A general version of this embedding process is illustrated in Fig. 3 and the inner LPSF module is depicted in Fig. 2.

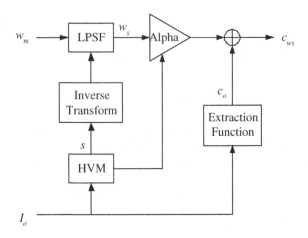

Fig. 3. Basic design of an embedder that uses LP synthesis filter

4 Watermark Detector

To detect the watermark, w_m on the cover data c_u extracted from the received image I_u, the linear correlation calculated as

$$\rho = \frac{1}{N}\widehat{c}_u \cdot w_m = \frac{1}{N}\sum_{i,j}\widehat{c}_u(i,j)w_m(i,j) \tag{7}$$

$$\widehat{c}_u = c_u - \mu_{cu} \tag{8}$$

is adopted, where N is the dimension number of c_u and w_m and μ_{cu} denotes the expectation of c_u.

Suppose P_{fp} is the prescribed limit on the probability of a false positive of the detector, the corresponding threshold τ is chosen so that

$$P(\rho \geq \tau | w_m \text{ is absent}) = P_{fp} \tag{9}$$

where $P(A|B)$ denotes the probability of an event A conditioned on an event B [21]. Under the condition I_u is unwatermarked with w_m, Equation (7) reduces to

$$\rho|_{co} = \frac{1}{N}\widehat{c}_o \cdot w_m = \frac{1}{N}\sum_{i,j}\widehat{c}_o(i,j)w_m(i,j) \tag{10}$$

where $\widehat{c}_o$ is defined as Equation (8). Because each component of w_m is satisfied with independently normal distribution and w_m is uncorrelated with c_o, it can be assumed that $\rho|_{co}$ is normally distributed [22]. Combining Equation (3), (8) and (10), it is easy to derive that the expectation, and standard deviation of $\rho|_{co}$ are respectively

$$\mu_\rho|_{co} = 0$$

and

$$\sigma_\rho|_{co} = \frac{\sqrt{N-1}}{N}\sigma_{co}\sigma_{wm} \qquad (11)$$

where

$$\sigma_{co} = \sqrt{\frac{1}{N-1}\sum_i\sum_j(c_o - \mu_{co})^2}$$

Therefore the equivalent expression for Equation (9) is

$$erfc(\frac{\tau}{\sigma_\rho|_{co}}) = P_{fp} \qquad (12)$$

where erfc denotes the complementary error function defined as

$$erfc(x) = \frac{1}{\sqrt{2\pi}}\int_x^\infty e^{\frac{t^2}{2}}dt$$

Solving Equation (12), τ is obtained as

$$\tau = erfc^{-1}(P_{fp})\sigma_\rho|_{co} \qquad (13)$$

Conversely, if I_u is watermarked with w_m, Equation (7) is transformed into Equation (14) by substituting $\widehat{c}_u$ with c_{ws} in Equation (6).

$$\rho|_{ws} = \frac{1}{N}\widehat{c}_o \cdot w_m + \frac{\alpha_s}{N}\widehat{w}_s \cdot w_m \qquad (14)$$

where $\widehat{w}_s$ is defined as Equation (8). Performing the expectation operation, we obtain

$$\mu_\rho|_{ws} = \frac{\alpha_s}{N}E(\widehat{w}_s \cdot w_m) \qquad (15)$$

Then, substituting Equation (5) into Equation (15), we have

$$\mu_\rho|_{ws} = \frac{\alpha_s}{N}\sum_i\sum_j E\{[\sum_{m_1}\sum_{m_2}a(m_1,m_2)w_s(i-m_1,j-m_2)+Gw_m(i,j)]w_m(i,j)\} \qquad (16)$$

Finally, Equation (16) simplifies to

$$\mu_\rho|_{ws} = G\alpha_s\sigma_{wm}^2 \qquad (17)$$

Similarly, we can also obtain

$$\mu_\rho|_{wm} = \alpha_m\sigma_{wm}^2 \qquad (18)$$

The mean value, $\mu_\rho|_{ws}$ is also an important performance index for differentiating the watermarked and unwatermarked images. Equation (17) illustrates it is proportional to G. A factor to affect G is the dimension numbers of c_{ws} i.e., N, which is shown in Equation (1). Generally when large N is selected, $\mu_\rho|_{ws}$ is augmented, that is the performance of the detector is improved.

In addition, combining Equation (17) and (18), we have

$$r = \mu_\rho|_{ws}/\mu_\rho|_{wm} = G\alpha_s/\alpha_m$$

If $r > 1$ (it is generally satisfied), the linear correlation between c_{ws} and w_s is higher than that between c_{wm} and w_m, which shows the use of LP synthesis filter enhances the performance of the detector.

5   Experimental Results

In order to test the proposed approach, a specific watermarking is designed. Watson's DCT-based visual model is adopted [6]. The image itself is regarded as the cover data. The watermark is first perceptually shaped as Equation (5) and then embedded in the spatial domain as Equation (6), where the embedding strength α_s is adjusted by a given perceptual distance [14].

First, watermark invisibility is evaluated. In Fig. 4 (a), the original "lena" image is presented. The response of HVM, s is shown in Fig. 4 (b), which reflects the local perceptual characteristic of "Lena". Fig. 4 (c) is the watermarked copy with perceptual distance 40. Further, as shown in Fig. 5 (a), the spectrum of the shaped watermark simulates s well, while the method regarding JND as weighting factors of watermark does worse in Fig. 5(b) [14].

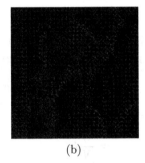

(a)   (b)   (c)

Fig. 4. Test on "Lena". (a) Original image "Lena"; (b) The response of Watson's DCT-based HVM with the input "Lena"; (c) The watermarked "Lena"

For illuminating the performance of the detector in the work, each of two hundred and fifty images from USC-SIPE Image Database is embedded with w_m and $-w_m$ when α_s is set to 0.5, and a total of 500 watermarked images are obtained. The detector is then applied. Fig. 6 shows the distribution of the detection value, ρ. It is observed that most absolute detection values of the watermarked images range between 2 and 4, and some of them are very large, even upper 7, which reflects the embedding strength is high. Such output results from the effect of G in Equation (17). In the designed watermarking, because the adopted HVM is based on 8*8 block, the LP is performed in each block. Therefore G as an accumulative quantity is not very large. If the used HVM is based on a larger space, the factor G enhances the performance of the detector greatly. Additionally, because there are two classes of images embedded in size 256*256, 512*512, their effect on G leads to two wave crests on each of both curves of the watermarked images in principle.

The results presented in the following allow us to evaluate the watermark embedding strength and the robustness of the designed watermarking from several respects including JPEG compression, additive noise, filtering, and cropping. All

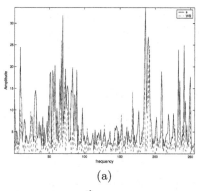 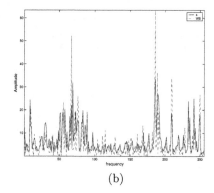

(a)   (b)

Fig. 5. The 250th row spectral coefficients of the shaped watermark and the JND. (a) the shaped watermark is obtained using 2-D LP synthesis filter; (b) the shaped watermark is obtained with the method regarding JND as weighting factors in frequency domain

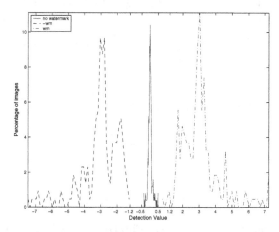

Fig. 6. Distributions of detection values resulting from a set of images embedded with $-w_m$ (left) and w_m (right) and their unwatermarked copies (middle)

the experiments were carried out on the Lena image (see Fig. 4) when the target perceptual distance is set to 50 and P_{fP} is 10^{-8}.

Fig. 7 shows the effect of JPEG compression on the detector. The detector response remains above the threshold, 0.83 corresponding to the imposed P_{fP} until a quality factor of 28 is reached. Fig. 8 illustrates that the algorithm is robust to the noise with the variance underneath 36. Fig. 9 shows the response of the detector after Gaussian, low-pass filtering with varying standard deviation (width). Other than noising, the detector is sensitive to filtering. The detection values begin falling off sharply when the filter width exceeds 0.4. However, principally the detection values are large. So the detector can tolerant filtering distortion with a relatively higher width. In Fig. 10, the detection values are given after a serial of cropping are applied to the watermarked image. It can be seen that the detection value is not proportional to the size of the cropped area. The reason is that the designed watermarking is based on 8*8 block and each block is operated independently.

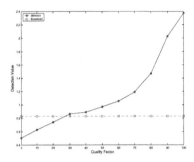

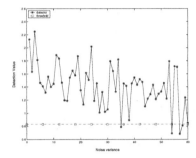

Fig. 7. Results of JPEG compression with a set of quality factors

Fig. 8. Results of Gaussian noise with zero mean and a set of variances

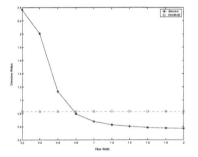

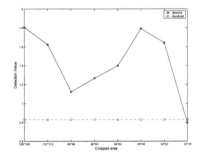

Fig. 9. Results of Gaussian low-pass filtering with a set of filter widths

Fig. 10. Results of cropping with a set of regions' parameters given

6   Conclusion

In this paper, a new approach using HVM for watermarking is proposed. The special LP synthesis filter is introduced to adapt the spectral structure of the watermark to that of the JND estimated by the adopted HVM. And its parameters are obtained by applying optimum linear prediction theory to the JND. Then the shaped watermark is embedded in inverse transform domain of HVM. Through the analysis of the linear correction detector, we derive that the gain of the filter can increase the detection values, but it doesn't affect the false positive probability. The experimental results show that the shaped watermark is still invisible under the condition of high embedding strength. And large detection values improve the robustness of the algorithm.

References

1. I. Cox, M. L. Miller: A review of watermarking and the importance of perceptual modeling. Proc. Electronic Imaging, (Feb. 1997)
2. A. H. Tewfik, M. Swanson: Data hiding for multimedia personalization, interaction, and protection. IEEE Signal Processing Mag., **Vol. 14** (July. 1997) 41–44.
3. R. B.Wolfgang, C. I. Podilchuk, E. J. Delp: Perceptual watermarks for digital images and video. Proc. IEEE, **vol. 87** (July 1999) 1108-1126.
4. S. Voloshynovskiy, A.Herrigel, N.Baumgaetner, T.Pun: A stochastic approach to content-adaptive digital image watermarking. in Third International Workshop on Information Hiding, (1999).
5. N. Jayant, J. Johnston, R. Safranek: Signal compression based on models of human perception. Proc. IEEE, **Vol. 81** (Oct. 1993)
6. B. Watson: DCT quantization matrices optimized for individual images. Human Vision, Visual Processing, and Digital Display IV, SPIE-1913, (1993) 202-216.
7. A. B. Watson, G. Y. Yang, J. A. Solomon, J. Villasenor: Visual thresholds for wavelet quantization error. Human Vision and Electronic Imaging, SPIE-2657, (1996) 381-392.
8. A. S. Lewis, G. Knowles: Image compression using the 2-D wavelet transform. IEEE Trans. Image Processing, **Vol. 1** (1992) 244-250.
9. C.I. Podilchuk, W. Zeng: Image-adaptive watermarking using visual models. IEEE J. Selected Areas Comm.. **Vol. 16, no. 4** (May 1998) 525–539
10. M. Barni, F. Bartolini, V. Cappellini, A. Piva: A DCT-domain System for Robust Image Watermarking. IEEE Transactions on Signal Processing. **Vol. 66, no. 3** (1998) 357-372
11. J. F. Delaigle, C. De Vleeschouwer, B. Macq: Watermarking Algorithm Based on Human Visual Model. IEEE Transactions on Signal Processing. **Vol. 66, no. 3** (1998) 319-335
12. Y. S. Kim, O. H. Kwon, R. H. Park: Wavelet based watermarking method for digital images using the human visual system. ISCAS '99. Proceedings of the 1999 IEEE International Symposium on Circuits and Systems. **Vol. 4, no. 30** (June 1999)
13. C. D. Vleeschouwer, J. F. Delaigle, B. Macq: Invisibility and application functionalities in perceptual watermarking an overview. Proceedings of the IEEE. **Vol. 90, Issue: 1** (Jan. 2002) 64–77
14. Ingemar J. Cox, Matthew L. Miller, Jeffrey A. Bloom: Digital Watermarking. San Francisco: Academic Press. (2002)
15. Y. Rangsanseri, W. Thitimajshima: Copyright protection of images using human visual masking on DCT-based watermarking. APCCAS '02. 2002 Asia-Pacific Conference on Circuits and Systems. **Vol. 1** (Oct. 2002) 28–31
16. M. Barni, F. Bartolini, A. Piva: Improved Wavelet-Based Watermarking Through Pixel-Wise Masking. IEEE Transactions on Image Processing. **Vol. 10, no. 5** (May 2001) 783-791
17. V. Saravanan, P.K. Bora, D. Ghosh: Oblivious Image-Adaptive Watermarking Using Quantization Index Modulation. The Eighth National Conf. On Communications, India. (Jan. 2002) 26-37
18. Simon Haykin: Adaptive Filter Theory. 3nd edition: Prenticee Hall. (1998)
19. S. Lawrence Marple Jr.: Two-dimensional Lattice Linear Prediction Parameter Estimation Method and Fast Algorithm. IEEE Signal Processing Letters. **Vol. 7** (June 2000) 164-168

20. Kuo, Shyh-Shiaw, Johnston, J.D.: Spatial Noise Shaping Based on Human Visual Sensitivity and Its Application to Image Coding. IEEE Transactions on Image Processing. **Vol. 11, no. 5** (May 2002) 509–517

21. M. L. Miller, J. A. Bloom: Computing the probability of false watermark detection. Proceeding of the Third International Workshop on Information Hiding. (1999) 146-158

22. C. W. Helstrom: Statistical Theory of Signal Detection. New York: Pergamon Press. (1960)

Watermarking System for QoS Aware Content Adaptation

Tae Meon Bae, Seok Jun Kang, and Yong Man Ro

IVY Lab., Information and Communication University (ICU),
119, Munjiro, Yuseong-gu, Deajeon, 305-714, Korea
{heartles, impedance99, yro}@icu.ac.kr

Abstract. Video transcoding technology is useful for seamless video service to guarantee quality of service (QoS). But video transcoding would distort the watermark signal embedded in the video content. In this paper, we propose a watermarking system that guarantees detecting watermark signal even after video transcoding. We analyzed the effect of video transcoding for watermark signal. Based on the analysis, metadata based approach is proposed to keep watermark in the video transcoding under QoS guaranteeing service environment. We performed experiments with widely used watermark algorithms to verify that the proposed watermarking system is useful.

1 Introduction

Recently, various multimedia services are becoming a unified service with ubiquitous computing and networking so that one could enjoy multimedia contents anytime and anywhere. For example of ubiquitous service environment, multimedia contents could be delivered by various channels such as ADSL, wireless LAN, and mobile network. At the same time, user terminals for consuming multimedia could be diverse in their characteristics from handset, PDA to HDTV. Definitely it needs a means to protect content when the content is distributing. Among various technologies for copyright protection in DRM system, digital watermarking is used for owner identification and tracking. Watermarking can be utilized to find that media contents are illegally consumed outside of the DRM system.

To guarantee quality of service in the diverse consuming environment, content adaptation is required [1,2]. But content adaptation could distort the embedded watermark signal. The DRM system, which uses digital watermark as a way of property protection, should take into account the distortion.

In this paper, we propose a scheme for watermark validity in content adaptation. By using the proposed metadata that describes watermarking conditions, watermarking can be safely used as an intellectual property protection for DRM system in ubiquitous environment. In the experiment, we performed widely used watermark algorithms to verify that the proposed watermarking system is useful for the content adaptation.

The paper is organized as follows: In section 2, content adaptation to guarantee QoS is explained. And, in section 3, we explain the video transcoding and its effect on watermark. In section 4, the watermarking system under the content adaptation is

I.J. Cox et al. (Eds.): IWDW 2004, LNCS 3304, pp. 77–88, 2005.

proposed. And in section 5, we experimented digital watermarking with and without proposed scheme in the condition of video transcoding. And then, finally, we conclude our work in section 6.

2   Content Adaptation to Guarantee QoS

Digital content adaptation is a technique that provides content suitable for user environment by converting display size, bitrate, and the complexity of the content processing. Content consumption in ubiquitous environment is restricted by the bandwidth of network, computational capability and display size of terminal. Digital content adaptation could be useful for the consumption of multimedia in ubiquitous environment. Currently, research and standardization about content adaptation is going on in MPEG-21 [3]. Content adaptation to guarantee QoS can be considered according to the characteristics of transmission channel and user terminal. MPEG-21 defines these characteristics related with QoS.

The performance of video streaming depends on characteristics of the transmission channel. When video contents are streamed, network characteristics related with QoS are network bandwidth, transmission delay, and transmission error rate. Table 1 shows the network characteristics and related content adaptations for QoS.

Table 1. Content adaptation related with network characteristics

Network characteristics	Adaptation function
Network capability (bandwidth)	Bit rate reduction
Network condition (delay, error rate)	Bit rate reduction
	Error resilient coding

In ubiquitous environment, diverse characteristics of terminals should also be considered. Table 2 shows the terminal capabilities and related adaptation functions. The kind of decodable codec, computational capability, display resolution, and pixel depth are considered as terminal capability.

Table 2. Content adaptation related with terminal capability

Terminal capability	Adaptation function
Codec capability	Format conversion
Codec parameter	Re-encoding
Display capability	Resizing

3   Watermarking in Video Transcoding for Terminal and Network QoS

The objectives of transcoding are seamless streaming and provision of best quality of video. In transcoder, one needs to consider these objectives as deciding encoding parameter value. The specific algorithm of video coding depends on the encoding scheme, but generally MPEG-2 and MPEG-4 are generic codecs which share basic encoding schemes such as block based motion estimation, quantization in the DCT domain, and variable length coding (VLC). Therefore, the transcoding parameter set for QoS constraint is the same for MPEG-based codecs. In [4], quantization step size, special scaling, and frame rate are considered as transcoding parameters.

Because embedded watermark signal could be distorted by video transcoding, it is difficult to use digital generic watermarking with transcoding technique. To solve this problem, one needs to analyze requirements of digital watermarking that could work even under video transcoding.

The transcoding parameters could affect the embedded watermark signal. Changing transcoding parameter value can be considered as an attack to watermark. In general, there are three transcoding operations which are frame size conversion, increasing quantization step, and frame rate conversion. In case of frame size conversion, the effect is similar to the geometric attack on watermark [5]. Increasing quantization step size also distorts embedded watermark signal. For frame rate conversion, it can distort embedded watermark if watermarking algorithm uses temporal information, e.g., 3D DCT and 3D wavelet based algorithm. Many algorithms robust to geometric attack, quantization error and frame rate conversion are being developed [5,6]. But these algorithms are not enough to detect watermark after generic transcoding. And, when the combination of the transcoding operation is applied, the watermark detection becomes harder.

To analyze the effect of the video transcoding for embedded watermark signal, it needs to know the effect of the spatial scaling and quantization and their combination. Because these two factors of transcoding parameter are also applicable to still image conversion, we test in JPEG compression that is similar to MPEG I-frame encoding.

Four image based watermarking algorithm including the spread spectrum based algorithm working on DCT domain proposed by Cox [7] and 3 wavelet based algorithms [8-10] are used in the test. Similarity measure proposed by Cox is used to indicate watermark detection response, where the detectable threshold is six [7]. Watermark signal the length of which is 1000 is embedded to 512x512 sized Lena image. With spatial scaling down ratio from 1/4 to 1/64, we performed transcoding. For frame rate conversion, we can assume the result. In the experiment, we added watermark for each frame, thereby frame dropping doesn't affect detection ratio. Figure 1 shows that watermarking algorithms are not robust to spatial scaling down, where 1/4 down scaling is acceptable. Figure 2 shows the watermark signal robustness with varying quantization step size in JPEG, where quality factor is inverse proportional to quantization step size.

We tested video transcoding effect for spread spectrum based algorithm [7] with "Foreman" MPEG-4 test sequence and MPEG-4 ASP (advanced simple profile) encoder. Watermark detection ratio indicates the number of frames that watermark is detected after transcoding per total number of frames. Generally, transcoder changes both spatial scaling factor and quantization step size to satisfy QoS. As seen at table 3, watermark detection ratio is significantly decreased when both transcoding parameters are simultaneously changed, which means that watermark detection constraint should be considered in determining transcoding parameter set with given QoS.

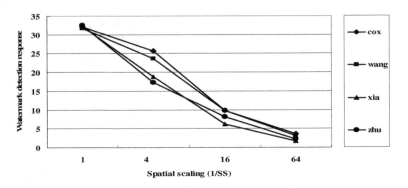

Fig. 1. Watermark detection response according to spatial down scaling

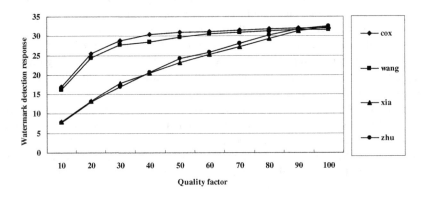

Fig. 2. Watermark detection response with quality factor variation for JPEG compression

Table 3. Watermark detection ratio after transcoding

Spatial down scaling ratio	1			¼	
Compression ratio	30	50	94	94	188
Watermark detection ratio	100%	99%	90%	49%	40%

We also tested video watermarking algorithms [11-12]. The video watermarking algorithms working on compressed domain [11] and 8x8 DCT based ones [12] failed to detect watermark. In result, these algorithms cannot be used with video transcoding.

4   Proposed Watermarking System for Video Transcoding

Watermark under video transmission with content adaptation does not work correctly as a copyright protection function due to the distortion of the embedded watermark. It should guarantee that the embedded watermark is detectable after transcoding to use watermarking as the copyright protection. Devising a new watermarking algorithm robust to transcoding or making a mechanism that prevents corrupting embedded watermark can be solutions for this problem. But in the algorithmic approach, current research shows that watermark algorithms are vulnerable to geometric and quantization attack [13].

In the systemic approach, it is possible to prevent corruption of watermark by using additional information. If we know the exact information about the robustness of embedded watermark and it can be possible for transcoder to avoid watermark corrupting decision or reducing the degree of the distortion.

Figure 3 shows the procedure of the proposed system. When watermark is embedded to a video content, watermark robustness is measured with varying possible encoding parameter sets. And the measured robustness is saved to metadata. In the transcoding process, transcoding parameter decision engine determines optimal transcoding parameter set with a given QoS constraint and the metadata that indicates the robustness of watermark signal against for each parameter set. And video transcoding is performed using the parameter set.

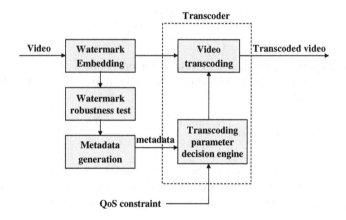

Fig. 3. The proposed watermarking system process

To describe the proposed system, it needs to define some notations.

$RQ=[RQ_1, RQ_2,..., RQ_N]$, $RQ_i^j \in [RQ^0,..,RQ^K]$, $i=1,..., N$, $j=0,...K$, where RQ_i is the requantization parameter of ith frame, N is the total number of frames in the video.

$TS=[TS_1, TS_2,..., TS_N]$, $TS_i \in \{0, 1\}$, $i=1,..., N$, where TS is a set of temporal scaling operation and one means no-skipping and zero does frame skipping.

$SS=[SS_1, SS_2,..., SS_N]$, $SS_i^j \in (SS^0, SS^1,..., SS^L]$, $i=1,..., N$, where SS is a set of spatial scaling operation, and one means the original video and 1/4 means half spatial down scaling; SS^0 is 0 and SS^L is 1.

R_i : bitrate of ith frame.

D_i : distortion of ith frame.

R_{Max} : maximum bit.

$\{RQ^*, TS^*, SS^*\}$: optimal transcoding parameter set.

4.1 Watermark Detectable Region in Transcoding Parameter Space

Metadata used in the proposed system describes video transcoding environment, and the robustness of watermark against for each transcoding parameter set. About transcoding environment, transcoder type such as MPEG-2, MPEG-4, H.263, and H.264 is specified.

The robustness information about watermark signal is expressed by boundary line B which describes the border of watermark detectable and non-detectable region in the transcoding parameter space. Figure 4 shows how boundary line B divides the parameter space into watermark detectable and non-detectable regions. If a video content is transcoded by parameter set selected in the watermark detectable region, the transcoded content contains watermark signal that is detectable.

The watermark detectable/non-detectable region can be expressed in terms of similarity function. The similarity measure for watermark detection is suggested by cox[7] like

$$\text{sim}(W,W') = \frac{<W,W'>}{\sqrt{|W\ \|\ W'|}}.$$

$$(1)$$

And using the similarity function, detectable region can be defined similarity value is larger than predefined threshold value. And by defining watermark valid function $V(RQ,TS,SS)$ as follows

$$V(RQ,TS,SS) = \left(\begin{array}{l} 1,\ \text{sim}(W,W'|_{RQ,TS,SS}) > Th_{sim}) \\ -1,\ \text{otherwise} \end{array} \right).$$

$$(2)$$

Watermark detectable region is where the value of watermark valid function is one.

The transcoding parameter space is three-dimensional. But, if we consider frames that transcoded into Intra mode, TS is not considered in the watermark detectable region description.

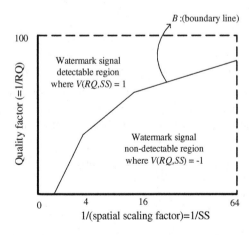

Fig. 4. Watermark detectable and non-detectable region in transcoding parameter space

Because the range of *RQ* is 1 to 31, and if we consider spatial scaling 1, 1/4, 1/16, 1/64, the number of discrete points belongs to the parameter space is 128 per one frame. If each region has only one segment and there exist one boundary line that divides the regions like figure 4, we can express the segmentation information by just indicating the boundary line that has only 3 points.

But if more than one segment for each region could exist as seen in figure 5, one should present watermark detectable region by representing all region points. Therefore it is meaningful to study the characteristics of boundary line.

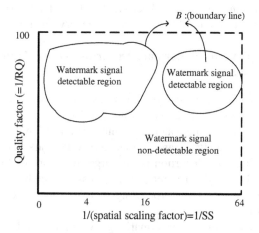

Fig. 5. Watermark detectable and non-detectable regions that has more than one segment in transcoding parameter space

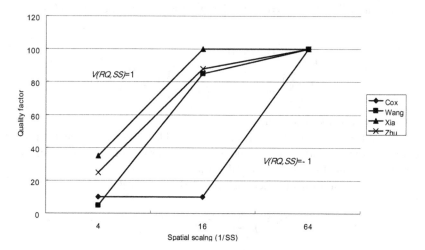

Fig. 6. Boundary line in transcoding parameter space

Figure 5 shows boundary line for each watermarking algorithm in the transcoding parameter space. Left-top region of the boundary line in figure 5 is watermark detectable region where the transcoder should choose transcoding parameter set that belongs to this region.

In MPEG, it is hard to describe the watermark detectable condition due to the diverse configurations of motion estimation such as I, B, P and the distance between referenced and estimated frames. Current video watermarking algorithms hints about this problem [14], where I (Intra) frame is used for watermarking. Therefore, if only I-frames are considered in watermarking detection, we can verify the detection of watermark with the metadata. But, because we don't know which frame will be encoded into I-frame, metadata should contain boundary line for every frame.

4.2 The Characteristics of Watermark Distortion Versus Transcoding Parameter Space

To understand the characteristics of the boundary line, it needs to analyze the effects of quantization and spatial scaling to the watermark signal.

For blind watermarking, the watermark embedded position in transformed domain is possibly missed due to attack, and in this case, watermark distortion can be large even though overall image distortion is not large. But, for non-blind watermarking, the exact watermark embedded points are not missed, thereby watermark distortion and image distortion due to some processing such as compression and resizing show similar characteristics.

In the transformed domain watermarking, watermark embedding is performed using the following equation.

$$v'_i = (v_i + \alpha w_i) \tag{3}$$

Assuming that $E[W]=0$, $\sigma_W = 1$, and the watermark distortion ε and watermark signal is independent,

$$sim(W, W') = \frac{\frac{1}{K}\sum_{i=0}^{K-1}(w_i(w_i + \varepsilon_i))}{\frac{1}{K}\sqrt{\sum_{i=0}^{K-1}(w_i + \varepsilon_i)^2}} = \sqrt{\frac{K}{1 + \frac{1}{K}\sum_{i=0}^{K-1}\varepsilon_i^2}} = \sqrt{\frac{K}{1 + D_W}}, \tag{4}$$

where D_W is watermark distortion.

As shown Eq. 4, because the distortion of embedded watermark signal is inversely increasing to the similarity value, studying the distortion of watermark signal is a good way to measure the robustness of the watermark.

In this paper, distortion of watermark signal D_W is defined as

$$D_W = \frac{1}{K}\sum_{i=0}^{K-1}(w_i' - w_i)^2 . \tag{5}$$

where, K is the length of watermark signal.

The relation between spatial scaling and watermark distortion could reveal the characteristics of boundary line. Distortion due to spatial scaling is the difference between the watermarked image I_w and the low pass filtered image $I_{w|LPF}$, which can be expressed like

$$D_w(SS) = E[(I_w - I_{w|LPF})^2]$$

$$= E[(I_{W|high})^2] = \frac{1}{\pi} \int_{\omega_c}^{\pi} P(\omega)d\omega, \text{ where } P(\omega) \geq 0, \tag{6}$$

where ω_c is cutoff frequency of LPF, $P(\omega)$ is power spectrum of I_W at the frequency ω. From Eq (6), we can see the following fact.

$$\frac{dE[(I_{W|high})^2]}{d\omega_c} = -P(\omega_c) \leq 0. \tag{7}$$

Because the cut off frequency ω_c of low pass filter is monotonically increasing to spatial scaling factor,

$$\frac{d\omega_c}{dSS} \geq 0. \tag{8}$$

So, the derivative of D_w by SS is

$$\frac{dD_w(SS)}{dSS} = \frac{dE[(I_{W|high})^2]}{d\omega_c} \times \frac{d\omega_c}{dSS} = -P(\omega_c)\frac{d\omega_c}{dSS},$$

$$\therefore \frac{dD_w(SS)}{dSS} \leq 0. \tag{9}$$

Therfore, D_w is monotonically decreasing with SS.

Because distortion of watermark signal for spatial scaling value is monotonically increasing,

If quantization parameter for each spatial scaling is uniquely determined in the boundary line, which can be achievable by selecting minimum RQ for each SS, boundary line can be expressed by functional form. Therefore, we can define boundary line as function BL like,

$$RQ^j = BL(SS^j) = \underset{(RQ)}{\arg\min}\{V(RQ, SS|_{SS^j}) = -1\}, \tag{10}$$

where SS^j is given spatial scaling value and RQ^j is correspond quantization parameter in the boundary line.

4.3 Transcoding Parameter Decision Considering Watermark Constraint

Video transcoding aims to satisfy network and terminal QoS. With watermark validation metadata, it can be possible to considering embedded watermark robustness in transcoding process. In [4], video transcoder measures rate-distortion for each candidate transcoding parameter set that satisfies QoS constraint. Transcoding parameter set decision is optimization problem in the point of rate-distortion model, and it is expressed as follows.

$$\{RQ*,TS*,SS*\} = \arg \min_{RQ,TS,SS} \sum_{i=1}^{N} D_i(RQ,TS,SS),$$

$$\text{subject to } \sum_{i=1}^{N} R_i(RQ,TS,SS) < R_{max}. \tag{11}$$

The solution of the Eq. (11) depends on how to model $D_i(RQ, TS, SS)$ function.

With given metadata indication watermark robustness, we can reject candidate transcoding parameter sets in the non-detectable region of the transcoding parameter space. From Eq. (10), the watermark detection condition for candidate transcoding parameter set (RQ,SS) can be written as

$$RQ - BL(SS) < \Delta_{RQ}, \tag{12}$$

where, Δ_{RQ} is defined as marginal distortion for the robustness of watermark signal after transcoding. By using Eq. 12, parameter space to be searched with constraint of Eq. (11) is restricted into watermark detectable region. In general, video transcoding can be required in real-time operation, and the content creator and who use transcoder for the video service can be different. Because only creator or property holder should have watermark information, finding BL function values for each spatial scaling during video transcoding is not an appropriate way. Instead, BL function should be offered by property holder.

Finding BL function is very time consuming work because it should search all transcoding parameter space to find global minima of the watermark distortion.

By using Eq. (12), parameter space to be searched in the point of Eq. (1) is restricted into watermark detectable region. And to find watermark safe transcoding parameter set, the R-D optimization problem stated at Eq. (11) should be re-written as follows:

$$\{RQ*,TS*,SS*\} = \arg \min_{RQ,TS,SS} \sum_{i=1}^{N} D_i(RQ,TS,SS),$$

$$\text{subject to } 1. \sum_{i=1}^{N} R_i(RQ,TS,SS) < R_{max},$$

$$\text{subject to } 2. \ RQ - BL(SS) < \Delta_{RQ}. \tag{13}$$

5   Experiment and Discussion

In the experiment, we tested the watermark detection ratio with and without proposed watermarking scheme under video transcoding. We performed transcoding by using transcoder suggested by [4]. We used network bandwidth restriction as target QoS. "Foreman" CIF video is used as test sequence. We changed frame size to 256x256 to easily apply Cox's algorithm. And the test video is encoded at 500Kbps by MPEG-4 ASP and used as an input of transcoder. Watermark is embedded before video encoding process.

First, we extracted watermark validation metadata from the test video for every frame. Table 4 shows the estimated operations which generate the target rate 80Kbps. When the parameter set (*RQ, TS, SS*) is (6, 1/5, 1/4), the estimated RMSE is minimum, thereby transcoding is performed by this parameter set. But from the metadata, the watermark cannot be detected in the video transcoded by the selected parameter set. In stead of (6, 1/5, 1/4), (19, 1/5, 1) is chosen by the proposed system, which guarantees detection of the watermark signal. As seen table 5, transcoding using the watermark validation metadata always guarantees watermark signal detection.

Table 4. The estimated transcoding parameter that can generate the target rate 80Kbps

RQ	TS	SS	RMSE	Watermark detection ratio	Metadata indication
6	1/5	1/4	50.5	46%	Non-detectable
9	1/3	1/4	84.1	48%	Non-detectable
12	1/2	1/4	92.0	40%	Non-detectable
19	1/5	1	100.0	100%	Detectable
30	1/3	1	108.0.	100%	Detectable

Table 5. The watermark detection after transcoding

Bitrate (Kbps)	R-D optimized system		Proposed system	
	Parameter set	Watermark detection ratio	Parameter set	Watermark detection ratio
80	(6, 1/5, 1/4)	46%	(19, 1/5, 1)	100%
200	(3, 1/5, 1/4)	49%	(8, 1/5, 1)	100%
400	(4, 1, 1/4)	100%	(4, 1, 1/4)	100%

6 Conclusion

In this paper, we propose a framework for watermarking system to be able to use video transcoding with digital watermarking. To guarantee the safe use of watermark technology with video transcoding, we propose a metadata based transcoding. We focused on spatial scaling and quantization from the MPEG based transcoding parameter set. Using the metadata that contains watermark robustness against transcoding parameter set, video transcoder can perform with guaranteeing that the watermark in the distributed content is valid.

References

1. T. C. Thang, Y. J. Jung, and Y. M. Ro: On Some QoS Aspects of User Profile in Universal Multimedia Access, IEEE TENCON, Bangalore, India, Oct. (2003) 591-595
2. Y. J. Jung, H. K. Kang, and Y. M. Ro: Metadata Hiding for Content Adaptation, IWDW2003, (2003) 456-467
3. MPEG-21 Requirements on Digital Item Adaptation, ISO/IEC/JTC1/SC29/WG11 N4684, Jeju, March (2002)
4. Y.J. Jung, and Y. M. Ro: Joint Spatio-SNR-Temporal Rate Control and Distortion Modeling for Quality Tradeoffs in Video Transcoding, WIAMIS, Portugal, April, (2004)
5. M. Alghoniemy, and A. H. Tewfik: Geometric Distortions Correction in Image Watermarking, IEEE International Conference on Multimedia and Expo, (2000) 82-89
6. Ozer, I., Ramkumar, and M., Akansu, A.: A New Method for Detection of Watermarks in Geometrically Distorted Images, Procedding of IEEE International Conf. on Accoustic, Speech, and Signal Processing, June, (2000) 5-9
7. I.J. Cox and M.L. Miller: A Review of Watermarking and the Importance of Perceptual Modeling, Proc. SPIE Conf. on Human Vision and Electronic Imaging II, Vol. 3016, Feb. (1997) 92-99
8. H. M. Wang, P. C. Su, and J. Kuo: Wavelet-based digital image watermarking, Optic Express, Vol. 3, Dec. (1998) 491-496
9. X.G. Xia, C.G. Boncelet, and G.R. Arce: Wavelet transform based watermark for digital images, Optics Express, Vol. 3, Dec. (1998) 497-506
10. W. Zhu, Z. Xiong, and Y.Q. Zhang: Joint wavelet compression and authentication watermarking, Proceedings of the IEEE International Conference on Image Processing, Oct. (1998) 465-467
11. G. C. Langelaar, R. L. Lagendijk, and J. Biemeond: Real-Time Labeling of MPEG-2 Compressed Video, Journal of Visual Communication and Image, Vol. 9, No. 4, Dec. (1998) 256-270
12. G. C. Langelaar and R. L. Lagendijk: Optimal Differential Energy Watermarking of DCT Encoded Image and Video, IEEE Transaction on Image Processing, Vol. 10, No.1, Jan, (2001)
13. I.J. Cox and M.L. Miller, J. A. Bloom: Digital Watermarking, Morgan Kaufmann publishers, (2002) 240-277
14. George, M., Chouinard, J. V., Georganas, N.: Digital watermarking of images and video using direct sequence spread spectrum techniques, IEEE Canadian Conference on Electrical and Computer Engineering, Vol. 1, May (1999) 116-121

Weighted Segmented Digital Watermarking

Glen E. Wheeler, Reihaneh Safavi-Naini, and Nicholas Paul Sheppard

School of Information Technology and Computer Science,
The University of Wollongong,
NSW 2522, Australia
{gew75, rei, nps}@uow.edu.au

Abstract. We introduce the notion of weighted watermarking for proof-of-ownership watermark protection of multimedia works that are the product of more than one author and where each author is considered to be of different importance relative to the other authors. We specifically examine weighted segmented watermarking for still images and generalise previous work on performance measurement of watermark embedding patterns in the presence of cropping attacks.

1 Introduction

Many multimedia works are the product of more than one author, and it is often the case that the relative importance of one contribution to a work is greater than that of another contribution. In this paper, we consider proof-of-ownership watermarking in which it is desirable for this disparity in importance to be reflected in watermark protection of the work.

More specifically, where one contributor is considered to be more important than others, we would like to afford greater protection to that contributor than to less important contributors. That is, it should be harder for an attacker to successfully remove that contributor's watermark than other watermarks.

Multiple watermarking, and, in particular, segmented watermarking [4] is one method by which the contribution of several authors to a work can be recognised by a multimedia protection system. In this paper, we introduce the notion of *weighted* segmented watermarking in which each contributor to a multimedia work is assigned an integer weight reflecting his or her relative importance amongst the contributors to the work, and contributors are afforded greater or lesser levels of protection according to their assigned weight.

In segmented watermarking, the work to be watermarked is divided into a series of individual *segments* and each segment is watermarked independently. In particular, in this paper we consider segmented watermarking of still images in which segments are formed by dividing the image into square blocks, each of which contains one contributor's watermark. If a watermark is present in one or more segments of the work, the owner of that watermark is reported to be an owner of the work as a whole by an arbiter.

An obvious attack on this kind of system is to crop the image so that one or more of the watermarked segments is (either intentionally or coincidentally)

I.J. Cox et al. (Eds.): IWDW 2004, LNCS 3304, pp. 89–100, 2005.

removed from the work. In general, each contributor to a work may have his or her watermark contained in more than one segment, which gives some resistance to a cropping attack, but if all of the segments assigned to one contributor are removed, the attack can be considered successful.

We will generalise the work of Atallah and Frikken [1] and Scealy, et al. [3] to examine watermark embedding patterns that minimise the risk of watermarks being destroyed in this way, while taking into account the weighting assigned to contributors. We present generalised metrics for comparing the performance of weighted embedding patterns in the face of cropping attacks, and compare the performance of several embedding patterns using the generalised metrics.

2   Previous Work

Guo and Georganas [2] propose a "joint watermarking" scheme based on cryptographic secret sharing techniques. In their scheme, part of the watermark pattern is made to be dependent on a shared secret which can only be recovered if some approved subset of the watermark owners comes together and re-constructs the secret according to the underlying secret sharing scheme.

Many secret-sharing schemes have mechanisms by which some parties can be made more important than others in the sense that fewer parties with important shares are required to re-construct the secret than parties with less important shares. In this way, some watermark owners can be made more important than others by distributing more important shares to these owners.

Guo and Georganas' approach gives an all-or-nothing result: either a given set of watermark owners can recover the watermark completely, or they cannot recover it at all. In weighted watermarking, watermark detection degrades gracefully when one or more watermark owners are unavailable, and, furthermore, the detector can recover the relative importance of each watermark owner by comparing the detector response for each owner.

Atallah and Frikken [1] and Scealy et al. [3] describe some performance metrics for cropping-resistance of square-block segmented watermarking of still images, as we do in this paper. These metrics are based on the notion of *completeness*: a region of an image is said to be *complete* if and only if it contains at least one copy of every watermark from each contributor. In these papers, all watermark owners were considered to be equally important.

Atallah and Frikken define a worst-case metric called the *maximum non-complete area* (MNCA) as the largest rectangular region of a watermarked image missing at least one watermark (i.e. is not complete), which gives an indication of the largest possible cropping attack that might succeed. We will later define a generalised form of this metric to account for the existence of watermark owners of disparate importances.

Scealy, et al. further define two average-case metrics called the *all-exclusion* and *single-exclusion* metrics. The all-exclusion metric gives a measure of how likely an arbitrary cropping attack is to succeed in removing a watermark owner; the single-exclusion metric is similar but applies greater penalties if cropping attacks can remove multiple watermark owners. In this paper, the degree of success of a cropping attack is measured by the relative importance of the watermark owners that are removed, and we will define a generalised form of the all-exclusion metric in order to capture this.

3   Definitions

In this paper, we consider watermarking of a rectangular still image X by dividing it into a series of $t \times t$ square blocks $X(1,1), X(1,2), \ldots$. Each block $X(x,y)$ contains one watermark according to some underlying still-image watermarking scheme. We have m watermark owners $1, \ldots, m$ and each author i has

- some watermark q_i according to the underlying watermarking scheme; and
- an integer weight w_i measuring his or her relative importance amongst the authors, with higher weights indicating greater importance.

We assume that the weights are assigned by some dealer and that watermarking is done by some embedder under the control of the dealer. The protection system should ensure that protection is distributed according to the supplied weights, i.e. authors with higher weights should be better protected in some sense than authors will lower weights.

An *embedding pattern* is a mapping $\phi : \mathcal{N} \times \mathcal{N} \to \{1, \ldots, m\}$ mapping an image segment $X(x,y)$ to a watermark owner $\phi(x,y)$. The design and evaluation of embedding patterns that reflect the weighting assigned to the owners is the subject of this paper.

We will use the same model for a cropping attack as that used by Scealy, et al., that is, as the selection of a rectangular area of the segementation grid. We can assume this because

- non-rectangular images are unlikely to have any value for proving ownership due to the obvious nature of the tampering; and
- each partial segment included in a cropped image is either large enough for reliable watermark detection (in which case this segment can be considered wholly present), or it is not.

4   Metrics

The desirability of a given embedding pattern for a given set of weights can be judged according a variety of different measurements reflecting different aspects of the pattern. In this section, we propose two metrics that measure the worst-case and average-case performance of the pattern.

4.1   Generalised Maximum Non-complete Area (GMNCA)

Atallah and Frikken [1] define an area of the segmentation grid to be *complete* if and only if at least one copy of each watermark is present in that area. The *maximum non-complete area* (MNCA) of an embedding pattern ϕ is then the size of the largest rectangle of ϕ in which at least one watermark is not present. The maximum non-complete area is a measure of the largest possible region that an attacker can crop from the image while removing at least one watermark; all larger regions contain all watermarks.

We define the *generalised maximum non-complete area* as a vector $\alpha = (\alpha_1, \ldots, \alpha_m)$ with α_i being the size of the largest rectangle of ϕ not containing at least one copy of watermark q_i.

4.2   Generalised All-Exclusion (GAE)

An embedding pattern is said to be *periodic* if $\phi(\delta x, \delta y) = \phi(x, y)$ for some fixed integers δx and δy. Scealy, et al. define the "all-exclusion metric" in terms of the proportion of *minimal cropping regions* found to be complete over one period of the embedding pattern. All of the embedding patterns used by Scealy, et al., and also in this paper, are periodic.

Scealy, et al. determine the set of all minimal cropping regions for an area T as the set of all rectangles with area at least T, and minimal in each dimension. Formally, a minimal cropping region for area T is an $a \times b$ rectangle such that

- if $a \le b$ and $a \le \sqrt{T}$, then $b = \lceil \frac{T}{a} \rceil$; and
- if $a > b$ and $b \le \sqrt{T}$, then $a = \lceil \frac{T}{b} \rceil$.

For example, the minimal cropping regions for $T = 5$ are the rectangles of size 5×1, 3×2, 2×3 and 1×5.

Scealy, et al. argue that testing all minimal cropping regions for area m (the number of watermark owners) gives a good indication of how the embedding pattern can be expected to perform in the face of an arbitrary region being cropped from the image. This is because all regions smaller than the minimal cropping regions for m cannot possibly be complete, while all regions larger than the minimal cropping regions for m encompass one or more minimal cropping regions. Thus the all-exclusion metric gives an indication of the likelihood of success for an arbitrary cropping attack, while reducing the complexity of the test as compared to testing all possible cropping regions.

Let $C = \{C_1, \ldots C_r\}$ be the set of all minimal cropping regions for area m over one period of the embedding pattern ϕ. Note that the embedding pattern is considered to "wrap around" at the edges so that minimal cropping regions at the edges of the period will effectively extend into the next period of the pattern. We define the *generalised all-exclusion* (GAE) metric to be a vector $\eta = \eta_1, \ldots, \eta_m$ with

$$\eta_i = \frac{|\{C_k \in C : q_i \notin C_k\}|}{|C_k|}, \tag{1}$$

that is, the proportion of minimal cropping regions that do not contain watermark q_i. The higher the value of η_i, the more likely q_i is to be eliminated by a cropping attack.

Note that our definition for generalised all-exclusion is the dual of that used for ordinary all-exclusion by Scealy, et al., in which all-exclusion is defined as the proportion of minimal cropping regions that are complete, that is, *do* contain the required watermarks. By using the dual definition, all of the metrics considered in this paper indicate better performance by lower values.

5   Evaluation of Embedding Patterns

5.1   Mean

In general, lower values for the elements α_i and η_i indicate that the corresponding watermark q_i is more difficult to remove by cropping. An embedding pattern that reduces these values therefore reduces the susceptibility of a watermarked image to cropping attacks.

A simple method of measuring the overall resistance of the embedding pattern to cropping attacks is to take the means of the GMNCA and GAE vectors. We will therefore define the *GMNCA mean* to be

$$\mu_\alpha = \frac{\sum_{i=1}^m \alpha_i}{m} \tag{2}$$

and the *GAE mean* similarly as

$$\mu_\eta = \frac{\sum_{i=1}^m \eta_i}{m} \tag{3}$$

Lower values of μ_α and μ_η indicate greater overall resistance to cropping attacks.

5.2   Divergence

If owner i has a high weight w_i, then a good embedding pattern should have

- only relatively small areas not containing q_i (i.e. low α_i); and
- relatively few minimal cropping regions from which q_i is absent (i.e. low η_i).

We can quantify this in terms of the products $w_i\alpha_i$ and $w_i\eta_i$: we would like $w_i\alpha_i$ to be roughly the same for all i, and similarly for $w_i\eta_i$.

We define the *GMNCA divergence* θ_A to be the angle between the GMNCA product vector $\hat{\alpha} = (w_1\alpha_1, \ldots, w_m\alpha_m)$ the all one vector, that is

$$\cos(\theta_\alpha) = \frac{\hat{\alpha} \cdot \mathbf{1}}{|\hat{\alpha}|\sqrt{m}} \tag{4}$$

where $\mathbf{1} = (1, \ldots, 1)$. A GMNCA divergence close to zero indicates that the embedding pattern is more faithful to the supplied weights insofar as it is harder to find regions without q_i if w_i is high than if w_i is low.

We similarly define the *GAE divergence* θ_η to be the angle between the GAE product vector $\hat{\eta} = (w_1\eta_1, \ldots, w_m\eta_m)$ and the all one vector, that is,

$$\cos(\theta_\eta) = \frac{\hat{\eta} \cdot \mathbf{1}}{|\hat{\eta}|\sqrt{m}} \tag{5}$$

As for the GMNCA divergence, a GAE divergence of close to zero indicates that the embedding pattern is more faithful to the supplied weights.

6   Embedding Patterns

An obvious method of distributing watermarks according to their relative weights is to form a basic pattern in which each watermark q_i appears w_i times, and then repeat this pattern as necessary to fill the image to be watermarked. All of the embedding patterns considered in this paper follow this paradigm, and are differentiated in the way they determine the basic pattern and in the way they repeat the pattern throughout the image.

6.1   Cyclic Embedding

Scealy, et al. [3] show that their metrics favour embedding patterns based on the *cyclic* paradigm, in which each row of the embedding pattern is a cyclic shift of the row above it (and similarly for columns).

Given a set of watermarks and corresponding weights, we can form a vector S of length $\ell = \sum_{i=1}^{m} w_i$ with w_i elements set to q_i and use this vector as the input to the cyclic embedding algorithm. In this way, watermarks will appear with frequency proportional to their weight.

Given an initial vector S, a cyclic embedding can be defined as

$$\phi(x, y) = S((xH + yJ \bmod m) + 1) \qquad (6)$$

for some integer step sizes H and J. Scealy, et al. set $J = 1$ for all of their experiments, and observe that H is usually best chosen to be as large as possible – specifically, equal to the largest number less than $\lceil \frac{\ell}{2} \rceil$ that is relatively prime to ℓ – in order to maximise the difference between two adjacent rows of the embedding.

It remains to determine how the initial vector S should be arranged. Intuitively, for resistance to cropping, we want each watermark to be spread evenly throughout the image, since clustering a watermark in one area will lead to large areas elsewhere in which it is not present. Without loss of generality, assume that the weights $w_1, \ldots, w_m$ are arranged in non-increasing order. Then the following is a simple algorithm for distributing the watermarks $q_1, \ldots, q_k$ evenly through a string such that each watermark appears a number of times equal to its weight:

```
create w₁ strings S₁, . . . , S_{w₁} with S_i = q₁
set k = 1
for i = 2 to m
    for j = 1 to w_i
        append q_i to S_k
        set k = k + 1
    end for
end for
set S = S₁ ‖ · · · ‖ S_{w₁}
```

where '‖' denotes concatenation. We will use this algorithm in all of our experiments.

Figure 1 shows a vector S and cyclic embedding pattern ϕ for four authors with $w = 3, 2, 2, 1$. The q's have been omitted from the figures for clarity, that is, only the authors' numbers are shown.

<table>
<tr><td></td><td>1 2 3 1 2 4 1 3</td></tr>
<tr><td></td><td>3 1 2 3 1 2 4 1</td></tr>
<tr><td></td><td>1 3 1 2 3 1 2 4</td></tr>
<tr><td>1 2 3 1 2 4 1 3</td><td>4 1 3 1 2 3 1 2</td></tr>
<tr><td></td><td>2 4 1 3 1 2 3 1</td></tr>
<tr><td></td><td>1 2 4 1 3 1 2 3</td></tr>
<tr><td></td><td>3 1 2 4 1 3 1 2</td></tr>
<tr><td></td><td>2 3 1 2 4 1 3 1</td></tr>
</table>

(a)   (b)

Fig. 1. (a) S and (b) one period of ϕ for cyclic embedding with $w = 3, 2, 2, 1$ and $H = J = 1$

6.2   Tile Rotation

Scealy, et al. also propose a "tile rotation" method in which a basic pattern is rotated each time it is repeated, so that (if the image is large enough) every watermark appears at least once in every row and every column. This method obtains better results than the cyclic method for some special values of m where the cyclic method performed relatively poorly.

Let L be an $a \times b$ matrix such that

$$ab = \ell = \sum_{i=1}^{m} w_i \tag{7}$$

with exactly w_i entries set to q_i for all $1 \leq i \leq m$. Scealy, et al. then derive the formula

$$\phi(x, y) = L(x + \lfloor \tfrac{x}{a} \rfloor \bmod a, y + \lfloor \tfrac{y}{b} \rfloor \bmod b) \tag{8}$$

for rotating the basic tile L over the whole image.

If $a = 1$ or $b = 1$, this method reduces to the cyclic method since L becomes a vector, and this vector is rotated for every row of the embedding pattern. Scealy, et al. do not allow $a = 1$ or $b = 1$, but their results show that the tile rotation method consequently performs poorly for prime m (which is equal to ℓ when there are no weights), since in this case L has empty entries. In this paper, we will use $a = \ell$ and $b = 1$ for prime ℓ so that this method will perform as well as the cyclic method in these cases.

In choosing the layout of the base tile L, we have a similar problem to the one we had in choosing the layout of the initial vector S for cyclic embedding. We can define the initial tile by use of the algorithm described in Section 6.1:

given the output vector S, we place the first a elements of S on the first row of L, the second a elements on the second row, and so on, that is

$$L(x, y) = S(a(y - 1) + x). \qquad (9)$$

Figure 2 shows the tile rotation pattern for the same parameters used in Fig. 1, with $a = 4$ and $b = 2$. Again, the q's have been omitted for clarity.

```
                                    1 2 3 1 2 4 1 3
                                    2 4 1 3 1 2 3 1
                                    1 1 2 3 3 2 4 1
            1 2 3 1                  3 2 4 1 1 1 2 3
            2 4 1 3                  3 1 1 2 1 3 2 4
                                    1 3 2 4 3 1 1 2
                                    2 3 1 1 4 1 3 2
                                    4 1 3 2 2 3 1 1
```

(a)   (b)

Fig. 2. (a) S and (b) one period of ϕ for tile rotation embedding with $w = 3, 2, 2, 1$ and $a = 4$ and $b = 2$

7   Experiments

In general, we would expect different weight vectors to result in different performances from any given embedding method. There is an infinite number of possible weight vectors, though not all of them seem very likely in practice. We ran two series of tests:

- the *lead authorship* case in which a single important author is assigned a weight of 2 and all other authors are assigned a weight of 1;
- the *bimodal authorship* case in which the authors are evenly divided into two groups, with the more important group being assigned weight 2 and the less important group being assigned weight 1. For odd m, there is one more author in the less important group than in the more important group.

Lead authorship models the case where artistic direction is taken by a single lead author (or production company), who is then assisted by secondary authors to fill out details. Bimodal authorship of tests models a collaboration in which a core group of designers outsource minor tasks to other authors.

For each set of weights, we computed the mean and divergence of the GMNCA and GAE for each of the embedding paradigms described in Section 6 for 2 up to 10 authors. For the cyclic method, we chose $J = 1$ and H to be the largest integer less than $\lceil \frac{\ell}{2} \rceil$ relatively prime to ℓ, as suggested by Scealy, et al.

Figure 4 shows the GMNCA mean and divergence for each embedding pattern and each set of weights, using the graph legend shown in Fig. 3. Figure 5 similarly shows the GAE mean and divergence.

	Cyclic	Tile Rotation
Lead author	—o—	·····o·····
Bimodal authors	—■—	·····■·····

Fig. 3. Graph legend

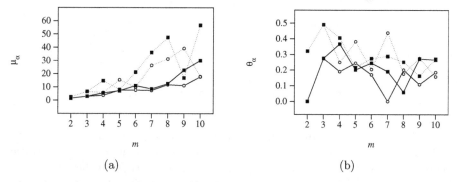

(a)   (b)

Fig. 4. (a) GMNCA mean and (b) GMNCA divergence

8   Discussion

The results are very similar for both models of authorship used for our experiments. The cyclic method obtains better results in most cases, though there are a significant number of cases in which the tile rotation method has scored better, particularly for the GAE metric. The cyclic method appears to be somewhat less erratic than the tile rotation method, however.

As we would expect, the GMNCA mean increases as the number of authors is increased, since more area is required to fit in more watermark owners. The GAE mean is much more erratic than the GMNCA mean and it is difficult to draw conclusions about any trends that the GAE mean may show, though there is at least arguably a slight upward trend as we would expect.

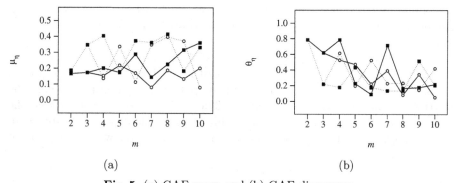

(a)   (b)

Fig. 5. (a) GAE mean and (b) GAE divergence

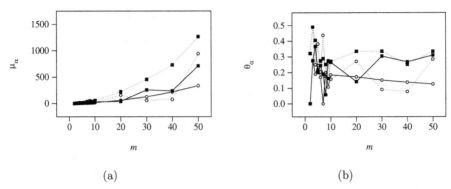

Fig. 6. (a) GMNCA mean and (b) GMNCA divergence for large m

Unlike the means, the divergence measures seem to exhibit a downward trend as the number of authors is increased, though this is slight and rather erratic except in the GAE divergence of lead authorship (Fig. 5(b)). In the latter case, this might be explained by the embedding pattern becoming closer and closer to the simple case in which all authors have equal weight, and in which divergence is zero for any reasonable embedding pattern.

In the other divergence cases, the results may be too erratic to draw conclusions with great confidence, but it seems plausible to suggest that the behaviour of an embedding pattern is "evening out" as it grows larger. For a greater number of authors, the period of the embedding pattern and the number of minimal cropping regions increases, and a greater number of tests are performed. The sample population used to compute the divergence score is thus larger and may therefore show less variance.

In general, our generalised measures are somewhat more erratic than the unweighted measures reported by Scealy, et al. Scealy, et al. note that certain numerical properties of m – such as the whether or not there are numbers near $\frac{m}{2}$ relatively prime to m in the cyclic method, or m is prime in the tile rotation method – have a significant impact on the formation of embedding patterns. In introducing weights, we may have increased the opportunity for some chance property of the input parameters to dramatically affect the properties of the embedding pattern. For larger values of m we might expect the proportion of troublesome m's and w's to grow smaller, also contributing to a reduced variance in the results.

Figures 6 and 7 show graphs of the GMNCA and GAE metrics, respectively, for $m = 10, 20, \ldots, 50$ in addition to the smaller m's shown in the earlier graphs. We stopped at $m = 50$ as the amount of computation required to calculate the metrics becomes prohibitive for larger m. The extended graphs confirm that the means increase as m increases, as we would expect. The divergences appear to decrease slightly, but find a level at around $m = 20$, after which they do not decrease any further.

Of course, it does not seem very likely that a single image would be the result of the collaboration of an extremely large collection of authors and so the

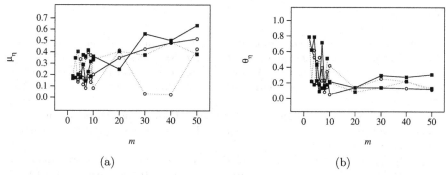

Fig. 7. (a) GAE mean and (b) GAE divergence for large m

behaviour of the divergence (or any other measurement) for very high m may not hold much interest in practice, at least in the image case we are considering here. For larger works such as video where large numbers of authors may be more realistic, our metrics would need to be extended to their three-dimensional forms.

9   Conclusion

We have introduced the notion of weighted segmented digital watermarking, and generalised previous work on cropping-resistance in segmented watermarking to provide performance measures for the weighted case. As in the unweighted case embedding patterns based on the cyclic paradigm typically give the best results though the similar tile rotation method sometimes obtains better scores.

The addition of weights, however, has made the results somewhat more erratic than observed in the unweighted case. We have conjectured that this is due to the greater number of interacting parameters used in forming embedding patterns. In small objects, such as still images, this erratic performance may be inevitable given the difficulty of satisfying a large number of parameters in a relatively small solution space.

Our metrics, and the earlier ones from which they have been derived, are quite narrow in that they measure only the effectiveness of an embedding pattern in defeating a cropping attack specific to segmented watermarking. For a complete comparison of multiple watermarking techniques, more broad-based metrics need to be defined. These broader metrics are likely to be computed in quite different ways to the metrics presented in this paper, though we think notions such as the division between mean (measuring overall goodness) and divergence (measuring faithfulness to a particular parameter set) may also be useful in a broader sense than the sense in which we have used them here.

Acknowledgements

This work was partly funded by the Co-operative Research Centre for Smart Internet Technology, Australia.

References

1. M. Atallah and K. Frikken. Cropping-resilient segmented multiple watermarking. In *Workshop on Algorithms and Discrete Structures*, pages 231–242, 2003.
2. H. Guo and N. D. Georganas. A novel approach to digital image watermarking based on a generalized secret sharing scheme. *Multimedia Systems Journal*, 9:249–260, 2003.
3. R. Scealy, R. Safavi-Naini, and N. P. Sheppard. Performance measurement of watermark embedding patterns. In *International Workshop on Digital Watermarking*, pages 77–85, Seoul, Korea, 2003.
4. N. P. Sheppard, R. Safavi-Naini, and P. Ogunbona. On multiple watermarking. In *Workshop on Security and Multimedia at ACM Multimedia*, pages 3–6, Ottawa, Canada, 2001.

Robust Estimation of Amplitude Modification for Scalar Costa Scheme Based Audio Watermark Detection

Siho Kim and Keunsung Bae

School of Electronics & Electrical Engineering, Kyungpook National University,
1370 Sankyuk-dong, Puk-gu, Daegu, 702-701, Korea
{si5, ksbae}@mir.knu.ac.kr
http://mir.knu.ac.kr/

Abstract. Recently, informed watermarking schemes based on Costa's dirty paper coding are drawing more attention than spread spectrum based techniques because these kinds of watermarking algorithms do not need an original host signal for watermark detection and the host signal does not affect the performance of watermark detection. For practical implementation, they mostly use uniform scalar quantizers, which are very vulnerable against amplitude modification. Hence, it is necessary to estimate the amplitude modification, i.e., a modified quantization step size, before watermark detection. In this paper, we propose a robust algorithm to estimate the modified quantization step size with an optimal search interval. It searches the quantization step size to minimize the quantization error of the received audio signal. It does not encroach the space for embedding watermark message because it just uses the received signal itself for estimation of the quantization step size. The optimal searching interval is determined to satisfy both detection performance and computational complexity. Experimental results show that the proposed algorithm can estimate the modified quantization step size accurately under amplitude modification attacks.

1 Introduction

Digital audio watermarking is the technique that a watermark signal is added to the original audio content as imperceptible as possible. It is now drawing much attention as a new method of providing copyright protection to digital audio content. Over the last few years, considerable audio watermarking algorithms have been proposed such as SS (spread spectrum) coding [1], phase coding [2], echo hiding [2, 3, 4, 5], and so on. Especially, blind spread spectrum and echo hiding schemes are paid more attention than others because they do not need the original audio signal for detecting watermark, which kinds of watermarking scheme is called blind watermarking. But the blind SS and echo coding suffer significantly from the host signal interference. On the other hand, recently, informed watermarking scheme [7, 8, 9] based on Costa's dirty paper coding [6], which is the scheme that a host signal interference can be eliminated if the host signal is used as side information

I.J. Cox et al. (Eds.): IWDW 2004, LNCS 3304, pp. 101–114, 2005.
© Springer-Verlag Berlin Heidelberg 2005

by the watermark encoder, is rapidly going to replace SS-based techniques. These kinds of watermarking do not need original host signals for watermark detection and host signals do not affect the performance of watermark detection. Therefore they can have larger capacity and better detection performance than those of SS-based schemes. Using Costa's result, Chen, et al [7] proposed QIM (Quantization Index Modulation), and Eggers, et al [8] proposed SCS (Scalar Costa Scheme). Both schemes use uniform scalar quantizers for practical implementation.

If the quantization step sizes used in embedding and extracting are different due to amplitude modification of a watermarked signal, the detection performance can be degraded severely. In other words, scalar quantization based watermarking schemes are very vulnerable against amplitude modification attack. Thus, it is required to estimate the modified quantization step size before extracting watermark information. To solve this problem, some kinds of algorithms are proposed lately. Eggers, et al [10] used a pilot-based estimation scheme, which embed a pilot sequence via secure SCS watermarking and estimated the possible amplitude modification using securely embedded pilot sequence before watermark detection. This method requires a large number of samples for a pilot signal and the embedding space for watermark message is encroached due to a pilot signal. Lee, et al [11] proposed a preprocessed decoding scheme for estimation of a scale factor using the EM (Expectation Maximization) algorithm, which does not encroach on the watermarking capacity because it uses the received signal itself for the estimation of the scale factor. However, EM algorithm needs a large number of samples for accurate estimation of a scale factor and then it can cause the impractical complexity.

In this paper, we propose a novel algorithm to estimate the modified quantization step size with an optimal searching interval. It searches the quantization step size to minimize the quantization error of the received audio signal. It does not need a pilot signal and just use the received signal itself as Lee, et al [11] did. However, in this algorithm, it is important to select the optimal searching interval, which depends on the property of audio signal, the quantization step size in embedding, and so on. Hence we investigate the optimal searching interval that satisfies both detection performance and computational complexity simultaneously. Experimental results show that the proposed algorithm can estimate the modified quantization step size accurately under amplitude modification attacks. This paper is organized as follows. In section 2, we briefly review the blind watermarking schemes with scalar quantizers based on Costa's dirty paper coding. In the next section, the proposed algorithm for estimation of modified quantization step size with an optimal searching interval is explained in detail. In section 4, experimental results are shown with our discussions, and finally we make a conclusion in the last section.

2   Watermarking Schemes Based on Scalar Quantization

In quantization-based watermarking scheme such as QIM or SCS, the binary watermark message $d \in \{0, 1\}$ is embedded into host signal using dithered scalar quantizer, $Q_{\Delta,d}$, which is defined as equation (1) and (2)

$$Q_{\Delta,d}(x) \equiv Q_\Delta\left(x + \frac{\Delta}{2} \cdot d\right) - \frac{\Delta}{2} \cdot d \tag{1}$$

$$Q_\Delta(x) \equiv \left\lfloor \frac{x}{\Delta} + 0.5 \right\rfloor \cdot \Delta \tag{2}$$

where $Q_\Delta(\cdot)$ is uniform scalar quantizater and Δ is quantization step size. Then the watermarked signal, s, is obtained from host signal, x, as follows

$$s = x + \alpha \cdot [Q_{\Delta_e,d}(x) - x] \tag{3}$$

where α and Δ_e are embedding parameters. For a given watermark power or embedding distortion, σ_w^2, these parameters are related by

$$\alpha = \sqrt{\frac{12 \cdot \sigma_w^2}{\Delta_e^2}} \tag{4}$$

As shown in equation (4), selecting optimal α is equivalent to finding the optimal quantization step size Δ_e. However, it is hard to find analytically the optimal value of α for the structured codebook. Hence in SCS, the optimal α and Δ_e are selected based on numerical optimization and the resulting optimal values are approximated by

$$\Delta_{e,opt} = \sqrt{12 \cdot (\sigma_w^2 + 2.71\sigma_v^2)} \tag{5}$$

where σ_v^2 denotes the power of additive white Gaussian noise(AWGN). On the other hand, in the scheme of Moulin[9], Δ_e is determined by

$$\Delta_{e,opt} = \sqrt{12 \cdot \frac{(\sigma_w^2 + \sigma_v^2)^2}{\sigma_w^2}} \tag{6}$$

where σ_w^2 satisfies the condition of $(\sigma_w^2 + \sigma_v^2) \ll \sigma_x^2$. QIM corresponds to a special case of Costa's transmission scheme, where $\alpha = 1$ regardless of the noise variance σ_v^2.

If the amplitude modification attack that scales the watermarked signal by a scaling factor g, and AWGN attack are conducted, then the received signal r is written by equation (7)

$$r = g \cdot (s + v) \tag{7}$$

As a result, the quantization step size in received signal becomes $\Delta_d = g \cdot \Delta_e$. Hence it is necessary to estimate the scale factor g before decoding process. If we use Δ_e instead of the changed step size Δ_d in decoding process, the watermark detection performance may be degraded seriously. Using the Δ_d, the estimated watermark signal, $\hat{d}$, is obtained by comparing the quantization error with $\Delta_d/4$ as follows:

$$e = r - Q_{\Delta_d,0}(r) \tag{8}$$

$$\hat{d} = \begin{cases} 0, & |e| \le \Delta_d/4 \\ 1, & |e| > \Delta_d/4 \end{cases} \tag{9}$$

3   Estimation of Modified Quantization Step Size

3.1   Estimation Scheme of Modified Quantization Step Size

The received watermarked signal that is attacked by amplitude scaling and AWGN can be rewritten by equation (10).

$$
\begin{aligned}
r &= g \cdot (s + v) \\
&= g \cdot x + g \cdot \alpha(Q_{\Delta_e,d}(x) - x) + g \cdot v \\
&= g \cdot Q_{\Delta_e,d}(x) + g(1 - \alpha)(x - Q_{\Delta_e,d}(x)) + g \cdot v \\
&= g \cdot Q_{\Delta_e,d}(x) + w' + v'
\end{aligned}
\tag{10}
$$

where w' and v' are defined as $g(1 - \alpha)(x - Q_{\Delta_e,d}(x))$ and $g \cdot v$, respectively. In general, the means of w' is zero but v' may be not. Since the mean of an audio signal can be assumed zero, however, we remove the mean of the received watermarked signal before processing. To find the modified quantization step size $g \cdot \Delta_e$, we define an error function as follows.

$$
QE(\Delta) = E\left[(r - Q_\Delta(r))^2\right]
\tag{11}
$$

The error function QE has minimum value when the quantization step size, Δ, of a uniform scalar quantizer, $Q_\Delta(r)$, is equal to $g \cdot \Delta_e/2$. The estimated quantization step size, $\hat{\Delta}_d$, is then obtained by equation (12).

$$
\hat{\Delta}_d = 2 \cdot \underset{\Delta}{\arg \min}\left(QE(\Delta)\right)
\tag{12}
$$

Figure 1(a) shows an example of the QE function for one frame of an audio signal. The value of QE increases according to the quantization step size Δ but it has minimum value, zeros, at $\Delta = 64(\Delta_e = 128)$, which is a quantization step size used in embedding. The value of QE except the neighborhood of $\Delta = 64$, follows the curve of quantization noise power, $\Delta^2/12$. Therefore we normalize QE function with $\Delta^2/12$ and define it as a normalized $QE(\equiv QE_N)$ as given in equation (13). Then the equation (12) can be rewritten as (14). Figure 1(b) illustrates the curve of QE_N

$$
QE_N(\Delta) = 1 - \frac{12}{\Delta^2} \cdot QE(\Delta)
\tag{13}
$$

$$
\hat{\Delta}_d = 2 \cdot \underset{\Delta}{\arg \max}\left(QE_N(\Delta)\right)
\tag{14}
$$

The searching range of Δ in equation (12) or (14) can be properly selected in the neighborhood of the quantization step size, $\Delta_e/2$ used in embedding process. For example, we can select $0.5 \cdot \Delta_e/2 \le \Delta \le 1.5 \cdot \Delta_e/2$. Then, how can we find it in case that scaling factor is over 1.5 or under 0.5? But it is out of the question because we normalize the audio signal to predefined power in embedding process and do same in decoding process. The important thing is to estimate the scaling

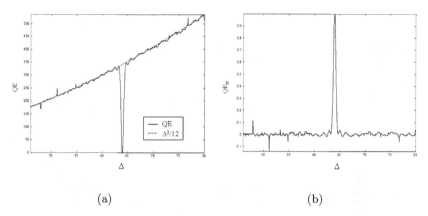

(a)   (b)

Fig. 1. Example of QE curve for an audio signal: (a) QE (b) QE_N

factor that changes slightly according to time. The important problem in our proposed algorithm is thus to select an appropriate searching interval. Both computational load and detection accuracy of a modified quantization step size depend on the searching interval. By making the searching interval smaller, we can detect the exact peak point but it requires more computational load. Otherwise for low complexity, we may miss the peak of QE_N curve. Therefore in the next section, we investigate the optimal searching interval satisfying both detection performance and computational complexity at the same time.

3.2   Selecting Optimal Searching Interval

In this section, we analyze the curve of QE function that quantizes the audio signal, which was quantized with Δ_q in embedding process, with quantization step size Δ. For simplicity, we consider the QIM method with $\alpha = 1$. We define the host signal quantized with Δ_q as s_{Δ_q}, and quantization error caused by quantizing s_{Δ_q} with Δ as $e_\Delta(k)$. As shown in figure 2, $e_\Delta(k)$ increases in proportion to k, that is to say, $e_\Delta(k) = k(\Delta_q - \Delta)$. However if the value of $e_\Delta(k)$ exceeds $\Delta/2$, it becomes $-\Delta/2$ because it is quantized with next codeword. Finally we can obtain $e_\Delta(k)$ like figure 2(b), which is identical with general quantization error shape except its distribution is discrete. Therefore the quantization error, $e_\Delta(k)$, can be represented as follows.

$$e_\Delta(k) = mod\left((\Delta_q - \Delta)\cdot k + \frac{\Delta}{2}, \Delta\right) - \frac{\Delta}{2}, \quad k = 0, \pm 1, \pm 2, ... \quad (15)$$

where mod denotes modulo operation. If the slope, i.e., difference between Δ_q and Δ, is large, the power of $e_\Delta(k)$, QE, follows the quantization noise error, $\Delta^2/12$, but in a small slope, it shows different curve, which will be analyzed from now. If we denote the probability density function of a host signal as $f(x)$, then QE function can be rewritten by equation (16).

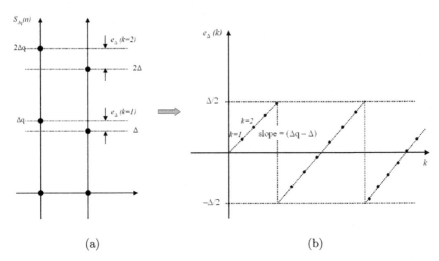

Fig. 2. Quantization error caused by quantizing s_{Δ_q} with Δ: (a) Quantization error (b) Quantization error function

$$QE(\Delta) = \sum_{k=-\infty}^{\infty} \left[\Delta_q \cdot f(k\Delta_q) \cdot e_\Delta(k)^2 \right] \tag{16}$$

First, we analyze the curve of QE function for the case of the uniform and Gaussian probability density function. The uniform probability density function is given by equation (17).

$$f(x) = \begin{cases} 1/(2 \cdot MAX) & , |x| \le MAX \\ 0 & , |x| > MAX \end{cases} \tag{17}$$

The curve of QE in small difference between Δ_q and Δ is shown in figure 3(a). Figure 3(b) shows some error functions at the intersections between the curve of QE and that of $\Delta^2/12$.

To find the crossing point of QE and $\Delta^2/12$, first we define $d\Delta \equiv \Delta_q - \Delta$. Then from figure 3(b)-(1), we can obtain the equation (18).

$$\frac{MAX}{\Delta_q} \cdot d\Delta_{(1)} = \frac{\Delta}{2} \tag{18}$$

If we substitute $\Delta = \Delta_q - d\Delta_{(1)}$ into (18) and rearrange them, $d\Delta_{(1)}$ is obtained as follows.

$$d\Delta_{(1)} = \frac{\Delta_q^2}{2 \cdot MAX + \Delta_q} \cong \left. \frac{\Delta_q^2}{2 \cdot MAX} \right|_{\Delta_q \ll MAX} \tag{19}$$

In the same manner, $d\Delta_{(2)}$ and $d\Delta_{(3)}$ can be obtained as follows.

$$d\Delta_{(2)} \cong 2 \cdot \frac{\Delta_q^2}{2 \cdot MAX} \quad \text{and} \quad d\Delta_{(3)} \cong 3 \cdot \frac{\Delta_q^2}{2 \cdot MAX} \tag{20}$$

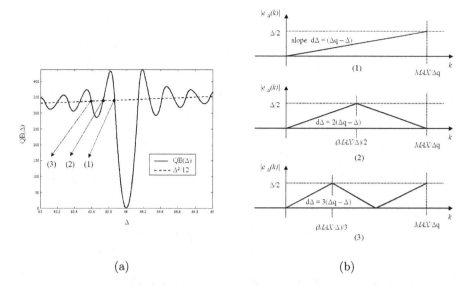

Fig. 3. QE and error functions with small value of $(\Delta_q - \Delta)$: (a) Curve of QE (b) Shape of some error functions, $e_\Delta(k)$

Thus $d\Delta_{(m)}$ can be generalized as shown in equation (21).

$$d\Delta_{(m)} \cong m \cdot \frac{\Delta_q^2}{2 \cdot MAX} \tag{21}$$

From the result of (21), we can conclude that width of the peak, $d\Delta_{(1)}$, increases in proportion with square of Δ_q.

Subsequently, we analyze the curve of QE for Gaussian probability density function. Generally, an audio signal can be modeled with Gaussian distribution with zero mean. Its probability density function is given in equation (22).

$$f(x) = \frac{1}{\sqrt{2\pi\sigma_s^2}} \cdot e^{\frac{x^2}{2\sigma_s^2}} \tag{22}$$

Figure 4 shows an example of the curve of QE for Gaussian distribution with $\sigma_s = 3000$ in comparison with that for uniform distribution with $MAX = 32767$. We can see that the QE also has a similar shape to Gaussian distribution. The width of a valley seems to increase inversely to the standard deviation σ_s of an audio signal, which will be confirmed experimentally later.

The purpose of this section is to determine an optimal searching interval using the property of QE function, where the optimal searching interval means the minimum interval not to miss the peak of QE_N. In other words, we should find the minimum searching interval that can detect the value which exceeds some threshold of the peak of QE_N, i.e., $\beta \cdot QE_N$. We then can obtain $d\Delta$ satisfying equation (23).

$$QE_N(\Delta_q + d\Delta) = \beta \cdot QE_N(\Delta_q)|_{0<\beta<1} \tag{23}$$

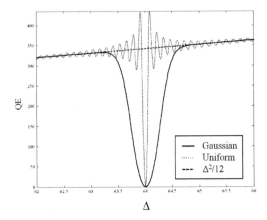

Fig. 4. Curve of QE for Gaussian distribution

Therefore the minimum searching interval, $w(\Delta)$, is calculated by

$$w(\Delta_q) = 2 \cdot d\Delta \qquad (24)$$

Assume that the shape of QE_N in neighborhood of Δ_q is Gaussian distribution. If we substitute the Gaussian density function with σ_p and $\mu = \Delta_q$ into (23) and arrange them, $d\Delta$ is obtained as follows.

$$d\Delta = \sqrt{2} \cdot \sigma_p \cdot \sqrt{\ln\left(\frac{1}{\beta}\right)} \qquad (25)$$

$$d\Delta \propto \sqrt{\ln\left(\frac{1}{\beta}\right)} \qquad (26)$$

where σ_p depends on the standard deviation of an input audio signal, σ_s, and quantization step size, Δ_q, but it is hard to find their relation analytically. Hence we find the relation between the parameter, Δ_q, σ_s, β, and $d\Delta$ numerically. As shown in equation (21), $d\Delta$ is in proportion to Δ_q^2 for uniform distribution. Similarly, we could confirm numerically that $d\Delta$ is in proportion to Δ_q^2 for Gaussian distribution of an input audio signal. Therefore we can express the relationship between $d\Delta$ and Δ_q as equation (27). Figure 5(a) shows the graph of the relationship between $d\Delta$ and Δ_q.

$$d\Delta \propto \Delta^2 \qquad (27)$$

Subsequently, we could obtain numerically that $d\Delta$ is inversely proportional to σ_s as shown in the figure 5(b). Hence the relationship between $d\Delta$ and Δ_q can be expressed by equation (28).

$$d\Delta \propto \frac{1}{\sigma_s} \qquad (28)$$

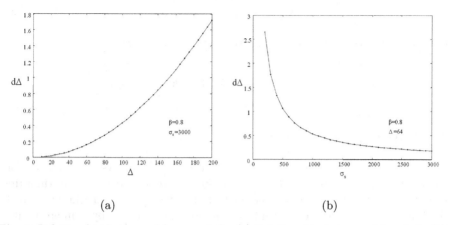

(a)   (b)

Fig. 5. Relationship between $d\Delta$, σ_s and Δ_q: (a) Relationship between $d\Delta$ and Δ_q (b) Relationship between $d\Delta$ and σ_s

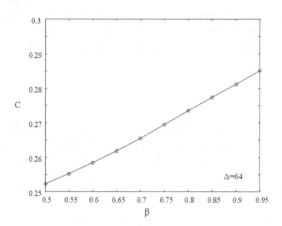

Fig. 6. Variation of C according to β

Considering collectively equations (26), (27), and (28), $d\Delta$ can be written by the formula as follows.

$$d\Delta = C \cdot \sqrt{\ln\left(\frac{1}{\beta}\right)} \cdot \frac{\Delta_q^2}{\sigma_s} \qquad (29)$$

where C is a constant that should be determined. But actually, C is not a constant but slightly varies depending on β because the shape of QE function is not exact Gaussian distribution. Therefore we measure the variation of C according to β and the result is shown in figure 6.

Figure 6 shows that the constant C varies directly depending on β, and especially is very close to a linear line in the range of from 0.7 to 0.95. Therefore we model the variation of C according to β as a linear equation and measure the slope and intercept. The result is as given equation (30)

$$C(\beta) = 0.0783 \cdot \beta + 0.2106 \tag{30}$$

Finally, we get the $d\Delta$ expressed by the formula as follows.

$$d\Delta(\Delta_q, \beta, \sigma_s) = (0.0783 \cdot \beta + 0.2106)\sqrt{\ln\left(\frac{1}{\beta}\right)} \cdot \frac{\Delta_q^2}{\sigma_s} \tag{31}$$

4   Experimental Result

In order to validate the proposed algorithm and evaluate its detection performance, we applied it to an audio watermarking system. The audio watermarking system used in the experiments is illustrated in figure 7, which simply embeds the binary watermark message into an audio signal sample by sample in time domain. Since we focus on solving the weakness for the amplitude modification attack, we did not make much effort to improve the performance of a baseline watermarking system. The audio signal is normalized to the predefined power σ_N^2 before watermark embedding and extracting. In the extractor, Δ estimation block consists of two components, which are coarse searching and fine searching. In coarse searching process, it searches the coarse position of peak of QE

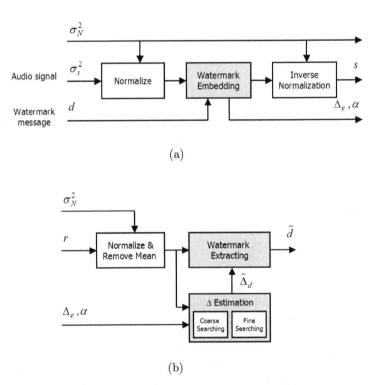

(a)

(b)

Fig. 7. Audio watermarking system used in experiments: (a) Embedder (b)Extractor

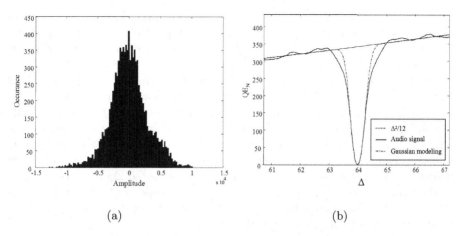

(a)   (b)

Fig. 8. Distribution of an audio signal and QE function: (a) Distribution of a real audio signal (b) Shape of QE for an audio signal and its Gaussian modeling

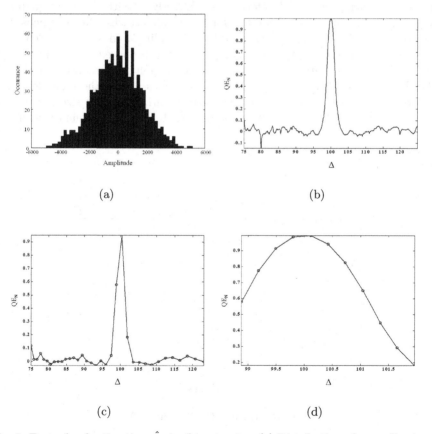

(a)   (b)

(c)   (d)

Fig. 9. Example of estimating $\hat{\Delta}_d$ in the extractor: (a) Distribution of an audio signal (b) QE_N function (c) Coarse searching (d) Fine searching

using the searching interval suggested in equation (31). Then, in fine searching process, the neighborhood of the coarse peak position is searched by dense interval. It provides the detection of an exact quantization step size with low computational load.

First, we compared the shape of QE for an original audio signal and its Gaussian modeling, which is shown in figure 8. It shows that the shape of QE for Gaussian modeling of an audio signal fits well with that of QE for a real audio signal. Figure 9 illustrates the result of coarse searching and fine searching for one frame of an audio signal. In coarse searching, the detector extracts comparatively well the neighborhood of the peak value and it detects more exact position in fine searching. Figure 10 shows the trace of the estimated $\hat{\Delta}_d$ on a frame basis. In the figure, D1 and D2 mean σ_w^2 and $(\sigma_w^2 + \sigma_v^2)$, respectively. When D2/D1 is 1.1 or 1.3, the estimated value of $\hat{\Delta}_d$ is almost exact but it provides inaccurate results occasionally in case of D2/D1= 1.5.

We evaluated the detection error rate (BER: Bit Error Rate) in presence of the AWGN. Figure 11 shows the results and we can see that BER increases proportionally to AWGN. The figure shows the result for three different methods for extracting watermark information: 'Exactly' is with the exact quantization step size $g \cdot \Delta_e$ that we modified for amplitude attacks, 'Not compensated' with the quantization step size Δ_e used for embedding, and 'Compensated' with the estimated quantization step size $\hat{\Delta}_d$ using the proposed algorithm. As expected, 'Not compensated' shows the poorest detection performance even though AWGN is weak. But the proposed method provides almost the same detection performance with that of an exact modified quantization step size in range of $1.0 < D2/D1 < 1.4$. As D2/D1 increases over 1.4, the performance begins to

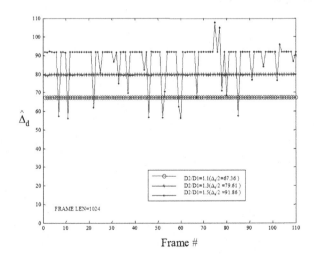

Fig. 10. Trace of the estimated $\hat{\Delta}_d$

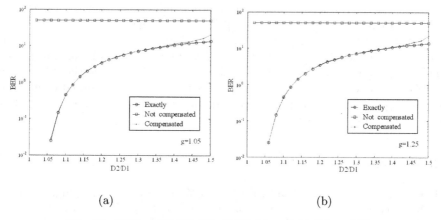

(a)   (b)

Fig. 11. BER as D2/D1 (N=1024) (a) g=1.05 (b) g=1.25

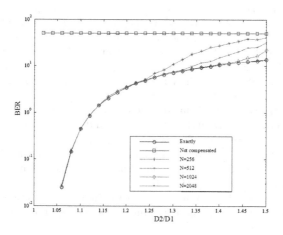

Fig. 12. Comparison of BER for different N (g=1.25)

decrease. The experimental result in figure 11 is conducted under frame size of 1024 samples (N=1024). The BER for different frame size is shown in figure 12. As N increase, BER decrease. The BER of the proposed method has shown to have almost same to that of 'Exactly' in case of N=2048.

5   Conclusions

In this paper, we proposed a robust algorithm to estimate the modified quantization step size with an optimal searching interval. It searches the modified quantization step size under amplitude modification as well as AWGN attack to minimize the quantization error of the received audio signal in a given searching range. The equation to determine the optimal searching interval is derived, which can satisfy both detection performance and computational complexity simultaneously. The estimation process consists of two steps, coarse searching using the optimal searching interval and fine searching within the range detected by coarse searching. The experimental results demonstrate that the proposed estimation algorithm provides good performance under amplitude modification and AWGN attacks with restricted power.

References

1. Boney, L., Tewfik, A., Hamdy, K.: Digital Watermarks for Audio Signals. IEEE Int. Conference on Multimedia Computing and Systems (1996) 473–480
2. Bender, W., Gruhl, D., Morimoto, N., Lu, A.: Techniques for data hiding. IBM Systems Journal, Vol.35, Nos 3&4 (1996) 313–336
3. Gruhl, D., Lu, A.: Echo Hiding. Information Hiding Workshop, Cambridge University, U.K. (1996) 295-315
4. Oh, H. O., Youn, D. H., Hong, J. W., Seok, J. W.: Imperceptible Echo for Robust Audio Watermarking. AES 113th Convention, Los Angeles, CA, USA, Oct. (2002)
5. Kim, S., Kwon, H., Bae, K.: Modification of Polar Echo Kernel for Performance Improvement of Audio Watermarking. International Workshop on Digital Watermarking 2003, Seoul, (2003) 477–487
6. Costa, M. H. M.: Writing on dirty paper. IEEE Transactions on Information Theory, Vol.29, No.7, (1983) 439–441
7. Chen, B., Wornell, G. W.: Quantization Index Modulation: A Class of Provably Good Methods for Digital Watermarking and Information Embedding. IEEE Transaction on In-formation Theory, Vol.47, No.4, (2001)
8. Eggers, J. J., Su, J. K., Girod, B.: A Blind Watermarking Scheme Based on Structured Codebooks. in Secure Image and Image Authentication. Proc. IEE Colloquium, London, UK, (2000) 4/1–4/6
9. Moulin, P., Mihcak, M. K., Lin, G. I.: An Information-theoretic model for image water-marking and data hiding. IEEE Int. Conference on Image Proc., Vancouver, B. C., September (2000)
10. Eggers, J. J., Bauml, R., Girod, B.: Estimation of amplitude modifications before SCS watermark detection. SPIE: Multimedia Systems and Applications IV, Vol.4675, San Jose, USA, (2002) 387–398
11. Lee, K., Kim, D., Kim, T., Moon, K.: EM Estimation of Scale Factor for Quantization-based Audio Watermarking. International Work-shop on Digital Watermarking 2003, Seoul, (2003) 335–346

Reversible Data Hiding Using Integer Wavelet Transform and Companding Technique

Guorong Xuan[1], Chengyun Yang[1], Yizhan Zhen[1],
Yun Q. Shi[2], and Zhicheng Ni[2]

[1] Tongji University, Shanghai, P.R. of China
grxuan@public1.sta.net.cn
[2] New Jersey Institute of Technology, NJ, USA
shi@njit.edu

Abstract. This paper presents a novel reversible data-embedding method for digital images using integer wavelet transform and companding technique. This scheme takes advantage of the Laplacian-like distribution of integer wavelet coefficients in high frequency subbands, which facilitates the selection of compression and expansion functions and keeps the distortion small between the marked image and the original one. Experimental results show that this scheme outperforms the state-of-the-art reversible data hiding schemes.

1 Introduction

Data hiding has drawn increasingly extensive attention recently. Most multimedia data hiding techniques modify and, hence, distort the cover media in order to insert the additional information. Even though the distortion is often small and imperceptible to human visual systems (HVS), the original cover media usually cannot be restored completely. In other words, they are irreversible data hiding. The irreversibility is not admissible to some sensitive applications, such as legal and medical imaging. For these applications, reversible data hiding is desired to extract the embedded data as well as recover the original host signal. Reversible, also often referred to as lossless, invertible, or distortion-free, data hiding has been a very active research subject in the last a few years. In particular, the scheme by Fridrich et al. [1] losslessly compresses the bit planes in the spatial domain and saves the space to embed the data and bookkeeping data to achieve reversible data hiding. The payload of this technique is quite small owing to the lower compression ratio. Based on this, Celik et al. [2] propose a general LSB embedding technique in spatial domain. The payload, visibility and flexibility of this technique are largely improved because of the more efficient compression technique. Xuan et al. [3] proposed a reversible data hiding algorithm carried out in the integer wavelet transform (IWT) domain. By exploiting the features of superior decorrelation and being consistent with HVS of wavelet transform, this technique embeds the data into high frequency subband coefficients achieving high payload and visual quality. Similarly, Tian [4] embeds the data using the difference expansion technique and results in one of the best reversible

I.J. Cox et al. (Eds.): IWDW 2004, LNCS 3304, pp. 115–124, 2005.
© Springer-Verlag Berlin Heidelberg 2005

data hiding method among all the existing reversible data hiding techqniues. Recently, Yang et al. [5] proposed a reversible data hiding technique using the companding technique. This technique, however, embeds data in discrete cosine transform (DCT) coefficients. Inspired by the techniques reported in [3] and [5], this paper applies the companding technique to the integer wavelet transform domain and selects a more suitable companding function for IWT high frequency coefficients, thus resulting in a reversible data hiding technique that outperforms the state-of-the-art [4]. Both theoretical analysis and experimental results demonstrate the superiority of the proposed technique. The rest of the paper is organized as follows. A brief introduction to companding technique is provided in Section 2. The proposed algorithm is detailed presented in Section 3. Some experimental results and performance analysis are presented in Section 4. The conclusion is drawn in Section 5.

2   Companding Technique

Companding, the processing pair of compression and expansion, is a technique utilized to implement nonuniform quantization in speech communications in order to achieve high signal noise ratio. This has been detailed introduced in many digital communications texts, say, in [6]. Specifically, this procedure first compresses a signal and then expands it. Uniform quantization is carried out after the compression and before the expansion. As a result, with the companding and uniform quantization, nonuniform quantization is equivalently performed. Instead of data compression, compression here means that the dynamic range of the original signal is mapped to a narrower range. After the expansion of the compressed signal, the expanded signal is close to the original signal. In ideal situation, this companding operation can be expressed as

$$E(C(x)) = x$$

where C stands for compression function, E stands for expanding function. If this assumption is satisfied, this technique can be successfully applied to the reversible data hiding. We apply companding in our proposed lossless data hiding.

2.1   Companding Technique Used for Reversible Data Hiding

A simple realization is as follows:

(1) Compression function C is applied to the original signal x to obtain a new signal $y = C(x)$. Assume the binary expression of y is $p_1 p_2 \cdots p_n$, where $p_i \in \{0,1\}$.

(2) A bit $b \in \{0,1\}$ is appended after the least significant bit (LSB) of y. In this way, y becomes $y' = p_1 p_2 \cdots p_n b$, which means $y' = 2 \times y + b$. For generality, we use P to express this appending operation, which means $y' = P(y)$.

(3) If $y' \approx x$, then the modification of the signal will be small and hardly be perceived.

(4) In the hidden data extraction stage, we only need to extract the LSB bit of signal y', which means $b = LSB(y')$ and recover the signal $y = \dfrac{y'}{2}$.

(5) After obtaining the signal y, we can recover the original signal by expansion, i.e., $x = E(y)$.

From the above steps, we can see that the function C, E and P should satisfy the following two conditions:

(1) $E(C(x)) = x$
(2) $P(C(x)) \approx x$ and $P(C(x))$ is within the range of the original signal x, which means overflow/underflow problem can be avoided.

In dealing with digital signal, however, the above two conditions are difficult to be exactly met owing to the nature of digitization. This is because the quantized companding functions C_Q and E_Q have to be utilized instead, where

$$C_Q = Q(C), \; E_Q = Q(E)$$

and Q denotes the quantization function. Obviously, right now for some signal x, we may have

$$E_Q(C_Q(x)) \neq x$$

namely the difference (error) value is $r = E_Q(C_Q(x)) - x \neq 0$.

Hence in order to recover the original signal x, we must record the difference value r. This is to say that the difference value r and the to-be-embedded data both need to be embedded into the host signal x as overhead and   pure payload, respectively.

2.2   Selection of Compression Function in the Companding Technique

Through the analysis of companding function, we find that if Condition (2) were not considered, then any one-to-one mapping function F can be utilized as a compression function. For example, the simplest linear function $F(x) = x$ can be considered as a compression function. If multiple x values are mapped to a single value of y, it indicates that it will not be straightforward to find corresponding x value from the given y value. This function can, however, still be used as a compression function under the condition that some payload must be sacrificed to record the multiplicity, thus resolving the uncertainty. For example, if x_1, x_2 are compressed to the same y_0, in order to express this mapping relationship, we need to use one bit to record which x is mapped to y_0, say, bit 0 to indicate x_1 and bit 1 to indicate x_2. These overhead data used for recording is also need to be embedded into the original signal.

For speech signals, the following compression and expanding functions may be considered to use:

$$C(x) = \frac{1}{2}\sqrt{x} , \quad E(x) = (2x)^2$$

in which x is normalized to the range [0,1]. As discussed, obviously, quantized compression and expanding functions should be used in digital data hiding system. In reality, it is difficult to find a function which satisfies both one-to-one mapping and Condition (2). For example, the linear function $F(x) = x$ does not satisfy Condition (2) if the input signal x is large since y' is almost as large as twice of x value and y' may encounter overflow or underflow problem. From the histogram of many images, it is observed that the images are different from speech signals in that the former often has large magnitude while the latter has small magnitude predominantly. Therefore, for digital images, the above functions are not suitable for companding [5] because of the different nature between aural and visual signals. The selection of compression and expanding functions plays a key role when used in the invertible data hiding.

3   Integer Wavelet Transform Based Reversible Data Hiding Using Companding Technique

Wavelet transform is widely applied in different tasks image processing. Since wavelet coefficients are highly decorrelated, have compact energy concentration and are consistent with the feature of the HVS, it is also widely applied in image data hiding. The study on human visual system points out that slight modification on wavelet high frequency subband coefficients is hard to be perceived by human eyes. Through out the investigation of wavelet coefficients, we find that if companding technique is applied to wavelet coefficients, the restriction listed in condition (2) will be largely decreased. The followings are detailed discussion.

3.1   Integer Wavelet Transform (IWT)

To recover the original image losslessly, reversible wavelet transform should be used. Hence we employ the integer wavelet transform which maps integer to integer [7] and can reconstruct the original signal without any distortion. Although various wavelet families can be applied to our reversible embedding scheme, through experimental comparison study we have discovered that CDF(2,2) is better than other wavelet families in terms of high embedding capacity and visual quality of marked images. CDF(2,2) format has also been adopted by JPEG2000 standard.

3.2   Distribution of IWT Coefficients in High Frequency Subbands and Selection of Companding Function

For most of images, the distribution of high frequency coefficients of integer wavelet transform obeys in general a Laplacian-like distribution. The following two features exist in the distribution.

(a) Most high frequency integer wavelet transform coefficients are very small in magnitude. It is then convenient to select the compression function. For example the linear function $F(x) = x$ can be considered as compression function since even though y' is about twice the x value, it is still in the range of x.

(b) Although most of high frequency IWT coefficients are small in magnitude, there are still some IWT coefficients having large magnitude. For these large coefficients, compression function selection should consider the restriction of condition (2). In this case, the linear function $F(x) = x$ is no longer suitable to serve as a compression function.

Considering the above two situations, we propose to adopt the following piecewise linear function as the compression function.

$$C(x) = \begin{cases} x, |x| < T \\ sign(x) \cdot (\dfrac{|x| - T}{2} + T), |x| \geq T \end{cases}$$

where T is a pre-defined threshold. $C(x)$ is depicted below in Figure 1.

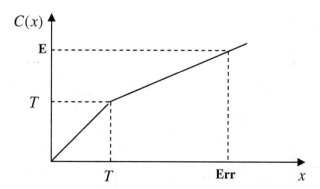

Fig. 1. Compression function $C(x)$

As discussed above, in actual realization, however, we have to adopt the compress function in quantized version, namely

$$Q(C) = C_Q(x) = \begin{cases} x, |x| < T \\ sign(x) \cdot \left(\left\lfloor \dfrac{|x| - T}{2} \right\rfloor + T \right), |x| \geq T \end{cases}$$

It can be derived from the above equation that when $|x| \geq T$, x and $(x+1)$ (or $(x-1)$) are compressed to correspond to a same y value. Hence according to the previous discussion, x and $(x+1)$ (or $(x-1)$) are need to be recoded and the recording data need to be embedded as overhead into the wavelet coefficients. From the above discussion, T is a critical value. When T is small, the coefficients alterations are small and good visual quality of marked image is achieved. When T is large, a larger payload can be achieved. In the actual embedding, we select the T value according to the payload.

3.3   Histogram Modification

For a given image, after data are embedded into some high frequency IWT coefficients, it is possible to cause overflow and/or underflow, which means that after inverse integer wavelet transform the grayscale values of some pixels in the marked image may exceed the upper bound (255 for an eight-bit grayscale image) and/or the lower bound (0 for an eight-bit grayscale image). In order to prevent the overflow and underflow, we adopt histogram modification to narrow the histogram from both sides. The bookkeeping data generated in histogram modification need to be embedded into image as a part of overhead data, which will be used late in the recovery of the original image. For details about histogram modification, readers are referred to [3].

Following Figure 2 is a block diagram for the proposed data embedding and extaction procedures.

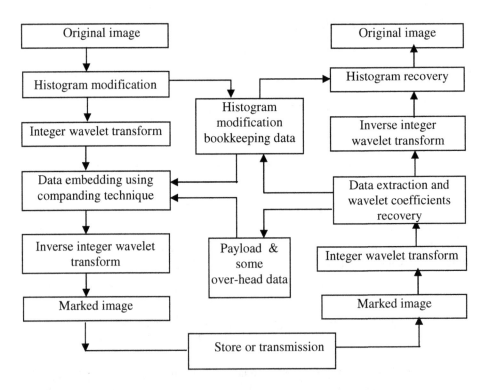

Fig. 2. Block diagram of reversible data hiding diagram. Left: data embedding, Right: data extraction

4   Experimental Results and Analysis

We applied the proposed reversible data hiding algorithm to some frequently used images. Tables 1, 2, 3, and 4 contain the experimental results on four grayscale level images, Lena, Baboon, Barbara and Goldhill of size 512×512 shown in Figure 3. For an image of size of 512×512, a payload 1 bpp (bits per pixel) means that 262,144 (namely 512×512) bits are embedded in the image. The data in these tables indicate that the proposed reversible data hiding algorithm can embed a large payload, while maintaing the high PSNR (peak signal-to-noise-ratio) of the marked image versus the original image. In Figure 4, the comparison results between the difference expansion method [4] and our proposed method are shown. It is observed that our proposed technique can obtain better visual quality in the same payload. More than 2 dB improvement in PSNR has been achieved.

Lena   Baboon

Barbara   Goldhill

Fig. 3. Some test images

Table 1. PSNR vs. payload for Lena image

Payload (bpp)	0.1	0.2	0.3	0.4	0.6	0.7
PSNR (dB)	49.53	46.23	44.04	42.28	39.43	37.48

Table 2. PSNR vs. payload for Baboon image

Payload (bpp)	0.1	0.2	0.3	0.4	0.5
PSNR (dB)	43.45	39.66	36.42	33.61	31.51

Table 3. PSNR vs. payload for Barbara image

Payload (bpp)	0.1	0.2	0.3	0.4	0.5	0.6
PSNR (dB)	49.47	46.84	44.70	42.33	40.13	36.77

Table 4. PSNR vs. payload for Goldhill image

Payload (bpp)	0.1	0.2	0.3	0.4	0.5	0.6
PSNR (dB)	47.85	44.74	42.37	40.40	38.36	36.68

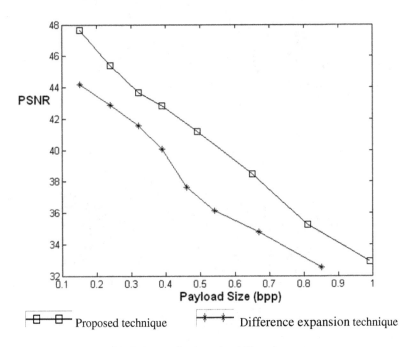

Fig. 4. Comparison results on Lena image

We should point out that this proposed technique can be applied to an image more than once for multiple embedding. For an already embedded image, we can embed it again with another payload. Since we embed data in three high frequency subbands of

IWT, each embedding has a payload capacity less than 0.75 bpp. Results reported in Tables 1, 2, 3, and 4 are the results after the first time embedding. In practice, the payload capacity limit of each embedding will decrease gradually, as the redundancy becomes less and less. To explore the redundancy as much as possible, a recommended strategy is to select different positions of images as beginning points of IWT. For example, at the first embedding, we can begin IWT from first row and first column; at the second embedding, we begin from the second row and second column, and so forth. An example of two embedding on Lena is presented in Figure 5.

0.6 bpp, PSNR: 39.43 dB, one embedding   1.3 bpp , PSNR: 31.1 dB, two embedding

Fig. 5. Visual quality on Lena image for different payload

5   Conclusion

This paper proposes a reversible data hiding technique based on the integer wavelet companding technique. Experimental results and the comparison with the difference expansion (Figure 4) method demonstrate that this proposed technique can obtain a better visual quality of the marked image at the same payload. It is expected that this reversible data hiding technique will be deployed for a wide range of applications in the areas such as secure medical image data system, law enforcement, e-government, image authentication and covert communication.

Acknowledgement

This research is supported in part by China NSFC: The Research of Theory and Key Technology of Lossless Data Hiding (90304017), and by New Jersey Commission of Science and Technology via NJWINS.

References

[1] Fridrich, J., Goljan, M., Du, R.: Invertible Authentication. In: Proc. SPIE Photonics West, vol. 3971, Security and Watermarking of Multimedia Contents III, San Jose, California January (2001) 197-208.

[2] Celik, M., Sharma, G., Tekalp, A. M., Saber, E.: Reversible Data Hiding. In: Proceedings of the International Conference on Image Processing 2002, Rochester, NY, September (2002).

[3] Xuan, G., Zhu, J., Chen, J., Shi, Y. Q., Ni, Z., Su, W.: Distortionless Data Hiding Based on Integer Wavelet Transform. In: IEE Electronics Letters, December (2002) 1646-1648.

[4] Tian, J.: Reversible Data Embedding Using a Difference Expansion. In: IEEE Transactions on Circuits and Systems for Video Technology, August (2003) 890-896.

[5] Yang, B., Schmucker, M., Funk, W., Busch, C., Sun, S.: Integer DCT-based Reversible Watermarking for Images Using Companding Technique. In: Proceedings of SPIE Vol. #5306, 5306-41.

[6] Sklar, B.: Digital Communications: Fundamentals and Applications. Englewood Cliffs, New Jersey: PTR Prentice Hall (1988).

[7] Calderbank, A. R., Daubechies, I., Sweldens, W., Yeo, B.-L.: Wavelet Transforms that Map Integers to Integers. In: Applied and Computational Harmonic Analysis, July (1998) 332–369.

Alteration-Locating
Authentication Watermarking for Binary Images

Hae Yong Kim and Ricardo Lopes de Queiroz

[1] Escola Politécnica, Universidade de São Paulo, Brazil
hae@lps.usp.br
http://www.lps.usp.br/~{}hae
[2] Universidade de Brasília, Brazil
queiroz@ieee.org

Abstract. In image authentication watermarking, hidden data is inserted into an image to detect any accidental or malicious image alteration. In the literature, quite a small number of cryptography-based secure authentication methods are available for binary images. This paper proposes a new authentication watermarking method for binary images. It can detect any visually significant alteration while maintaining good visual quality for virtually all types of binary images (possibly excluding dispersed-dot halftones). As usual, the security of the algorithm lies only on the secrecy of a secret- or private-key. This paper also presents a variation of the proposed scheme that can locate the modified region with good spatial resolution. A possible application of the proposed technique is in Internet fax transmission, i.e. for legal authentication of documents routed outside the phone network.

1 Introduction

Classically, steganography (also known as data/information hiding) studies how to hide secret messages in other messages, such that the secret's very existence is concealed. In this paper, data hiding scheme simply means the technique to embed a sequence of bits in a still image and to extract it afterwards without worrying about the confidentiality of the secret's existence.

A watermarking technique makes use of a data-hiding scheme to insert some information in the host image, in order to make an assertion about the image later. Watermarking techniques can be classified as either "robust" or "fragile." Robust watermarks are useful for copyright and ownership assertion purposes. They cannot be easily removed and should resist common image-manipulation procedures such as rotation, scaling, cropping, brightness/contrast adjusting, lossy compression, printing, scanning, etc. On the other hand, fragile watermarks (or authentication watermarks) are easily corrupted by any image processing procedure. However, watermarks for checking the image integrity and authenticity can be fragile because if the watermark is removed, the watermark detection algorithm will correctly report the corruption of the image.

I.J. Cox et al. (Eds.): IWDW 2004, LNCS 3304, pp. 125–136, 2005.

In the literature, there are many authentication-watermarking techniques (AWTs) for continuous-tone images [27, 26, 22, 23, 17, 2, 13, 24, 3, 5]. Also, there are many techniques for data hiding in binary and halftone images [9, 18, 1, 6, 25, 10, 11, 21, 19]. However, quite a small number of secure AWTs are available for binary and halftone images. We mean by "secure AWT" a scheme where the security does not lie on the secrecy of the algorithm but only on the secrecy of the key. The watermarking algorithm and the fact that an image is watermarked may be made public without compromising the security. Hence, usually a secure AWT relies upon cryptography, and it seems to be very difficult to design a really secure AWT without making use of the solid cryptography theory and techniques. Moreover, a secure AWT must detect *any* visually significant change made to an image. A cryptography-based secure AWT [14, 15] was recently devised for dispersed-dot halftone images but the visual quality for a generic binary image is poor.

In a typical cryptography-based AWT, an authentication signature (AS) is computed from the whole image and inserted into the image itself. In cryptography, an AS is called message authentication code (MAC) using a secret-key cipher or digital signature (DS) using a public/private-key cipher. An AS contains information about the host image content that may be checked to verify its integrity. However, inserting the AS into the image alters the image itself, hence modifying its AS and invalidating the watermark. Typically, the image has to be somehow divided into at least two parts: a portion to maintain the image integrity and another portion to carry the AS. For continuous-tone images, many AWTs compute the AS from the image clearing the least significant bits (LSBs) and insert the AS in LSBs. In other words, the host image is divided in two parts: LSBs and the remainder of the image excluding LSBs. Clearly, the LSB-clearing technique cannot be applied to binary images.

In this paper, we propose a new cryptography-based secure AWT for binary images that has good visual quality when applied to generic binary images (excluding dispersed-dot halftones). It can be used in conjunction with secret-key or public/private-key ciphers. We also present a variation of the algorithm that can spatially locate the modifications (besides detecting them). This version does not lose its alteration-locating capability even with image cropping. A possible use of our method is to send faxes and documents over uncontrolled networks and the Internet. In this case, the receiver of a document can verify its integrity for a given originator.

2   Data Hiding and Authentication Watermarking

There are three basic ways of embedding a sequence of bits in binary/halftone images:

Pixel-wise: Change the values of (usually pseudo-randomly chosen) individual pixels [10, 11, 7]. This approach is well suited for dispersed-dot halftone images. However, visible salt and pepper noise will appear when applied to other types of binary images. It can be applied to the binary image or directly to the halftone screen in its design step [16].

Component-wise: Change the characteristics of pixel groups (for example, the position or the area of connected components) [18]. Unfortunately, the success of this approach depends on the type of the host image.

Block-wise: Divide the host image into blocks and modify some characteristics of each block [1, 12, 19, 25, 21].

Many data hiding schemes for binary images can be transformed into AWTs by simply dividing the host image Z in two regions: the first region Z_1 where the AS is to be stored, and the second region Z_2 from where the AS is to be computed. This idea was recently used to transform a pixel-wise data hiding scheme [10, 11] into an AWT for dispersed-dot halftone images that can detect even single pixel toggling [14, 15]. However, some caution must be taken when transforming a data-hiding scheme into an AWT, because although the region Z_2 is well protected (with the security assured by the cryptography theory), the region Z_1 is not. For example, let us take the component-wise data-hiding scheme that inserts one bit per connected component, forcing it to have an even or odd number of pixels. A connected component can be forced to have the desired parity by toggling one of its boundary pixels. This scheme can be transformed into an AWT by dividing the host image in regions Z_1 and Z_2, computing the AS of Z_2 and inserting it in Z_1. Yet, a malicious hacker can arbitrarily alter the region Z_1 without being noticed by the AWT, as long as all the parities of its connected components remain unaltered. For example, a character "a" in Z_1 region can be changed into an "e" (or any other character that contains only one connected component) as long as its parity remains unchanged. We refer to this as a "parity attack."

3   The Proposed Method

As we noted in previous section, there are some data hiding techniques for binary images. Among them, an interesting technique is template ranking [8, 25], which can be applied to most binary images with excellent visual quality. It can be summarized as follows:

- Divide the image Z to be marked into blocks (e.g. 8×8).
- The neighborhood of each pixel (usually a 3×3 template) is analyzed to rate its visual significance. A pixel with low visual significance may change its color with small visual impact. Figure 1 depicts two possible rankings of 3×3 templates. It seems that the most visually pleasant ranking depends on the nature of the image Z to be marked.
- Insert one bit in each block by forcing the block to have even or odd number of white pixels, to insert bits 0 or 1 respectively. If the block already has the desired parity, it is left untouched. Otherwise, toggle the pixel in the block with the lowest visual significance.

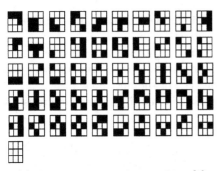

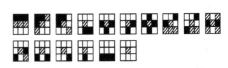

(a) A suggested template ranking [8].   (b) Another rank where hatched pixels match either black or white pixels (the score of a given pattern is that of the matching template with the highest impact).

Fig. 1. Two template rankings (in increasing visual significance order from left to right, top to bottom). Mirrors, transposes and reverses of each pattern have the same score. All white or all black patterns have the highest visual impacts

As different blocks may have different quantities of low-visibility pixels, it is suggested to shuffle image Z before embedding data. The template ranking data hiding technique can be employed in a secure AWT for binary images. That was hinted in [25] but not elaborated before. We refer to this technique as AWTR (Authentication Watermarking by Template Ranking). The first version of the AWTR insertion algorithm is:

Step 1) Let be given a binary image Z to be marked. Using a pseudo-random number generator with a seed, construct an auxiliary data structure called shuffling vector, so that the image Z can be viewed as a completely shuffled sequence of pixels $\tilde{Z}$. In the secret-key version of our technique, the secret-key is used as the seed of the pseudo-random generator. In the public/private-key version, the seed must be made public.

Step 2) Let n be the length of the adopted AS, and m be the number of pixels in each block. Divide the shuffled sequence $\tilde{Z}$ into two regions:
  – First region $\tilde{Z}_1$ with $n \times m$ pixels, where the AS is to be stored. This region is subdivided into n blocks with m pixels each. In each block, one bit of the AS will be inserted.
  – Second region $\tilde{Z}_2$: the remainder of the shuffled sequence $\tilde{Z}$. The insertion algorithm will compute AS of this region.

Step 3) Using a cryptographically secure hashing function H, compute the fingerprint of the second region $H = H(\tilde{Z}_2)$. Encrypt the fingerprint H using a secret- or private-key k, obtaining an authentication signature $S = E_k(H)$.

Step 4) Insert S into the first region, obtaining the watermarked image Z'. Insert one bit of S in each block as previously described.

We remark here that AS cannot be made too short without seriously compromising security. A 64-bits-long message authentication code does not withstand a birthday attack [3]. Usually, a message authentication code (MAC) with 128-bits is considered secure. The best known digital signature (DS), RSA, is considered secure with 1024 bits. A newer scheme, DSA, is considered secure with 320 bits. A brand new scheme, BLS, is supposedly secure with only 160 bits [4]. The reader is referred to introductory books on Cryptography for more details (for example, [20]). The verification algorithm of a watermarked image Z' is straightforward:

Step 1) Compute the same shuffling vector used in the insertion. Note that in the secret-key version, the secret-key is also the seed of the random number generator and consequently only the owner of the key can reconstruct the shuffling vector. However, in the public-key version, the seed is public and so is the shuffling vector.

Step 2) Divide the shuffled sequence $\tilde{Z}'$ into two regions $\tilde{Z}'_1$ and $\tilde{Z}'_2$, in the same way done in the insertion. Compute the fingerprint $H = H(\tilde{Z}'_2)$.

Step 3) Extract the authentication signature S stored in $\tilde{Z}'_1$ and decrypt it using the secret- or public-key k, obtaining the check data $D = D_k(S)$.

Step 4) If $D = H$, the watermark is verified. Otherwise, image Z' has been modified or a wrong key was used.

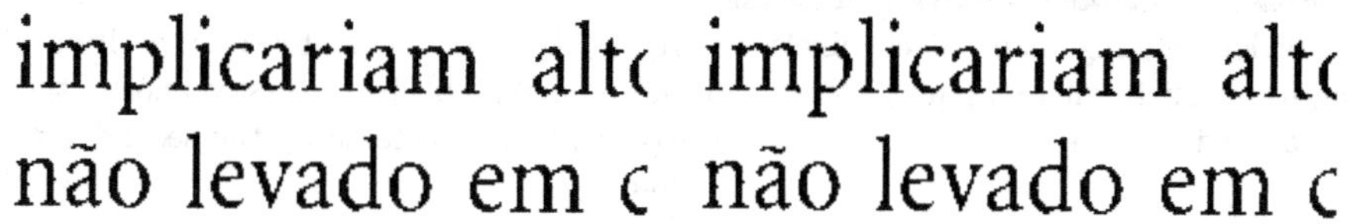

implicariam alt(implicariam alt(
não levado em c não levado em c

(a) Part of a page of magazine scanned at 300 dpi which can be considered as a "typical" binary document.

(b) AWTR-marked image (1024 bits embedded, enough for embedding the RSA digital signature).

(c) Exclusive-or between figures 2(a) and 2(b).

(d) Region-defining map: Black pixels belong to region 1, while white ones to region 2.

Fig. 2. Quality of a "typical" binary document marked with the AWTR

Figure 2(a) depicts a zoom of a magazine page scanned at 300 dpi, which can be considered as a "typical" binary document (3200×2432 pixels for the full page). Figure 2(b) is the corresponding image after embedding 1024 bits using 64-pixel blocks. Note in figure 2(c) that only a few pixels have changed their values.

Figure 3(a) shows a very small binary image (160 × 370 pixels) to be watermarked. Figure 3(b) shows the AWTR-watermarked image with 800 bits embedded using 64-pixel blocks. The quality of the marked image is acceptable, even though many bits have been embedded.

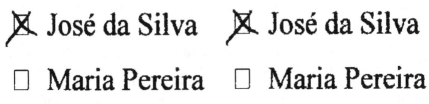

(a) A very small image (160 × 370) to be watermarked.

(b) Image with 800 bits embedded.

(c) Region-defining map: Black pixels belong to region 1, where a parity attack can be mounted.

(d) A fake image generated by a parity attack, undetectable by the first version of the AWTR, but detectable by the second version.

Fig. 3. Quality of a very small image marked with the AWTR and the parity attack

4   Parity Attack

The proposed method detects any alteration of the second region of a watermarked image, even if one single pixel is toggled. Indeed, the probability of not detecting a modification in this region is only 2^{-n} (n is the length of the AS), which can be neglected.

Unfortunately, any alteration that maintains the parities of the blocks in the first region cannot be detected by AWTR. For example, if two pixels that belong to the same block change their values, the parity of this block does not change and this modification will pass undetected. We named this a "parity attack." If the host image Z is large enough, pixels of the first region constitute isolated pixels randomly dispersed in the image and it is unlikely that a malicious attacker will be able to introduce any visually significant alteration by changing only the region-1 pixels (while maintaining the parities of all blocks). For example, in Fig. 2(d), black pixels belong to the region 1 and they are quite dispersed. Thus, no visually meaningful alteration will result by modifying only these pixels. As a rule of thumb, we can consider that no visually significant parity attack can occur if the number of pixels of the first region is, say, less than 5% of total host image pixels.

However, if image Z is small, region-1 pixels can form contiguous areas. This rises the possibility of a visually meaningful modification that would pass undetected. For example, Fig. 3(c) shows pixels that belong to region 1 in black. Any region-1 pixel can be modified, provided that another pixel in the same block is also modified. To obtain a fake image, a hacker changes a pixel p of block i. Then, the hacker looks for the pixel within block i with the lowest visibility and flips its value. Figure 3(d) shows a fake image constructed by repeating this idea. This alteration will pass undetected by AWTR.

Actually, the above described scenario only applies to the public-key version of the AWTR, where the locations of regions 1 and 2, as well as the subdivisions of region 1 into blocks are publicly known. Unfortunately, we could not find any technique to thwart the parity attack for public-key AWTR, except forcing region-1 to be much smaller than the size of the host image. This can be achieved by using small blocks and/or short digital signatures.

For secret-key AWTR, we do not have to worry *much* about a parity attack, because the secret-key is used to generate the shuffling vector. So, an attacker will not know how the watermarked image is divided into regions 1 and 2, and how region 1 is subdivided into blocks. However, we have to pay some attention to this potential attack because the hacker may have many different ways to obtain "clues" about the location of regions and blocks. For example, let us suppose that the hacker has access to a database of original and marked binary documents, all of the same size and all watermarked using the same secret-key. Then the hacker will know that all those pixels whose values are different in the original and the watermarked images belong to region-1 (although it will not be known how region-1 is subdivided into blocks). Nevertheless there are always means to make the division into regions to be image dependent, therefore unique for each image. In any case, in order to minimize the possibility of a parity attack, we suggest the following improvement of step 4 of the secret-key AWTR insertion algorithm:

Step 4) Insert S into the first region using the following algorithm, to obtain the watermarked image Z':
For $i \leftarrow 0$ to $n-1$ {
 - Insert bit i of S into the i-th block forcing it to have odd or even number or white pixels;
 - Compute the new AS S, feeding the hashing function with the content of block i, and encrypting it with the key k: $S \leftarrow E_k(H(S, \text{pixels of block } i))$;
}

In this way, block $n-1$ can still suffer a parity attack without being detected. However, if block $n-2$ is modified without modifying its parity, with 50% of chance this modification will be detected. If block 0 is changed (maintaining its parity), there is a probability of $1 - 2^{-(n-1)}$ of detecting this change. Obviously, the AWTR verification algorithm must be changed accordingly. Unfortunately, this idea cannot be used with the public-key AWTR, because the digital signature must be completely extracted before decrypting it with the public-key.

5   Locating Alterations

The AWTR can be transformed into an authentication watermarking capable of spatially locating the altered regions. Let us call this technique AWTRAL (Authentication Watermarking by Template Ranking with Alteration Locating). The naive idea of dividing the host image into sub-images and authenticating independently each sub-image is not safe. Wong [22,23] has proposed a similar idea to authenticate continuous-tone images and it was demonstrated later to be subject to many kinds of attacks, including the "cut and paste," "vector quantization counterfeiting" and "birthday" attacks [2,13,24,3]. A few works [24, 3,5] present different approaches to protect the host image against such attacks. Wong and Memon [24] propose a technique where the AS of each sub-image is dependent of its index and a unique identifier of the host image. However, the image identifier has to be somehow stored outside of the host image, what is a significant inconvenience. Barreto et al. [3] present a technique called "hash block chaining" that uses the contexts of sub-images and a non-deterministic digital signature to obtain the security. Using this technique, there is no more need to use an image identifier. However, the obtained spatial resolution is twice the size of each sub-image. Celik et al. [5] propose a hierarchical watermarking. The spatial resolution of this scheme is nearly the size of each sub-image. It does not lose its alterations-locating capability even with an image cropping: it can use a "sliding window" to resynchronize with sub-images. We will use the hierarchical watermarking with two layers to construct the AWTRAL. Two layers are sufficient to obtain the desired security.

The idea of AWTRAL is to divide the image to be marked into sub-images (say, with 128×128 pixels). Then, we watermark independently each sub-image with secret-key AWTR (first layer), and watermark the whole image (composed by all AWTR-marked sub-images) with another public- or secret-key AWTR (second layer). Note that if the host image is not large enough to hinder parity attacks, secret-key AWTR must be used in both watermark layers. Using secret/public-key AWTRAL, anyone can verify if the marked image is authentic using the public-key. If an image is found to be fraudulent, the owner of the secret-key can spatially locate the alterations to help discovering the intentions of the hacker. We describe below the secret/public-key AWTRAL:

Step 1) Let be given a binary image Z to be marked. Pseudo-randomly shuffle Z, obtaining the shuffled sequence of pixels $\tilde{Z}$.

Step 2) Divide the sequence $\tilde{Z}$ into two regions:
  - Region $\tilde{Z}_A$ with $n_2 \times m$ pixels, where the second-layer DS is to be stored (n_2 is the length of adopted DS and m is the size of each block).
  - Region $\tilde{Z}_{BC}$: the remainder of $\tilde{Z}$ from where the DS is to be computed. This region will be further subdivided into regions $\tilde{Z}_B$ and $\tilde{Z}_C$.

Step 3) Divide the original non-shuffled image Z into sub-images (say, with 128×128 pixels) $Z_1, Z_2, ..., Z_l$.

Step 4) Pseudo-randomly shuffle each sub-image Z_i, obtaining $\tilde{Z}_i$, and divide it into three sub-regions:
- Sub-region $\tilde{Z}_{iA}$, constituted by the pixels of sub-image $\tilde{Z}_i$ that belong to the region $\tilde{Z}_A$ determined in step 2.
- Sub-region $\tilde{Z}_{iB}$ with $n_1 \times m$ pixels, where the first-layer MAC is to be stored (n_1 is the length of adopted MAC and m is the size of each block).
- Sub-region $\tilde{Z}_{iC}$: the remainder of $\tilde{Z}_i$ from where the MAC is to be computed.

Step 5) For each shuffled sub-image $\tilde{Z}_i$, compute the fingerprint of sub-region $\tilde{Z}_{iC}$: $H_i = H(\tilde{Z}_{iC})$. Encrypt the fingerprint H_i with a secret-key, obtaining the MAC $S_i = E_k(H_i)$. Insert S_i into sub-region $\tilde{Z}_{iB}$, as described in sections 3 and 4.

Step 6) Compute the fingerprint of region $\tilde{Z}_{BC}$: $H = H(\tilde{Z}_{BC})$. Encrypt the fingerprint H with the private-key, obtaining the digital signature $S = E_k(H)$. Insert S into region $\tilde{Z}_A$, as described in sections 3 and 4.

The AWTRAL verification algorithm is:

Step 1) Given an AWTRAL-marked image Z', shuffle it as in the insertion, obtaining the shuffled sequence $\tilde{Z}'$.

Step 2) Divide the sequence $\tilde{Z}'$ into regions $\tilde{Z}'_A$ and $\tilde{Z}'_{BC}$, as before. Compute the fingerprint H of $\tilde{Z}'_{BC}$.

Step 3) Extract the DS S stored in $\tilde{Z}'_A$ and decrypt it using the public-key k, obtaining the check data $D = D_k(S)$.

Step 4) If $D = H$, the watermark is verified and no further processing is necessary. Otherwise, image Z' was modified and the following steps can determine the altered locations.

Step 5) Divide the watermarked non-shuffled image Z' into sub-images $Z'_1, Z'_2, ..., Z'_l$, as in the insertion.

Step 6) Shuffle each sub-image Z'_i, obtaining $\tilde{Z}'_i$, and divide it into three sub-regions $\tilde{Z}'_{iA}, \tilde{Z}'_{iB}$ and $\tilde{Z}'_{iC}$, as before.

Step 7) For each shuffled sub-image $\tilde{Z}'_i$, compute the fingerprint H_i of sub-region $\tilde{Z}'_{iC}$. Extract the MAC S_i stored in sub-region $\tilde{Z}'_{iB}$ and decrypt it, obtaining the check data $D_i = D_k(S_i)$. If $H_i = D_i$, the watermark of sub-image Z'_i is verified.

Let us make three remarks on the AWTRAL algorithm. First, the above-described algorithm loses its capability of locating alterations after row or column cropping. Celik et al. [5] suggest using a sliding window to obtain a cropping-surviving watermark. Step 5 of the verification algorithm may be modified as follows to locate alterations even after image cropping:

Step 5) Slide a window (of the same size as the sub-images used in the AW-TRAL insertion) over the non-shuffled image Z' to obtain all possible sub-images $Z'_1, Z'_2, ..., Z'_l$ within Z'.

Second, there may be some sub-images almost completely white (black) with only a few black (white) pixels. These sub-images have few low-visibility pixels and the watermark insertion may make visible salt-and-pepper noise. We suggest not watermarking neither verifying these sub-images, because it is not possible to introduce any visually significant alteration without significantly increasing the number of black (white) pixels. And if the number of black (white) pixels increases significantly, the MAC verification will detect the forgery.

Third, the first-layer MAC can be shorter than the usual 128 bits, because the AWTRAL cannot be assaulted by a conventional birthday attack. If a birthday attack takes place and a sub-image is replaced by another fake sub-image, the second-layer DS will detect this alteration. However, the AWTRAL can be assaulted by an "improved birthday attack" similar to that described in [3]. It consists in replacing simultaneously two sub-images by two fake sub-images such that the two sub-images' MACs and the DS of the whole image remain valid. Hence, the first-layer MAC must be longer than 64 bits: we recommend using a 96-bit or longer MAC.

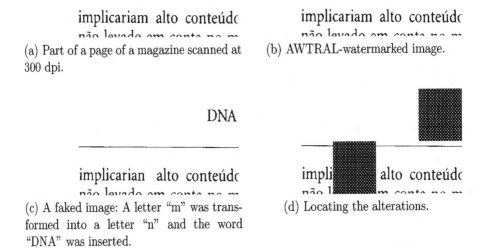

(a) Part of a page of a magazine scanned at 300 dpi.

(b) AWTRAL-watermarked image.

(c) A faked image: A letter "m" was transformed into a letter "n" and the word "DNA" was inserted.

(d) Locating the alterations.

Fig. 4. The use of the alteration-locating watermark AWTRAL

Figure 4 illustrates the AWTRAL. Figure 4(a) is part of a page of a magazine which was scanned at 300 dpi yielding 3200×2432 pixels per page. This image was marked by the AWTRAL, resulting in Fig. 4(b). The host image was subdivided into 475 sub-images each with 128×128 pixels. Each sub-image was marked with a 96-bits-long MAC, using blocks of 64 pixels. A 1024-bits-long DS, also using blocks of 64 pixels, was used to protect the whole image. Almost completely white (black) sub-images, with 6 or less black (white) pixels, were not marked. Figure 4(c) is a fake image, where a letter "m" was switched by the letter "n" and the word "DNA" was inserted. Figure 4(d) shows the result of the AWTRAL verification algorithm, where the modified sub-images are clearly marked.

6   Conclusions

This paper has proposed a new cryptographically secure authentication watermarking technique for binary images (AWTR). The proposed technique is suitable to watermark most binary images with excellent visual quality. We also described a variant of the AWTR that can locate the alterations, besides detecting them. The AWTR can be used in trusted FAX machines, i.e., to electronically sign binary documents. Further research is necessary to adapt the method to scanned documents.

Acknowledgements

The authors would like to express their gratitude to Dr. Paulo S. L. M. Barreto for warning us about the possibility of an improved birthday attack against the AWTRAL. One of the authors, H. Y. Kim, would like to thank FAPESP and CNPq for the partial financial supports of this work under grants 2003/13752-9 and 305065/2003-3, respectively.

References

1. Z. Baharav and D. Shaked, "Watermarking of Dither Halftone Images," Hewlett-Packard Labs. Tech. Rep. HPL-98-32, 1998.
2. P. S. L. M. Barreto and H. Y. Kim, "Pitfalls in Public Key Watermarking," Sibgrapi – Brazilian Symp. Computer Graphics and Image Processing, pp. 241-242, 1999.
3. P. S. L. M. Barreto, H. Y. Kim and V. Rijmen, "Toward a Secure Public-Key Blockwise Fragile Authentication Watermarking," IEE Proc. Vision, Image and Signal Processing, vol. 149, no. 2, pp. 57-62, 2002.
4. D. Boneh, B. Lynn and H. Shacham, "Short signatures from the Weil pairing," Advances in Cryptology - Asiacrypt'2001, Lecture Notes in Computer Science 2248, pp. 514-532, 2002.
5. M. U. Celik, G. Sharma, E. Saber and A. M. Tekalp, "Hierarchical Watermarking for Secure Image Authentication with Localization," IEEE Trans. Image Processing, vol. 11, no. 6, pp. 585-595, 2002.
6. Y.-Y. Chen, H.-K. Pan and Y.-C. Tseng, "A Secure Data Hiding Scheme for Binary Images," IEEE Symposium on Computers and Communications, pp. 750-755, 2000.
7. I. G. Chun and S. Ha, "A Robust Printed Image Watermarking Based on Iterative Halftoning Method," 2nd Int. Workshop on Digital Watermarking, Lecture Notes on Computer Science 2939, pp. 200-211, 2003.
8. R. de Queiroz and P. Fleckenstein, "Object Modification for Data Embedding through Template Ranking," Xerox Invention Proposal, 1999.
9. M. P. Deseilligny and H. Le Men, "An Algorithm for Digital Watermarking of Binary Images, Application to Map and Text Images," available at www-ima.enst.fr/~maitre/tatouage/MPdS_HK.ps, 1998.

10. M. S. Fu and O. C. Au, "Data Hiding by Smart Pair Toggling for Halftone Images," IEEE Int. Conf. Acoustics, Speech and Signal Processing, vol. 4, pp. 2318-2321, 2000.

11. M. S. Fu and O. C. Au, "Data Hiding Watermarking for Halftone Images," IEEE Trans. Image Processing, vol. 11, no. 4, pp. 477-484, 2002.

12. H. Z. Hel-Or, "Watermarking and Copyright Labeling of Printed Images," Journal of Electronic Imaging, vol. 10, no. 3, pp. 794-803, 2001.

13. M. Holliman and N. Memon, "Counterfeiting Attacks on Oblivious Block-wise Independent Invisible Watermarking Schemes," IEEE Trans. Image Processing, vol. 9. no. 3, pp. 432-441, 2000.

14. H. Y. Kim and A. Afif, "Secure Authentication Watermarking for Binary Images," in Proc. Sibgrapi – Brazilian Symp. on Comp. Graph. and Image Proc., pp. 199-206, 2003.

15. H. Y. Kim and A. Afif, "Secure Authentication Watermarking for Halftone and Binary Images," to appear in Int. J. Imaging Systems and Technology.

16. K. T. Knox and S. Wang, "Digital Watermarks Using Stochastic Screens, Color Imaging: Device-Independent Color, Color Hard Copy, and Graphic Arts II," SPIE Proc., vol. 3018, pp.316-322, Feb. 1997.

17. C. T. Li, D. C. Lou and T. H. Chen, "Image Authentication and Integrity Verification via Content-Based Watermarks and a Public Key Cryptosystem," IEEE Int. Conf. Image Processing, 2000, vol. 3, pp. 694-697.

18. N. F. Maxemchuk and S. Low, "Marking Text Documents," Int. Conf. Image Processing, vol. 3, pp. 13-17, 1997.

19. S. C. Pei and J. M. Guo, "Hybrid Pixel-Based Data Hiding and Block-Based Watermarking for Error-Diffused Halftone Images," IEEE Trans. on Circuits and Systems for Video Technology, vol. 13, no. 8, pp. 867-884, 2003.

20. B. Schneier, Applied Cryptography, John Wiley & Sons, 1996.

21. Y.-C. Tseng, Y.-Y. Chen and H.-K. Pan, "A Secure Data Hiding Scheme for Binary Images," IEEE Trans. on Communications, Vol. 50, No. 8, Aug. 2002, pp. 1227-1231.

22. P. W. Wong, "A Watermark for Image Integrity and Ownership Verification," IS&T PIC Conference, (Portland, OR), May 1998 (also available as Hewlett-Packard Labs. Tech. Rep. HPL-97-72, May 1997).

23. P. W. Wong, "A Public Key Watermark for Image Verification and Authentication," IEEE Int. Conf. Image Processing, 1998, vol. 1, pp. 455-459, (MA11.07).

24. P. W. Wong and N. Memon, "Secret and Public Key Image Watermarking Schemes for Image Authentication and Ownership Verification," IEEE Trans. Image Processing, vol. 10, no. 10, pp. 1593-1601, 2001.

25. M. Wu, E. Tang and B. Liu, "Data Hiding in Digital Binary Image," IEEE Int. Conf. Multimedia and Expo, ICME'00, New York, USA, 2000.

26. M. M. Yeung and F. Mintzer, "An Invisible Watermarking Technique for Image Verification," IEEE Int. Conf. Image Processing, 1997, vol. 1, pp. 680-683.

27. J. Zhao and E. Koch, "Embedding Robust Labels into Images for Copyright Protection," Proc. Int. Cong. Intellectual Property Rights, Knowledge and New Technologies, 1995, pp. 242-251.

On Security Notions of Steganographic Systems

Kisik Chang[†], Robert H. Deng[†], Bao Feng[†], Sangjin Lee[‡], and Hyungjun Kim[‡]

[†]InfoComm Service Division(ICSD),
Institute for Infocomm Research(I²R),
21 Heng Mui Keng Terrace 119613 Singapore
{stusck, deng, baofeng}@i2r.a-star.edu.sg
[‡]Center for Information Security and Technologies(CIST),
Graduate School of Information Security,
Korea University, 136-701, Republic of Korea
{sangjin, hyungjun}@korea.ac.kr

Abstract. We define the notion of pseudoprocessingness to formulate chosen-input-attack, chosen-stego-attack, and key-recovery. We then construct a efficient, provable secure steganographic algorithm against chosen-input-attack and key-recovery. So far as we know, this is the first paper dealing with those security notions.

1 Introduction

Many research papers related to information hiding techniques have been published since Simmons proposed the *prisoners' problem* in [9]. In this problem, Alice and Bob are accomplices in a crime and have been arrested, and then they are put in two different cells. After that time, they try to conspire to escape but their all communications are listened to by a guardian named Warden. Since Warden suspect that Alice and Bob want to collude an escape plan, he will only permit the exchanges through not an encrypted message but a plain text. Under this restriction, on the other hand, Alice and Bob attempt to deceive Warden by finding a way of establishing an invisible communication channel between them in full view of the warden, even though the messages themselves contain no secret information. A couple of solutions has been proposed for the prisoners' problem; subliminal channel, covert channel, etc. There also have been introduced different approaches; steganography and digital watermarking. Especially, steganography is related to how Alice and Bob can construct a secret channel over a public channel without arousing Warden's suspicion. In other words, the goal of steganography is to conceal the existence of secret communication between Alice and Bob without being suspected by Warden. So the security of steganography it is important that Warden can not distinguish between a cover-object and a stego-object, and also the scheme hiding a message has not to leave any special feature on a stego-object. Although many researchers have studied the steganography in theoretic perspective and in practical, relatively little researchers have approached the security of steganography theoretically. First work

I.J. Cox et al. (Eds.): IWDW 2004, LNCS 3304, pp. 137–151, 2005.

was produced by Anderson[1]. He introduced some explanation of information hiding and present a couple of approaches to the theoretical security of steganography. And he also mentioned the computational security using polynomial-time turing machine. After publishing his paper, Cachin[2] and Zöllner *et al.*[11] proposed information theoretic security models separately. Cachin defined the security of steganography using *relative entropy*, while Zöllner *et al.* gave a different definition using *mutual information*. During that time, many theoretical and practical steganographic algorithms had been proposed and published, but almost all of them are identified as insecure[7, 6]. Katzenbeisser and Petitcolas defined the conditional security of steganography and gave a possibility for a provable secure steganography for the first time[8]. Hopper *et al.* introduced a provable secure steganographic algorithm in the sense of complexity theory[5]. However, the security of their algorithm just depends on not the algorithm itself but the security of the encryption algorithm used in their algorithm. In addition, it is different from a practical one because it is not efficient. Thus, we need more practical, efficient algorithms.

In this paper, we will introduce two new security notions, *pseudoprocessingness* and *key recovery*, and two adversary models, *chosen-input-attack* and *chosen-stego-attack*, in the sense of complexity theory. And we will also propose a practical, provable secure steganographic algorithm and prove that our model is secure under chosen-input-attack and key recovery attack.

2   Security Notions of Steganographic Systems

Since the goal of steganography is to conceal the existence of secret communications, we can say that steganography is broken when an adversary is able to detect the existence of steganography. So the secure steganography must be that no adversary can decide whether a given object is a cover-object or a stego-object without knowing the key. To formulate the secure steganography, we propose a steganographic decision problem.

Definition 1 (Steganographic Decision Problem(SDP)). *Given a suspected object $s \in C$, determine whether s has a message $m \in \{0, 1\}^*$ or not.*

Now we adopt complexity theory to define the computational security of steganography. Recall the situation which Warden monitors a public channel between Alice and Bob in the prisoners' problem. If Warden suspects that Alice sends Bob a stego-object, it is true that he can declare that the steganographic algorithm, which produces a stego-object in the embedding process, differs from a common algorithm making a cover-object. So we can transform SDP into the following proposition. Yet, the converse is not always true.

Proposition 1. *If Warden can distinguish a stego-object from a cover-object, then he can also differentiate a steganographic algorithm from a common algorithm, which is used for creating a cover-object*

Proposition 1 says that if Warden has an ability to discriminate between two algorithms, then he is capable of identifying the difference between input-output behaviors of the two algorithms. In this case, what kind of an algorithm could become a common one? It depends on the type of a cover-object. For example, an image could be used as a cover-image. It is obtained through a general image processing operation such as enhancement or contrast. On the other hand, most of practical steganographic algorithms produce a stego-image by substituting a message for the redundant parts of a cover-image or by modifying them. This alteration causes the degradation in quality or the statistical change in unnecessary data[10]. If we consider its modification as one of image processing operations, in this sense, we can say that Warden is capable of separating these two operations into a steganographic function and a general image processing. Therefore, Proposition 1 gives us a tip for the computational security of steganography. Now we define a symmetric-key steganographic system as follows;

Now we will introduce some notions used in proving the security from the complexity theoretic point of view. Following definitions are imported from Goldwasser and Bellare's lecture notes[4], but these notions are enough to be modified reasonably for steganographic security.

First, we define the symmetric-key steganographic system before constructing an algorithm for the prisoners' problem. An easy computation is one which can be carried out by a probabilistic polynomial time algorithm and a function is *negligible* if it vanishes faster than the inverse of any polynomial[4].

Definition 2 (Negligible Function). *A function $\nu : \mathbb{N} \to \mathbb{R}$ is a negligible if for every constant $c \geqslant 0$, there exits an integer k_c such that $\nu(k) < k^{-c}$ for all $k \geqslant k_c$.*

Definition 3 (Symmetric-Key Steganographic System). *A symmetric-key (or secret-key) steganographic system $\mathcal{SKS}$ = (Keys, Emb, Ext) consists of three polynomial-time algorithms. On input 1^k (the security parameter), the key generation algorithm Keys($\cdot$) outputs produces a string k, we write $K \xleftarrow{R}$ Keys(1^k). The embedding algorithm Emb($\cdot, \cdot, \cdot$) takes the key $K \in$ Keys(1^k), a cover-object $c \in \mathcal{C}$, and a message $m \in \mathcal{M}$ to return a stego-object $s \in \mathcal{C} \cup \{\bot\}$, we write $s \leftarrow$ Emb(K, c, m). The extracting algorithm Ext($\cdot, \cdot$) takes the key $K \in$ Keys(1^k) and a stego-object s to return a message $m \in \mathcal{M}(\cup\{\bot\})$, we write $m \leftarrow$ Ext(K, s). We require that for any key $K \in$ Keys(1^k), any cover-object $c \in \mathcal{C}$, and any message $m \in \mathcal{M}$, if Emb(K, c, m) returns a stego-object $s \neq \bot$, that is, $s \leftarrow$ Emb(K, c, m), then $\mathbf{Pr}[s \leftarrow$ Emb(K, c, m)] = 1 and $\mathbf{Pr}[$Ext($K, s) \neq m]$ is negligible.*

Note that the embedding algorithm must be probabilistic. If an embedding algorithm is randomized, in particular using embedding algorithm twice on the same inputs, it may not returns the same stego-objects. So if the same message was sent twice with the same cover-objects, Warden can always discriminate between the former stego-object and the later. This is similar to *collusion attack* in digital fingerprinting. That's why most people think that the embedding algorithm has to be deterministic for both a cover-object and a message. However, what happens if it is deterministic? Suppose that a sender uses a deterministic algorithm twice on a cover-object for two different messages. Then, Warden can always notice the difference between two communication sessions. This also causes most people some worry that the cover-objects, used in previous communication, must not be revealed and even not be reused them. But how we can guarantee that Warden is not capable of acquiring them? It is appropriate that he can acquire the original cover-objects used in previous steganographic communication and will be able to know them to be applied in the future. This fact should be considered as the extended version of Kerchoff's principle for a cover-object.

In addition, for a message and a couple of different cover-objects, an embedding algorithm should not make stego-objects related to each others. In other words, those stego-objects must not leak any partial information for the embedded message. For example, assume that an embedding algorithm substitute message bits sequentially for the LSB(Least Significant Bit) of pixels in a digital image. If the scheme embeds a message into several cover-images, then it returns several stego-images with LSBs, related between them, so they must not leak any information.

Definition 4 (Processing Function). *A processing function is a map* Proc : $\mathcal{C} \times \mathcal{M} \rightarrow \mathcal{S}$, *where* $\mathcal{C} = \{0, 1\}^{\ell}$, $\mathcal{M} = \{0, 1\}^{l}$, *and* $\mathcal{S} = \{0, 1\}^{L}$ *are finite sets, and* $\ell, l, L \geqslant 1$ *be integers. And the inverse of an processing function is defined as* $\mathsf{Proc}^{-1} : \mathcal{S} \rightarrow \mathcal{M}$.

The processing function $\mathsf{Proc}^{\mathcal{C} \times \mathcal{M} \rightarrow \mathcal{S}}$ takes two inputs, an element $c \in \mathcal{C}$ and a message $m \in \mathcal{M}$, and returns an output $s \in \mathcal{S}$ denoted by $s \leftarrow \mathsf{Proc}(c, m)$. We call a member of $\mathsf{Proc}^{\mathcal{C} \times \mathcal{M} \rightarrow \mathcal{S}}$ an *instance* of a processing function. Especially, we call the processing function an *image processing function* when $\mathcal{C}$ is a set of digital images. Then the set of instances of $\mathsf{Proc}^{\mathcal{C} \times \mathcal{M} \rightarrow \mathcal{S}}$ could be considered as the set of all digital image processing operations. Theoretically, the enlargement operation in image processing can't be a function because a pixel is mapped onto multiple pixels. Yet, although we will include this operation and consider it as one of the scaling operation, the key space of $\mathsf{Proc}^{\mathcal{C} \times \mathcal{M} \rightarrow \mathcal{S}}$ is invariable. So it is no matter that we include the enlargement operation among image processing functions.

Note that a message m does not play a key role in the operation of Proc. It's just a auxiliary input value, so it can be used with the internal coin of Proc to determine the parameter of the processing, or it might not be used. The inverse of a processing function Proc^{-1} takes an element of $s \in \mathcal{S}$ and returns a bit string m' denoted by $m' \leftarrow \mathsf{Proc}^{-1}(s)$. Strictly speaking, Proc^{-1} is not an inverse of a processing function. Since we are now comparing an processing function with an extracting algorithm, it is appropriate that we consider an inverse of the processing function as a function which withdraw a bit string from an input data as if it were an extracting algorithm. For example, a hash function could be an inverse of the image processing function; it takes an image and outputs a hash value of input. We have an interest in the input-output relation of the function which is randomly selected in the embedding function.

Now, it will be difficult for a person who uses a function like a black box to decide whether a given function is selected in an embedding function or in a processing function. So if he can't distinguish two function families, neither can't he do between a cover-image and a stego-image. We define *pseudorprocessingness* as the degree of the similarity between an embedding function and processing. To measure the pseudoprocessingness, we will formulate the pseudoprocessing function.

Definition 5 (Pseudoprocessing Function). *The input-output behavior of a random instance of the embedding function is computationally indistinguishable from that of a processing function.*

Let's fix an embedding function $\mathsf{Emb} : K \times \mathcal{C} \times \mathcal{M} \to \mathcal{S}$ and suppose that a function $p : \mathcal{C} \times \mathcal{M} \to \mathcal{S}$ is given to Warden so that whenever he provides a cover-object c and a message m, he receives an output $p(c, m)$. He can only input the restricted questions chosen on the cover-object set $\mathcal{C}$ and the message set $\mathcal{M}$ of a function, and he will receive the output from the range $\mathcal{S}$. In this environment, what Warden can only see is the input-output behavior of the function p. Now assume that p will be chosen in two different sets as follows:

Set 0: The function p is chosen randomly from $\mathsf{Proc}^{\mathcal{C} \times \mathcal{M} \to \mathcal{S}}$, denoted by $p \xleftarrow{R} \mathsf{Proc}^{\ell \times l \to L}$. This means that p is a random processing function from $\mathcal{C} \times \mathcal{M}$ to $\mathcal{S}$.

Set 1: The function p is chosen randomly from an embedding function Emb, denoted by $p \xleftarrow{R} \mathsf{Emb}$. This means that a key is selected via $K \xleftarrow{R} \mathsf{Keys}$ and then p is set to Emb_K.

The set and the corresponding function p is predetermined, and Warden can't know which set is selected. The set won't be changed until a session is finished. What Warden has to do is to decide which set is selected. To do so, what he can do is only to give several input pairs $(c_1, m_1), \ldots, (c_q, m_q)$ and to get back an output $p(c_1, m_1), \ldots, p(c_q, m_q)$. The experiment and study will help him to determine which computer replied for queries. Now the pseudoprocessingness of an embedding function can be considered as the measure difficult of decision in SDP. The experiment simulates plainly a method which uses an embedding function p in practical. So if it is impossible to distinguish the input-output behavior of a random instance from an embedding function and one's a processing function. The action of Warden could be considered as the notion of a *distinguisher* that an algorithm queries an oracle for a function p and tries to determine whether a function p is a processing function(set 0) or an embedding function(set 1). A distinguisher can only interact with the function by giving inputs, and getting back and examining outputs, but it can't inspect the function itself so that he can't know the key used in the function. We denote $\mathcal{W}^p$ the distinguisher $\mathcal{W}$ that has an oracle for the function p. Intuitively, an embedding function could be considered as *pseudoprocessing* if the probability that Warden says 1 is roughly the same regardless of which room's computer is connected. We define this mathematically as following definition.

Definition 6 (Pseudoprocessing Function Experiment). *Let* Emb : Keys× $C \times M \to S$ *be an embedding functions, and let* W *be an algorithm that takes an oracle for a function* $p : C \times M \to S$, *and returns a bit* d. *We consider following two experiments:*

Experiment $\mathbf{Exp}_{\mathsf{Emb},W}^{PPF\text{-}1}$	Experiment $\mathbf{Exp}_{\mathsf{Emb},W}^{PPF\text{-}0}$
$K \xleftarrow{r} \mathsf{Keys}$	$p \longleftarrow \mathsf{Proc}^{C \times M \to S}$
$d \longleftarrow W^{\mathsf{Emb}(K,\cdot,\cdot)}$	$d \longleftarrow W^p$
Return d	Return d

The advantage for a pseudoprocessing function of a distinguisher W, *PPF-advantage, is defined as*

$$\mathbf{Adv}_{\mathsf{Emb},W}^{PPF} = \left| \; \mathbf{Pr}\left[\; \mathbf{Exp}_{\mathsf{Emb},W}^{PPF\text{-}1} = 1 \; \right] - \mathbf{Pr}\left[\; \mathbf{Exp}_{\mathsf{Emb},W}^{PPF\text{-}0} = 1 \; \right] \right|$$

For any t, q, μ, *we define the PPF-insecurity of an embedding function* Emb

$$\mathbf{InSec}_{\mathsf{Emb}}^{PPF}(t, q, \mu) = \max_{W} \left\{ \mathbf{Adv}_{\mathsf{Emb},W}^{PPF} \right\}$$

where the maximum is over all distinguishers W *having time-complexity* t *and making at most* q *oracle queries, the sum of the lengths of these queries being at most* μ *bits. An embedding function* Emb *is* (t, q, μ, ε)-*pseudoprocessing function or* (t, q, μ, ε)-*pseudoprocessing when* $\mathbf{InSec}_{\mathsf{Emb}}^{PPF}(t, q, \mu) \leqslant \frac{1}{2} + \varepsilon$, *where* ε *is negligible.*

In Definition 6, the information of the key K is not used in defining the insecure function $\mathbf{InSec}_{\mathsf{Emb}}^{PPF}(t, q, \mu)$. Although the insecure function is a function of the key K, it is difficult to find what kind of function without knowing about Emb itself. Actually, neither the key information nor the key length doesn't play an important role in the passive adversary model. What matters is just the advantage a distinguisher can gain. In SDP, Warden is enough to suspect Alice for a steganographic communication with confidence larger than 1/2-probability. Moreover, Definition 6 does not give any kinds of strategies of which a distinguisher is capable. It only put a limit on its resources, so Warden can use any method, instrument, or process to distinguish the function as long as it stays within the specified resource bounds.

What does 'secure PPF' mean? Definition 6 does not show any clear context about a secure function. It address only about a PPF-insecurity of a function. Intuitively, we just can say informally that Emb is secure when the insecurity is low for the practical input parameters. In a well-designed steganographic system, the value of the advantage must be $\frac{1}{2}$. But this is really an ideal. Practically, it should be close to $\frac{1}{2}$ value. As you know, security is not some absolute or boolean attribute, but a function of the resources available to Warden. Like cryptographic systems, we have to assume that all steganographic systems are breakable in principle. To solve the SDP, we can use some resources; a cover-object, a message and a stego-object. Depending on the available resources, there are several kinds of adversary models for the steganographic systems[7], and Hoper *et al.* also introduced independently several adversary models close to cryptographic adversary model[5]. They considered a cover-object not as an external, annexational input but as an output data chosen internally in encoding process. So their models are quite a bit different from the others. In this paper, we will treat only two kinds of adversary models;

Chosen-Input-Attack(CIA). Adversary can choose a message and a cover-object and use the embedding algorithm.

Chosen-Stego-Attack(CSA). Adversary can choose not only a messages and a cover-object, but a stego-object. In addition, he can use both the embedding and extracting algorithm.

This classification is based on the algorithms which an adversary can use as an oracle. Although this is different from the others' model, it includes all of notions previously introduced. As you see, our category is very simple and more reasonable than previous one. Therefore, it is enough to consider these two attacks for the security. In above classification, the adaptive adversary models can be applied as the cryptographic models, however we will imagine that the chosen models include the adaptive adversary models in this paper.

Now, we will define the security for each adversary models corresponding to the accessible oracle in Pseudo-Processing Function Experiment. In CIA model, the adversary is accessible to an embedding oracle, so he can inquire of an embedding oracle with different cover-objects for distinct messages. So, in the sense of PPF-CIA, the security is defined as follows;

Definition 7 (PPF-CIA Security). *Let* $\mathsf{Emb} : \mathsf{Keys} \times \mathcal{C} \times \mathcal{M} \to \mathcal{S}$ *be an embedding functions, and let* $\mathcal{W}$ *be an algorithm that takes an oracle for a function* $p : \mathcal{C} \times \mathcal{M} \to \mathcal{S}$*, and returns a bit* d*. We consider following two experiments:*

$$
\begin{array}{c|c}
\text{Experiment } \mathbf{Exp}_{\mathsf{Emb},\mathcal{W}}^{\text{PPF-CIA-1}} & \text{Experiment } \mathbf{Exp}_{\mathsf{Emb},\mathcal{W}}^{\text{PPF-CIA-0}} \\
K \xleftarrow{r} \mathsf{Keys} & p \longleftarrow \mathsf{Proc}^{\mathcal{C} \times \mathcal{M} \to \mathcal{S}} \\
d \longleftarrow \mathcal{W}^{\mathsf{Emb}(K,\cdot,\cdot)} & d \longleftarrow \mathcal{W}^p \\
\text{Return } d & \text{Return } d
\end{array}
$$

The advantage for a pseudoprocessing function of a distinguisher $\mathcal{W}$*, PPF-CIA-advantage, is defined as*

$$
\mathbf{Adv}_{\mathsf{Emb},\mathcal{W}}^{\text{PPF-CIA}} = \left| \mathbf{Pr}\left[\mathbf{Exp}_{\mathsf{Emb},\mathcal{W}}^{\text{PPF-CIA-1}} = 1 \right] - \mathbf{Pr}\left[\mathbf{Exp}_{\mathsf{Emb},\mathcal{W}}^{\text{PPF-CIA-0}} = 1 \right] \right|
$$

For any t, q, μ*, we define the PPF-insecurity of an embedding function* Emb

$$
\mathbf{InSec}_{\mathsf{Emb}}^{\text{PPF-CIA}}(t, q, \mu) = \max_{\mathcal{W}} \left\{ \mathbf{Adv}_{\mathsf{Emb},\mathcal{W}}^{\text{PPF-CIA}} \right\}
$$

where the maximum is over all distinguishers $\mathcal{W}$ *having time-complexity* t *and making at most* q *oracle queries, the sum of the lengths of these queries being* *at most μ bits. An embedding function* Emb *is* (t, q, μ, ε)-*pseudoprocessing function under Chosen-Input-Attack(CIA) or* (t, q, μ, ε)-*pseudoprocessing under CIA when* $\mathbf{InSec}_{\mathsf{Emb}}^{\mathrm{PPF\text{-}CIA}}(t, q, \mu) \leqslant \frac{1}{2} + \varepsilon$, *where ε is negligible.*

In CIA setting, an adversary can use two resources, a message and a cover-object for a query. He is capable of fixing a cover-object and then varying a message, or the other way. In this case, μ should be the total sum of the length of a fixed input and the sum of the length of varied one. We can immediately draw an important consequence. Steganographic systems which simply substitute message bits sequentially for the LSB(Least Significant Bit) of pixels in a digital image are not secure.

Proposition 2. *Let $F :$ Keys $\times \{0, 1\}^{\ell} \times \{0, 1\}^{l} \to \{0, 1\}^{L}$ be an LSB substitution steganographic algorithm, where l is the maximum capacity of a cover-object $c \in \{0, 1\}^{\ell}$. Then, for any $t, q, q(\ell + \frac{1}{2} \cdot l)$, and non-negligible ε,*

$$\mathbf{InSec}_{F}^{\mathrm{PPF\text{-}CIA}} \left[t, \ q, \ q \cdot \left(\ell + \frac{1}{2} \cdot l \right) \right] \geqslant \frac{1}{2} + \varepsilon.$$

Proof. In CIA setting, Warden $\mathcal{W}$ takes an oracle for an embedding function, so he give some queries and get them back. Since his methods is not constrain, he can use a patterns analysis[6], a visual analysis[10], or a statistical analysis[10]. These analyses require at least a half size of the maximum message length to determine whether a given image is a stego-image or not with a fairly high probability. So for non-negligible ε, we get the following equation;

$$\mathbf{Adv}_{\mathsf{Emb}, \mathcal{W}}^{\mathrm{PPF\text{-}CIA}} = \left| \mathbf{Pr} \left[\mathbf{Exp}_{\mathsf{Emb}, \mathcal{W}}^{\mathrm{PPF\text{-}CIA\text{-}1}} = 1 \right] - \mathbf{Pr} \left[\mathbf{Exp}_{\mathsf{Emb}, \mathcal{W}}^{\mathrm{PPF\text{-}CIA\text{-}0}} = 1 \right] \right|$$
$$\geqslant \frac{1}{2} + \varepsilon.$$

If he has an ability to distinguish between an embedding algorithm and a processing algorithm, he is capable of finding out the difference between outputs of distinct messages for a fixed cover-object, or even of different cover-objects for a fixed message. Similarly, in CSA setting, Warden can access both an embedding oracle and an extracting. So in the sense of PPF-CSA, the security is defined as follows;

Definition 8 (PPF-CSA Experiment). *Let* Emb $:$ Keys $\times \mathcal{C} \times \mathcal{M} \to \mathcal{S}$ *be an embedding functions, and let $\mathcal{W}$ be an algorithm that takes an oracle for a function $p : \mathcal{C} \times \mathcal{M} \to \mathcal{S}$, and returns a bit d. We consider following two experiments:*

Experiment $\mathbf{Exp}_{\mathsf{Emb}, \mathcal{W}}^{\mathrm{PPF\text{-}CSA\text{-}1}}$	Experiment $\mathbf{Exp}_{\mathsf{Emb}, \mathcal{W}}^{\mathrm{PPF\text{-}CSA\text{-}0}}$
$K \xleftarrow{r}$ Keys	$p \longleftarrow \mathsf{Proc}^{\mathcal{C} \times \mathcal{M} \to \mathcal{S}}$
$d \longleftarrow \mathcal{W}^{\mathsf{Emb}(K, \cdot, \cdot), \mathsf{Ext}(K, \cdot)}$	$d \longleftarrow \mathcal{W}^{p, p^{-1}}$
Return d	Return d

The advantage for a pseudoprocessing function of a distinguisher $\mathcal{W}$, PPF-CSA-advantage, is defined as

$$\mathbf{Adv}_{\mathsf{Emb},\mathcal{W}}^{\text{PPF-CSA}} = \left| \mathbf{Pr}\left[\mathbf{Exp}_{\mathsf{Emb},\mathcal{W}}^{\text{PPF-CSA-1}} = 1 \right] - \mathbf{Pr}\left[\mathbf{Exp}_{\mathsf{Emb},\mathcal{W}}^{\text{PPF-CSA-0}} = 1 \right] \right|$$

For any $t, q_c, \mu_c, q_s, \mu_s$, we define the PPF-insecurity of an embedding function Emb

$$\mathbf{InSec}_{\mathsf{Emb}}^{\text{PPF-CSA}}(t, q_c, \mu_c, q_s, \mu_s) = \max_{\mathcal{W}}\left\{ \mathbf{Adv}_{\mathsf{Emb},\mathcal{W}}^{\text{PPF-CSA}} \right\}$$

where the maximum is over all distinguishers $\mathcal{W}$ having time-complexity t and making at most q_c oracle queries to the p oracle, the sum of the lengths of these queries being at most μ_c bits, and also making at most q_s queries to the p^{-1} oracle, the sum of the lengths of these queries being at most μ_s bits. An embedding function Emb is $(t, q_c, \mu_c, q_s, \mu_s, \varepsilon)$-pseudoprocessing function under Chosen-Stego-Attack(CSA) or $(t, q_c, \mu_c, q_s, \mu_s, \varepsilon)$-pseudoprocessing under CSA, when $\mathbf{InSec}_{\mathsf{Emb}}^{\text{CSA-PPF}}(t, q_c, \mu_c, q_s, \mu_s) \leqslant \frac{1}{2} + \varepsilon$, where ε is negligible.

Definition 8. does not say any comment about the inverse processing of p. It depends on the behavior of an extracting function to be analyzed. For instance, if an extracting algorithm returns a LSB-string of pixels, the inverse of the processing function should be dealt with the function which simulates an extracting function. In PPF-CSA setting, an adversary is capable of accomplishing effectively a chosen-input-attack. Thus there is a relation between PPF-CIA and PPF-CSA as follows;

Proposition 3. Let Emb : Keys $\times \mathcal{C} \times \mathcal{M} \to \mathcal{S}$ be an embedding function. Then, for any t, q, μ,

$$\mathbf{InSec}_{\mathsf{Emb}}^{\text{PPF-CIA}}(t, q, \mu) = \mathbf{InSec}_{\mathsf{Emb}}^{\text{PPF-CSA}}(t, q, \mu, 0, 0).$$

There is no work that attempts to deal with the notions of key-recovery attack. Even though security against key-recovery is not sufficient as a notion of security for steganography, it is certainly among necessary conditions. That is, if key-recovery is easy, we can say that the algorithm is insecure. So we want to show that any embedding function which is insecure under key-recovery is also insecure as a PPF. In this attack model, we consider that Warden tries to find the key K based on input-output behavior of an instance Emb_K of a function Emb. The insecurity of an embedding algorithm is defined as the probability that Warden succeeds in finding K. The probability is over the random choice of K and any random choices of Warden himself. We suppose that Warden can access the oracle Emb_K to study the input-output examples of his selection. Moreover, this definition contains all types of key-recovery attacks such as exhaustive key search. As the previous adversary models, we do not constrain Warden's method used to find K. We give the following definition.

Definition 9 (Key-Recovery Experiment). Let Emb : Keys $\times \mathcal{C} \times \mathcal{M} \to \mathcal{S}$ be an embedding functions, and let $\mathcal{W}_{\text{KR}}$ be an algorithm that takes an oracle for a function $p : D \to R$, and returns a string $K^\star$. We consider following two experiments:

$$\text{Experiment } \mathbf{Exp}^{\text{KR}}_{\text{Emb}, \mathcal{W}_{\text{KR}}}$$
$$K \xleftarrow{r} \text{Keys}$$
$$K^\star \longleftarrow \mathcal{W}^{\text{Emb}(K,\cdot,\cdot)}_{\text{KR}}$$
$$\text{If } K = K^\star \text{ then return 1 else return 0}$$

The KR-advantage of $\mathcal{W}_{\text{KR}}$ is defined as

$$\mathbf{Adv}^{\text{KR}}_{\text{Emb}, \mathcal{W}_{\text{KR}}} = \mathbf{Pr}\left[\, \mathbf{Exp}^{\text{KR}}_{\text{Emb}, \mathcal{W}_{\text{KR}}} = 1 \,\right].$$

For any t, q, μ, we define the KR-insecurity of an embedding function Emb

$$\mathbf{InSec}^{\text{KR}}_{\text{Emb}}(t, q, \mu) = \max_{\mathcal{W}_{\text{KR}}} \left\{ \mathbf{Adv}^{\text{KR}}_{\text{Emb}, \mathcal{W}_{\text{KR}}} \right\}$$

where the maximum is over all $\mathcal{W}_{\text{KR}}$ having time-complexity t and making at most q oracle queries, the sum of the lengths of these queries being at most μ bits.

3   Proposed Algorithm

In this section, we propose a provable secure steganographic algorithm in the sense of PPF. As we described earlier, most of previously suggested algorithms are detectable because they don't modify a cover-object by a natural processing method. Thus the embedding algorithm must hide a message using a cover-object-based processing. First, we define the processing algorithm, which is a subroutine of the embedding algorithm, as follows:

Algorithm PROCESSING(K, c, m)
Input: key K, cover-object c, message m
    Repeat
        $s \leftarrow \text{Proc}(c)$
    Until $\text{Hash}(K, s) = m$
Output: stego-object s

In this algorithm, the function $\text{Proc}(\cdot)$ plays the leading role in the processing algorithm. It could be any natural processing method, such as a contrast stretching, an enhancement, an interpolation or a point processing when a cover-object is an image. When input vectors are given, $\text{Proc}(\cdot)$ flips coins internally and uses the results from flipping to vary the parameters used in processing the cover-object. It repeats the processing until $\text{Hash}(K, s) = m$. Then it returns s satisfying $\text{Hash}(K, s) = m$. Note that the iteration count is bounded to $2^{|m|}$. That is, we always get s with probability 1. Now we construct the embedding algorithm and the extracting as follows;

Algorithm EMBEDDING Emb(K, c, m)
Input: key K, cover-object c, message m
  Parse c as $c_1||c_2||\cdots||c_\ell$
  Parse m as $m_1||m_2||\cdots||m_\ell$
  for $i = 0$ to ℓ
    $s_i \longleftarrow$ PROCESSING(K, c_i, m_i)
    $s \longleftarrow s||s_i$
Output: $s = s_1||s_2||\cdots||s_k$

Algorithm EXTRACTING $Ext(K, s)$
Input: key K, stego-object s
  Parse s as $s_1||s_2||\cdots||s_\ell$
  for $i = 0$ to ℓ
    $m_i \longleftarrow$ Hash(K, s_i)
Output: $m = m_1||m_2||\cdots||m_\ell$

The idea of the above algorithms is very simple. The embedding algorithm divide the cover-object and the message into ℓ parts each. Then, it applies the processing to the sub-cover-objects c_i repeatedly until it finds a processed object s_i, so called a sub-stego-object, such that Hash$(K, s_i) = m_i$. Note that the length of each c_i should not be the same. When the length is not fixed, the sender and the receiver need to synchronize each length of each sub-object so that the recipient can extract the message. At this time, the key should be used for synchronization. And there is also another consideration in using our algorithm. It is the length of sub-messages; that is, the longer the length of a message becomes, the larger the number of the iteration time does. In addition, this may make some sub-objects not be matched well to the neighbor sub-objects so that the result could not be an acceptable output. So the sender should choose a proper length for the processing function Proc$(\cdot)$.

While Hoper *et al.*'s S1. algorithm looks similar to the proposed one, that has some weaknesses as compared with this; see Table 1. Since their algorithm is based on the encryption algorithm, it is strong as the security of the used encryption algorithm. There exist a probability that their embedding algorithm doesn't success in finding a cover-object even though the probability is low. In addition, its efficiency is very low because it only just embeds 1 bit into a cover-object. So we should prepare a large number of cover-object before embedding a message. And moreover, in (passive) adversary, Hoper *et al.* dealt with only chosen-message-attack, whereas in practical, attacker can choose a message and a cover-object separately. So we have to consider the adversary model more broadly, variously. Now we claim that if the proposed algorithm is a secure PPF, then it is also secure against CIA.

Table 1. Comparison between Hoper *et al.*'s S1. algorithm and the proposed algorithm

	Hoper *et al.*	Propose Algorithm
Security basis	encryption function (pseudorandomnessn)	processing function (pseudoprocessingness)
Failure rate in embedding	low, but positive value	never fail
Embedding rate per a cover-object	1 bit	variable length
(passive) Adversary Models	chosen-message-attack	chosen-input-attack chosen-output-attack key-recovery-attack

Theorem 1. *Let* $\mathsf{Emb} : \mathsf{Keys} \times \mathcal{C} \times \mathcal{M} \to \mathcal{S}$ *be the proposed embedding function, where* $\mathsf{Keys} = \{0,1\}^k$, $\mathcal{C} = \{0,1\}^\ell$, $\mathcal{M} = \{0,1\}^l$, *and* $\mathcal{S} = \{0,1\}^L$. *Then for any* t, q *with* $q < 2^{\ell+l}$ *we have*

$$\mathbf{InSec}_{\mathsf{Emb}}^{\mathrm{PPF\text{-}CIA}}(t, q, q(\ell + l)) \;\leqslant\; \mathbf{InSec}_{\mathsf{Emb}}^{\mathrm{PPF}}(t', q, q(\ell + l)).$$

Proof. We will show that given any adversary $\mathcal{W}$ whose resources are restricted to $t, q, \ell + l$, we can construct an adversary $\mathcal{A}_{\mathcal{W}}$, using $t, q, q(\ell + l)$, such that

$$\mathbf{Adv}_{\mathsf{Emb}}^{\mathrm{PPF\text{-}CIA}}(t, q, q(\ell + l)) \;=\; \mathbf{Adv}_{\mathsf{Emb}}^{\mathrm{PPF}}(t', q, q(\ell + l)).$$

$$
\begin{array}{c}
\text{Adversary } \mathcal{A}_{\mathcal{W}} \\[4pt]
c \longleftarrow \mathcal{C} \\
m \longleftarrow \{0,1\}^l \\
d \longleftarrow \mathcal{W}^{\mathsf{Emb}_K(c,m)} \\[4pt]
\text{Return } d
\end{array}
$$

The adversary $\mathcal{A}_{\mathcal{W}}$ chooses a key K, a cover-object c, and a message m randomly. When necessary, he selects more cover-objects and messages. Then he simply runs $\mathcal{W}$ with the selected inputs and returns a bit d after seeing the output of $\mathcal{W}$. Since the results of queries are just outputs of a processing function Proc, the advantage of $\mathcal{W}$ is determined by the pseudoprocessingness. Moreover, the advantage of $\mathcal{A}_{\mathcal{W}}$ depends on the advantage of $\mathcal{W}$. Thus, the advantage is computed as follows;

$$
\begin{aligned}
\mathbf{Adv}_{\mathsf{Emb},\mathcal{A}_{\mathcal{W}}}^{\mathrm{PPF}} &= \left| \mathbf{Pr}\left[\mathbf{Exp}_{\mathsf{Emb},\mathcal{A}_{\mathcal{W}}}^{\mathrm{PPF\text{-}1}} = 1 \right] - \mathbf{Pr}\left[\mathbf{Exp}_{\mathsf{Emb},\mathcal{A}_{\mathcal{W}}}^{\mathrm{PPF\text{-}0}} = 1 \right] \right| \\
&\geqslant \left| \mathbf{Pr}\left[\mathbf{Exp}_{\mathsf{Emb},\mathcal{W}}^{\mathrm{PPF\text{-}CIA\text{-}1}} = 1 \right] - \mathbf{Pr}\left[\mathbf{Exp}_{\mathsf{Emb},\mathcal{W}}^{\mathrm{PPF\text{-}CIA\text{-}0}} = 1 \right] \right| \\
&= \mathbf{Adv}_{\mathsf{Emb},\mathcal{W}}^{\mathrm{PPF\text{-}CIA}}.
\end{aligned}
$$

And if the proposed algorithm is a secure PPF, then it is also secure against all key-recovery attacks.

Theorem 2. *Let* $\mathsf{Emb} : \mathsf{Keys} \times \mathcal{C} \times \mathcal{M} \to \mathcal{S}$ *be the proposed embedding function, where* $\mathsf{Keys} = \{0,1\}^k$, $\mathcal{C} = \{0,1\}^\ell$, $\mathcal{M} = \{0,1\}^l$, *and* $\mathcal{S} = \{0,1\}^L$. *Then for any* t, q *with* $q < 2^{\ell+l}$ *we have*

$$\mathbf{InSec}_{\mathsf{Emb}}^{\mathrm{KR}}(t, q, q(\ell + l)) \;\leqslant\; \mathbf{InSec}_{\mathsf{Emb}}^{\mathrm{PPF}}(t', q+1, (q+1)(\ell + l)) + \frac{1}{2^L}.$$

Proof. We will show that given any adversary $\mathcal{W}_{\mathrm{KR}}$ whose resources are restricted to $t, q, q(\ell + l)$, we can construct an adversary $\mathcal{W}$, using $t, q, (q+1)(\ell + l)$, such that

$$\mathbf{Adv}_{\mathsf{Emb},\mathcal{W}}^{\mathrm{PPF}} \;\geqslant\; \mathbf{Adv}_{\mathsf{Emb},\mathcal{W}_{\mathrm{KR}}}^{\mathrm{KR}} - \frac{1}{2^L}.$$

As per Definition 9., adversary $\mathcal{W}$ will be provided an oracle for a processing function $p : \{0,1\}^\ell \longrightarrow \{0,1\}^L$, and will to determine in which room it is. To do so, he will run adversary $\mathcal{W}_{\mathrm{KR}}$ as a subroutine. Adversary $\mathcal{W}$ is constructed as follows;

Adversary $\mathcal{W}$

    $i \longleftarrow 0$

    Run adversary $\mathcal{W}_{\mathrm{KR}}$, replying to its oracle queries as follows

    When $\mathcal{W}_{\mathrm{KR}}$ makes an oracle query x do

        $i \longleftarrow i+1;\ c_i \longleftarrow c;\ m_i \longleftarrow m$

        $s_i \longleftarrow p(c_i)$

        Return s_i to $\mathcal{W}_{\mathrm{KR}}$ as the answer

    Until $\mathcal{W}_{\mathrm{KR}}$ stops and outputs a key $K^\star$

    Let $c \notin \{c_1, c_2, \ldots, c_q\}$ and $m \notin \{m_1, m_2, \ldots, m_q\}$

    $s \longleftarrow p(c, m)$

    If $\mathsf{Enc}(K^\star, c, m) = s$

        then return 1

        else return 0

Since adversary $\mathcal{W}$ is running $\mathcal{W}_{\mathrm{KR}}$ as a subroutine, $\mathcal{W}$ passes oracle queries of $\mathcal{W}_{\mathrm{KR}}$ to its oracle p and transfers the outputs of p to $\mathcal{W}_{\mathrm{KR}}$ again. When $\mathcal{W}_{\mathrm{KR}}$ completes his work, it returns a $K^\star \in \{0,1\}^k$, which $\mathcal{W}$ tests by checking whether $\mathsf{Emb}(K, c, m) \stackrel{?}{=} p(c, m)$. c or m is a value different from any that $\mathcal{W}_{\mathrm{KR}}$ queried previously, so we require the condition $q < 2^{\ell+l}$. Now the PPF-advantage of the embedding function is computed as follows;

$$\mathbf{Adv}^{\mathrm{PPF}}_{\mathsf{Emb},\mathcal{W}} = \left| \mathbf{Pr}\left[\mathbf{Exp}^{\mathrm{PPF-1}}_{\mathsf{Emb},\mathcal{W}} = 1 \right] - \mathbf{Pr}\left[\mathbf{Exp}^{\mathrm{PPF-0}}_{\mathsf{Emb},\mathcal{W}} = 1 \right] \right|.$$

How can we calculate the above two probabilities? First, let's consider the experiment $\mathbf{Exp}^{\mathrm{PPF-1}}_{\mathsf{Emb},\mathcal{W}}$. In this experiment, the oracle p is $\mathsf{Emb}_K(\cdot, \cdot)$ for some key K, which is the oracle that adversary $\mathcal{W}_{\mathrm{KR}}$ can access, and thus $\mathcal{W}_{\mathrm{KR}}$ acts as the adversary in $\mathbf{Exp}^{\mathrm{KR}}_{\mathsf{Emb},\mathcal{W}_{\mathrm{KR}}}$. Furthermore, if $\mathcal{W}_{\mathrm{KR}}$ is successful in the experiment, then it outputs the $K^\star$ which equals the key K. Thus $\mathcal{W}$ will return 1. There is also the possibility that $\mathcal{W}$ might return 1 even though $\mathcal{W}_{\mathrm{KR}}$ failed to find the key, meaning if $K^\star \neq K$ but $\mathsf{Emb}(K^\star, c, m) \neq \mathsf{Emb}(K, c, m)$. Therefore, we get the following inequality;

$$\mathbf{Pr}\left[\mathbf{Exp}^{\mathrm{PPF-1}}_{\mathsf{Emb},\mathcal{W}} = 1 \right] \geqslant \mathbf{Adv}^{\mathrm{KR}}_{\mathsf{Emb},\mathcal{W}_{\mathrm{KR}}}.$$

Now look at the second experiment $\mathbf{Exp}^{\mathrm{PPF-0}}_{\mathsf{Emb},\mathcal{W}}$. In this experiment, the probability

$$\mathbf{Pr}\left[\mathbf{Exp}^{\mathrm{PPF-0}}_{\mathsf{Emb},\mathcal{W}} = 1 \right]$$

means that adversary $\mathcal{W}$ returns 1 when the oracle is a random processing function. Since the oracle p is random and since c or m is never queried before by adversary $\mathcal{W}_{\mathrm{KR}}$, it can't get any information about the $p(c, m)$. Anyway, $\mathcal{W}_{\mathrm{KR}}$ outputs some key $K^\star$ after querying. At that time, $\mathsf{Emb}(K^\star, c, m)$ is already defined. So the probability is computed as

$$\mathbf{Pr}\left[p(c, m) = \mathsf{Emb}(K^\star, c, m) \right] = \frac{1}{2^L}.$$

Therefore, we can get the following inequality

$$\begin{aligned} \mathbf{Adv}_{\mathsf{Emb},\mathcal{W}}^{\mathrm{PPF}} &= \left| \mathbf{Pr}\left[\ \mathbf{Exp}_{\mathsf{Emb},\mathcal{W}}^{\mathrm{PPF\text{-}1}} = 1 \right] - \mathbf{Pr}\left[\ \mathbf{Exp}_{\mathsf{Emb},\mathcal{W}}^{\mathrm{PPF\text{-}0}} = 1 \right] \right| \\ &\geqslant \mathbf{Adv}_{\mathsf{Emb},\mathcal{W}_{\mathrm{KR}}}^{\mathrm{KR}} - \frac{1}{2^L}. \end{aligned}$$

Corollary 1. *Let* Emb : Keys$\times\mathcal{C}\times\mathcal{M} \to \mathcal{S}$ *be the proposed embedding function, where* Keys $= \{0,1\}^k$, $\mathcal{C} = \{0,1\}^\ell$, $\mathcal{M} = \{0,1\}^l$, *and* $\mathcal{S} = \{0,1\}^\ell$. *Then for any* t, q *with* $q < 2^{\ell+l}$ *we have*

$$\mathbf{InSec}_{\mathsf{Emb}}^{\mathrm{KR}}(t, q, q(\ell+l)) \leqslant \mathbf{InSec}_{\mathsf{Emb}}^{\mathrm{PPF\text{-}CIA}}(t', q+1, (q+1)(\ell+l)) + \frac{1}{2^\ell - q}.$$

Proof. Proof is similar to Theorem 1. In the second experiment, adversary $\mathcal{W}_{\mathrm{KR}}$ already queried q times, so there left only $2^\ell - q$ things. So the second term could be the probability that it takes the one from $2^\ell - q$ things.

4   Conclusion

Many practical steganographic algorithms have been introduced to construct a secret communication channel as a part of solutions for the prisoners' problem. But almost all of them are revealed as insecure. Recently, Hopper *et al.* introduced a provable secure steganographic algorithm in the sense of complexity theory. However, the security of their algorithm just depends on not the algorithm itself but the security of the encryption algorithm used in their algorithm. In addition, it is different from a practical one because it is not efficient. Thus, we need more practical, efficient algorithms.

So we have introduced some security notions in steganography in this paper; pseudoprocessingness, three kinds of adversary models; Chosen-Input-Attack(CIA), Chosen-Stego-Attack(CSA) and Key-Recovery(KR), and the security notions against each adversary. Then, with these notions, we constructed a efficient algorithm and proved that it is secure against CIA as well as KR.

Acknowledgement

This work was supported in part by the Ministry of Information & Communications, Korea, under the Information Technology Research Center (ITRC) Support Program.

References

1. R.J. Anderson, "Stretching the Limits of Steganography," in *Information Hiding: First International Workshop*, Lecture Notes in Computer Science 1174, Cambridge, U.K, May 30–June 1, Proceedings: Springer-Verlag, 1996, pp.39–48.

2. C. Cachin, "An Information-Theoretic Model for Steganography," in *Information Hiding - Second International Workshop*, Lecture Notes in Computer Science 1525, Portland, Oregon, USA, April 14–17, 1998, Proceedings: Springer-Verlag, 1998, pp.306–318.

3. S. Craver, "On Public-Key Steganography in the presence of an Active Warden," in *Proceedings of the Second International Workshop on Information Hiding*, Lecture Notes in Computer Science 1525, Springer-Verlag, 1998, pp.255–368.

4. G. Goldwasser and M. Bellare, Lecture Notes on Modern Cryptography, August, 2001. Available at `http://www-cse.ucsd.edu/users/mihir/papers/gb.html`.

5. N.J. Hopper, J. Langford, and L. von Ahn, "Provably Secure Steganography," in *Proceedings of Crypto'02*, Lecture Notes in Computer Science 2442, Springer-Verlag, 2002, pp.77–92.

6. N.F. Johnson, Z. Duric, and S. Jajodia, *Information Hiding: Steganography and Watermarking Attacks and Contermeasures*, Kluwer Academic Publishers, 2001.

7. S. Katzen Beisser and F.A.P. Petitcolas, *Information Hiding - techniques for steganography and digital watermarking*, Artech House Books, 1999.

8. S. Katzenbeisser and F.A.P Petitcolas, "Defining Security in Steganographic Systems," in *Proceeding of the SPIE*, vol.4675, Security and Watermarking of Multimedia Contents IV, 2002, pp.50–56.

9. G.J. Simmons, "The Prisoners' Problem and the Subliminal Channe," in *Advances in Cryptology: Proceedings of Crypto'83*, Plenum Press, New York, 1984, pp.51–67.

10. A. Westfeld and A. Pfitzmann, "Attacks on Steganographic Systems," in *Information Hiding - Third International Workshop, IH'99*, Lecture Notes in Computer Science 1768, Springer-Verlag, 1999, pp.61–76.

11. J. Zöllner, H. Federrath, H. Klimant, A. Pfitzmann, R. Piotraschke, A. Westfeld, G. Wicke, and G. Wolf, "Modeling the Security of Steganographic Systems," in in *Information Hiding - Second International Workshop*, Lecture Notes in Computer Science 1525, Portland, Oregon, USA, April 14–17, 1998, Proceedings: Springer-Verlag, 1998, pp.344–354.

A Multi-feature Based Invertible Authentication Watermarking for JPEG Images

Ye Deng-Pan, Mao Yao-Bin, Dai Yue-Wei, and Wang Zhi-Quan

Department of Automation, Nanjing University of Science & Technology,
Nanjing, P.R China 210094
yedp2001@163.com

Abstract. Invertible authentication techniques have been used in some special applications (such as medical or military applications), where original data can be recovered after being authenticated. In this paper, we proposed a new scheme combine features (relation of coefficients) in DCT domain with content features (edges or textures) of JPEG image into multi-feature, which is useful to authenticate images in both spatial and frequency domains. A novel invertible data embedding mechanism based on random walk is proposed. Experimental results show that the algorithm is sensitive to intended tampers while accepting appropriate JPEG recompressions, and even more, it has the ability to locate corrupt areas. Compared with authentication scheme based on features extracted from single domain, the "miss alarm" probability of our scheme is much lower.

1 Introduction

With the development of web communication and multimedia technology, more and more digital multimedia signal can be transmitted through Internet. This made multimedia data vulnerable to various attacks. Among today's information security techniques, multimedia authentication techniques have been developed greatly and become a kind of powerful tool for protecting multimedia content. Multimedia authentication techniques can be divided into two groups including digital signature and watermarking [1]. The former utilizes encryption algorithm to extract hash codes from image or other multimedia data as signature, and the hash code is saved in header file or other extra space transmitting with the image. When authentication is needed, signature produced in the same way will be compared with signature saved before. If they match, then received multimedia data is authenticated. The latter is that the feature codes (such as hash value or message authentication code [1]) of object to be authenticated are self-embedded as watermark, and then feature extracted in the same way will be compared with the watermark retrieved to determine if there are any changes. Compared with digital signature method, the authentication scheme with watermark has the advantage that it does not need extra space to save authentication code. However, due to the added redundant information within image, visual quality will be degraded more or less. And in some applications where high perceptual quality is needed, this degradation will be obviously unacceptable.

I.J. Cox et al. (Eds.): IWDW 2004, LNCS 3304, pp. 152 – 162, 2005.

Another kind of improved authentication technique (invertible authentication watermarking method) has been proposed and original signal will be recovered after authentication [2,3,6,7,8]. This new authentication method does not need extra space for saving MAC or hash value like digital signature, moreover, it can invert original signal if the watermarked image is thought as authentic, which is impossible in previous watermarking methods (non-invertible). In paper [2], Fridrich presented two methods for the authentication of JPEG images using invertible watermarking. In both methods LSB embedding algorithm and hash function were adopted. Invertible authentication for JPEG image can be implemented well in two schemes. However, they are too sensitive to many kinds of modifications such as appropriate JPEG compression and other noise. In practical applications these schemes seem too fragile. In addition, because hash bit stream was embedded into the DCT coefficients in fixed locations, a good security property could not be achieved. Recently some scholars presented other invertible schemes [6,7,8]. However, either imperceptibility or robustness/frangibility of watermarking system is not good enough in practice.

In this paper, we present a new invertible authentication scheme based on multi-feature instead of hash bit stream. The algorithm proposed in our paper aims at overcoming the two drawbacks mentioned above of methods given in paper [2]. Furthermore, due to extracting multi-feature from both spatial domain and frequency, the message authentication code (MAC) can accurately describe the block content. This can make the probability of "miss alarm" very low. Here we select edge feature as spatial content feature and the relation of two mid-frequency DCT coefficients closest to DC coefficient as frequency features. The two features are combined into a multi-feature based MAC, which is embedded into JPEG image as watermark in an invertible manner used for authentication. Without the authentication key, one can neither notice any trace of MAC hidden in JPEG image nor implement authentication process. If image to be test is deemed authentic, the original image can be recovered by anyone who possesses the authentication key.

In next section we summarize different ways of feature extraction and illustrate our consideration on multi-feature authentication. Details about the invertible authentication scheme are described in section 3. We give the experimental results and discussion in section 4 and conclude it in last section.

2   The Multi-feature Based Authentication Idea

In general authentication system, feature construction is an important issue. How to utilize feature of image (or other multimedia objects) to construct a string of unique code that can represent image to the greatest extent is the problem that designers should care about. Different features were used in multimedia authentication in different papers. Bhattacha and Kutter proposed an authentication method that extracts "salient" image feature points by using a scale interaction model and Mexican-Hat wavelets [4]. They generate digital signature based on the location of these feature points. A most drawback maybe that it is not sensitive enough to some crop-and-replace manipulations inside the objects. Queluz proposed a way to generate digital signatures based on edges [5]. Edge-based features may be a good choice for image authentication because the contour of objects should keep consistent for acceptable manipulations. One drawback is that the length of signature should be reduced. In paper [1], Lin used the relation of DCT coefficients of same positions in different blocks as feature to detect malicious modifications. He mainly considered the robustness of MAC to JPEG compression but not the actual semantic meanings that MAC represented. An intended attack may be successful if statistical analysis method to DCT coefficients is adopted.

All authentication methods above adopted features extracted from one-fold domain (either spatial domain or frequency domain). As we know, in authentication system, multi-feature content descriptor is more nicely to denote image content than the one based on single domain. To reduce the probability of "miss alarm" and improve the security of authentication system, we propose a new multi-feature based authentication scheme that will more exactly authenticate original signal from both spatial and frequency domain.

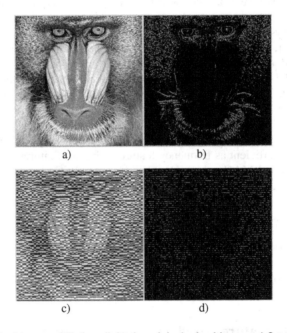

Fig. 1. a) The original image of "baboon", b) the original edge bit map, c) Intentional tampers aiming at the relation DCT coefficient of (2,1) and (2,2), d) corresponding edge bit map

Edge-features are adopted to classify types of 8x8 pixel blocks and relations of DCT coefficient pairs closest to DC coefficient that represent frequency feature. If 8x8 block contains edges, then define feature code as "1", else as "0". The combination of two features and detailed algorithm will be seen in the next section. In common DCT coefficient's relation based authentication schemes, an intentional attacker most probably destroys visual content of images aiming at certain DCT coefficients (such as the ones of (2,1) and (2,2) in our scheme) while successfully cheating the authentication system. In figure 1 an experimental example is given to show the efficiency of multi-feature authentication compared with single domain based one. In this example, although the attacker successfully cheating DCT domain based authentication system, the edge features before and after tampers will tell us the visual content have been modified.

Here we propose a new idea for feature extraction, that in future works more than two features fused together for authentication purpose will be considered. In spatial domain, geometry characters such as edges and textures, all can be used for authentication. Features of different transform domains such as relations of energy or transformed coefficients in block are all good candidate for generating multi-feature code.

3   The Invertible Authentication Scheme for JPEG Image

In JPEG images, there exist many zero coefficients due to compression. Thus invertible data embedding can be easily realized by utilizing these zero coefficients. Our invertible authentication watermarking has several advantages compared with previous ones. Firstly, the multi-feature are adopted, consequently the probability of "miss alarm" is reduced. Secondly, it can resist both small noise interference and appropriate JPEG compression. In addition, the positions for embedding feature in every block are randomly selected under the control of authentication key. This method has better security than the ones selecting fixed locations [2]. An attacker using statistical analysis based on quantized coefficients cannot find any trace of hidden MAC in watermarked image.

3.1 Multi-feature Extraction

Our scheme is based on 8x8 blocks. Assume that B_i represent a typical block in JPEG image, $i \in [1, L]$, L is the total number of blocks in image. Edge based message authentication code is defined by a binary sequence. Use edge-detecting method to classify types of blocks. If block B_i contains edges, let edge based MAC for B_i be "1", else be "-1".

In DCT domain, we select two coefficients $D_i(1,0)$ and $D_i(1,1)$ as a feature pair. In normal quantization table, the quantized steps according to the two positions both equal to 12 (see the normal quantization table). So it can be predicted that the relation of the pair should be robust to JPEG recompression. If $D_i(1,0) >= D_i(1,1)$, then let DCT based MAC for B_i be "1", else be "-1". So multi-feature code for B_i can be represented by two bits, which will be embedded into JPEG image in a novel invertible manner.

3.2 Invertible Watermarking Algorithm

Suppose a JPEG image is qualified by a factor of Q.

1)   Assume that current block is B_i, $i \in [1, L]$, L is total number of blocks in image. MAC for block B_i is $\{a_i, b_i\}$, $a_i, b_i = \pm 1$. The MAC should be randomly permuted with a secret key.

2) Divide 60 DCT coefficients except $D_i(0,0)$, $D_i(1,0)$, $D_i(0,1)$ and
    $D_i(1,1)$ into two groups. Following zigzag scan, the former group is constituted
    by coefficients i of which equal to $\{4,7,9,11,13,....63\}$, and the latter group is
    constituted by $\{6,8,10,12,14,....64\}$ coefficients. Discard the coefficients in
    high frequency and then the candidate positions are changed to be group
    A$\{4,7,9,11,13,....31\}$ and group B$\{6,8,10,12,14,....32\}$ that will be used for
    watermarks embedding. In general, DCT coefficients after the 30th one are zeros.
    If not, we should increase the cut index to keep that at least one zero in the last
    positions of the two groups of every block. The algorithm's precondition is that
    coefficients in the last position are both zeros.

3) Assume that authentication key is $\vec{K}$. The key corresponding to the block B_i
    is $\vec{k}_i = \{k_{i1}, k_{i2}\}$.   Then   search   the   two   first   non-zero   coefficient
    D_j, $j \in \{4,7,9,...29\}$ and D_k, $k \in \{6,8,10,...30\}$ following a random non-
    intersecting walk through group A and group B respectively from the 31th and the 32th
    position. The random walk in two groups are respectively controlled by secret key
    k_{i1} and k_{i2}. Then define the previous neighboring coefficients of D_j and D_k in random
    walk as D'_j and D'_k . Then let $D'_j = q'_j * sign(a_i)$ and $D'_k = q'_k * sign(b_i)$.
    Go to the next block till the end of all blocks.

4) Do the inverse DCT transformation to the pixel domain.

3.3 Watermarking Retrieval and Verification Algorithm

The steps of authenticating JPEG image are simple and given as following.

1) DCT transform image by 8x8 blocks.

2) In current block B_i, $i \in [1, L]$, the corresponding key is $\vec{k}_i = \{k_{i1}, k_{i2}\}$. Search
    the first two non-zero coefficients D''_j and D''_k following a random non-intersecting
    walk through group A and group B. Then let $a'_j = sign(D''_j)$, $b'_j = sign(D''_k)$.
    Go to the next block till the end of all blocks. The whole MAC can be calculated by
    inversely permuting $\{(a'_1, b'_1), (a'_2, b'_2),....(a'_i, b'_i),....(a'_L, b'_L)\}$ with
    the secret key used before.

3) Compare the watermark with MAC extracted from image in the same way
    described in section 3.1. If they match, the JPEG image will be deemed authentic.
    Otherwise some tampers must have happened. Output the index of mismatch
    blocks indicating the location that has been tampered.

3.4 Original Signal Recovery

According to secret key $\vec{k}_i = \{k_{i1}, k_{i2}\}$, we implement the random non-intersecting
walk through the group A and B, and search the first two non-zero DCT coefficients. Then
we may set the two coefficients as zero. Thus the original JPEG image can be recovered.

3.5   A Simple Example

To illustrate our algorithm better, a simple example is given as following. Given the normal test JPEG image "baboon" with Q_0 equal to 80 and select the first 8x8 pixel block of 'banboon'. The original pixel and DCT coefficient matrix are showed in table 2 and 3.

Using edge's statistical analyzing method, we know this block does not contain any edges. Then $a_1=-1$. On the other hand, $D_1(1,0)=45$ and $D_1(1,1)=-15$, so $b_1=1$. The MAC for block B_1 is {-1, 1}.

Table 1. The original pixel values matrix

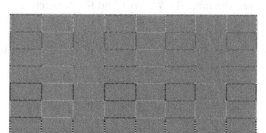

Table 2. The original DCT coefficients matrix

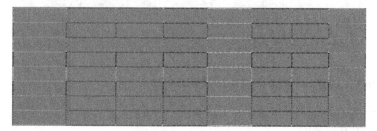

Let us see the group A are composed by the coefficients corresponding to positions of {4, 7, 9, 11,..., 31}. Look up table 3, they are {17.5, 0, 0, 0,100, 0, -32.5, -27.5, 0, -43.75, 0, 0, 0, 0}. In group B, they are {37.5, 17.5, 17.5, 21.25, -47.5, 0, 30, 27.5, 0, 0, -50, 0, 0, 0}. According to the random walk controlled by the key $\bar{k}_1 = \{k_{11}, k_{12}\}$, the two sequences maybe arranged as following (table 3).

Table 3. The two coefficients sequence following random walk

Now MAC for B_1 is $\{-1, 1\}$. In practical implementation, the MAC for block B_1 should be embedded into another block B_i and the index i of B_i are selected under the control of the secret key. Here we simplify the algorithm and embed the MAC into the block B_1 itself. The first non-zero coefficient is $A_3=100$, then we set $A_2=q(2,1)*\mathrm{sign}(-1)=-13/0.8=-16.25$. Another non-zero coefficient is $B_2=17.5$, so we set $B_1=q(3,4)*\mathrm{sign}(1)=51/0.8=63.75$. Consequently, the embedded DCT coefficient matrix is given in table 5. it can be seen in table 5 that the embedded DCT matrix has the same properties as common 8x8 JPEG DCT matrix and an attacker can not find any trace of hidden data.

When authentication is needed, according to the random walk controlled by the key $\vec{k}_1 = \{k_{11}, k_{12}\}$, we search the first non-zero coefficient respectively in group A and group B again (see the table 4). We will find the non-zero coefficients are $A_2 = -16.2500$ and $B_1=63.7500$. So the watermark bit is $\{-1, 1\}$. Remove A_2 and B_1, the original signal can be recovered (assume that no manipulation has happened). Using the original image to extract MAC and comparing it with watermark help us conclude that whether or not modification has happened.

Table 4. The embedded DCT coefficients matrix

4   Experimental Results and Discussion

Figure 2 (a), (b) and (c), each with size 512x512, are used as the cover images in our experiments ($Q_0=80$).

In our scheme one quantized step is adopted as magnitude of watermarking. The capacity of watermark is invariably two bits per 8x8block. To achieve higher robustness to JPEG or other accepted manipulation, the magnitude of watermarking can be adjusted to a lager one (two steps or more). However, the visual quality will be affected. Our experiments are implemented based on one step's watermark magnitude. Q_0 is the original quality factor of JPEG images. With $Q_0=80$, three test JPEG images are watermarked with MAC which can be used to verify the JPEG images. In figure 2 we can see the visual effect of these three watermarks.

Using JPEG images with different quality factor Q_0 for embedding authentication watermarks, the distortions are showed in figure 3. We can see that the PSNR rises with the increasing of Q_0. The reason is that larger step is corresponding to lower JPEG quality.

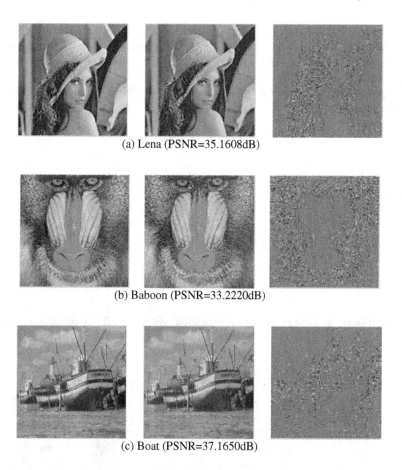

(a) Lena (PSNR=35.1608dB)

(b) Baboon (PSNR=33.2220dB)

(c) Boat (PSNR=37.1650dB)

Fig. 2. Three original JPEG images (left Q_0=80) and (middle) their watermarked images embedded with MAC and (right) corresponding watermarks (different $W=I_w-I$)

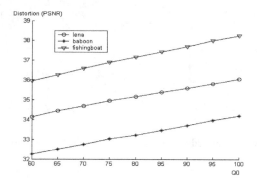

Fig. 3. Distortion for invertible JPEG authentication for three test images ("lena", "baboon", "boat") and different quality factors (Q_0)

Because a watermark bit is represented by one quantized step with Q_0, it can be predicted that watermarks should be robust to recompression with quality Q_1 (round $(Q_1/Q_2)>1/2$). However, DCT features may not endure large compression ratio. Experimental results are given in figure 4.

Edge-based features show good robustness to JPEG compression. The visual results are given in figure 5.

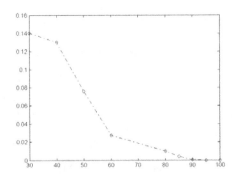

Fig. 4. Figure 4 Robustness of authentication system to JPEG recompression (Round $(Q_1/Q_2)>1/2$)

Fig. 5. The robustness of edge bit map to JPEG compression with different Q (100,90,80,60,50,40)

Some tampered visual effect of three JPEG images with $Q_0=80$ are given in figure 6. In (left) figure 6 (a) and (b) two kinds of tampering are imposed on

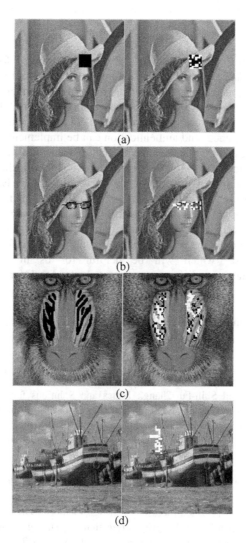

Fig. 6. Tampered JPEG images and authentication results. (a) (Left) Tampered image 1 of "lena" and authentication result (right). (b) (Left) Tampered image 2 of "lena" and authentication result (right). (c) (Left) Tampered image of "baboon" and authentication result (right). (d) Tampered image of "boat" and authentication result (right)

"lena". Authentication results are shown in (a) and (b) (right). In figure 6 (c), several black lines are added into image of "baboon" (left), and the authentication result is given on the right. In figure (d)(left), the lighthouse is removed from image of "boat" and the authentication result is given on the right. From figure 6 we can see that our scheme can correctly detect malicious modifications and more, locate corrupt area approximately. Each tampered block is marked in white color.

5 Conclusion

A novel multi-feature based invertible authentication method for JPEG images is proposed in this paper. Using multi-feature helps us exactly describe original multimedia content and can be expected to resist the statistical attack that maybe successful to the authentication system based on single relation of DCT coefficients. With a key only known to the owner, original JPEG image can be recovered if no manipulation has happened, and authentication can be implemented. Due to randomly selecting embedding position the scheme has better security than embedding strategy based on fix position [2]. Moreover robustness can be achieved by adjusting magnitude of watermarks within allowable vision distortion. Experimental results show that the invertible authentication scheme can detect malicious modifications in high precise. In applications of invertible authentication such as military communication and remote medical care, our scheme will have good feasibility. Future work will focus on the research of the relation between feature extraction and authenticating precise, which will be helpful for us in designing invertible authentication schemes with different precision adapted for different applications.

Acknowledgements. This work is supported by the project of China NSF-60374066 and the project of Jiangsu Province NSF-BK2002101.

References

[1] Ching-Yung Lin and Shih-Fu Chang.: Issues and Solutions for Authenticating MPEG Video. SPIE Conf. on Security and Watermarking of Multimedia Contents, Vol. 3657, pp.54-65, San Jose, CA, Jan. 1999.

[2] Fridrich, J., Goljan, M., Du, R.: Invertible Authentication Watermark for JPEG Images. ITCC 2001, Las Vegas, Nevada, April 2-4, 2001, pp. 223–227.

[3] Honsinger, C.W., Jones, P., Rabbani, M., Stoffel, J. C.: Lossless Recovery of an Original Image Containing Embedded Data, US Patent # 6,278,791 (Aug 2001)

[4] Bhattacharjee, S., Kutter, M.: Compression Tolerant Image Authentication," IEEE International Conf. On Image Processing, Chicago, October 1998.

[5] M.P.Queluz.: Content-based Integrity Protection of Digital Images. SPIE Conf. on Security and Watermarking of Multimedia Contents, Vol. 3657, pp.85-93, San Jose, CA, Jan. 1999.

[6] Tian, J.: Wavelet-based reversible watermarking for authentication. In Proc.Security and Watermarking of Multimedia Contents IV, Electronic Imaging 2002, vol.4675. (20-25 Jan 2002) 679-690

[7] Vleeschouwer, C.D., Delaigle, J.F., Macq, B.: Circular Interpretation of Bijective Transformations in lossless Watermarking for Media Asset Management. In IEEE Transaction on Multimedia, (Mar 2003)

[8] Mohammad Awrangjeb, Mohan S. Kankanhalli: Lossless Watermarking Considering the Human Visual System. IWDW 2003: 581-592

Steganographic Scheme Using a Block Cipher*

Jeong Jae Yu, Chang-ho Jung, Seok-Koo Yoon, and Sangjin Lee

Center for Information Security Technologies, Korea University, Seoul, Korea
{shakehds, zangho, skyoon}@cist.korea.ac.kr
sangjin@korea.ac.kr
http://cist.korea.ac.kr

Abstract. Westfeld[1] detected the stegoed–image by measuring the frequencies of PoVs(pairs of values) in the suspicious images. Fridrich[4] proposed another detection method, so-called RS steganalysis. In this paper we propose a steganographic scheme using a block cipher, which minimizes the embedding changes of a cover object utilizing not only the LSBs of the cover object's strings but also the whole bits of the cover object. The proposed scheme is a kind of the coding scheme which minimizes changed bits for message embedding without sharing the secret code–book. The experimental result shows that the proposed scheme efficiently evades the χ^2–statistical test and RS steganalysis.

1 Introduction

Steganography is a study about the invisible communication which aims that no one is able to know the existence of this secret channel except two parties of communicators. In many cases, it was first invented for the military communication or criminal purpose with the technical or linguistic ways[3]. Therefore it was studied in the restricted area. But thanks to the improvement of Internet, it becomes easy to copy or transmit digital data, more and more people are interested in the steganography that utilizes the digital data as cover-media. Nowadays, whoever wants to conceal a secret message in the innocent-looking digital data may easily get some steganographic tools on the web. Many of them simply substitute the least significant bits(LSB) of the cover data for a secret message since it is easy to implement. Because the redundant parts of a cover are imperceptible, some believes intuitively that these parts are random and the LSB substitution would not be detected. But Westfeld[1] obtained the experimental result that the redundant parts of digital data are not random and proposed the blind steganalytic method called χ^2–statistical test. It is based on the statistical analysis of PoVs(pairs of values) that are exchanged during message embedding. Provos[5] also extended this method by re-sampling the test interval to detect

---

* This work was supported (in part) by the Ministry of Information and Communications, Korea, under the Information Technology Research Center (ITRC) Support Program.

I.J. Cox et al. (Eds.): IWDW 2004, LNCS 3304, pp. 163–170, 2005.

the randomly spread steganography. After that,Fridrich[4] introduced a RS steganalysis which is based on the partition of an image' pixels as three groups ; Regular, Singular, Unusable groups. This method can estimate the embedded message length in case of the LSB substitution steganography.

As a rule, the fewer bits is changed after message embedding, the harder it is for an attacker to determine whether the given data contain a secret message or not. A secure block cipher must have an avalanche effect; The small amounts of an input value's change causes a large amounts of an output value's change. If this property is applied to steganography, we can embed an enough amount of the message in the cover object without changing the same size of the message bits. The proposed scheme can give an effect of the compression coding which minimizes the embedding changes of a cover object without pre-sharing any other information except a secret key. The changed bits after the same size of message embedding by the proposed scheme is decreased about 40% comparing with the simple LSB embedding scheme. The experiment shows that the proposed scheme also evades well the χ^2–statistical test and RS steganalysis. We explain the details of the proposed scheme in section 2 and the experimental results are followed in section 3. Then, we conclude this paper in section 4.

2   The Proposed Scheme

The fewer bits is changed after message embedding, the harder it is for an attacker to determine whether the given data contain a secret message or not. If we use the LSB embedding steganographic method, then the best secure case is to find the cover whose LSBs are exactly the same as the message bits. If the unmodified cover contains the secret message, the system which can find this cover in the polynomial time bound is called the perfect steganographic system[2] but it is not a practical system.

The block cipher has the property that for a few changes in the input value, there are many changes in the output value. If this property is applied to steganographic system, we can embed a message bits in the cover object within smaller changing bits than expectedly doing the half of the total message bits. We make the pre-computation to find the collision pair; the output of a block cipher and an embedding message block. The details of the scheme is as follows. With a convenience, we implemented this algorithm with an image file, especially at a BMP format.

1. First, the encoding algorithm divide the cover object C into the same blocks, $c_{11} \ldots c_{1\ell} \parallel c_{21} \ldots c_{2\ell} \parallel \ldots$, whose length is ℓ bits. The divided block is split again into the subblocks in which there should be at least 2 changeable bits. We took subblock as a pixel value(8 bits) in the next section. One bit out of the changeable bits must be a message check bit. It's position is determined by the pseudo-random sequence generated from a shared key.
2. An embedding message M is also divided into suitable r bits blocks, $m_1 \parallel m_2 \parallel \cdots \parallel m_z$. The length of r bits block is flexible with a proportion to the collision with an output of a block cipher. In the next section, we took this block length as $r = 8$.

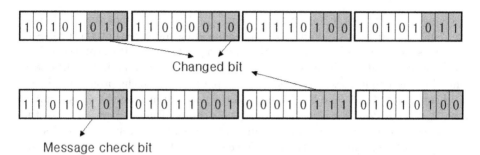

Fig. 1. Divided image block when $\ell = 64, r = 8$

3. With a shared key, generate a pseudo-random sequence to determine the position of a message check bit. For example, assume that $\ell = 64$, $r = 8$, a subblock is a pixel value(1 byte) and the changeable bits is located from the LSB to the 3rd LSB. If pseudo-random number is 12, then for all $3 \times 8 = 24$ changeable bits($0 \sim 23$), the position of a message check bit becomes 13th bit in a sequential order. See Fig.1.

4. Change a message check bit value into 1. Then compute the output value of a block cipher by setting this cover block as an input value. Compare the least r bits of an output value with the first embedding message block m_1.

$$E_k(c_{11} \ldots c_{1i} \ldots c_{1\ell}) \, (mod \, 2^r) \overset{?}{\equiv} m_1$$

If two values are same, then move to the next cover block and repeat the above steps. Otherwise, recover the previous changed bit and flip one of other changeable bit except the message check bit then compare it again. Until finding a collision of an embedding message block with an output block of the block cipher, continue flipping changeable bits within the permitted iterations. If the collision does not happen by the last iteration, then change the message check bit value into 0 and move to next cover block.

5. If before moving to the last cover block the whole secret message is not embedded, then the embedding process is a failure.

6. Decoding is more simple. Determine the position of a message check bit by a pseudo-random sequence. If the message check bit value is 1, then compute the cipher text by inputting this cover block and take the least r bits of the cipher text as an embedded message block.

$$E_k(s_{j1} \ldots s_{ji} \ldots s_{j\ell}) \, (mod \, 2^r) = m_j$$

Otherwise, the cover block is skipped.

Instead of changing more cover bits, we finds collision with a secret message. This scheme is more complex and time consuming than the simple LSB substitution steganography, but this computation minimizes the cover object's changes for message embedding. To get more security, the user can decrease the number of changeable bits or the length of collision bits. Other steganographic schemes are dependent on the randomness of an embedding message, but the proposed scheme is independent on the embedding message's property. If the attacker does not know a shared key, then he even doesn't know whether a plain text has been embedded or a cipher text has been. The simplest attack on the proposed scheme is a brute force attack on a block cipher. If the decoded message block is a cipher text, it gives a double encryption effect as a result. Table 3.1 and 3.2 are the pseudo code of an encoding and decoding processes respectively. c'_{ji} denotes the flipped bit of c_{ji}, and s'_{jt} is the message check bit of in the stego-image block.

Encode 3.1

Input: $K \in \{0,1\}^k$, $C = c_{11} \ldots c_{1\ell} \parallel c_{21} \ldots c_{2\ell} \parallel \cdots$,
$\qquad M = m_1 \parallel m_2 \parallel \cdots \parallel m_z, \ 0 \le |m_j| \le 2^r$

for $\quad j = 1, 2, \ldots$
$\qquad t = rand(K) \bmod \ell$
$\qquad s'_{jt} = c_{jt} = 1; \ tag = 0$
$\qquad temp = c_{j1} \ldots c_{ji} \ldots c_{j\ell}$
$\qquad$ for $\quad i \leftarrow 1$ to ℓ do
$\qquad\qquad$ if $\quad E_k(temp) \ (\bmod \ 2^r) = m_j$
$\qquad\qquad\qquad s_{j1} \ldots s_{ji} \ldots s_{j\ell} = temp$
$\qquad\qquad\qquad tag = 1$
$\qquad\qquad\qquad$ **break**
$\qquad\qquad$ **else**
$\qquad\qquad\qquad temp = c_{j1} \ldots c_{ji} \ldots c_{j\ell}$
$\qquad\qquad\qquad temp = c_{j1} \ldots c_{j(i-1)} c'_{ji} \ldots c_{j\ell}$
$\qquad$ if $\quad tag = 0$
$\qquad\qquad s'_{jt} = 0$
Output: $S = s_{11} \ldots s_{1\ell} \parallel s_{21} \ldots s_{2\ell} \parallel \cdots$

Decode 3.2

Input: $K \in \{0,1\}^k$,
$\qquad S = s_{11} \ldots s_{1\ell} \parallel s_{21} \ldots s_{2\ell} \parallel \cdots$
for $\quad j = 1, 2, \ldots$
$\qquad t = rand(K) \bmod \ell$
$\qquad$ if $\quad s'_{jt} = 1$
$\qquad\qquad E_k(s_{j1} \ldots s_{ji} \ldots s_{j\ell}) \ (\bmod \ 2^r) = m_j$

Output: $M = m_1 \parallel m_2 \parallel \cdots \parallel m_z$

---

3 Experimental Result

We used AES[6] as a block cipher and implemented at a bmp file format image as a cover object. We set the 128 bits input block which consists of $n = 64$ bits

Fig. 2. Nothing is embedded(L) and the visual test(R)

Fig. 3. stego-image embedded 65KB message(L) and the visual test(R)

cover images and $n = 64$ bits padding, then fix a secret message block size $m = 8$ bits. We randomly select one bit as a message check bit out of 24 changeable bits that are located from the LSB to the 3rd LSB of the subblock(pixel value=8 bits) and use 1bit for the message check bit, 3 bits for message embedding out of the rest 23 changeable bits. To avoid being concentrated the changed bits(or flipped bits) on a special bit-plain, we flipped the changeable bits from having minimum hamming distance and controlled not to exceed at most two changed bits in the same bit plain. Then every input block can be changed to become the 648 ways of a different input block; classified as the cases none of bits are changed, only one bit is changed, two bits are changed, three bits are changed, respectively.

$$1 + \binom{23}{1} + \left\{ 2 \binom{7}{1} \binom{8}{1} + \binom{8}{1} \binom{8}{1} \right\} + \binom{7}{1} \binom{8}{1} \binom{8}{1} = 1 + 23 + 176 + 448 = 648$$

Fig. 4. stego-image embedded 65KB message(L) and the χ^2–statistical test(R)

Assume that for given inputs, the output value of AES operation is random, then the probability of a collision this output with an embedding message block in one AES operation is $(\frac{1}{2})^8$. The total probability of successful collision after 648 AES iterations becomes $1 - (1 - (\frac{1}{2})^8)^{648} \simeq 0.920834$. For the test of the scheme, we collected the various kind(natural images, true color cartoon images and fractal images etc) of images which are acquired from a digital camera, scanner and internet. All of them are fitted to size as $512 \times 379 \times 24$ bits $\cong$ 570kbytes. We selected the 160 sample images whose detection probabilities are all zero by the χ^2–statistical test and the RS steganalysis. Then we embedded 30kbytes and 65kbytes of ciphertext into the selected images respectively using the proposed algorithm. **Table.**1 shows the result of the 160 sample

Table 1. Results of 160 sample images

	30kbytes	65kbytes
χ^2–statistical test	0/160	0/160
Extended χ^2–test	15/160	30/160
RS steganalysis	9/160	15/160

images for the χ^2–statistical test, the extended χ^2–statistical test and the RS steganalysis respectively whose detecting threshold is set to 5%. As the result shows, the χ^2–statistical test can not detect at all regardless of the embedded message size and the RS steganalysis can hardly estimate the approximation of the embedded message size. This fact shows that the proposed scheme has the spread embedding property cause of a block cipher computation. Fig.2,3 show the visual tests of a pure cover image and a stego-image embedded 65KB secret message by the proposed scheme. With a only filtered images, we cannot tell the difference between a cover and a stego-image. **Table.**2 shows the objective

Table 2. SNR of the tested image

	SNR(dB)
Lena.bmp(**Fig**.4)	46.751
JJH1.bmp(**Fig**.3)	47.108

distortion metric, SNR(signal to noise ratio) of the tested images. The proposed scheme is a kind of the coding scheme which minimizes changed bits for message embedding without sharing the secret code–book. Naturally, the changed bits with the proposed scheme is decreased about 40% comparing with the simple LSB substitution method. **Table**.3 shows the total numbers of flipped bits after embedding by the proposed scheme and the LSB substitution respectively. The numbers in the round bracket denote the embedding efficiency. The embedding efficiency rate(EER) is defined by **Eq. (1)**–where TML denotes the total embedded message length and CML denotes the actually changed message length.

$$EER = \frac{TML}{CML} \tag{1}$$

Table 3. numbers of the flipped bits for 65KB embedding

	the proposed scheme	the LSB substitution
Lena.bmp(**Fig**.4)	171910 (3.02)	275421 (1.89)
JJH1.bmp(**Fig**.3)	165512 (3.14)	288457 (1.80)

4   Conclusion

In this paper, we proposed a secure steganographic scheme which minimizes the changes of a cover object but has a sufficient embedding capacity by using a block cipher. The spread bit-plain embedding property of the proposed scheme makes hard to estimate the approximation of the embedded message size by the RS steganalysis. Because the proposed scheme needs not any other cryptographic subroutine to encrypt an embedding message, the changed bits of a cover object are independent on the randomness of the ciphertext. Therefore the proposed scheme can not detected by the steganalytic methods which are based on the randomness of an embedding message.

References

1. A. Westfeld and A. Pfitzmann: *"Attacks on Steganographic Systems,"* Information Hiding 1999: pp.61-76. 21.
2. C. Cachin, "An Information-Theoretic Model for Steganography," in *Proceedings of the Second International Workshop on Information Hiding*, vol. 1525 of *Lecture Notes in Computer Science*, Springer,1998, pp.306-318.

3. D. Kahn, , *The Codebreakers-The Story of Secret Writing,* New York,USA: Scribner,1996. *Proceedings of CRYPTO'83*, Plenum Press, 1984, pp.51-67.
4. J. Fridrich, M. Goljan, and R. Du, *"Detecting LSB steganography in color and grayscale image,"* Magazine of IEEE Multimedia, 2001, pp. 22-28.
5. N. Provos, *"Defending Against Statistical Steganalysis,"* in Proceedings of the 10th USENIX Security Symposium, 2001, pp.323-335.
6. http://csrc.nist.gov/publications/fips/fips197/fips-197.pdf.

Watermarking Attack: Security of WSS Techniques

François Cayre[1], Caroline Fontaine[2], and Teddy Furon[1]

[1] INRIA projet TEMICS
{francois.cayre,teddy.furon}@irisa.fr
[2] CNRS LIFL, Université des Sciences et Technologies de Lille
Caroline.Fontaine@lifl.fr *

Abstract. Most of watermarking techniques are based on Wide Spread Spectrum (WSS). Security of such schemes is studied here in adopting a cryptanalysis point of view. The security is proportional to the difficulty the opponent has to recover the secret parameters, which are, in WSS watermarking scheme, the private carriers. Both theoretical and practical points of view are investigated when several pieces of content are watermarked with the same secret key. The opponent's difficulty is measured by the amount of data necessary to estimate accurately the private carriers, and also by the complexity of the estimation algorithms. Actually, Blind Source Separation algorithms really help the opponent exploiting the information leakage to disclose the secret carriers. The article ends with experiments comparing blind attacks to these new hacks. The main goal of the article is to warn watermarkers that embedding hidden messages with the same secret key might is a dangerous security flaws.

1   Introduction, Context and Notation

A lot of digital watermarking techniques have been designed those last years. They mainly aim at embedding an invisible watermark into the document in a robust manner. Several kinds of schemes have been proposed, but this article only deals with blind robust watermarking. The reliability is usually evaluated through benchmark tests aiming at removing the watermark [1].

Benchmarking is not really a *security* evaluation, but mainly a *robustness* evaluation. In [2], Kalker defines *robust* watermarking as a communication channel multiplexed into original content in a non-perceptible way, and whose "*capacity [...] degrades as a smooth function of the degradation of the marked content*", and *security* as "*the inability by unauthorized users to access the communication channel*" established by a robust watermark. Accessing the communication channel means to remove, read, or write the hidden message. Hence, *security* deals

---

* This work is supported by the french ACI Fabriano and the european Network of Excellence ECRYPT.

with intentional attacks, excluding those already encompassed in the robustness category since the watermark is assumed to be robust.

This paper adopts a cryptanalytic approach, in the sense that the attacker first recovers the secret that has been used for the generation of the watermark. This approach is certainly not the only one but secret disclosure is a very powerful hack: it gives the access of the communication channel at the lowest distortion price to hack content. The key idea of this security analysis is that information about the secret key might leak from the observations. Hence, the *a posteriori* ignorance of the opponent decreases as he makes more and more observations. As suggested by Diffie and Hellman [3], different contexts of attack are investigated according to the type of observations available to the opponent.

1. In *Known Original Attack – KOA* – the opponent observes N_o pairs of (watermarked / original contents).
2. In *Known Message Attack – KMA* – the opponent has access to N_o (watermarked contents / hidden messages) pairs.
3. In *Watermark Only Attack – WOA* – the opponent has only access to N_o watermarked contents.

As Shannon did [4], it is worth distinguishing what can be stated as a theoretical fact, and the practical tools making the attack really work. Hence, for each of the above-mentioned contexts of attack, the security analysis aims at evaluating two criteria: the *security level*, that is, the theoretical number of observations needed to disclose the secret key, and the *work*, that is, the complexity of the algorithm extracting information about the secret key from observations.

Such a security analysis can only be assessed for a given watermarking algorithm. Here, we decided to focus on spread spectrum based techniques, which are widely used for still images watermarking. Theoretical studies [5] and practical implementations [6] focus on the optimization of operational capacity-robustness functions for a given embedding distortion.

The novelty of this paper resides in the practical implementation of the new watermarking security paradigm whose theoretical background is exposed in [7]. The algorithms we found to hack wide spread spectrum (WSS) techniques come from the Blind Source Separation (BSS), community like Principal Component Analysis (PCA) and Independent Component Analysis (ICA). This use of PCA and ICA in watermarking security analysis is new, as the only other papers mentioning PCA/ICA in the watermarking community have different purposes. González-Serrano *et al* [8] and Bounkong *et al* [9] used ICA to design a watermarking embedder. Du *et al* [10] presented a technique for estimating the watermark by observing only one image. Their purpose is the simple erasure of the whole watermark signal and not the disclosure of the secret parameters. Our approach allows a complete access to the watermarking communication channel to remove, read or write hidden data[1].

---

[1] We have discovered after submission a similar approach uniquely devoted to watermark removal and only based on PCA in [11].

The paper is organized as follows. Section 2 summarizes the theoretical discussions about the measurement of the secret information leakages from the observations and the *security level*. Section 3 focuses on the *work* as the complexity of the tools. In particular, extremely high complexity renders the attacks hardly possible. We discuss some possible strategies to decrease the work to an acceptable amount. In both sections, the three contexts (KOA, KMA, WOA) are investigated. Section 4 finally presents some practical results on watermarked images, where adaptation of the tools to real signals was necessary.

2   Theoretical Results

We present a model for WSS watermarking and the methodology applied in the rest of this section. Details in proofs are omitted but can be found in [7].

2.1   Watermarking Model

Let us denote by x a vector of N_v samples extracted from original content. The embedding is the addition of the watermark signal, giving $y = x + w$. The watermark signal w is the modulation of N_c private carriers u_i:

$$w = \frac{\gamma}{\sqrt{N_c}} \sum_{k=1}^{N_c} a(k) u_k, \tag{1}$$

where $\gamma > 0$ is a small gain fixing the embedding strength and $\|u_k\| = 1$, $1 \le k \le N_c$. An inverse extraction function puts back the watermarked vector y into the media to produce the watermarked piece of content.

The symbols a_k represent the message to be hidden/transmitted through content. In the case of a BPSK [12], symbols $a(i)$ take one of the following values $\{-1, +1\}$. Note that this model also covers some side-informed watermarking techniques called spread transform [13, 14], where $a(k)$ are real values uniformly distributed in $[-\Delta/2, \Delta/2]$. In all cases, the WSS aims at increasing the signal to noise ratio by projecting signals on a smaller subspace of dimension N_c. This implies that $N_v > N_c$. Moreover, to cancel inter-symbol interferences at the decoding side, the carriers are two-by-two orthogonal. For security reason, they are private and issued by a pseudo-random generator fed by the secret key.

In the sequel, the security analysis considers several watermarked vectors y_j $(1 \le j \le N_o)$, with different embedded symbols $a_j = (a_j(1) \dots a_j(N_c))^T$ being linearly mixed by the $N_v \times N_c$ matrix $\mathcal{U} = (u_1 \dots u_{N_c})$. Index i denotes the ith samples of a given signal, whereas j indices the different signals. Thus, there are N_o watermarked vectors or, equivalently, with the $N_v \times N_o$ matrix $\mathcal{Y} = (y_1 \dots y_{N_o})$, and the $N_c \times N_o$ matrix $\mathcal{A} = (a_1 \dots a_{N_o})$:

$$y_j = x_j + \frac{\gamma}{\sqrt{N_c}} \mathcal{U} a_j \quad \text{is equivalent to} \quad \mathcal{Y} = \mathcal{X} + \frac{\gamma}{\sqrt{N_c}} \mathcal{U} \mathcal{A}. \tag{2}$$

2.2   Methodology

Some preliminary works have already adapted the classical guidelines of crypt-analysis to watermarking [15, 16]. Their first assumption is given by the Ker-ckhoffs' principle [17] stating that the encryption/watermarking algorithm is public, but parametrized by a secret key. In watermarking, it means that the attacker knows the extraction and inverse extraction functions. Thus, if he has access to a watermarked piece of content, he can observe its extracted vector $\boldsymbol{y}_j$.

Now, as Shannon did in [4], we consider that several pieces of content have been watermarked with the same key K. The opponent's goal is to disclose K by observing these pieces of content (i.e. their extracted vectors $\{\boldsymbol{y}_j\}$). Shannon named the *equivocation* $e(N_o)$ the entropy of K knowing N_o observations. It measures the ignorance of the attacker after having observed N_o pieces of content, as the following equation holds:

$$e(N_o) = H(K) - I(K; \mathcal{Y}), \tag{3}$$

where $H(K)$ is the entropy of K (i.e. the ignorance of the attacker before ob-serving any content) and $I(K; \mathcal{Y})$ is the mutual information (i.e., a measure of the information about K that leaks from signal set $\{\boldsymbol{y}_j\}_{j=1}^{N_o}$). A physical inter-pretation readily comes: when $e(N_o^\star) = 0$, the attacker has enough observations to disclose the secret key. The security level of the system is of $N_o^\star$ observations.

Does Information Leak? However, the knowledge of the carriers is sufficient to hack a WSS watermarking scheme: these private parameters allow the de-coding, the embedding and the removal of the watermark. It is not necessary to disclose the secret key K that fed the pseudo-random generator issuing the carriers [2]. The real issue then concerns the information leakage about $\boldsymbol{w}$ from watermarked signal $\boldsymbol{y}$. For instance, suppose that host signal $\boldsymbol{X} \sim \mathcal{N}(\boldsymbol{0}, \mathcal{R}_{\boldsymbol{X}})$ and $\boldsymbol{w}$ is picked up randomly among sequences distributed as $\mathcal{N}(\boldsymbol{0}, \mathcal{R}_{\boldsymbol{W}})$. Then, $p_{\boldsymbol{Y}} = \mathcal{N}(\boldsymbol{0}, \mathcal{R}_{\boldsymbol{X}} + \mathcal{R}_{\boldsymbol{W}})$ and $p_{\boldsymbol{Y}|\boldsymbol{W}=\boldsymbol{w}} = \mathcal{N}(\boldsymbol{w}, \mathcal{R}_{\boldsymbol{X}})$. This gives:

$$I(\boldsymbol{W}; \boldsymbol{Y}) = \frac{1}{2} \log \frac{\det \mathcal{R}_{\boldsymbol{X}} + \mathcal{R}_{\boldsymbol{W}}}{\det \mathcal{R}_{\boldsymbol{X}}} \geq 0. \tag{4}$$

This equation is extremely important as it shows that there is a leak of information about $\boldsymbol{W}$ from $\boldsymbol{Y}$.

Information Measurement Yet, Shannon's definition of equivocation based on conditional entropy, is inappropriate in the watermarking field. As we now deal with continuous random vectors, $H(\boldsymbol{W})$ and $H(\boldsymbol{W}|\{\boldsymbol{y}_i\}_{i=1}^{N_o})$ do not mea-sure a quantity of information. The physical interpretation of (3) does not hold anymore. This is the reason why we change the information measurement tools.

In statistics, Fisher was the first to introduce the measure of the amount of information supplied by the observations about unknown parameters. In our case, FIM (Fisher Information Matrix) is defined as:

$$\mathrm{FIM}(\theta) = E\psi\psi^T \quad \text{with} \quad \psi = \nabla_\theta \log p_{\mathcal{X}}(\mathcal{Y} - \mathcal{W}(\theta)). \tag{5}$$

θ denotes the unknown parameter vector. In the KMA case, $\theta = (\boldsymbol{u}_1^T \dots \boldsymbol{u}_{N_c}^T)^T$, whereas, in the WOA context, $\theta = (\boldsymbol{u}_1^T \dots \boldsymbol{u}_{N_c}^T \, \boldsymbol{a}_1^T \dots \boldsymbol{a}_{N_o}^T)^T$.

The Cramér-Rao theorem gives a lower bound of the covariance matrix of an unbiased estimator whenever the FIM is inversible:

$$\mathcal{R}_{\hat{\theta}} \geq \text{FIM}(\theta)^{-1}, \tag{6}$$

where $\mathcal{B} \geq \mathcal{C}$ means that $\mathcal{B} - \mathcal{C}$ is definite non-negative. Equation (6) provides a physical interpretation: the bigger the information leakage, the more accurate the estimation of the secret parameters. In the sequel, we will see that the trace of $\text{FIM}(\theta)^{-1}$ is proportional to N_o^{-1} if the N_o observations are statistically independent. We define the security level $N_o^\star$ by the slope of the line such that $\text{tr}(\text{FIM}(\theta)^{-1}) = N_o^\star / N_o$. The accuracy of the estimation of θ increases significantly when the number of observations increases of $N_o^\star$.

2.3   Security Levels

We apply in this section the methodology to the three contexts of attack.

Known Original Attack (KOA) The reader might be surprised that this context deserves any attention. Seemingly, there is no need to attack watermarked content when one has the original version. The pirate does not hack these contents, but his goal is to gain information about the secret key, in order, later on, to hack different pieces of content watermarked with the same key.

Only One Carrier: In this case, the opponent has access to $\boldsymbol{x}$ and $\boldsymbol{y} = \boldsymbol{x} + \gamma a(1)\boldsymbol{u}_1$. The game is over with just one observation as a good estimation of the secret carrier is $\widehat{\boldsymbol{u}_1} = (\boldsymbol{y} - \boldsymbol{x})/\|\boldsymbol{y} - \boldsymbol{x}\|$. However, note that it is impossible to disclose $\boldsymbol{u}_1$ up to a sign, as the estimation depends on the sign of $a(1)$.

Several Carriers: In this case, the situation is more complicated because the knowledge of $\boldsymbol{w}$ does not directly give the opponent the carriers. Indeed, he observes several instances of $\boldsymbol{d}_j = \boldsymbol{y}_j - \boldsymbol{x}_j = \gamma \sum_{k=1}^{N_c} a_j(k)\boldsymbol{u}_k/\sqrt{N_c}$. And he is interested in guessing the N_c secret carriers $\boldsymbol{u}_k$. However, note that it is impossible to disclose them up to a sign and a permutation of the order.

Theorem 1. *The security level of WSS watermarking schemes against the Known Original Attack is in the order of N_c pairs $\{(\boldsymbol{x}_j, \boldsymbol{y}_j)\}$. However, this attack reveals the secret carriers up to sign and permutation.*

If the goal of the pirate is to remove the watermark signal, then, he has to render whatever watermarked vector $\boldsymbol{y}$ orthogonal to all estimated $\{\hat{\boldsymbol{u}}_k\}$. If his goal is to decode or encode without authorization, he has not enough information. The ambiguity about the sign and order prevents him to decode the hidden symbols. Yet, he notes whether hidden symbols change from a watermarked content to another. Moreover, the accidental knowledge of hidden symbols in few watermarked pieces of content may fix this ambiguity.

Known Message Attack (KMA) In this subsection, the opponent has access to (watermarked signals/hidden messages) pairs: $\{\boldsymbol{y}_j, \boldsymbol{a}_j\}_{j=1}^{N_o}$. For simplicity reason, we assume that each occurrence of random vector $\boldsymbol{X}$ is independently drawn from $\mathcal{N}(\boldsymbol{0}, \sigma_X^2 \mathcal{I}_{N_v})$. The following theoretical derivations can be easily adapted to colored original signals.

The Fisher Information Matrix is, here, equal to

$$\text{FIM} = \frac{\gamma^2}{N_c \sigma_x^2} \mathcal{A}\mathcal{A}^T \otimes \mathcal{I}_{N_v} \overset{N_o \to +\infty}{\longrightarrow} N_o \frac{\gamma^2 \sigma_a^2}{N_c \sigma_x^2} \mathcal{I}_{N_v N_c}, \tag{7}$$

where $\otimes$ denotes the Kronecker product and $\mathcal{I}_N$ the identity matrix of size N. The information leakage is linear with the number of observations, and the slope is given by the watermark to original power ratio per carrier $\gamma^2 \sigma_a^2 / N_c \sigma_x^2$.

Theorem 2. *The security level of WSS watermarking schemes against the Known Message Attack is $N_o^\star = N_c \sigma_x^2 / \gamma^2 \sigma_a^2$ of $\{(\boldsymbol{y}_j, \boldsymbol{a}_j)\}_j$ pairs.*

Watermarked Only Attack (WOA) In this subsection, messages are unknown so that they must be regarded as nuisance parameters. It is well-known that these nuisance parameters usually render estimation less accurate. Moreover, constraints must be added to the estimation problem to remove unidentifiability and singularity of the Fisher Information Matrix. The main rationale of this presentation was used in [18] to give an alternative expression for the bound in the case where the unconstrained problem is unidentifiable. We add $N_c(N_c - 1)/2$ constraints: the estimated carriers must be orthonormal.

The Fisher Information Matrix is then equal to

$$\text{FIM} = \frac{N_o \sigma_a^2 \gamma^2}{N_c \sigma_x^2} (\mathcal{U}^\perp \mathcal{U}^{\perp T})^{-1}, \tag{8}$$

where $\mathcal{U}^\perp$ is a basis of the complementary space of $\text{Span}(\mathcal{U})$. The information leakage is linear with the number of observations, and the slope is given by the watermark to original power ratio per carrier $\gamma^2 \sigma_a^2 / N_c \sigma_x^2$.

Theorem 3. *The security level of WSS watermarking schemes against the Watermarked Only Attack is in $N_o^\star = N_c \sigma_x^2 / \gamma^2 \sigma_a^2$ watermarked vectors $\{\boldsymbol{y}_j\}$. However, the secret carriers are revealed up to sign and permutation.*

3   Practical Tools

The main tools come from Blind Source Separation like Principal Component Analysis and Independent Component Analysis. Their principles will be recalled when needed, through the analysis of the three cases KOA, KMA and WOA.

3.1   Known Original Attack (KOA)

Actually, this case is related to the well known problem of signal processing called Blind Source Separation (BSS) with no noise. A lot of papers have already been written on BSS, and we will just recall here its goals and well-known algorithms. The main idea of BSS is that several source signals are linearly mixed, and that only the mixed signals are available. The goals are the reconstruction of the source signals and the identification of the mixing matrix.

For each observation j, the source signal $\boldsymbol{a}_j$ is linearly mixed by matrix $\mathcal{U}$:

$$d_j = \frac{\gamma}{\sqrt{N_c}} \, \mathcal{U} \boldsymbol{a}_j \,. \tag{9}$$

This system is not unique as for whatever $N_c \times N_c$ invertible matrix $\mathcal{P}$, we have $\boldsymbol{d}_j = \gamma \widetilde{\mathcal{U}} \widetilde{\boldsymbol{a}}_j / \sqrt{N_c}$ with $\widetilde{\mathcal{U}} = \mathcal{U}\mathcal{P}$ and $\widetilde{\boldsymbol{a}}_j = \mathcal{P}^{-1}\boldsymbol{a}_j$. However, the mixing matrix is composed of orthonormal vectors: $\mathcal{U}^T\mathcal{U} = \mathcal{I}_{N_c}$. Thus, the system is now be determined, up to a unitary matrix $\mathcal{P}$ (i.e. a rotation).

To show how the accumulation of observations reveals the carriers, denote $\mathcal{D} = (\boldsymbol{d}_1 \ldots \boldsymbol{d}_{N_o})$. A Gram-Schmidt orthogonalization of vectors $\{\boldsymbol{d}_j\}_{j=1}^{N_o}$ yields ρ orthonormal vectors lying in Span($\mathcal{U}$) (this can also be done through a SVD of $\mathcal{D}\mathcal{D}^T$, as PCA does - see Sect. 3.3), with $\rho \stackrel{\Delta}{=}$ Rank $(\mathcal{A})$. Hence, the decomposition outputs a basis of Span($\mathcal{U}$) if the opponent has observed N_c pairs with linearly independent symbols $\{\boldsymbol{a}_j\}_{j=1}^{N_c}$.

Once a basis of Span($\mathcal{U}$) found, the opponent can focus the attack's noise in this subspace to far more efficiently jam the communication, or to nullify the watermarked signals projection in this subspace to remove the watermark. Yet, the vectors of this basis are not necessarily collinear with the private carriers. This is due to the rotation matrix $\mathcal{P}$ ambiguity mentioned above. The opponent cannot decode as projection of watermarked signals onto his basis gives a mixture of the hidden symbols as illustrated in Fig. 1. The same reason prevents him transmitting information in the hidden channel.

Nevertheless, under the assumption that the symbol vectors are *statistically* independent, the opponent can resort to a more powerful tool: the Independent Component Analysis (ICA). It is an extension of PCA that 'rotates' the basis until the estimated symbols are independent. This happens when the estimated carriers are collinear with the secret carriers, as illustrated in Fig. 1. For the opponent, ICA reduces the ambiguity from the set of rotation matrices $\mathcal{P}$ to the one of permutations with possible changes of sign matrices. In practice, an ICA

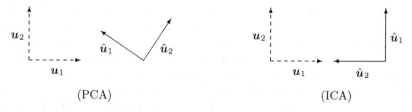

(PCA)   (ICA)

Fig. 1. PCA *v.s.* ICA. PCA finds the secret carriers up to a rotation, whereas ICA succeeds to align the estimated carriers $\{\hat{\boldsymbol{u}}_k\}_{k=1}^{\hat{N}_c}$ with $\{\boldsymbol{u}_l\}_{k=1}^{N_c}$ (Here, $N_c = \hat{N}_c = 2$). An ambiguity remains about their order (permutation) and their orientation (sign)

algorithm needs $N_o > N_c$ observations to converge. A good tutorial on ICA is [19], and a welcome reference on the links between BSS and ICA is [20].

3.2 Known Message Attack (KMA)

The Maximum Likelihood Estimator (MLE) has been chosen because it converges to the Cramér-Rao bound. The log-likelihood is the logarithm of the probability of observing the data $\{y_j\}_1^{N_o}$ knowing the model:

$$\log L(\mathcal{Y}) = cst - \frac{1}{2\sigma_x^2} \sum_{j=1}^{N_o} \|y_j - \frac{\gamma}{\sqrt{N_c}} \mathcal{U}a_j)\|^2. \qquad (10)$$

The MLE can be defined by $\frac{\partial \log L}{\partial u_j} = \mathbf{0}$ for all $j \in \{1, \ldots, N_c\}$ giving $\widehat{\mathcal{U}} = \gamma^{-1} \mathcal{Y} \mathcal{A} (\mathcal{A}\mathcal{A}^T)^{-1}$. The complexity of this estimator is quite small. Assuming that $N_c \ll N_o < N_v$, a rough approximation gives an order of $O(N_v N_o{}^2 N_c)$ for the matrix multiplications, plus $O(N_c{}^3)$ for the inversion of $\mathcal{A}\mathcal{A}^T$.

3.3 Watermark Only Attack (WOA)

This case is similar to BSS with noise which is really harder than the previous ones. The covariance matrix of the observed signals is the following:

$$\mathcal{R}_y = \mathcal{R}_x + \frac{\gamma^2}{N_c} \mathcal{U} E\{\mathcal{A}\mathcal{A}^T\} \mathcal{U}^T = \sigma_X^2 \mathcal{I}_{N_v} + \frac{\sigma_a^2 \gamma^2}{N_c} \mathcal{U}\mathcal{U}^T. \qquad (11)$$

The PCA algorithm first estimates $\mathcal{R}_y$ by $\mathcal{Y}\mathcal{Y}^T$, and performs its SVD decomposition. A (noisy) estimation of a basis of $\text{Span}(\mathcal{U})$ is given by the eigenvectors of $\mathcal{R}_y$ related to the N_c biggest eigenvalues. Then, ICA rotates this basis until the decoded symbols look-like statistically independent.

From a complexity point of view, the bottleneck is the SVD of the covariance matrix whose size is $N_v \times N_v$. In practical cases, schemes spread the watermark on very long extracted signals. This prevents the feasibility of the attack, as is.

A first idea, to make the attack work, is to split the extracted vectors in order to process smaller vectors of size $N_v' = N_v/p$. Yet, the problem then is to put them back together because the ambiguity about the sign and the order completely messes the pieces. The idea shall be given up.

We design an hybrid strategy, mixing this idea of splitting with the MLE algorithm used in the KMA case. The principle of the attack is resumed in Fig. 2. When the ICA algorithm process one block, it outputs N_c estimated carrier blocks and the estimated symbols. Taking N_v' as the biggest size the ICA algorithm can manage (this depends on the available computing power), one has a chance to receive reliable hidden symbols. The pirate can now switch to the KMA context to estimate the whole carriers at a low complexity. Thanks to the Kerkhoff's principle, the decoding process is public. The pirate estimates again the symbols with the estimated carriers. It is likely that this produces a better result than the ICA on small vectors. The iteration of the two last operations is

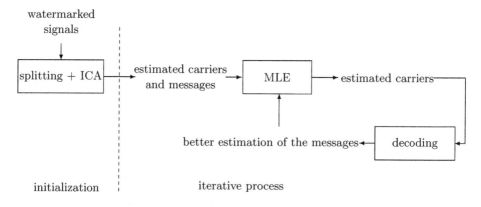

Fig. 2. Final attack for the WOA case

indeed the transcription to our case of the Expectation Maximization algorithm invented by Dempster *et al* [21]. Let us summarize the algorithm:

- **Initialization: ICA algorithm.** Split the extracted vectors by chunks of size N_v', so that the ICA algorithm works on pieces. It estimates not only pieces of carriers but also hidden symbols $\hat{\mathcal{A}}(0)$.
- **Iteration: EM algorithm.**
  - Maximization step. From the estimated symbols $\hat{\mathcal{A}}(k)$, the MLE algorithm estimates the carriers: $\hat{\mathcal{U}}(k) = \text{MLE}(\mathcal{Y}, \hat{\mathcal{A}}(k))$.
  - Expectation step. The decoding algorithm gives a new estimation of the hidden symbols: $\hat{\mathcal{A}}(k+1) = \text{Decoder}(\mathcal{Y}, \hat{\mathcal{U}}(k))$.

4   Experimental Works

This section shows experiments about the estimation of the secret carriers with KMA and WOA, and the exploitation of this knowledge to forge pirated images.

4.1   Robust Watermarking

We have chosen a robust watermarking technique [12] embedding $N_c = 8$ bits in still images of size 512×512. It spreads the watermark signal on $N_v = 205008$ coefficients in the wavelet domain. Wavelet coefficients are modeled as independent random variables having their own distribution $\mathcal{N}(0, \sigma_{X_i}^2)$. The watermark amplitude factor is proportional to this variance: $\gamma_j(i) = G_j \sigma_{X_{i,j}}$. G_j is set for each image in order to fulfill a distortion constraint expressed by PSNR in dB (set to 38 dB in the experiments).

4.2   Adaptation to Real Images

We need to adapt the estimators that are based on the too simple model of Sect. 2.1. Note that normalized coefficient $y_j'(i) = y_j(i)/\sigma_{X_{i,j}}$ is distributed as

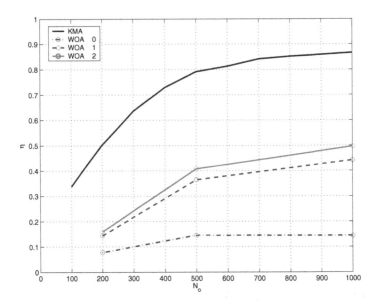

Fig. 3. Mean normalized correlation η between the estimated carriers and the secret ones as the number of observations increases. With circles, correlations with $\hat{\mathcal{U}}(0), \hat{\mathcal{U}}(1)$, and $\hat{\mathcal{U}}(2)$ (see EM algorithm in Sect. 3.3). The WOA EM-algorithm is initialized with the FastICA algorithm [22] on $N_v' = 2048$

$\mathcal{N}(G_j w_j(i), 1)$. The rewriting of the likelihood of $\mathcal{Y}'$ shows that $\boldsymbol{y}_j$ must be weighted by $G_j/1 + G_j^2$. The opponent does not know G_j, but he estimates it with the variances $\hat{\sigma}_{X_{i,j}}$. Algorithms are run with these weighted vectors.

4.3 Secret Carriers Estimation

We think that it is more natural for watermarkers to measure the efficiency of the attack by a normalized correlation of estimations with the secret carriers, rather than by a mean square error power (as the Cramér-Rao theorem would recommend). Hence, the criteria is defined as $\eta = \text{tr}\ (\mathcal{U}^T \hat{\mathcal{U}})/N_c$. For this purpose, the estimated carriers are normalized. Moreover, the sign and order ambiguity is automatically removed before measuring the efficiency (we know the secret carriers during the simulations but, of course, a pirate can not do this in real life). Fig. 3 shows the experimental results.

4.4 Hacking Content

Fifty other 512×512 images were watermarked. Two opponents try to pirate them. They succeed if the decoded message is not equal to the hidden one (even if just one bit is different). Pirate A uses a blind attack (i.e. pertaining to *robustness*). He scales the size of the images by $1/4$, compresses with JPEG at quality factor Q, and he scales them back to the original size. Pirate B uses the

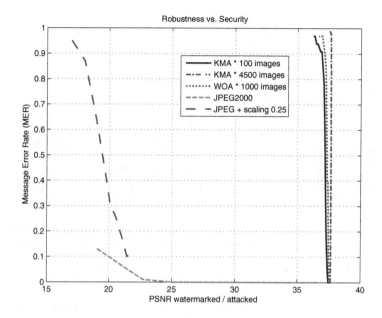

Fig. 4. MER against the attack distortion - PSNR in dB

following hack (i.e. pertaining to *security*). He has estimated the private carriers (KMA or WOA contexts). For each image, he estimates the hidden message and he tries to flip one bit. The first step is to find the carrier leading to the lowest correlation in absolute value:

$$k^\star = \arg\min_{1 \leq k \leq N_c} |\hat{\boldsymbol{u}}_k^T \boldsymbol{y}| . \tag{12}$$

This maximizes the chance of flipping the corresponding bit at the lowest distortion. The second step is the alteration of the corresponding bit. The attacked vector $\boldsymbol{z}$ is formed as follows:

$$z(i) = y(i) - G_{hack}.\sigma_{X_i}.\text{sign}(\hat{\boldsymbol{u}}_{k^\star}^T \boldsymbol{y}).\hat{u}_{k^\star}(i) \quad \forall i \in \{1 \dots N_v\}, \tag{13}$$

and the inversion extraction function concludes the hack.

Three contexts have been tested: KMA with $N_o = 100$ image/message pairs ($\eta \sim 0.3$), WOA with $N_o = 1000$ images ($\eta \sim 0.5$), and KMA with $N_o = 4500$ image/message pairs ($\eta \sim 0.9$). To compare the two strategies, we measure the probability of success (i.e. the Message Error Rate - MER) against the attack distortion between original and pirated content. For this purpose, pirate A decreases quality factor Q of the JPEG compression and pirate B increases parameter G_{hack}. Figure 4 clearly shows the power of smart attacks. They need a far smaller distortion budget than the blind attack (a difference of 15 dB!). In our experiment, pirate A's images are so damaged that any exploitation is impossible, as illustrated by Fig. 5. Indeed,

(a) Pirate A. Best quality for a successful attack: PSNR=21.8 dB.

(b) Pirate B. Best quality for a successful hack: PSNR=35.8 dB.

Fig. 5. Comparison between the two pirated Lena images

we selected in purpose such a robust technique to better illustrate the danger of information leakages. Moreover, the slope of the MER/distortion characteristics of smart attacks is very high. It means that pirate B can really trust in his attack, whereas pirate A is never sure he succeeded until the decoding process happens.

5   Conclusion

This article is an illustration of the recent theory about watermark security. Practical tools from the BSS community help us creating estimators for the KOA, KMA and WOA contexts. However, a double adaptation was necessary. First, real images require a more complex statistical model than the one used in BSS and in the theoretical study of the security levels. Secondly, an ICA algorithm cannot be used as is because it is too complex for such long signals. This is the reason why we develop an EM-like algorithm. However, ICA, working on small pieces of extracted vectors, is necessary to initialize the process. Figure 4 is key fact of the paper. It shows that a robust WSS watermarking technique might be secure iff the embedder changes the secret key for each image. As soon as one secret key is used to watermark several images, there exist information leakages imperilling the security of the watermarking primitive.

References

1. Petitcolas, F., Steinebach, M., Raynal, F., Dittmann, J., Fontaine, C., Fates, N.: Public automated web-based evaluation service for watermarking schemes: Stirmark benchmark. In: IS&T/SPIE International Symposium on Electronic Imaging 2001. Volume 4314. (2001) 575–584 Security and Watermarking of Multimedia Contents III.

2. Kalker, T.: Considerations on watermarking seccurity. In: Proc of the IEEE Multimedia Signal Processing workshop, Cannes, France (2001) 201–206
3. Diffie, W., Hellman, M.: New directions in cryptography. IEEE Trans. on information theory **22** (1976) 644–54
4. Shannon, C.: Communication theory of secrecy systems. Bell system technical journal **28** (1949) 656–715
5. Moulin, P.: The role of information theory in watermarking and its application to image watermarking. Signal Processing **81** (2001) 1121–1139
6. Cox, I., Miller, M., Bloom, J.: Principles and Practice. Morgan Kaufmann Publisher (2001)
7. Cayre, F., Fontaine, C., Furon, T.: Watermarking security: Theory and Practice (2004) accepted to IEEE transactions of Signal Processing.
8. González-Serrano, F., Murillo-Fuentes, J.: Independent component analysis applied to image watermarking. In: ICASSP'01. (2001)
9. Bounkong, S., Toch, B., Saad, D., Lowe, D.: ICA for watermarking digital images. Journal of Machine Learning Research **1** (2002) 1–25
10. Du, J., Lee, C.H., Lee, H.K., Suh, Y.: Watermark attack based on blind estimation without priors. In: IWDW 2002. Lecture Notes in Computer Science, Springer-Verlag (2002)
11. Doërr, G., Dugelay, J.L.: Danger of low-dimensional watermarking subspaces. In: Proc. ICASSP. Volume 3., Montrea, Canada, IEEE (2004)
12. Pateux, S., Guelvouit, G.L.: Practical watermarking scheme based on wide spread spectrum and game theory. Signal Processing: Image Communication **18** (2003) 283–296
13. J.Eggers, Baüml, R., Tzschoppe, R., B.Girod: Scalar costa scheme for information embedding. IEEE Trans. on Signal Processing **51** (2003) 1003–1019
14. Chen, B., Wornell, G.: Quantization index modulation: A class of provably good methods for digital watermarking and information embedding. IEEE Trans. on Information Theory **47** (2001) 1423–1443
15. Barni, M., Bartolini, F., Furon, T.: A general framework for robust watermarking security. Signal Processing **83** (2003) 2069–2084 Special issue on Security of Data Hiding Technologies, invited paper.
16. Furon, T., Duhamel, P.: An asymmetric watermarking method. IEEE Trans. on Signal Processing **51** (2003) 981–995 special issue on signal processing for data hiding in digital media & secure content delivery.
17. Kerckhoffs, A.: La cryptographie militaire. Journal des sciences militaires **9** (1883) 5–38
18. Stoica, P., Ng, B.: On the cramer-rao bound under parametric constraints. IEEE Signal Processing Letters **5** (1998) 177–179
19. Hyvärinen, A., Oja, E.: Independent component analysis: a tutorial. Neural Networks **13** (2000) 411–430
20. Douglas, S.: Blind source separation and independent component analysis: a crossroad of tools and ideas. In: Proceedings of Fourth International Symposium on Independent Component Analysis and Blind Signal Separation, ICA2003. (2003)
21. Dempster, A., Laird, N., Rubin, D.: Maximum likelihood from incomplete data via the em algorithm. J. Roy. Stat. Soc. (1977) 1–38
22. Hyvärinen, A.: Fast and robust fixed-point algorithms for independent component analysis. IEEE Transactions on Neural Networks **10** (1999) 626–634

Flaws in Generic Watermarking Protocols Based on Zero-Knowledge Proofs

Raphael C.-W. Phan[1] and Huo-Chong Ling[2]

[1] Information Security Research (iSECURES) Lab,
Swinburne University of Technology (Sarawak Campus), 93576 Kuching, Malaysia
rphan@swinburne.edu.my
[2] Center for Cryptography & Information Security (CCIS),
Faculty of Engineering, Multimedia University, 63100 Cyberjaya, Malaysia
hcling@mmu.edu.my

Abstract. Recently, two generic watermarking protocols were proposed, based on a popular zero-knowledge identification protocol. In this paper, we show that both protocols are flawed and therefore fail to achieve their purpose of allowing a prover to prove to a verifier of his ownership of a watermarked image. We also give some suggestions to fix these flaws.

Keyword: Watermark detection protocol, generic, zero knowledge proof, identification, flaws.

1   Introduction

Most information, documents and contents these days are stored and processed within a computer in digital form. However, since the duplication of digital content results in perfectly identical copies, the copyright protection issue is a main problem that needs to be addressed. *Digital watermarking* [14, 6, 17, 19, 3] is a technique used to solve this problem by imperceptibly embedding an *owner-specific* watermark, which upon extraction enables provable ownership.

Recently, two very similar watermarking protocols were proposed [15, 16], the latest being presented at the IWDW 2003 [16]. Their aim was to develop a generic watermark detection protocol that is independent of the underlying watermark embedding and detection scheme.

Nevertheless, in this paper, we present several flaws in these two protocols that undermine their security and hence show they do not guarantee that the content owner's copyright is protected.

In section 2, we briefly review the variant of the zero-knowledge identification protocols used by the two generic watermarking protocols proposed in [15, 16]. We then review these two protocols in Section 3. In Section 4, we present the flaws in the two protocols and further suggest how to fix them. We conclude in Section 5.

I.J. Cox et al. (Eds.): IWDW 2004, LNCS 3304, pp. 184–191, 2005.

2   The Feige-Fiat-Shamir Zero Knowledge Identification Protocol

The best-known identification protocol based on zero-knowledge proofs was due to Feige, Fiat and Shamir [4, 5]. Zero-knowledge proofs allow a prover, P to prove to a verifier, V that he knows a secret, without letting V know what that secret is. The reader is referred to [11] for a more candid description of this interesting concept.

There are several versions of the Feige-Fiat-Shamir zero-knowledge identification protocol. Here, we shall describe the version used by Then and Wang [15, 16] in their generic watermark detection protocols. We refer the reader to [4, 5] for detailed descriptions of all Feige-Fiat-Shamir versions.

Initialization Phase

1. A trusted third party, T chooses a large modulus, n as the product of two secret primes, p and q, and a pseudorandom function, $f(.)$. Then, n and f are made public.
2. T further chooses k distinct numbers, v_i for $i = 1 \ldots k$ such that $x^2 = v_i$ mod n has a solution and v^{-1} mod n exists. This string, $(v_1, v_2, \ldots, v_k)$ is the *public key* of P.
3. T then calculates the smallest s_i such that $s_i = \sqrt{v_i^{-1}}$ mod n. This string, $(s_1, s_2, \ldots, s_k)$ is the *private key* of P.

Identification Phase

1. P picks a random number, $r < n$ and computes $x = r^2$ mod n and sends x to V.
2. V sends P a random binary string of k bits: $b_1, \ldots, b_k$.
3. P computes $y = r \times s_1^{b_1} \times s_2^{b_2} \times \cdots \times s_k^{b_k}$ mod n, and sends y to V.
4. V verifies that $x = y^2 \times v_1^{b_1} \times v_2^{b_2} \times \cdots \times v_k^{b_k}$ mod n.

P and V repeat this several times until V is convinced that P knows $(s_1, s_2, \ldots s_k)$. Since only P is supposed to know these values, then V assumes that it is really P.

3   Two Generic Watermarking Protocols

In this section, we briefly review the two recently proposed generic watermarking protocols [15, 16], which are very similar to each other, except that one [15] requires a trusted third party while the other [16] does not. Both consist of two phases, namely the *initialization phase* in which they differ, and the *watermark detection phase* in which they are identical. Note that though not explicitly stated in [15, 16], the initialization phase actually includes the watermark embedding process.

3.1   Generic Protocol with Trusted Third Party

We first describe the generic protocol *with* trusted third party presented in [15], as follows:

Initialization Phase

1. A trusted third party, T chooses a large modulus, n as the product of two secret primes, p and q, and a pseudorandom function, $f(.)$. Then, n and f are made public.
2. T further computes several values of $v_i = f(com(WM)^{A(I_w, par)}, i)$ for small values of i where WM is the watermark, $com(WM)$ is the commitment on WM, $A(.)$ is the watermark detection scheme, I_w is the watermarked image and par represents the parameters for $A(.)$.
3. T then chooses k distinct values of v_i such that v_i is a modulus of n, and calculates the smallest s_i such that $s_i = \sqrt{v_i^{-1}} \bmod n$. The strings $(v_1, v_2, \ldots, v_k)$ and $(s_1, s_2, \ldots, s_k)$ are respectively the public and private keys of P. The values of $(s_1, s_2, \ldots, s_k)$ are published to P.

Watermark Detection Phase

1. P sends $com(WM)$ and $A(I_w, par)$ to V.
2. V generates $v_i = f(com(WM)^{A(I_w, par)}, i)$ for $i = 1 \ldots k$.
3. P picks a random number, $r < n$ and computes $x = r^2 \bmod n$ and sends x to V.
4. V sends P a random binary string of k bits: $b_1, \ldots, b_k$.
5. P computes $y = r \times s_1^{b_1} \times s_2^{b_2} \times \cdots \times s_k^{b_k} \bmod n$, and sends y to V.
6. V verifies that $x = y^2 \times v_1^{b_1} \times v_2^{b_2} \times \cdots \times v_k^{b_k} \bmod n$.

Again, P and V repeat this several times until V is convinced that P knows $(s_1, s_2, \ldots s_k)$. Since only P is supposed to know these values, then V assumes that it is really P.

3.2   Generic Protocol Without Trusted Third Party

We next describe the generic protocol *without* any trusted third party presented in [16]. Since only the initialization phase is different from that in Section 3.1, while the watermark detection phase is identical, it suffices only to describe the initialization phase, as follows:

Initialization Phase

1. The prover, P chooses a large modulus, n as the product of two secret primes, p and q, and a pseudorandom function, $f(.)$. Then, n and f values are published to V.
2. P further computes several values of $v_i = f(com(WM)^{A(I_w, par)}, i)$ for small values of i where $com(WM)$, $A(.)$, I_w and par are as in Section 3.1.

3. P then chooses k distinct values of v_i such that v_i is a modulus of n, and calculates the smallest s_i such that $s_i = \sqrt{v_i^{-1}}$. The strings, $(v_1, v_2, \ldots, v_k)$ and $(s_1, s_2, \ldots, s_k)$ are respectively the public and private keys of P. Publish $(v_1, v_2, \ldots, v_k)$ to V.

3.3   Comparing Between the Two Protocols

We briefly compare in Table 1 between the two protocols proposed in [15, 16], highlighting their differences.

Table 1. Comparison Between the Two Generic Protocols

[15]	[16]
P registers its watermark, WM with the trusted third party	No trusted third party
The trusted third party binds the watermark to the watermarked image by computing v_i as a function of both and binds this to P's private key, s_i	P himself binds the watermark to the watermarked image by computing v_i as a function of both and binds this to his private key, s_i
s_i is computed by the trusted third party and sent to P	s_i is computed by P himself
n is chosen by the trusted third party so only it knows the factorization of n	n is chosen by P so it knows the factorization of n

4   Flaws in the Protocols, and Some Fixes

In this section, we point out some serious flaws in the two generic watermarking protocols in [15, 16], and then suggest how the flaws could be fixed.

4.1   Flaws in Both Protocols

We first give in this subsection some flaws in *both* protocols.

No Proof of Watermark Existence. Step 2 of the watermark detection phase only proves to V that v_i is a function of $com(WM)$ and the watermarked image, I_w, but this does not prove that P's watermark has really been embedded into the image. Further, V does not compute any watermark detection procedure, $A(I_w, par)$, but is merely computing the f function by using the values $com(WM)$ and $A(I_w, par)$ that it received from P in Step 1 of the watermark detection phase. In fact, V would not be able to compute $A(I_w, par)$ even if it were asked to, since I_w is not sent to V, without which one would not be able to compute $A(.)$ at all.

No Revelation of Commitment. Yet another flaw in the two generic protocols is that the commitment, $com(WM)$, which is supposed to be P's commitment that its watermark is really contained within it, is not even proven to V that it really does contain WM. Therefore, V cannot be convinced that $com(WM)$ really contains P's watermark, WM.

Further, even if it can be proven that $com(WM)$ really does contain WM, P does not prove to V that this watermark is really the same as the one that has been embedded in the watermarked image, I_w. In contrast, note that in their usage of the commitment to prove content ownership, Adelsbach and Sadeghi [1]'s protocol did consider how V can be convinced that the commitment contains the same watermark that has been embedded into the image.

No Binding Between Knowledge and Ownership. Since the two generic protocols are very similar to the Feige-Fiat-Shamir zero-knowledge identification protocol, they inherit the same problem as the Feige-Fiat-Shamir [13]. The problem is that in the Feige-Fiat-Shamir protocol, P does not really prove its identity but is proving that it knows a piece of secret information. It is then assumed that since P knows this secret, it must be P himself. One could abuse this link between the knowledge of the secret and the real identity, especially in the case when P willingly or intentionally discloses this secret to others such that V thinks others are P. This is discussed in more detail in [13].

In the same way in the context of the two generic watermark detection protocols, the prover, P is not really proving that it owns the watermarked image, but is instead proving that it knows some secret information, and by this knowledge, it is assumed that P must be the owner of the image. Though it appears that the attacks that abuse this assumption [13] do not apply to the watermark detection context, they apply to the fingerprinting context used to trace illegal copies of watermarked contents [18, 20, 9, 10, 8].

4.2   Further Flaws in the Protocol Proposed at IWDW '03

We give further flaws in one of the two generic watermarking protocols, in particular the one that does not involve any trusted third party and that was proposed at IWDW '03 [16].

Keys Not Binding on the Prover. Note that all the v_i for $i = 1 \ldots k$ are provided by P himself, with no involvement nor certification from any trusted third party. Further, the value of the modulus, n is also chosen by P. Obviously it would then be very easy for P to prove to V that it knows the private values, s_i corresponding to all the v_i. In this case, the protocol fails to authenticate the real identity or ownership of P since the values v_i could well be chosen or generated by anyone not necessarily P.

In contrast, all versions of the Feige-Fiat-Shamir protocol [4, 5] as well as Adelsbach-Sadeghi [1] require a trusted third party, T to assure V that the secret values s_i are really bound to the identity of P. Therefore, T's presence is necessary and is the binding factor that guarantees to V regarding the authenticity of P's identity (or ownership in the case of watermarking protocols). More discussion of this in our concluding remarks.

Contradictions. The description of the generic protocol in IWDW '03 [16] has some self-contradicting remarks. In Section 4 of the protocol description, it is mentioned that P computes the modulus, n and chooses the function, f. Nevertheless, in Section 5.3, it is mentioned that n and f must be computed by V. This is a direct contradiction!

Further, the description in Section 5.3 is very misleading where it is mentioned that P computes $\sqrt{(v_i)}$ with the help of V who knows this, and that P should not know the factorization of n. Both P and V know v_i, but only P can compute $\sqrt{(v_i)}$ since only P knows the factorization of n.

4.3   Fixing the Flaws

We now give some suggestions to fix the flaws presented in the previous subsection. First, we remark that the flaws have to do with some erroneous or contradictory steps, or necessary steps missing from the protocol specifications, for example how it can be proven to V that the watermark in the commitment is indeed the watermarked embedded in the image, etc. Therefore, some obvious fixes can be identified by going through the previous subsections 4.1 and 4.2, and including the missing steps or correcting the flawed steps in the protocols. We leave this to the designers of [15, 16] and to the reader as a straightforward exercise.

Second, we suggest that one should first try to directly turn existing watermarking protocols (such as that presented in [1]) into generic ones, rather than designing a generic one from scratch or converting protocols used for other purposes such as the Feige-Fiat-Shamir protocol. Alternatively, if one really desires to customize the Feige-Fiat-Shamir protocol for the watermarking context, then at least develop a non-generic one first before converting that to a generic version.

Our point is that though we do agree that generic watermarking protocols are nice to have, the authors of [15, 16] in attempting to present a truly generic protocol, have left some necessary steps missing and unanswered − as described in Section 4.1 − resulting in incomplete protocols.

As an aside, to improve on the efficiency of the generic protocols, we suggest that all flaws notwithstanding, v_i should be computed as a simple hash of the $com(WM)$ and $A(I_w, par)$ values since one really just wants v_i to be an irreversible (one-way) function of these two values. This will eliminate the need to compute any exponentiations which are slow and resource-intensive.

5   Concluding Remarks

We have compared between the two generic watermark detection protocols [15, 16] and highlighted serious flaws, especially for the version presented at IWDW

'03 [16]. We also remark that the schemes in [15, 16] are merely straightforward adaptations of the Feige-Fiat-Shamir zero-knowledge identification protocol by having the prover's public and private keys be functions of the watermark and the watermarked image, and therefore do not contain much novelty.

Our work suggests that more caution should be exercised when proposing generic protocols, and that though one desires to generalize as much as possible, some steps are still necessary and should not be overlooked. We also hope that our work would trigger off further analysis of the two generic protocols and that the flaws be fixed immediately.

It also appears that the protocol version proposed in [15] that requires a trusted third party, when compared to the version without any trusted third party [16], is more secure against attacks and provides authentication since all the important parameters of the protocols, such as n, $com(WM)$ or $A(I_w, par)$, are chosen or computed by the trusted third party. In this case, V is at least assured of the authenticity of these values. On this note, Then and Wang [16] have misunderstood the basic principle of watermark-based proofs of ownership: that a trusted third party (who is the registration center) *must* be involved in the watermark embedding stage because otherwise any party could simply embed their own watermarks into an image as they like and claim it to be theirs. To suggest otherwise as was done in [16] is preposterous, and the scheme should henceforth be withdrawn.

An interesting problem is how to adapt the Feige-Fiat-Shamir zero-knowledge identification protocols to the context of fingerprinting, in which the watermark of a content buyer is embedded into the content in order to trace illegal distributions. As we discussed in Section 4.1, the problem inherited from the Feige-Fiat-Shamir protocols would cause attacks if these protocols are adapted for fingerprinting.

Acknowledgement

We thank the anonymous referees of IEEE Transactions on Image Processing, IEEE Signal Processing Letters, and IWDW '04 for their numerous comments and suggestions which have helped to improve this paper considerably. We also thank God for His many blessings (Ps. 122).

References

1. A. Adelsbach, A.-R. Sadeghi, *Zero Knowledge Watermark Detection and Proof of Ownership*, Information Hiding (IH '01), LNCS 2137, pp.273-288, 2001.
2. D. Boneh, J. Shaw, *Collusion-Secure Fingerprinting for Digital Data*, Crypto '95, LNCS 963, pp.452-465, 1995.
3. I.J. Cox, M.L. Miller, J.A. Bloom, *Digital Watermarking*, Morgan Kaufmann, 2002.
4. U. Feige, A. Fiat and A. Shamir, *Zero Knowledge Proofs of Identity*, 19th Annual ACM Symposium on the Theory of Computing, pp. 210-217, 1987.
5. U. Feige, A. Fiat and A. Shamir, *Zero Knowledge Proofs of Identity*, Journal of Cryptology, vol. 1, no. 2, pp. 77-94, 1988.

6. F. Hartung, M. Kutter, *Multimedia Watermarking Techniques*, Proc. IEEE, vol. 87, pp. 1079-1107, July 1999.
7. A.J. Menezes, P.C. van Oorschot, S.A. Vanstone, *Handbook of Applied Cryptography*, CRC Press, 1997.
8. B. Pfitzman, A.R. Sadeghi, *Coin-Based Anonymous Fingerprinting*, Eurocrypt '99, LNCS 1592, pp.150-163, 2000.
9. B. Pfitzman, M. Schunter, *Asymmetric Fingerprinting*, Eurocrypt '96, LNCS 1070, 1996, pp. 84-95.
10. B. Pfitzman, W. Waidner, *Anonymous Fingerprinting*, Eurocrypt '97, LNCS 1233, pp. 88-102, 1997.
11. J.-J. Quisquater, L.C. Guillou, T.A. Berson, *How to Explain Zero-Knowledge Protocols to Your Children*, Crypto '89, LNCS 435, pp. 628-631, 1989.
12. R.L. Rivest, A. Shamir, L. Adleman, *A Method for Obtaining Digital Signatures and Public-Key Cryptosystems*, Communications of the ACM, vol. 21, no. 2, pp.120-126, 1978.
13. B. Schneier, *Applied Cryptography: Protocols, Algorithms, and Source Code in C*, John Wiley & Sons, 1996.
14. M. Swanson, M. Kobayashi, A. Tewfik, *Multimedia Data Embedding and Watermarking Technologies*, Proc. IEEE, vol. 86, pp. 1064-1087, June 1998.
15. P.H.H. Then and Y.C. Wang, *Towards Generic Zero Knowledge Protocol for Blind Watermark Detection*, International Conference on IT in Asia (CITA '03), pp. 278-282, 2003.
16. H.H.P. Then and Y.C. Wang, *Towards Generic Detection Scheme in Zero Knowledge Protocol for Blind Watermark Detection*, International Workshop on Digital Watermarking (IWDW '03), LNCS 2939, pp. 570-580, 2003.
17. G. Voyatzis and I. Pitas. *The Use of Watermarks in the Protection of Digital Multimedia Products*. Proc. IEEE, vol. 87, pp. 1197-1207, July 1999.
18. N.R. Wagner, *Fingerprinting*, IEEE Symposium on Security and Privacy, pp.18-22, 1983.
19. R. Wolfang, C. Podilchuk, E. Delp, *Perceptual Watermarks for Digital Images and Video*, Proc. IEEE, vol. 87, pp. 1108-1126, July 1999.
20. J. Zhao, E. Koch, *Embedding Robust Labels Into Images For Copyright Protection*, International Congress on Intellectual Property Rights for Specialized Information, Knowledge and New Technologies, Vienna, 1995.

Cryptanalysis of a Wavelet Based Watermarking Scheme

Tanmoy Kanti Das[1,*], Jianying Zhou[2], and Subhamoy Maitra[1]

[1] Applied Statistics Unit, Indian Statistical Institute,
203, B T Road, Calcutta 700 108, India
{das_t, subho}@isical.ac.in
[2] Infocomm Security Department, Institute for Infocomm Research,
21 Heng Mui Keng Terrace, Singapore 119613
jyzhou@i2r.a-star.edu.sg

Abstract. In this paper we cryptanalyze the wavelet based watermarking scheme by Wang et al, 2002. By cryptanalysis we mean the removal of the watermark using a single watermarked copy which is equivalent to cipher text only jamming attack. The watermark embedding process replaces a particular middle frequency band of the host image (in wavelet domain) with the watermark. In the scheme, the key consists of three secrets: (i) the watermark, (ii) the random filter bank used for wavelet transform and (iii) the wavelet band where the watermark is inserted. First we observe that the secret random filter bank does not provide any security since it can be replaced by any filter bank from a large class. Further, it is possible to discover the secret wavelet band used to watermark the host image. Though in cryptography the random nature of secret key provides the security, in contrary here we show that the random nature of the watermark actually helps in identifying the secret wavelet band and consequently one can remove the watermarking signal from that band to mount the successful cryptanalytic attack.

Keywords: Correlation, Cryptanalysis, Digital Watermarking, Wavelet Transform.

1 Introduction

Over the past years digital media have grown rapidly in terms of popularity. However, with all the obvious advantages of digital media, it comes with some disadvantages, especially in copyright protection. Digital media can be copied with ease without any loss of fidelity as several copy control mechanisms have failed miserably. Content providers wonder whether their contents might be pirated more frequently than ever before. In this scenario, the subject of watermarking has been developed to a large extent to protect the copyright of digital

---

* Some portion of this work has been done while the author was visiting the Institute for Infocomm Research, Singapore during 2003–2004.

I.J. Cox et al. (Eds.): IWDW 2004, LNCS 3304, pp. 192–203, 2005.

media. The aim of digital watermarking is to embed visible or invisible marks into the digital objects for copyright protection. Recently researchers have taken active interest in the design of robust invisible watermarking schemes. Current state of the art watermarking schemes are robust against standard signal processing attacks. Unfortunately, few attempts have been made to analyze each of the popular watermarking schemes and to study customized attacks in highlighting their weaknesses. It should be noted that this kind of analysis is needed before any commercial use of these schemes. Otherwise, pirates may find it easy to break the watermarking scheme, causing considerable financial loss to the media owner. In this paper we concentrate on a specific watermarking scheme described in [17] and present an attack that successfully removes the watermark from the watermarked image.

Let us now briefly introduce some concepts about invisible watermarking schemes for digital images. A digital image I can be seen as a two dimensional matrix. In spatial domain, each cell of the matrix represents pixel value of a particular pixel. Several transform domain representations like Fast Fourier Transform (FFT), Discrete Cosine Transform (DCT), Wavelet Transform, etc. are also possible. If one alters the values in the image matrix by a small amount, visually the image may still remain indistinguishable from the original image I. We define the set of images which are indistinguishable from I as the neighbourhood of image I. Let us denote this set by $N(I)$. Usually digital watermarking schemes add a signal $s^{(i)}$ to the original image I in such a manner that watermarked image $I^w = I + s^{(i)}$ remains in $N(I)$. This image is given to the ith buyer.

It is expected from any robust watermarking scheme that it will be able to identify the malicious buyer properly and never wrongly implicate an honest buyer. Consider that during the watermark extraction process, the image $I^{\#}$ (may be attacked) is at hand and let $s^{\#} = I^{\#} - I$. Correlation between embedded signal $s^{(i)}$ and recovered signal $s^{\#}$ is used as a measure of confidence, i.e., buyer i is suspected if correlation between $s^{\#}$ and $s^{(i)}$ is significant. Thus given a watermarked image I^w, the challenge to the attacker is to construct an image $I^{\#}$ in such a manner that $I^{\#} \in N(I)$ and $s^{\#}$ is uncorrelated with $s^{(i)}$. Then it is not possible to identify the malicious buyer i any more. A robust watermarking scheme should defend such an attack, i.e., a scheme is considered to be secured if an attacker, who has access to the algorithmic principle of the scheme but has no access to the key, should not be able to tamper with the watermark. This model is accepted in the literature as evident from [1, 8, 10].

Most of the recently proposed watermarking schemes survive image processing based attacks [10, 15, 14]. On the other hand, majority of recent watermarking schemes are vulnerable to collusion attack [7]. However, collusion attack requires large number of copies, that may not be available in practice. On the other hand, single copy attack, which is based on only a single watermarked copy, is a very strong candidate in cryptanalysing many watermarking schemes [11, 9, 13]. Replacement attack presented in [11] utilizes presence of redundancy in multimedia content. Analyzing multimedia contents, it may be identified that there are several segments which are almost exact replica of others. One can replace these segments by perceptually similar (but different) segments generated from any combination of those replicas. Thus replacement attack is basically some kind of collusion attack. Our attack is different as we never assume the availability of such redundancy in the content. There is another class of attack [9, 13] which considers a decoder is available in the public domain and the attacker can gain knowledge about the watermark by using the decoder as an oracle. However, we do not consider any such facility available in our model. For more details on different single copy attacks one may refer to [3, 4, 5].

In this paper, we look into the watermarking scheme from the cryptographic point of view and present an attack which is analogous to cipher text only jamming attack. We mount a singe copy attack on a very recent wavelet based watermarking scheme [17], that removes the watermark successfully. In Section 2, we describe the scheme proposed in [17] and the attack is described in Section 3.

2 The Wavelet Based Watermarking Scheme

Before presenting the exact scheme, let us first provide a brief introduction on Wavelet transform. Wavelet transform cuts up data or functions into different frequency components to study each component with resolution matched to its scale. Given a signal $f(t)$, one may be interested in its frequency component locally in time. The standard Fourier transform provides the frequency component of f, but information about time-localization can not be read easily from Fourier transform. Time-localization can be achieved in windowed Fourier transform, where one cuts only a localized slice of f and takes its Fourier transform. Wavelet transform is able to provide time-frequency description better than windowed Fourier transform. Detailed study on Discrete wavelet transform is available in [6].

Most simple wavelet transform uses Haar basis [16]. We first explain, using an example, how an one dimensional image can be decomposed using Haar wavelet basis. Consider the following one dimensional signal $I = [11, 5, 7, 15]$ consisting of four samples. Haar wavelet transform first takes the pairwise averages and then calculates the half of the subtracted values. So, after first level of wavelet transform the coefficients look like $I_{wav}^{L=1} = [\frac{11+5}{2}, \frac{7+15}{2}, \frac{11-5}{2}, \frac{7-15}{2}] = [8, 11, 3, -4]$. First two coefficients are averages and known as low frequency components. Last two coefficients (half of the subtracted values) are known as detail or high frequency coefficients. In the next level of wavelet transform, normally the low frequency coefficients are subjected to further processing. Thus, $I_{wav}^{L=2} = [\frac{8+11}{2}, \frac{8-11}{2}, 3, -4] = [9.5, -1.5, 3, -4]$. As, in this example, there is only one low frequency component, we can not proceed further. Note that, one can also choose the high frequency coefficients at any level for next level of wavelet transform. This recursive computation of wavelet coefficients is based on the filter bank. Form the wavelet coefficients one can get back the original signal by pairwise addition and subtraction. For example, we can get back the coefficients of the previous level by the operation 9.5 ± -1.5.

To extend these ideas to images, we consider an image as a 2D signal and apply wavelet transform separately, first along the rows and then along the columns. In each level of wavelet transform four different bands are generated and they are denoted as LL, HL, LH, HH. One of the four bands is selected for next level of wavelet transform and the structure looks like a tree (see Figure 1). This tree is termed as a decomposition structure in [17]. In Figure 1, one such decomposition structure D_1 is depicted where the watermark is embedded in $LL5$. For our description we also need to use another decomposition structure D_2. This is nothing but the same decomposition structure as D_1 with only the last level removed. Note that the decomposition structure D_1 has been used for experiments in [17].

There are several classes of wavelet filter banks, one such important class of filter bank is "Two-Channel Orthonormal FIR Real coefficient Filter Bank" (TOFRFB) [16, 17]. This class of wavelet filter bank is used for watermark embedding in [17].

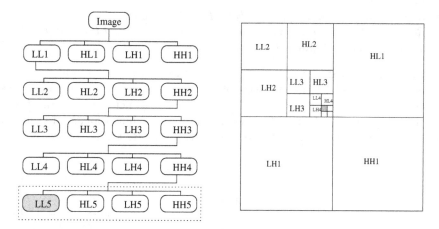

Fig. 1. Decomposition Structure (left) and 2D Wavelet Transform (right)

2.1   Watermark Embedding

Let us present the scheme due to Wang et al [17] in detail. It is well known that lossy compression eliminates the high frequency components of the image. Thus any watermarking information present in the high frequency component of the image gets destroyed easily by lossy compression. So, the authors choose to embed the watermarking information into the middle frequency band. This takes care of two conflicting requirements, robustness against compression and perceptual invisibility of the watermark. Randomly generated orthonormal filter banks are used for wavelet transform and they are also a part of secret key. Information regarding the particular middle frequency band, used to embed the watermark, is also kept secret along with the watermark. Thus there are three major secrets which constitute the private key. The watermark embedding algorithm of [17] is as follows.

Algorithm 1

1. *Determine the number of wavelet decomposition level L depending on the input image size and watermark size. Value of L is fixed in such a manner so that after wavelet transform size of each band at level L is equal to the size of watermark.*
2. *Generate $2L + 2$ sets of orthonormal filter banks F randomly. Filter bank F is part of the secret key and required during watermark extraction.*
3. *Use the analysis filters from F to decompose (forward wavelet transform) the image into I_{wav}.*
4. *Identify the particular middle frequency band R for watermark embedding. It should be one of the four bands at the highest level of decomposition and its size must be the same as that of the watermark.*
5. *Read the binary watermark. Transform it into a real valued one and scramble it (see below for more details about scrambling). Scrambled watermark w_s is multiplied by a suitable factor for energy adjustment to generate the watermark w.*
6. *Replace the pre-selected wavelet band R of I_{wav} by w.*
7. *Reconstruct the watermarked image I_w by inverse wavelet transform of I_{wav} using the synthesis filters from F.*

Scrambling of Watermarks. The watermark is generated from a pattern of values either $+1$ or -1. Let the size of the data (considered as a two dimensional matrix or image) be $n \times n$. The authors construct a vector $\vec{v_0}$ of size $n^2 \times 1$ by interpreting the two dimensional data as one dimensional data set and then compute $\vec{v_1} = R_1 R_2 \vec{v_0}$, where the matrices R_1, R_2 are as follows respectively.

$$\begin{bmatrix} \begin{smallmatrix} \cos\theta_1 & -\sin\theta_1 \\ \sin\theta_1 & \cos\theta_1 \end{smallmatrix} & & \\ & \ddots & \\ & & \begin{smallmatrix} \cos\theta_{n^2-1} & -\sin\theta_{n^2-1} \\ \sin\theta_{n^2-1} & \cos\theta_{n^2-1} \end{smallmatrix} \end{bmatrix}, \begin{bmatrix} 1 & & & \\ & \begin{smallmatrix} \cos\theta_2 & -\sin\theta_2 \\ \sin\theta_2 & \cos\theta_2 \end{smallmatrix} & & \\ & & \ddots & \\ & & \begin{smallmatrix} \cos\theta_{n^2-2} & -\sin\theta_{n^2-2} \\ \sin\theta_{n^2-2} & \cos\theta_{n^2-2} \end{smallmatrix} & \\ & & & 1 \end{bmatrix}$$

One can interpret R_1, R_2 as a series of rotations. The embedded watermark is generally same for each image. To make it different for different host images one can scramble the vector $\vec{v_1}$ to get another vector $\vec{v_2}$ using a permutation $\vec{s}$ of the integers $1, \ldots, n^2$. Now $v_2(i) = v_1(s(i)), (i \in 1..n^2)$. This scrambling process can also be used to insert user specific watermark, i.e., one permutation will correspond to one buyer. An $n \times n$ matrix w_s is generated from the one dimensional data $\vec{v_2}$. We refer to [17] to get the detailed description of how the energy is adjusted to get w from w_s as this has not much implication to the cryptanalysis process.

2.2   Watermark Detection

The watermark detection process is correlation based. If the correlation is greater than some predefined threshold value then one can claim the image under examination is watermarked. Exact watermark retrieval procedure is as follows.

Algorithm 2

1. *Read the key, i.e., information about the filter bank used, decomposition structure and particular middle frequency band R used to embed the watermark.*
2. *Decompose (i.e., forward wavelet transform) the image using the above information.*
3. *Let C_i^w be the coefficients at middle frequency band R.*
4. *Divide C_i^w into four parts and use the last set of analysis filters to get the data w_0.*
5. *Use $\overrightarrow{s}$ to de-scramble w_0 into w_1.*
6. *Normalize the energy of w_1 to get w_2. Interpret w_2 as a single dimensional data $\overrightarrow{v}_1{}'$.*
7. *Calculate the correlation coefficient (r) between $\overrightarrow{v}_1, \overrightarrow{v}_1{}'$.*
8. *If $r > t$, the image is considered to be watermarked using $\overrightarrow{v}_1$, otherwise not. Here t is a predefined threshold and taken to be 0.4 for experimentation in [17–page 83].*

3   Attack on the Scheme

Let us first give a few important observations about the scheme presented in [17]. It is pointed out that the low frequency noise is more visible and high frequency components get removed due to compression, thus it is preferable to introduce the watermark in the middle frequency band. However, there is some problem with this approach. For an attacker, who is looking for the watermark location, the search space is reduced due to this assumption. Though the scheme performs well against normal signal processing attacks, it is not robust against the attacks designed for it. According to the authors [17] robustness of the scheme depends on the following two factors.

1. Knowledge of particular middle frequency band used to embed the watermark.
2. Choice of filter banks to decompose the host image.

In [17], it has been pointed out that even with the knowledge of decomposition structure it is not possible to remove the watermark, unless the exact filter bank is known. However we will show, it is not difficult to find out the secret middle frequency band used to embed the watermark even without the knowledge of exact filter bank used to decompose the image at the time of watermarking. After our attack, the image quality stays reasonably good and the watermark information gets removed.

3.1   Cross Correlation of an Image

The pixels of a natural image are highly correlated. It is important to understand how the correlation between an original image and its shifted version varies with the amount of shift. Let us first describe what do we mean by shift here. A row or column of an image can be interpreted as an array. By shift we mean circular shifting the elements of the array. Given a data set $a_1, a_2, \ldots, a_{n-1}, a_n$, its one element shift can be seen as $a_n, a_1, \ldots, a_{n-2}, a_{n-1}$. Thus if there are n elements in an array, number of possible shifts is $n - 1$ because if we shift by n element it will be the original array. As an image can be described as a collection of rows or as a collection of columns, then by shift we mean circular shifting either all the rows or all the columns.

In case of an image, pixels that are close to each other are very highly correlated. Thus for any image it is expected that correlation falls very slowly with amount of shift. On the other hand, if we consider a matrix whose cells are filled with random numbers, the situation becomes completely different. In that case, correlation should be negligible (close to zero) after a single (or more) shift(s), which is the property of good pseudo random patterns. Let M an original matrix of size $a \times b$ and $M[n_1, n_2]$ denotes its shifted version generated by circular shifting all the rows of M by n_1 elements and then shifting all the columns by n_2 elements. Correlation between M and $M[n_1, n_2]$ will be high when the value of both n_1 and n_2 are less than some small integer value δ or $(a - \delta < n_1 < a)$ and $(b - \delta < n_2 < b)$.

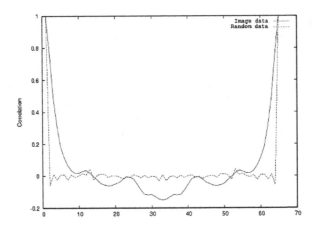

Fig. 2. Image Data (in wavelet domain) vs Random Data (in wavelet domain)

This property of an image also holds good for low or mid frequency wavelet bands. Thus if a wavelet band is replaced by random elements, that band can be easily differentiated from others by studying the cross-correlation. This helps to identify the wavelet band used to watermark the image. If we measure the correlation between wavelet coefficients of a particular band W and $W[n_1, n_2]$, for all possible values of n_1 and n_2, except the band where the watermark is embedded, correlation will follow the pattern that of an image. However, in the case of a band where the random watermark has been embedded, the correlation will follow the pattern that of a random matrix (see Figure 2). Thus one can identify the exact wavelet band used to embed the watermark by exhaustively searching all possible decomposition structures. As pointed out earlier that search space is greatly reduced due to choice of middle frequency band. Hence it is possible to exhaustively search all the available bands to find out the band where the watermark is embedded. Also we would like to point out that unlike cryptography, where randomness provides security, here randomness helps in identification of secret wavelet band used to watermark the image.

3.2   Cryptanalysis: Decomposition Structure Known

Here we like to argue that the secrecy of the filter bank chosen for the watermarking scheme is not of much effect as one can choose a random 'Two-Channel Orthonormal FIR Real coefficient Filter Bank" for the attack.

Let us consider a situation where the exact middle frequency band and the corresponding decomposition structure is known but the filter bank used is unknown. This case has been considered in [17] and it has been demonstrated that the scheme can withstand this type of attack. However, little variation of this attack, can successfully remove the watermark. Instead of replacing one of the wavelet bands at the final level, all four wavelet bands should be replaced to remove the watermark. To this end, an attacker first constructs his own filter banks and decomposes the image according to the known decomposition structure and replaces the coefficients of all the bands at the final level by random values.

As an example, refer to the Figure 1. Let $LL5$ be the middle frequency band used to embed the watermark. Now decompose the image according to decomposition structure D_2 and replace the $HH4$ by the same process as in watermark embedding algorithm. That is the data in $HH4$ is replaced by some random pattern having same energy. The watermark can be destroyed by this strategy as evident from Table 1. The exact algorithm is as follows.

Algorithm 3

1. *Read the watermarked image I^w.*
2. *Read the decomposition structure D.*
3. *Generate random filter bank for wavelet decomposition.*
4. *Decompose (forward wavelet transform) the image I^w according to D.*
5. *Consider the wavelet band used to generate the final four wavelet bands (in one of which the watermark is embedded). Replace this by a random data R having same energy according to step 5 of Algorithm 1.*
6. *Reconstruct the attacked image $I^\#$ by inverse wavelet transform.*

Algorithm 3 is basically an extension of watermark embedding Algorithm 1. Thus the attack can be seen as a re-watermarking attack with the knowledge of decomposition structure. Though the filter bank used for watermarking have large side lobes (i.e. watermark signal is distributed across different frequencies), that does not really prevent the attacker from removing it as the attack is mounted at the previous level. It is considered in [17] that the attacker replaces one of the final bands (which is used for watermark embedding) by zero to remove the watermark and then commented that this does not bring down the correlation below the threshold. Our attack is stronger as we basically replace all four bands at the final level (implemented by concentrating on the single band at the previous level) using a technique similar to watermarking.

Table 1. Correlation After the Attack when Decomposition Structure is Known

Image	Watermark size	Band	Decomposition	Correlation	PSNR(a,w)
Lena	16×16	LL5	D_1	0.31	37.15
Lena	16×16	HL5	D_1	0.28	37.67
Lena	16×16	HH5	D_1	0.21	38.10
Lena	16×16	LH5	D_1	0.23	37.52
Baboon	16×16	LL5	D_1	0.30	36.87
Baboon	16×16	HL5	D_1	0.28	37.12
Baboon	16×16	HH5	D_1	0.246	37.24
Baboon	16×16	LH5	D_1	0.252	37.16
Peppers	16×16	LL5	D_1	0.28	36.40
Peppers	16×16	HL5	D_1	0.26	35.83
Peppers	16×16	HH5	D_1	0.22	36.92
Peppers	16×16	LH5	D_1	0.26	35.42

Thus the 'new' watermark will be distributed over all the frequencies, which will suppress the previous watermark and brings down the correlation below the threshold. As the new watermark is introduced into the middle frequency bands, image quality remains acceptable after inverse wavelet transform. Table 1 provides the simulation result. During verification, if the correlation between recovered and embedded signal is above 0.4, then it is assumed that the watermark is present. Note that in Table 1, PSNR(a,w) means PSNR of attacked image with respect to watermarked image. Once again note that in the experiments we have used different filter banks at the time of attack than the ones used in embedding the watermark. Thus the secrecy of the filter bank is of no effect and the attack mentioned here turns out to be successful.

3.3   Find Out the Decomposition Structure

To use the Algorithm 3 to remove the watermark, the decomposition structure needs to be identified. In that case, the attacker has to identify possible location(s) where the watermark may have been embedded by the owner. This can be accomplished by checking cross-correlation of wavelet bands in every level before proceeding to the next level. Also search space can be greatly reduced if one searches only the middle frequency bands, as it is expected that the watermark is present in one of the middle frequency bands only. As discussed in

Subsection 3.1, the wavelet coefficients are highly correlated and their cross-correlation should behave in that manner. However, if any band manifests any large variation from this, that can be attributed to watermark embedding. In such a way we can identify the wavelet band used for watermark embedding. Exact algorithm for band identification is as follows.

Algorithm 4

1. *Read the watermarked image I^w.*
2. *Generate the set of all possible decomposition structures $D_1, \ldots, D_k$.*
3. *Select a two channel orthonormal filter bank F.*
4. *For $i = 1 \ldots k$ Do*
   (a) *Decompose the image according to decomposition structure D_i using F.*
   (b) *Let number of wavelet bands be m.*
   (c) *For $j = 1 \ldots m$ Do*
      i. *For wavelet band W_j inspect the cross-correlation nature for all possible shifts.*
      ii. *If cross-correlation pattern follows that of a random matrix then store D_i along with W_j as the target wavelet band.*

It is already known that the watermarking bits used during embedding are random in nature. Thus it is expected that despite the use of different filter banks, wavelet band used for watermarking will retain its random nature. When a proper decomposition structure is used in the above algorithm, wavelet coefficients W_j will be random and cross-correlation property will be that of a random matrix. There is some possibility of false alarm as the filter bank used for watermark embedding has large side lobs which spread the watermark over different frequencies. Since the filter bank used for decomposition is different from the one used during watermark embedding, traces of watermark could be found in more than one places. One way to solve this is to check the cross-correlation of the suspected bands with different random filter bank(s). During experiments we found that this technique reduces the number of suspected bands to at most 3. Even in some cases this technique is able to reduce the number of suspected bands to exactly one also. Now for all the suspected bands we run the Algorithm 3. As we are talking about searching all the available bands, we must have some idea about the search space. Let the size of the watermarked image is $2^n \times 2^n$. Then, atmost we can perform $(n - 1)$ level of wavelet transform. So total number of possible wavelet bands, that can be generated is $4^1 + 4^2 + 4^3 \ldots + 4^{n-1} = \frac{4^{n-1} - 4}{3}$. For a typical image of size 256×256, the number of possible bands comes out to be 5460. It is already known that only middle frequency bands are used to watermark the image, then the number of possible middle frequency bands to be searched comes out to be as low as 84. Table 2 shows the result obtained for different images which shows that our attack is successful. Let us point out once again that for successful watermark detection, correlation should be higher than 0.4 [17–page 83]. The PSNR(a,w) value in the table presents the image quality after the attack. To present the visual indistinguishability, we provide the Figure 3.

Fig. 3. Original, Watermarked and Attacked Images (from left to right)

Table 2. Correlation After the Attack

Image	Watermark size	Number of Suspect Band(s)	Correlation	PSNR(a,w)
Lena	16 × 16	3	0.23	33.43
Lena	16 × 16	3	0.24	33.62
Lena	16 × 16	3	0.22	33.38
Lena	16 × 16	2	0.26	33.27
Baboon	16 × 16	2	0.21	32.42
Baboon	16 × 16	2	0.22	32.56
Baboon	16 × 16	2	0.22	32.61
Baboon	16 × 16	2	0.24	32.14
Peppers	16 × 16	3	0.26	32.86
Peppers	16 × 16	3	0.25	33.04
Peppers	16 × 16	3	0.26	33.17
Peppers	16 × 16	1	0.31	32.93

4   Conclusion

In this paper we have presented a successful cryptanalytic attack on the wavelet based watermarking scheme presented in [17]. Here we exploit the random nature of the watermark to break the scheme. This is in sharp contrast with the notion of cryptographic security where randomness provides the security.

References

1. R. J. Anderson and F. A. P. Petitcolas. On The Limits of Steganography. *IEEE Journal of Selected Areas in Communications. Special Issue on Copyright and Privacy Protection*, 16(4):474-481, May 1998.
2. I. J. Cox, J. Kilian, T. Leighton and T. Shamoon. Secure Spread Spectrum Watermarking for Multimedia. *IEEE Transactions on Image Processing*, 6(12):1673–1687, 1997.

3. T. K. Das and S. Maitra. Cryptanalysis of Optimal Differential Energy Watermarking (DEW) and a Modified Robust Scheme. In *INDOCRYPT 2002*, number 2551 in Lecture Notes in Computer Science, Page 135–148, Springer Verlag, December 2002. An extended version of this paper has been accepted in IEEE Transactions on Signal Processing, to be published in February 2005.

4. T. K. Das. Cryptanalysis of Block Based Spatial Domain Watermarking Schemes. In *Indocrypt 2003*, volume 2904 in Lecture Notes in Computer Science, pages 363–374, Springer-Verlag, December 2003.

5. T. K. Das and S. Maitra. Cryptanalysis of Correlation Based Watermarking Schemes using Single Watermarked Copy. *IEEE Signal Processing Letters*, pages 446–449, 11(4), April 2004.

6. I. Daubechies. Ten Lectures on Wavelets. SIAM, 1992.

7. F. Ergun, J. Kilian and R. Kumar. A Note on the Limits of Collusion-Resistant Watermarks. In *Eurocrypt 1999*, Lecture Notes in Computer Science, Springer Verlag, 1999.

8. F. Hartung and M. Kutter. Multimedia Watermarking Techniques. *Proceedings of IEEE*, 87(7), July 1999.

9. T. Kalker, J. P. M. G. Linnartz and M. v. Dijk. Watermark Estimation through Detector Analysis. In *International Conference on Image Processing*, 1998.

10. S. Katzenbeisser and F. A. P. Petitcolas. *Information Hiding Techniques for Steganography and Digital Watermarking*. Artech House, USA, 2000.

11. D. Kirovski and F. A. P. Petitcolas. Replacement Attack on Arbitrary Watermarking Systems. In ACM workshop on *Digital Rights Management*, 2002.

12. G. C. Langelaar and R. L. Lagendijk. Optimal Differential Energy Watermarking of DCT Encoded Images and Video. *IEEE Transactions on Image Processing*, 10(1):148–158, 2001.

13. J. P. M. G. Linnartz and M. v. Dijk. Analysis of the Sensitivity Attack Against Electronic Watermarks in Images. In *Workshop on Information Hiding 1998*, Lecture Notes in Computer Science, volume 1525, pages 258–272, Springer-Verlag, 1998.

14. F. A. P. Petitcolas, R. J. Anderson, M. G. Kuhn and D. Aucsmith. Attacks on Copyright Marking Systems. In *2nd Workshop on Information Hiding*, Lecture Notes in Computer Science, volume 1525, pages 218–238, Springer Verlag, 1998.

15. F. A. P. Petitcolas and R. J. Anderson. Evaluation of Copyright Marking Systems. In *IEEE Multimedia Systems*, Florence, Italy, June 1999.

16. M. Vetterli and J. Kovacevic. *Wavelets and Subband Coding*. Prentice-Hall PTR, 1995.

17. Y. Wang, J. F. Doherty and R. E. VanDyck. A Wavelet-Based Watermarking Algorithm for Ownership Verification of Digital Images. *IEEE Transactions on Image Processing*, 11(2):77–88, 2002.

A Generalized Method for Constructing and Proving Zero-Knowledge Watermark Proof Systems

Xianfeng Zhao, Yingxia Dai, and Dengguo Feng

The State Key Laboratory of Information Security, Graduate School of
Chinese Academy of Sciences, PO Box 3908, Beijing 100039, P. R. China
{xfzhao, dyx, fengdg}@is.ac.cn

Abstract. Zero-knowledge watermark proof systems for copyright verification are not only theoretically appealing but also practically possible. However, most existing proposals concentrate on specific skills and neglect to give a formal proof of their zero-knowledge property. To improve the situation, the paper proposes a generalized framework for constructing and validating such systems. First, the theoretical foundations are investigated. Second, the paper shows that the existence of a secured equivalent operation, which enables watermark detection in a blinded domain, is one of the prerequisites of the systems' existence. In this view, the paper constructs a generalized zero-knowledge watermark proof system and verifies its zero-knowledge property. Third, the existing systems are investigated under the above framework, and a new system, which overcomes some defects of the existing ones, is proposed as a concrete instance of applying the generalized methods.

1 Introduction

As one of the countermeasures against the unauthorized copy of digital contents, watermarking gives a feasible way of ownership verification [1]. It embeds ownership message into an original without perceptually degrading the distributed version, implementing the so-named imperceptibility, and tries to preserve the embedded watermark in case of various attacks afterwards, implementing the so-named *robustness*. Similar to a cryptosystem, watermarking has to face the problem of key management. Typically, a detection key might consist of an original and a watermark, or only the latter. If both of them are needed, the watermarking is called a *private scheme*; if only the watermark is needed, it is called a *public scheme*. Since a public scheme disposes of the original and needs only the watermark in the detection, it is considered more convenient and secure for key management [1,2].

However, a watermark reveals sensitive information about the embedding so that it can help to damage the hidden watermark more precisely in the cases of dishonest users or a distrustful environment for transporting and storing the keys [2,3]. To avoid the damage, various techniques have been proposed. Some researchers borrowed the idea of public cryptosystem from cryptography and proposed a series of so-named *asymmetric watermarking* schemes, of which detection keys are different from the embedded

I.J. Cox et al. (Eds.): IWDW 2004, LNCS 3304, pp. 204–217, 2005.

watermarks [2]. Nevertheless, such schemes often sacrifice the robustness for the security, and most of them could still expose the sensitive information through an asymmetric key [3]. Hence it is not strange why applying the principles of zero-knowledge proof system to watermarking became a research interest in the literature [4,5]. In general, *zero-knowledge watermark proofs* (ZKWP) are proofs that yield nothing beyond the validity of the assertion that a watermark exists. In the principle of computational theory and cryptography, a functional interactive proof (IP) system and a collection of applicable one-way functions imply the existence of a zero-knowledge proof (ZKP) system [6]. The IP system is used to provide a probabilistic algorithm and the one-way functions are used to secure the knowledge. As for a ZKWP system, that requires it should be able to detect watermarks in a secured domain. Craver suggested using permutation to protect the watermark from being revealed [4]. He also proposed another scheme that hides the key in many false keys acquired by reverse engineering [4]. Adelsbach and Sadeghi found that some commitment protocols can be used by committing data that will never be opened [7]. To detect a watermark in a ciphered domain, Gopalakrishnan et al. exploited the homomorphic property of RSA cryptosystem [8].

Through our investigation, however, we found there is both theoretical and practical room for improvement in the existing ZKWP proposals. First, they all concentrate on specific skills, neglecting to give a generalized method at the level of computational theory. H. Then and Y. Wang [9] tried to make the ZKWP independent of specific detections and proposed the so-called generic detection that just proves a detected value. But we think it is insufficient because a value can be claimed and the verifier may want to detect the watermark by him or herself. Second, none of the existing ZKWP proposals gave a formal proof of the system's zero-knowledge property. Third, the detection often has no chance to examine the validity of a claimed key so that it just proves the existence of a detectable watermark that might be illegally computed through reverse engineering. Although the invertible problem [10] is challenging for watermarking, more and more schemes need at least control it to some extent [4]. Forth, the security of some systems is too weak to protect data, and those having strong security are often much complicated [7].

To improve the ZKWP systems, this paper is to propose a generalized method for constructing them and proving their zero-knowledge properties. In the subsequent discussion, Sect. 2 studies the foundations of such systems, and proves that the existence of a *secured equivalent operation* (SEO), which enables watermark detections in a blinded domain, is a prerequisite of the systems' existence. Through a generalized ZKWP system, it also gives the framework for constructing and verifying the systems. Sect. 3 investigates the existing proposals under the framework. And a new scheme is proposed and experimented in Sect. 4 as a concrete instance of applying the generalized method. Finally, Sect. 5 draws the conclusions.

2   The Generalized ZKWP System

This section is to give the generalized method for constructing and validating ZKWP systems by investigating a generalized such system. The theory of the ZKP systems

[6] does help the study, but it will be found that a ZKWP system has its own problem to solve since the watermark detection has to be executed in a secured domain.

2.1 Preliminaries

To deal with our topics more formally, the subsection is to review the concepts and theories that underlie our research. Let us begin with the following definition [6]:

Definition 1 (IP System): Let $c, s : N \to R$ be functions and $c(n) > s(n) + 1 / p(n)$ for a polynomial $p(\cdot)$. Let L denote a class or set, $\Pr(\cdot)$ denote a probability, and $|\cdot|$ denote the size of an input. A pair of interactive algorithms, a prover P and a verifier V, is called an (generalized) IP system for class L if V is of polynomial-time and the following two conditions hold:

(1) Completeness. $\forall x \in L$, $\Pr\big([P(y), V(z)](x) = 1 \big) \geq c(|x|)$. (1)

(2) Soundness. $\forall x \notin L, \forall P$, $\Pr\big([P(y), V(z)](x) = 1 \big) \leq s(|x|)$. (2)

Here, x is available for both parts and called the common input; the optional y and z are accessible for P and V respectively and called private inputs. $\forall$ is for 'every'. □

An IP system has more computational power than a non-interactive system [6,11]. Moreover, its error probability can be efficiently controlled. That is ensured by:

Lemma 1 (Error Minimization of IP): In Definition 1 let the executions on x be independent each time. Then for every polynomial $p(n)$, there exists a $p(n)$-time IP system for the class L, with an error probability bounded by $2^{-p(n)}$.

Proof. Please see [6,11], or other textbook of computational theory. □

IP systems can be characterized by their probabilities of the completeness and soundness. We found that the following class of systems, which we named the *one and a half IP* (OHIP) systems, is closely related to most ZKWP schemes:

Definition 2 (OHIP System): If the system defined by Definition 1 satisfies:

(1) Completeness. $\forall x \in L$, $\Pr\big([P(y), V(z)](x) = 1 \big) = 1$. (3)

(2) Soundness. $\forall x \notin L, \forall P$, $\Pr\big([P(y), V(z)](x) = 1 \big) \leq 1/2$. (4)

Then the system is called a one and a half IP system for class L. □

Likewise, we are interested in controlling the overall error probability. Supported by the next lemma, the efficiency and correctness of the systems can be guaranteed.

Lemma 2 (Error Minimization of OHIP): If there exists an OHIP system for class L, for every polynomial $p(n)$, there also exists a $p(n)$-time IP system for class L, with an error probability bounded by $2^{-p(n)}$.

Proof. Executing the IP system many times apparently decreases the overall error probability P_e. To give an explicit expression of it, we first replace Eq.(4) with

$$\Pr\big([P(y),V(z)](x) = 1 \big) = \varepsilon, \ 0 \leq \varepsilon \leq 1/2, \tag{5}$$

where ε is the error probability of one execution when $x \notin L$. Then suppose that, after k rounds of the execution, the overall error probability P_e is equal to the desired $2^{-p(n)}$. Then we have $P_e = \varepsilon^k = 2^{-p(n)}$. Apparently there exists a constant C satisfying $(\varepsilon^{-1})^C = 2$, or equivalently $C = \log_{\varepsilon^{-1}} 2$. Then

$$k = -\log_{\varepsilon^{-1}} P_e = -\log_{\varepsilon^{-1}} 2^{-p(n)} = -\log_{\varepsilon^{-1}} \big(\varepsilon^{-1}\big)^{-C \cdot p(n)} = C \cdot p(n). \tag{6}$$

Thus the lemma has been proved, and we also find it holds even when $0 \leq \varepsilon < 1$.   □

An IP system makes it possible to prove assertions without revealing any knowledge [6,11]. But as we know, what is zero-knowledge is particularly difficult to define. Anyhow, there is a widely accepted paradigm to verify the zero-knowledge property [6]. It assumes that a verifier has not acquired any knowledge if and only if it can simulate the prover and produce the interactions identically distributed to the real interactions within polynomial-time. Then we can define a ZKP system as follows:

Definition 3 (ZKP System): An IP system defined by Definition 1 is called a (computational) zero-knowledge proof system if for every probabilistic polynomial-time verifier V there exists an probabilistic polynomial-time algorithm $S*$ so that for every $x \in L$ the interactions generated by the following two systems are identically distributed (computationally indistinguishable): (1) $[P(y),V(z)](x)$; (2) $S*(x)$.   □

In addition, we think it is necessary to define a generalized watermarking both for our subsequent discussion and for the readers not familiar with it. Since a ZKWP system is often based on a *public watermarking scheme* (PWS) [2,3], which does not require the original in detection, we just define such a scheme as follows:

Definition 4 (Public Watermarking Scheme, PWS): Let u be an original or one of its transform domains, and w the coded watermark. The watermark is embedded into u by $x = e(u, w)$, where x denotes the distributed version and e the embedding. The assertion of w in x is to be verified by $c = r(x, w)$, where x might be attacked and w be fabricated. The assertion is validated only if $c \geq T$, where T is a threshold. The game among the embedder and the verifier is called a PWS.   □

2.2 Constructing and Verifying the Generalized ZKWP System

If we change the terminology used in the theory of computation into that used in watermarking, we immediately define a generalized ZKWP system as follows:

Definition 5 (ZKWP System): An IP system defined by Definition 1 is called a (computational) ZKWP system if for every probabilistic polynomial-time verifier V there exists a probabilistic polynomial-time algorithm $S*$ so that, in case that $[P(w),V](x)$ is designed to verify the assertion of a watermark in x, the interactions generated by the following two systems are identically distributed (computationally indistinguishable): (1) $[P(w),V](x)$; (2) $S*(x)$.   □

By Definition 4, a watermark apparently should not be sent to the verifier in plaintext. Hence we think that the detection can be equivalently executed in a blinded domain. We formally define the concept (Fig.1) as follows:

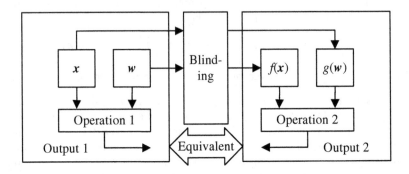

Fig. 1. An illustration of the secured equivalent operation defined by Definition 6

Definition 6 (Secured Equivalent Operation, SEO): Let X, $\tilde{X}$, C and $\tilde{C}$ be domains, and $O_x = \{\mu, \cdots : X \to \tilde{X}\}$ and $O_w = \{\gamma, \cdots : X \to \tilde{X}\}$ be two collections of blinding functions. Suppose the equation $r(x, w) = c \in C$, $x, w \in X$, and the equation $\tilde{r}(f(x), g(w)) = \tilde{c} \in \tilde{C}$, $f \in O_x$ and $g \in O_w$, imply each other, that is

$$r(x, w) = c \in C \;\Leftrightarrow\; \tilde{r}(f(x), g(w)) = \tilde{c} \in \tilde{C}, \tag{7}$$

then $\tilde{r}$ is named the secured equivalent operation of r. □

Although we have not constructed a ZKWP system yet, one might perceive that, with the aid of an IP system, the system could be constructed if the watermark detection has its SEO and the blinding functions are sufficiently secure. The intuition is proved by the following theorem.

Theorem 1 (Construction and Verification): Let $r(x, w) = c$ denote the detection of a watermark w in a distributed version x. If its secured equivalent operation, $\tilde{r}(f(x), g(w)) = \tilde{c}$, exists, and the blinding functions are sufficiently secure, then, for every polynomial $p(n)$, a $p(n)$-time ZKWP system with an error probability bounded by $2^{-p(n)}$ exists.

Proof. The proof will construct an IP system to detect watermarks, prove the validity and efficiency of the system, and finally verify its ZKP property by the simulators.

Construction 1 (Generalized ZKWP): Let x be the common input of an IP system, and w be the private input of P. Then the system, $[P(w), V](x)$, can do:

(a) P randomly selects $f \in O_x$, computes $\tilde{x} = f(x)$ and sends the value to V.

(b) V randomly selects $\sigma \in \{0,1\}$ and sends the value to P.

(c) P receives σ. If $\sigma = 0$, P sends f to V; if $\sigma = 1$, P selects $g \in O_w$ so that $\tilde{r}(f(x), g(w)) = \tilde{c}$, computes $\tilde{w} = g(w)$ and sends the value to V.

(d) If $\sigma = 0$, V receives f and computes $\hat{x} = f(x)$. If $\hat{x} = \tilde{x}$, V returns 1; or else V returns 0 and stops the execution. If $\sigma = 1$, V receives $\tilde{w}$ and computes $\tilde{r}(\tilde{x}, \tilde{w}) = \tilde{c}$. If $\tilde{c}$ implies a c that indicates the existence of the watermark, V returns 1; otherwise, V returns 0 and stops the execution.

(e) Executing again the above steps until the error probability is negligible.

In each round of the above execution, there exists

$$\Pr\big([P(w), V](x) = 1 \big) = 1, \quad \text{for any } w \text{ that exists in } x. \tag{8}$$

And for every prover P, there exists

$$\Pr\big([P(w), V](x) = 1 \big) = 1/2, \quad \text{for any } w \text{ that does not exist in } x. \tag{9}$$

Hence the system is an OHIP system, and by Lemma 2, for every polynomial $p(n)$, there exists a $p(n)$-time IP system with error probability bounded by $2^{-p(n)}$.

To prove the zero-knowledge property, we can construct a simulator $S*$ required by Definition 3 and 5. It further consists of two parts as follows:

Construction 2 (Simulator of the System Returning 1, S_1*): Suppose the simulator S_1* is to interact with itself, and $e(\cdot, \cdot)$ embeds a watermark. The following steps are to generate data identically distributed or computationally indistinguishable to the interactions of Construction 1 that returns 1.

(a) S_1* computes $x' = e(x, w')$, where w' is a randomly fabricated watermark and x is the distributed version.

(b) S_1* randomly selects $\sigma_S \in \{0,1\}$.

(c) If $\sigma_S = 0$, S_1* is to simulate the step (a) of Construction 1. It randomly selects $f \in O_x$ and computes $\tilde{x} = f(x)$. If $\sigma_S = 1$, S_1* is to simulate the step (c) of Construction 1. It randomly selects $f \in O_x$ and $g \in O_w$ so that they satisfy $\tilde{r}(f(x'), g(w')) = \tilde{c}$, and computes $\tilde{x}' = f(x')$ and $\tilde{w}' = g(w')$.

(d) S_1* randomly selects $\sigma_V \in \{0,1\}$. If $\sigma_S \neq \sigma_V$, S_1* discards all data of this round from the step (b); or else it arranges the data into the desired order.

(e) Going to the step (b) until sufficient interactions are collected.

Construction 3 (Simulator of the System Returning 0, S_0*): Since P is cheating or the claimed watermark is undetectable, S_0*, as a simulating 'deceiver', can just follow the P's steps in Construction 1 and will be caught in the step (d) by itself.

The validity of the simulators is easy to check. In the cases of Construction 2 and $\sigma_S = \sigma_V = 1$, since x' contains w', $\tilde{r}(\tilde{x}', \tilde{w}') = \tilde{c}$ implies a c that indicates the existence of a watermark. Because $\tilde{x}'$ and $\tilde{w}'$ are all blinded so that they are identically distributed or computationally indistinguishable to $\tilde{x}$ and $\tilde{w}$ in Construction 1 respectively. In the cases of Construction 2 and $\sigma_S = \sigma_V = 0$, or in Construction 3, $S*$ does the same thing as P, so the above property also holds.   □

Hence we concluded that the vital step of constructing a ZKWP system, or changing an old system into a ZKWP one, is searching for a secured equivalent operation that can be used to detect watermarks. However, since an attacker might have attacked and tampered with a distributed version, or have found another detectable watermark, two situations should be addressed here:

Corollary 1 (In Case of Attack or Reverse Engineering): (1) If a watermark cannot resist an active attack and becomes undetectable, the generalized ZKWP system does not prove its existence. (2) However, if V cannot differentiate a blinded false watermark from a blinded legal one, the system proves the existence of any detectable watermark, though it might be illegally claimed.

Proof. (1) Because $c = r(x, w) < T$ now does not imply the existence of w, P has little chance to make $\tilde{c} = \tilde{r}(f(x), g(w))$ imply a value larger than T in many rounds of the execution of Construction 1. The nonexistence is to be detected in step (d) of Construction 1 with the probability $1 - 2^M$, where M is the number of the execution rounds.

(2) Suppose the w in the inequality $r(x, w) \geq T$ can be feasibly replaced with w', saying the watermarking is invertible [10]. Since $r(x, w') = c \geq T$ holds, a dishonest prover can replace all w in Construction 1 with w', and send $\tilde{w}' = g(w')$ to V. Because V cannot tell it from a legal $\tilde{w} = g(w)$ in the blinded domain, V is also infeasible to examine the legality of a blinded watermark. V can only verify the validity of $\tilde{r}(\tilde{x}, \tilde{w}') = \tilde{c}$, which implies $r(x, w') = c \geq T$.   □

Now we can conclude that searching for an ideal SEO is vital for constructing a ZKWP system, but the system still needs the properties of robustness and noninvertibility, which are largely from the underlying watermarking scheme. In practice, constructing a strictly zero-knowledge and secure ZKWP system is very difficult. On one hand, the blinding functions are required not to conflict with the watermark detection so that the ways of constructing them are limited. On the other hand, the robustness and noninvertibility are not the totally settled problems. Anyhow, we will find that ZKWP systems with some levels of computational security and zero-knowledge property are possible.

3   Some Comments on the Existing Systems

Since the above discussion stems from the fully developed theories of computation and ZKP system, we think it gives a general method for investigating existing systems and designing new ones. In actuality, we found that almost all existing proposals [4,7,8] can be transformed into the above paradigm, and there is both theoretical and practical room for improvement in them. Our comments on them concentrate on four aspects as follows:

Zero-Knowledge Verification. None of the schemes gives a formal proof that can validate their claimed zero-knowledge property. By Definition 5, we know that a simulator of the system should be constructed to demonstrate that the interactions of a real system and those of the simulating one are identically distributed or computationally indistinguishable.

Blindness and Security. The method in [4] is based on the permutation of signal samples, but their values, especially the distinctive ones, compromise the one-wayness. Furthermore, most multimedia has several components, such as RGB in images and sound-channels in audios, so that a sample can be more peculiar. In [8], a correlation is computed sample-wise between two sequences encrypted by RSA algorithm. Since a RSA modulus is of the same size as each encrypted word, it has to be the common sample length of 8 or 16 bits. However, a secure RSA modulus should have 1024-1048 bits that can make the correlation meaningless.

Invertibility. By Corollary 1, a ZKWP system will accept an illegal claim if a dishonest prover has found another detectable watermark. The invertible problem is well recognized and very challenging, especially in case of public schemes [10]. However, it can be partly resisted by checking the features of a claimed watermark [4]. Unfortunately, a verifier in [7] and [8] has no chance to do it because the data is always strongly ciphered. Anyhow, in case of the permutation-based method [4], the situation is improved since many features remains in a permutated version.

Feasibility. The other approach proposed in [4] is based on the reversed engineering on watermarking [10]. However, it requires that a large number of inverted watermarks should be found such that it can be practically infeasible. And the method proposed in [7] embraces some complicated ZKP protocols that can make the implementation burdensome.

To sum up the comments, we think that the ZKWP systems need improving in the above four aspects. The next section is intended to give such improvements by combining the advantages and discarding the disadvantages of the existing schemes.

4   Constructing and Verifying a New ZKWP system

This section is to construct a new ZKWP system that not only brings the existing systems some improvements but also exemplifies our generalized method. By the above discussion, we know, besides proving the zero-knowledge property, it is also important to strengthen the blindness, control the invertibility and maintain feasibility. Hence we shall simply use both pseudo-random noise (PN) and permutation to blind the data, and examine the permuted data to control the invertibility.

4.1 Construction of the New System

By Theorem 1, we have to find a secured equivalent operation for watermark detection before constructing a ZKWP system. Thus we begin with the following lemma:

Lemma 3 (PN and Permutation Equivalent Correlation): Suppose a pseudo-random sequence p is orthogonal to w, that is, $< p, w > = 0$, where $< \cdot, \cdot >$ computes the inner product of two vectors. If x, w, and p are all permutated by $g(\cdot)$ into x', w', and p' respectively, then the correlations computed by

$$c_{x,w} = < x, w > / |w|, \quad c_{x'+p',w'} = < x' + p', w' > / |w'| \tag{10}$$

are equal, and the second computation can be the SEO of the first one. Here, $|\cdot|$ calculates the number of all elements in a vector.

Proof. Since p is orthogonal to w, we have $< p, w > = 0$. Because x, w, and p are permutated by g synchronously, we also have $< x, w > = < x', w' >$, $< p, w > = < p', w' >$, and $|w| = |w'|$. Thus

$$\begin{aligned} c_{x'+p',w'} &= < x' + p', w' > / |w'| \\ &= [< x', w' > + < p', w' >] / |w'| = < x, w > / |w| = c_{x,w}. \end{aligned} \tag{11}$$

Having permuted and added noise, the sample values of $x' + p'$ do not reveal the movement of positions. And so do not the sample values of w' since they can be designed to have less scales which are evenly distributed so that one value occupies many positions. Hence the computation of $c_{x'+p',w'}$ can be an SEO of that of $c_{x,w}$. □

Having found an SEO, we now show that it can be employed in the ZKWP system that is to be constructed from the watermarking scheme proposed by Balni et al. [12]. Let us give Balni's method first. Suppose that $U_{K+1 \sim K+L} = \{U_{K+1}, U_{K+2}, \cdots, U_{K+L}\}$ are selected DCT coefficients of an original u in zig-zag order. Let an L-length watermark $W_{1 \sim L} = \{W_1, W_2, \cdots, W_L\}$ modify them by $X_{K+i} = U_{K+i} + a |U_{K+i}| \cdot W_i$, $1 \leq i \leq L$, where a is a scale factor that adjusts the embedding energy. Then an inverse DCT transform over all the modified and intact DCT coefficients gives the distributed x. In detection, the correlation $c_{X,w} = < X_{K+1 \sim K+L}, W_{1 \sim L} > / L$, where $X_{K+1 \sim K+L}$ are selected DCT coefficients of x and was possibly attacked, is computed and compared with a threshold T. Now we can construct the ZKWP system as follows:

Construction 4 (Proposed ZKWP System): To improve the security, the watermark $W_{1 \sim L}$ is to be a pseudo-random sequence with only 2 values, -1 and +1, and to be generated through a valid permutation of a public-known sequence $G_{1 \sim L}$. The permutation π is the private input of P. The system $[P(\pi), V](X_{K+1 \sim K+L}, G_{1 \sim L}, T)$ can be as follows:

(a) P computes the watermark by $W_{1\sim L} = \pi(G_{1\sim L})$.

(b) P randomly selects f from

$$O_X = \{\forall \mu \mid \mu(X_{K+1\sim K+L}, W_{1\sim L}) = \psi(X_{K+1\sim K+L}) + \varphi(\psi, W_{1\sim L})\}, \tag{12}$$

where ψ is a randomly selected permutation, and φ randomly chooses a pseudo-random sequence R, also denoted by $\varphi(\psi, W_{1\sim L})$, from the solved sequences that satisfy $< R, \psi(W_{1\sim L}) > \approx 0$. P then computes $\tilde{X}_{K+1\sim K+L} = f(X_{K+1\sim K+L}, W_{1\sim L})$ and sends the value to V.

(c) V receives $\tilde{X}_{K+1\sim K+L}$, randomly selects $\sigma \in \{0,1\}$ and sends the value to P.

(d) P receives σ. If $\sigma = 0$, P sends ψ and R to V; or else P lets $g = \psi$, computes $\tilde{W}_{1\sim L} = g(W_{1\sim L})$ and sends the value to V.

(e)   If $\sigma = 0$, V receives ψ and R, and computes $\hat{X} = \psi(X_{K+1\sim K+L}) + R$. If $\tilde{X}_{K+1\sim K+L} = \hat{X}$, V returns 1; or else V returns 0 and stops the execution. If $\sigma = 1$, V receives $\tilde{W}_{1\sim L}$ and tests whether $c_{\tilde{X}, \tilde{W}} = < \tilde{X}_{K+1\sim K+L}, \tilde{W}_{1\sim L} > / L \geq T$ holds. If it is true, V returns 1; otherwise, V returns 0 and stops the execution. To resist the invertibility, V can also check that $\tilde{W}_{1\sim L}$ is a permutation of $G_{1\sim L}$.

(f)   Executing again the steps from (b) until the error probability is negligible.   □

4.2   Some Improvements and the Proof of the ZKWP Property

The potential improvements of Construction 4 lie in four aspects. First, all operations are very common so that the system is simple and feasible. Second, it strengthens the blindness by adding another pseudo-random sequence onto the permutated version. As a result, the sample values do not reveal the movements of samples. Third, it resists the invertibility by using the permuted versions of a known sequence as the blinded watermarks such that a verifier in each round has the chance to verify their validity. The known sequence can also be deduced from a seed that has legislative significance, such as a social security ID. Hence a reverse engineering becomes more infeasible because it has to search for a detectable watermark by only permuting one sequence. Finally, the efficiency and ZKWP property can be explicitly proved by:

Corollary 2 (Efficiency and ZKWP Property): If the SEO defined in Lemma 3 is secure, Construction 4 is a ZKWP system. And for every polynomial $p(n)$, it can be a $p(n)$-time system with the error probability bounded by $2^{-p(n)}$.

Proof. By Lemma 3, computing $< \tilde{X}_{K+1\sim K+L}, \tilde{W}_{1\sim L} > / L$ is an SEO of computing $< X_{K+1\sim K+L}, W_{1\sim L} > / L$. And in each round execution of Construction 4, there exists

$$\Pr\big([P(\pi), V](X_{K+1\sim K+L}, G_{1\sim L}, T) = 1\big) = 1, \text{ if } < X_{K+1\sim K+L}, W_{1\sim L} > / L \geq T. \tag{13}$$

And for every verifier V, there exists

$$\Pr\big([P(\pi), V](X_{K+1\sim K+L}, G_{1\sim L}, T) = 1\big) = 1/2, \text{ if } < X_{K+1\sim K+L}, W_{1\sim L} > / L < T. \tag{14}$$

Thus the system is an OHIP system. By Lemma 2, for every polynomial $p(n)$, it can be a $p(n)$-time IP system with the error probability bounded by $2^{-p(n)}$. Now the corollary can be proved if only we can give a simulator $S*$ of the system. It also consists of two parts. The part simulating the system returning 1 is as follows:

Construction 5 (Simulator of the System Returning 1, S_1*): Suppose that S_1* is to interact with itself. The following steps are to generate data identically distributed or computationally indistinguishable to the interactions of Construction 4 in case that a watermark exists.

(a) Original   (b) DCT of (a)   (c) Known Sequence

(d) Permuted Watermark   (e) (b) embedded by (d)   (f) Distributed

(g) Blinding Noise   (h) Permuted and Blinded (e)

Fig. 2. Images from one of the experiments (In (c), (d) and (g), the signal energy is increased to make them more visible; only the middle part of the DCT coefficients are used)

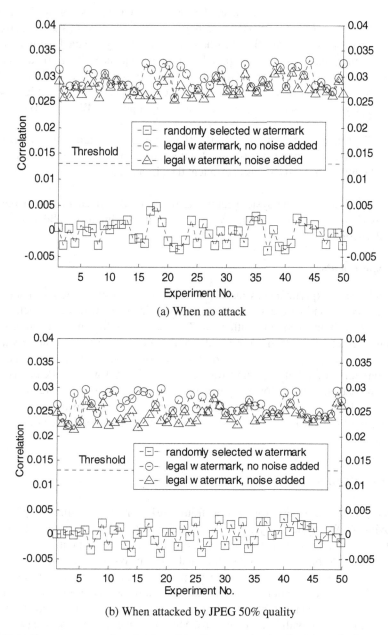

Fig. 3. Detection responses of randomly selected watermarks, legal watermarks in case of no pseudo-random noise, and legal watermarks in case of the noise respectively

(a) S_1^* computes $X'_{K+i} = X_{K+i} + a | X_{K+i} | W'_i$, $1 \leq i \leq L$, where $W'_{1 \sim L}$ is a fabricated watermark.

(b) S_1^* randomly selects $\sigma_S \in \{0,1\}$.

(c) If $\sigma_S = 0$, $S_1{}^*$ is to simulate the step (b) of Construction 4. It randomly selects $f \in O_X$ and computes $\widetilde{X}_{K+1 \sim K+L} = f(X_{K+1 \sim K+L}, W'_{1 \sim L}) = \psi(X_{K+1 \sim K+L}) + \varphi(\psi, W'_{1 \sim L})$, where ψ is a randomly selected permutation and φ randomly chooses a pseudo-random sequence R, also denoted by $\varphi(\psi, W'_{1 \sim L})$, from the solved sequences that satisfy $< R, \psi(W'_{1 \sim L}) > \approx 0$. If $\sigma_S = 1$, $S_1{}^*$ is to simulate the step (d) of Construction 4. It similarly selects $f \in O_X$, lets $g = \psi$, and computes $\widetilde{W}'_{1 \sim L} = g(W'_{1 \sim L})$ and $\widetilde{X}'_{K+1 \sim K+L} = f(X'_{K+1 \sim K+L}, W'_{1 \sim L})$.

(d) $S_1{}^*$ randomly selects $\sigma_V \in \{0,1\}$. If $\sigma_S \neq \sigma_V$, it discards all interactions of this round from the step (b); or else it arranges the data into the desired order.

(e) Going to the step (b) until sufficient data is collected.

The part simulating the system returning 0 can be described in almost the same words as Construction 3. And the two parts can all be similarly validated as in the proof of Theorem 1.   □

4.3 Experiments

The goal of the experiments is largely to make sure that the pseudo-random noise added in each round of the verification does not interfere with the detection, even when the distributed version is attacked. To further simplify the algorithm, we just randomly select noises with a normal distribution of zero mean and unity variance. Fig. 2 gives some images in one of the experiments. In each experiment, the detections for a randomly selected watermark and a legal watermark in case of no noise, and the detections for a legal watermark in case of noise are respectively tested. Fig.3 displays the results. They show that the influence of such a noise in each round of the verification is so slight that it is far from being able to change the conclusions.

5 Conclusions

In this paper, we have proposed a framework for constructing, verifying and improving ZKWP systems by giving a generalized ZKWP system. Our study shows that the vital step to construct such a system is to find a secured equivalent operation that enables watermark detection in a blinded domain. We also demonstrated that it is possible to verify the zero-knowledge property by constructing a simulator of the system. Because the simulator paradigm is widely accepted in the literature of computation theory and cryptography, we think we have given a more formal and rigorous way to deal with ZKWP systems. Moreover, the framework in case of active attack or reverse engineering is also studied. The outcome shows that a ZKWP system just gives a more secure way of watermark verification instead of a whole scheme. A watermarking scheme embracing a ZKWP system may still need to implement the properties of robustness and noninvertibility by specific skills. Finally, we constructed a new ZKWP system to exemplify the use of the generalized method.

References

1. G. C. Langelaar, I. Setyawan, R. L. Lagendijk. Watermarking digital image and video data, a state-of-the-art overview. IEEE Signal Processing Magazine, 17(5): 20-46, 2000.
2. J. J. Eggers, J. K. Su and B. Girod. Asymmetric watermarking schemes. In: Proc. of Sicherheit in Netzen and Mediendaten, Berlin, Germany, September, 2000.
3. S. Craver, S. Katzenbeisser. Security analysis of public-key watermarking schemes. In: SPIE Proc. of Mathematics of Data/Image Coding, Compression and Encryption, with Applications, Vol.4475: 172-182, 2001.
4. S. Craver. Zero knowledge watermark detection. In: Proc. of 3rd International Workshop on Information Hiding, Lecture Notes in Computer Science, Vol.1768: 102-116, Springer-Verlag, Berlin, Germany, 2000.
5. A. Adelsbach, S. Katzenbeisser, A. R. Sadeghi. Watermark detection with zero-knowledge disclosure. Multimedia Systems, 9: 266-278, 2003.
6. O. Goldreich. Foundations of Cryptography, Basic Tools. Cambridge University Press, Cambridge, United Kingdom, 2001.
7. A. Adelsbach, A Sadeghi. Zero-knowledge watermark detection and proof of ownership. In: Proc. of 4th International Workshop on Information Hiding, Lecture Notes in Computer Science, Vol.2137: 273-288, Springer-Verlag, Berlin, Germany, 2001.
8. K. Gopalakrishnan, N. Memon, P. L. Vora. Protocols for watermark verification. IEEE Multimedia, 8(4): 66-70, Oct.-Dec., 2001.
9. H. H. P. Then, Y. C. Wang. Towards generic detection scheme in zero knowledge protocol. In: Proc. of IWDW 2003, Lecture Notes in Computer Science, Vol.2939: 570-580. Springer-Verlag, Berlin, Germany, 2003.
10. S. Craver, N. Memon, B. L. Yeo B L, M. M. Yeung. Resolving rightful ownerships with invisible watermarking techniques: limitations, attacks, and implications. IEEE Journal on Selected Areas in Communications, 16(4): 573-586, 1998.
11. M. Sipser. Introduction to the Theory of Computation. Thomson Learning, Stamford, Connecticut, USA, 1997.
12. M. Barni, F. Bartolini, V. Capellini, A. Piva. A DCT-domain system for robust image watermarking. Signal Processing, 66(1998): 357-372, 1998.

Towards the Public but Noninvertible Watermarking

Xianfeng Zhao, Yingxia Dai, and Dengguo Feng

The State Key Laboratory of Information Security, Graduate School of
Chinese Academy of Sciences,
PO Box 3908, Beijing 100039, P. R. China
{xfzhao, dyx, fengdg}@is.ac.cn

Abstract. The public watermarking schemes, which do not need the originals in ownership verification, have been proved invertible in nature. However, this paper is to demonstrate that some public but noninvertible schemes exist in the cases of the ill-posed linear embedding or nonlinear embedding. Since attackers have to solve an ill-posed linear or nonlinear system, they have great difficulty dividing a released version into their claimed original data and scaled watermarks, and in the meantime making the latter be the particular adaptive results based on the former. Since the inverted solutions are drastically perturbed and perceptually unacceptable, they can fail to cheat the private schemes. Furthermore, because the owner has the embedded watermark which jointly defines the embedding system, he or she can do the reverse engineering more precisely and ultimately differentiate himself or herself from the attackers in a public scheme, achieving the public but noninvertible schemes.

1 Introduction

In digital surroundings, the ease of duplicating perfect contents results in the spread of unauthorized copies. As a countermeasure, watermarking [1] has been proposed to verify the ownership, especially for multimedia products. It embeds copyright message into an original without perceptually degrading the distributed version, implementing the so-named imperceptibility, and tries to preserve the embedded watermark in case of attacks afterwards, implementing the so-named robustness. Watermarking can be classified by its detection parameters. Typically, if both the original and the embedded watermark are needed, it is called a *private* scheme; if only the latter is needed, it is called a *public* scheme. A watermarking attack can just aim at destroying or damaging the hidden watermark, but it has to maintain the perceptual quality for commercial usage. Therefore, the widely recognized attacks are moderate *active attacks*, which slightly tamper with the distributed version [2,3].

To resist the attacks, researches on watermarking concentrate on improving the robustness [1-3], but they have to face the problem of *reverse engineering*. In cryptography, Kerckhoff's desiderata require that the security of algorithms should be built on keys, and it should be assumed that attackers know the algorithms [4]. However, to facilitate the applications, a watermarking scheme generally does not use an online authority. Attackers might then claim the ownership of an intact legally

I.J. Cox et al. (Eds.): IWDW 2004, LNCS 3304, pp. 218–231, 2005.

released version by fabricating keys and data according to the well known algorithms. In some scenarios, a real owner might even gain no advantages. Craver et al. [5,6] named the situation the *invertibility of watermarking*. On the assumption that a scale factor for adjusting the embedding energy is constant, they researched the problem thoroughly. They found that the noninvertibility could be achieved by the cryptographic method, which generates the watermark from the hash value of an original. In actuality, the noninvertibility comes from the one-way hash function, which makes an attacker infeasible to divide a released version into their claimed original and watermark with the latter being the hash value of the former. From then on, the topic has been further discussed. Qiao et al. [7] adopted the method in constructing the noninvertible video watermarking. Adelsbach et al. [8] investigated the security of the method. Nevertheless, the method obviously has its limitations because the hash value has to be recomputed from the original in verification. Hence it is only applicable to private schemes, which assume the availability of the original in verification. Craver et al. and Qiao et al. all concluded that a public scheme, which does not use the original in verification, is intrinsically invertible since anyone could claim a watermark in the legally distributed version!

With the development of *adaptive watermarking*, which adjusts the embedding energy according to the original [9,10], we think the invertible problem is worth further consideration. First, a variable scale factor can make the embedding be more complicated. Second, even in the cases that the embedding is linear, it might be ill-posed [11] so that its inverse processing can hardly be precise, particularly when a guessed watermark is used. Third, an adaptive embedding can be intrinsically nonlinear so that its reverse engineering can be also tough.

To answer the questions of how the changes influence the invertible problem and how to overcome it properly, especially in public schemes, this paper is to investigate the typical linear and nonlinear adaptive watermarking as well as the related reverse engineering. It will be found that adaptive watermarking can be noninvertible in nature if the scheme can induce and exploit the unavoidable perturbation in an attacker's reverse engineering properly. In the case of a private scheme, an attacker has great difficulty dividing a released version into their claimed original and scaled watermark, and in the meantime making the latter be the particular adaptive result based on the former. And in the case of a public scheme, an attacker can hardly exhibit a reverse engineering with a low level perturbation as a real owner, who has the embedded watermark that jointly defines the embedding system. In the subsequent discussion, Sect.2 introduces the invertible problem and points out the potentials of adaptive watermarking. Sect. 3 investigates two approaches to implementing the intrinsic noninvertibility for both the private and the public schemes. Sect. 4 gives the results of some image experiments. Sect. 5 draws the conclusions.

2   Cryptographic Noninvertibility Versus Intrinsic Noninvertibility

To express our thinking, the generalized private and public watermarking, together with their invertible problems, will be given first. Then, after the limitations of the current hash-function-based noninvertibility are pointed out, we shall give other possible approaches towards overcoming them.

2.1 The Generalized Watermarking and Its Invertibility

We first give a generalized embedding for both private and public schemes. Let x be a piece of an original or one of its transform domains which are all called an original in the sequel, w be ciphered copyright message, saying the watermark, and x' be the watermarked and distributed version. Then the embedding can be expressed as

$$x' = e(x, h(x) \otimes w) = e(x, a \otimes w) = e(x, s), \tag{1}$$

where $e(\cdot, \cdot)$, $h(\cdot)$ and $\otimes$ represents the embedding, the perceptual adaptation and the operator of direct element multiplication between vectors respectively. The output of $h(x)$, denoted by a, is called the *scale factor*. And s is the *scaled watermark* adjusted by a. When a is constant, the scheme degrades to non-adaptive watermarking. Because a piece of cipher-text can be claimed the result generated from other plain-text with a fabricated keystream, the research on the invertible problem does not consider ciphering and takes the watermark w as fully coded and ciphered data or just a piece of pseudo-random bits.

In the watermark verification of a generalized private scheme, the embedded watermark is to be extracted with the aid of the original and then compared with the claimed watermark. Suppose $e^{-1}(x', x)$ removes x from x', and $h^{-1}(x)$ scales down the output, where the superscript -1 indicates the reverse processing of an algorithm, or the inverse of a variant or vector, the extraction can be represented by

$$w' = h^{-1}(x) \otimes e^{-1}(x', x) = a^{-1} \otimes e^{-1}(x', x). \tag{2}$$

Then the retrieved hidden watermark w' is compared with w by

$$t = sim(w', w), \quad c_T(t) = \begin{cases} t < T \Rightarrow \text{No,} \\ t \geq T \Rightarrow \text{Yes.} \end{cases} \tag{3}$$

Here, with t for the similarity between w' and w and T for the recognition threshold, $c_T(t)$ draws the conclusion about the existence of w. $sim(\cdot, \cdot)$ often computes the correlation coefficient.

In the watermark verification of a generalized public scheme, the hidden watermark is to be detected by only the claimed watermark. Let $v(\cdot, \cdot)$ denote the detection. Then the verification can be expressed by

$$t = v(x', w), \quad c_T(t) = \begin{cases} t < T \Rightarrow \text{No,} \\ t \geq T \Rightarrow \text{Yes.} \end{cases} \tag{4}$$

The subsequent discussion will call an owner of an original Alice, and a deceiver Bob. Their data will be marked by subscripts A and B for Alice and Bob respectively whenever their differentiation is needed. For example, x_A and x_B are Alice's original and that claimed by Bob respectively, while x can represent either of them.

With the above generalized watermarking scheme, it is easy to define the concept of invertibility [5,6]. A private watermarking scheme, $(e, e^{-1}, sim, h, h^{-1})$, is invertible (noninvertible) if there exists an decomposition, $d(x'_A) = (x_B, w_B)$, which is computationally feasible (infeasible) to be found and satisfies

$$x'_A = e(x_B, h(x_B) \otimes w_B) = e(x_B, a_B \otimes w_B) . \tag{5}$$

As for a public watermarking scheme, (e, v, h, h^{-1}), it is invertible (noninvertible) if there exists a deduction, $d(x'_A) = w_B$, which is computationally feasible (infeasible) to be found and satisfies

$$t_B = v(x'_A, w_B) \geq T . \tag{6}$$

Eq.(5) shows that Bob has ever watermarked his original and produced x'_A, which is the version distributed by Alice. Eq.(6) shows that Bob can verify the existence of his watermark in x'_A. The significance is that the concepts disclose the probable existence of reverse engineering on x'_A at no price of any perceptual degradation that is otherwise unavoidably introduced by an active attack. This paper does not discuss the latter case because the active attacks and robustness are beyond its scope.

The mostly discussed reverse engineering [6] on Weber's law based watermarking [1,12], where the embedded values are a small proportion of the sample values of an original, can here serve as an example of the above concepts. Suppose a denotes the proportion and w a legal or arbitrarily assumed watermark, then the equation of the embedding or reverse engineering can be expressed by

$$x'_A = \left(\begin{bmatrix} w(0) & & & \\ & w(1) & & \\ & & \ddots & \\ & & & w(L-1) \end{bmatrix} \cdot \begin{bmatrix} a & & & \\ & a & & \\ & & \ddots & \\ & & & a \end{bmatrix}_{L \times L} + E \right) \cdot x_{L \times 1} = \begin{bmatrix} 1+a \cdot w(0) & & & \\ & 1+a \cdot w(1) & & \\ & & \ddots & \\ & & & 1+a \cdot w(L-1) \end{bmatrix} \cdot x, \tag{7}$$

where E is the identity matrix. The inverted original can be expressed by

$$x_B = \begin{bmatrix} 1+aw_B(0) & & & \\ & 1+aw_B(1) & & \\ & & \ddots & \\ & & & 1+aw_B(L-1) \end{bmatrix}^{-1} \cdot x'_A = \begin{bmatrix} (1+aw_B(0))^{-1} \cdot (1+aw_A(0)) & & & \\ & (1+aw_B(1))^{-1} \cdot (1+aw_A(1)) & & \\ & & \ddots & \\ & & & (1+aw_B(L-1))^{-1} \cdot (1+aw_A(L-1)) \end{bmatrix} \cdot x_A . \tag{8}$$

The watermarking scheme is obviously invertible. The false original x_B can be solved out feasibly at the cost of only $O(L)$. And the precision of the solution lies in the fact that $1+aw_B(i)$ is near or exactly 1 so that x_B is computationally stable. Moreover, the solved x_B is perceptually similar to x'_A or x_A because $1+aw_A(i)$ and $1+aw_B(i)$ are near or equal. Hence it is convincing also.

2.2   From Cryptographic Noninvertibility to Intrinsic Noninvertibility?

The existing countermeasure against the invertible problem is to make the embedded watermark one-way dependent on an original [6,7]. We here revise it so that it can cover the adaptive schemes. Let $hash(\cdot)$ represent a hash function [4], and $lfsr(\cdot)$ a linear feedback shift register (LFSR) [4]. Then the equation of the embedding or reverse engineering can be represented by

$$h(x) \otimes lfsr(hash(x)) + x = x'_A . \tag{9}$$

Here, the mostly used *additive watermarking* is used, that is, $e(\cdot, \cdot) = (\cdot) + (\cdot)$, and the LFSR is used to generate a watermark from the hash value. Obviously, the noninvertibility is based on the fact that Bob has difficulty dividing x'_A into x_B and $h(x_B) \otimes w_B$, and in the meantime satisfying $w_B = lfsr(hash(x_B))$. The infeasibility in solving Eq.(9) can be proven by hash function's one-way property [4]. Since the method borrows the idea from cryptography, we call the achieved property the *cryptographic noninvertibility*. However, its limitations are also apparent. First, the cryptographic operations make the embedding and the verification much complicated. Second, it is only applicable to private schemes since the watermark has to be regenerated from the original, which is unavailable in a public scheme's detection.

It is worth mentioning again that the current theories about the invertible problem were acquired on the assumption that the scale factor is constant [5,6]. However, we found that a reverse engineering can be more difficult in the case of adaptive embedding. Let us see, if $hash(\cdot)$ and $lfsr(\cdot)$ are omitted in Eq.(9), whether there still are potentials of the noninvertibility in the following revised equation:

$$h(x) \otimes w + x = x'_A . \tag{10}$$

Notably, $h(\cdot)$ might make the equation much complicated for the reverse engineering, and w can make the embedding become a ciphered and time-variant system [13]. Moreover, a pair of valid parameters, w and x, or only the w, can be reasonably required to satisfy the following criteria besides those expressed by Eq.(5) or Eq.(6):

Minor Computational Error. In a private scheme, a claimed watermark w and original x should satisfy Eq.(10) within a normal computational error. That can be expressed by $\| h(x) \otimes w + x - x'_A \| \leq \varepsilon$, where $\| \cdot \|$ represents a matrix or vector norm [14] and ε the upper bound of the allowed error norm. In actuality, an acceptable error can be so close to a rounding error of the embedding that Bob has to precisely solve the reverse equation. Other feasible methods [11,13], such as numerical estimation or signal restoration, can hardly be applicable.

Perceptual Similarity. In a private scheme, any claimed original x should be perceptually similar to the distributed version x'_A. As for a public scheme, if it requires a verifier, not an attacker, to restore x'_A to a false original x'' by the compulsory $R(x'_A, w)$, then $x''_A = R(x'_A, w_A)$ is expected to be more similar to x'_A than $x''_B = R(x'_A, w_B)$. The reason is that it is w_A, not the guessed w_B, that jointly defines the embedding such that it is the valuable knowledge to the restoration.

Statistical Semblance. To prevent an attacker from acquiring some special or easy-to-find solutions of the reverse equation, a claimed watermark should have statistical semblance, such as randomness, in either a private or a public scheme. In the sequel, we shall suppose that a verifier can use $S(w)$ to check the property.

Based on the above consideration, we think it is possible to make the embedding of Eq.(10), in either private or public schemes, noninvertible by constructing a $h(\cdot)$ so that a true owner can easily satisfy the criteria but a deceiver cannot. To acquire such a functional $h(\cdot)$, two approaches might exist. First, in principle of the inverse problems [11], an inverse processing of a linear system can have difficulty finding a numerically stable solution when the system is ill-posed. The inverse processing is sensitive to slight errors of its input or system. The errors can be drastically enlarged so that the output becomes meaningless [11,13]. Hence we can change the left side of Eq.(10) into an ill-posed linear embedding by designing $h(\cdot)$. Second, we can straightforwardly construct a nonlinear $h(\cdot)$ so that the reverse engineering has to deal with the tough work of solving a nonlinear system. In either of the cases, Bob encounters the numerical difficulties, which can be expressed by

$$\left.\begin{array}{l} S(w_B) = \text{TRUE} \\ \| h(x_B) \otimes w_B + x_B - x'_A \| \le \varepsilon \end{array}\right\} \Leftrightarrow \left\{\begin{array}{l} sim(x_B, x'_A) \ge T_1 \\ sim(x_B, x'_A) \ge sim(x_A, x'_A), \end{array}\right. \tag{11}$$

in a private scheme, and which can be expressed by

$$\left.\begin{array}{l} S(w_B) = \text{TRUE} \\ t_B = v(x'_A, w_B) \ge T \end{array}\right\} \Leftrightarrow \left\{\begin{array}{l} sim(x''_B, x'_A) \ge T_2 \\ sim(x''_B, x'_A) \ge sim(x''_A, x'_A), \end{array}\right. \tag{12}$$

in a public scheme. Here, $\Leftrightarrow$ means being infeasible to do something from left to right or vice versa. Since a scheme may reasonably require that any watermark should be coded from one alphabet, e.g. the simplest $\{0, 1\}$ or $\{-1, 1\}$, computing a valid w_B with an assumed x_B can be more difficult than computing a valid x_B with an assumed w_B. For example, having fabricated an x_B, Bob is unlikely to acquire a valid w_B whose elements are composed of only -1 and 1. Hence we shall only consider the difficulty of $\Rightarrow$.

In the above cases, we can expect that Alice gains advantages over Bob. First, she does not need to do a reverse engineering in a private scheme. Second, holding a correct watermark, she has more knowledge about the embedding so that x''_A can be more precise than x''_B in a public scheme. We shall show that it is just the advantages that ultimately differentiate Alice from Bob. Since the potential noninvertibility is a natural property of the embedding, we named it the *intrinsic noninvertibility*. The next section will investigate the methods that implement it.

3   Constructing the Intrinsically Noninvertible Private and Public Watermarking Schemes

This section is to construct and analyze the specific private and public watermarking schemes that fulfill our goal of implementing the intrinsic noninvertibility. The discussion will cover both the linear and the nonlinear approaches.

3.1 The Intrinsic Noninvertibility of Linear Watermarking

To facilitate the investigation, the embedding to be discussed in this subsection is modeled as a spatial linear system in matrix form [13]. Let us first deal with the 1-dimensional situation. Suppose an original is $x(n)$, $n = 0, 1, \cdots, L-1$, and the coefficients of an adaptive linear filter are $h(n)$, $n = 0, \pm 1, \cdots, \pm L_h$. Then the scale factor can be expressed by

$$a(n) = \sum_{m=-L_h}^{L_h} h(m)x_e(n-m), \quad n = 0, 1, \cdots, L-1, \tag{13}$$

where $x_e(n)$ extends $x(n)$ by zero-padding, symmetrical extension etc. When zero-padding is used, Eq.(13) can be expressed by $a_{L \times 1} = H_{L \times L} \cdot x_{L \times 1}$, where

$$a_{L \times 1} = [a(0) \ \cdots \ a(L-1)]^T, \quad x_{L \times 1} = [x(0) \ \cdots \ x(L-1)]^T, \tag{14}$$

and

$$H_{L \times L} = \begin{bmatrix} h(0) & \cdots & h(-L_h) & & \\ \vdots & \ddots & & \ddots & \\ h(L_h) & & \ddots & & h(-L_h) \\ & \ddots & & \ddots & \vdots \\ & & h(L_h) & \cdots & h(0) \end{bmatrix}. \tag{15}$$

Here, $H_{L \times L}$ denotes a matrix deduced from $h(n)$, and $[\cdot]^T$ the transpose of a matrix or vector. If $w(n)$, $n = 0, 1, \cdots, L-1$, represents a watermark, its diagonal form, denoted by $\hat{W}_{L \times L} = \mathrm{diag}(w(n))$, where $\hat{W}_{i,i} = w(i)$, and $\hat{W}_{i,j} = 0$ whenever $i \neq j$, is used to replace direct element multiplication with normal matrix multiplication. Then the equation of the embedding or reverse engineering can be expressed by

$$\begin{aligned} x'_A = s + x = a \otimes w + x &= \hat{W}_{L \times L} \cdot a_{L \times 1} + x_{L \times 1} \\ &= \hat{W} \cdot (H \cdot x) + x = (\hat{W} \cdot H) \cdot x + x = (\hat{W} \cdot H + E) \cdot x, \end{aligned} \tag{16}$$

where E is the identity matrix. Because $\hat{W} \cdot H + E$ is often a diagonally dominant and narrow band matrix [14], this paper presumes that its inverse always exists. The above model can be further extended to the 2-dimensional situation by the method in [13]. We do not give the steps for conciseness.

By Eq.(16), we can perceive that the embedded watermark can also be verified by common detections. For example, in the case of a private scheme, the verification can subtract the claimed original from the distributed version, and correlate the result with the claimed watermark [12]; in the case of a public scheme, the distributed version can be directly correlated with the claimed watermark [15].

The above embedding seems easy to be inverted by $x_B = (\hat{W}_B \cdot H + E)^{-1} \cdot x'_A$. However, in principle of inverse problems [11] and signal restoration [13], Bob may have great difficulty acquiring an acceptable original without the knowledge of Alice's ciphered watermark since it jointly defines her embedding system which is to be ill-posed. We have mentioned that the inverse processing of an ill-posed linear system is sensitive to errors of its system and input. Hence it would be better to see how the errors can affect the output before our further discussion. Suppose that

$C_A = \hat{W}_A \cdot H + E$, $C_B = \hat{W}_B \cdot H + E$ and $\delta C = C_B - C_A$. Let δx denote x's deviation resulting from the system error δC in solving $C_B \cdot x_B = (C_A + \delta C) \cdot (x_A + \delta x) = x'_A$. By the theory of linear equations [14,16], δx can be estimated by

$$\frac{\| \delta x \|}{\| x_A \|} \leq \frac{\| C_A^{-1} \| \cdot \| \delta C \|}{1 - \| C_A^{-1} \cdot \delta C \|} \leq \frac{\| C_A \| \cdot \| C_A^{-1} \| \cdot (\| \delta C \| / \| C_A \|)}{1 - \| C_A \| \cdot \| C_A^{-1} \| \cdot (\| \delta C \| / \| C_A \|)}, \tag{17}$$

where $\| \cdot \|$ represents a matrix or vector norm, e.g. the Euclidean norm. Moreover, the coding or rounding error $\delta x'$ of the released version x'_A can be regarded as Bob's observation error of the input. It introduces new deviation in an inverted original. We tentatively disregard the deviation resulting from δC. Thus we assume that the equation for Bob to solve is $C_B \cdot x_B = C_A \cdot (x_A + \delta x) = x'_A + \delta x'$. Likewise, by the theory of linear systems, we have

$$\frac{\| \delta x \|}{\| x_A \|} \leq \| C_A \| \cdot \| C_A^{-1} \| \cdot \frac{\| \delta x' \|}{\| x'_A \|}. \tag{18}$$

In actuality, $\| C \| \cdot \| C^{-1} \|$ is defined as the condition number of C, often denoted by cond(C). C is well-posed if cond(C) is around 1, and ill-posed if cond(C) is significantly larger than 1. In practice, the combined perturbation can be estimated by

$$\frac{\| \delta x \|}{\| x_A \|} \leq \text{cond}(C_A) \cdot \left(K \cdot \frac{\| \delta C \|}{\| C_A \|} + \frac{\| \delta x' \|}{\| x'_A \|} \right), \tag{19}$$

where K is a positive integer. Then we can assume that Bob is infeasible to acquire an acceptable original if the embedding system has a large condition number.

It is also necessary to investigate other probable ways of reverse engineering, though we have already pointed out that the methods based on numerical estimation and signal restoration are inapplicable under the restriction of minor computational error. First, exhaustively searching a functional w_B is infeasible because there are 2^L possible watermark. Second, one might attempt to retrieve an acceptable original in frequency domains. However, as we know, an ill-posed system is often low-pass, and vice versa [11,13]. For example, if Bob is to restore an original by

$$X_B(e^{n\omega j}) = \frac{X'_A(e^{n\omega j}) + \delta X'(e^{n\omega j})}{C_B(e^{n\omega j})} = \frac{X'_A(e^{n\omega j}) + \delta X'(e^{n\omega j})}{C_A(e^{n\omega j}) + \delta C(e^{n\omega j})}, \tag{20}$$

the errors will also be enlarged because the denominator of Eq.(20) has very small values over many frequency components. Third, the generalized inverse of matrices can be used in solving equations, but it cannot resist the ill-posedness also [14]. In addition, one might use iterative methods from the first sample to the last one or vice versa. However, each step of the iteration must assume the values used in the steps that follows. At the last stage of the iterations, no further assumptions can be made so that the values assumed just now have to validate both themselves and all the previously assumed ones. Hence the method is also infeasible, in particular when the filters or matrices with lager size are used.

If Bob is infeasible to acquire an acceptable original, he is already frustrated in a private scheme. However, how can we further frustrate him in a public scheme? To tackle the problem, we observe that Alice's reverse engineering, which we named the *self-inversion*, on the version distributed by herself provokes the slighter perturbation because δC is zero in Eq.(19). Then, although the original is not required by the verification so that Bob is able to claim a watermark in the distributed version, he has difficulty exhibiting a reverse engineering with a low level perturbation as Alice. In actuality, the verifier can use the claimed watermark to invert the ill-posed embedding by the above method and draw his or her conclusion by analyzing the output.

3.2 The Intrinsic Noninvertibility of Nonlinear Watermarking

Having investigated the intrinsic noninvertibility of the ill-posed linear embedding, we shall further consider the nonlinear case. Similarly, the embedding to be discussed uses a perceptually adaptive filter. However, since the filter now is nonlinear, the embedding becomes a nonlinear system. As we know, a nonlinear system can have various forms [16]. To deal with the problem in a wider context as in constructing the above linear embedding, let us begin with the discussion of the typical nonlinear embedding as follows:

$$
\begin{aligned}
x'_A(k) &= f_{w_A(k)}(x(k-L_h),\cdots,x(k)\cdots,x(k+L_h)) \\
&= x(k) + w_A(k) \cdot h(x(k-L_h),\cdots,x(k)\cdots,x(k+L_h)),
\end{aligned}
\tag{21}
$$

Here, $2L_h+1$ is the length of the adaptive filter, and $f_{w_A(k)}$ the nonlinear functions jointly defined by the different entries of a watermark and the nonlinearly adaptive filter $h(\cdot)$. Apparently, the nonlinear system is time-variant and much complicated. Nevertheless, the nonlinear part of each above function is in practice only used for scaling the watermark such that the embedding has most properties of additive watermarking. Hence the widely used detection methods [12,15] are also applicable here in either a private or a public scheme.

The noninvertibility of the above embedding lies in the well recognized difficulty of inverting a nonlinear system. In general, most nonlinear system cannot be solved directly. And inverting a time-variant nonlinear system, of which some parameters are unknown, is particularly infeasible under our previously mentioned restrictions. The current numerical algorithms for solving nonlinear system of equations, such as Newton's method, Broyden's method, the steepest descent method, homotopy method etc. [16], all require the specific knowledge about the system they are facing, and almost all of them are iterative. They can be expressed as

$$
F_w(x) = 0 \Rightarrow x = R_w(x) \Rightarrow x^{(k+1)} = R_w(x^{(k)}), k = 0,1,\cdots,N .
\tag{22}
$$

Here, $x^{(k)}$ is the result of the kth step with the exception that $x^{(0)}$ is the assumed initial value. $F_w(x) = 0$ can be regarded as the equivalent form of Eq.(21), and $R_w(x)$ the iterative function of it. If the iteration converges, $x^{(N)}$ is expected to be more precise and perceptually acceptable in the case of a correct w, namely the w_A. For example, when Newton's method is used, Eq.(22) can be expressed by

$$\begin{cases} x^{(k+1)} = x^{(k)} + \Delta x^{(k)}, \\ F_w'(x^{(k)})\Delta x^{(k)} + F_w(x^{(k)}) = 0, \end{cases} \quad k = 0,1,\cdots,N, \tag{23}$$

where $F_w'(x^{(k)})$ is the discrete derivative of F_w at $x^{(k)}$ and $\Delta x^{(k)}$ is the kth-step enhancement of the final solution. Obviously, when w is guessed, both $F_w'(x^{(k)})$ and $\Delta x^{(k)}$ can have the deviation from what they should be.

Finally, Alice still gains advantages over Bob since she already has a precise original and knows the embedding system by holding the correct watermark. In a private scheme, she does not need to do the tough work of inverting a nonlinear system. In a public scheme, to differentiate Alice from Bob, a verifier can use the claimed watermark to invert the nonlinear system by the compulsory method and draw the conclusion by analyzing the output.

4 Experiments

We divided our experiments into 5 groups, named G1-G5 respectively. The embeddings in G1 and G2 are linear, and those in G3 are nonlinear. Though all linear, G1 is designed to test the well-posed situations, while G2 to test the ill-posed situations. G4 and G5 are used to test the self-inversions of G2 and G3 respectively.

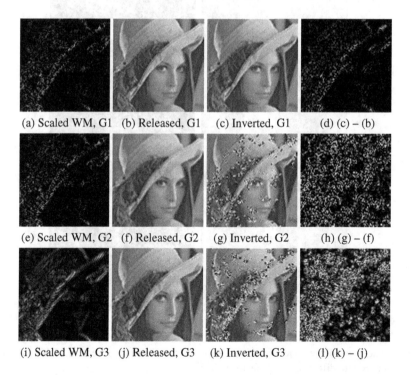

(a) Scaled WM, G1   (b) Released, G1   (c) Inverted, G1   (d) (c) – (b)

(e) Scaled WM, G2   (f) Released, G2   (g) Inverted, G2   (h) (g) – (f)

(i) Scaled WM, G3   (j) Released, G3   (k) Inverted, G3   (l) (k) – (j)

Fig. 1. A successful reverse engineering in G1 and two frustrated ones in G2 and G3 on image Lena (grayscales = 256, difference scale factor = 0.25)

Table 1. The condition numbers of 10 embedding systems in G1 and G2

λ	0.22	0.225	0.23	0.235	0.24	0.245	0.250	0.255	0.260	0.265
G1	2.563	3.139	3.294	3.503	3.793	4.137	4.738	5.267	5.972	6.176
G2	6.621	113.48	1278.9	19383	25783	30045	51291	63787	82786	72896

We here briefly introduce the methods that we used to design the experimental embeddings. Since the data perturbation often occurs in restoring low-passed signals [13], we decided using high-pass or low-pass embeddings to acquire the well-posed or ill-posed situations in G1 or G2 respectively. To hide the watermark, either a linear or a nonlinear embedding uses a perceptually adaptive filter h to analyze the degree of variation within local input. The more variable the input is, the more heavily the location is embedded. The filter estimates the variation by the mean difference of the gray levels between the processed pixel and its neighbors. In 1-dimensional cases, the filter coefficients can be represented by $h_1 = [-1/2 \ 1 \ -1/2]$ and $h_2 = [1/2 \ -1 \ 1/2]$ for high-passing and low-passing respectively. In 2-dimensional cases, it is easy to construct two separable filters, whose coefficients can be expressed by $\lambda \cdot h_1^T \cdot h_1$ and $\lambda \cdot h_2^T \cdot h_2$ respectively. Here, λ, called the *difference scale factor*, is used to adjust the

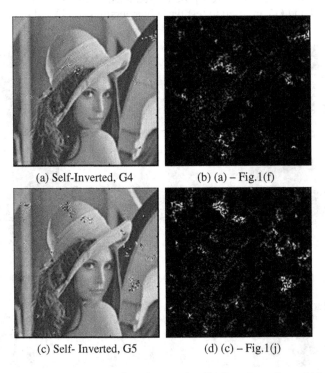

(a) Self-Inverted, G4   (b) (a) – Fig.1(f)

(c) Self- Inverted, G5   (d) (c) – Fig.1(j)

Fig. 2. The legal owner's reverse engineering on the distributed version of his or her own (grayscales = 256, difference scale factor = 0.25)

total embedding energy. The systems constructed by this way enlarge or decrease the condition numbers effectively (Table.1). In nonlinear cases, the second and third powers of the differences can be used. Anyhow, a watermark is then multiplied by the output of a filter, and embedded.

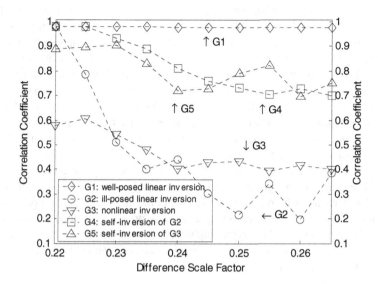

Fig. 3. The normalized correlation coefficients between the distributed version and those inverted in G1-G5 respectively

The experiments of the reverse engineering in different groups show different results (Fig.1). In G1, G2 and G4, the inverse of the embedding system's transfer matrix is use to do the reverse engineering on the linear systems, while in G3 and G5, Newton's method is used to solve the nonlinear systems. To be more efficient, an embedding and its inversion can each time use a block of enough large size, which in our experiments is of 150×150 pixels. The results from G1 demonstrate that inverting a well-posed embedding almost always provokes a low level perturbation, which means the success. The experiments in G2 and G3 show that inverting an ill-posed-linear or nonlinear embedding can be very tough in absence of the legal watermark. The inverted output is drastically perturbed and perceptually unacceptable. However, when the verifier or the owner, who has the hidden watermark, does the work, things become better (Fig.2). Hence the results of G4 or G5 not only differentiate themselves from those of G2 or G3, but also differentiate a legal owner from a deceiver. Fig.3 quantitatively depicts the differences through the correlation coefficients between the distributed version and those inverted in G1-G5 respectively.

5 Conclusions

The existing countermeasure against the invertible problem of watermarking adopts the cryptographic method that one-way generates the watermark from an original.

However, it complicates both of the embedding and the verification, and particularly, it is not applicable to the more preferred public watermarking because it has to regenerate the watermark from the original, which is unavailable in the verification.

To enhance or achieve the noninvertibility in both private watermarking schemes and public ones, this paper has introduced the concept of intrinsic noninvertibility and proposed two approaches to implementing it. The intrinsic noninvertibility means the naturally hard-to-invert property of an embedding. And we found such embeddings are often ill-posed-linear or nonlinear systems. In the case of a private scheme using the embedding, the attackers have great difficulty dividing a released version into their claimed original data and scaled watermark, and in the meantime making the latter to be the particular adaptive result based on the former. Their inverted solutions can even be drastically perturbed and not accepted by the scheme. In the case of a public scheme that exploits such noninvertibility, although a deceiver can still claim a watermark in the distributed version, he or she is infeasible to exhibit a reverse engineering by the claimed watermark with a low level perturbation like the real owner. The latter always gains advantages over an attacker because he or she holds the legal watermark, which jointly defines the embedding system. Compared with the existing countermeasure for private schemes, our proposed method is more efficient because it disposes of the cryptographic processing. And we also suggested a promising approach towards making a public scheme, which is widely considered intrinsically invertible, noninvertible.

References

1. G. C. Langelaar, I. Setyawan, R. L. Lagendijk. Watermarking digital image and video data, a state-of-the-art overview. IEEE Signal Processing Magazine, 17(5): 20-46, 2000.
2. I. J. Cox, J. M. G. Linnartz. Some general methods for tempering with watermarks. IEEE Journal on Selected Areas in Communications, 6(4): 587-593, 1998.
3. M. Kutter, F. Petitcolas. A fair benchmark for image watermarking systems. In: SPIE Proc. of Security and Watermarking of Multimedia Contents, Vol.3657: 226-239, Apr. 1999.
4. A. J. Menezes, P. C. van Oorschot, S. A. Vanstone. Handbook of Applied Cryptography. CRC Press, Inc., Boca Raton, Florida, 1997.
5. S. Craver, N. Memon, B. L. Yeo, M. M. Yeung. On the invertibility of invisible watermarking techniques. In: Proc. of 1997 International Conference on Image Processing of IEEE Signal Processing Society, Vol.3: 540-543, Oct. 1997.
6. S. Craver, N. Memon, B. L. Yeo, M. M. Yeung. Resolving rightful ownerships with invisible watermarking techniques: limitations, attacks, and implications. IEEE Journal on Selected Areas in Communications, 16(4): 573-586, 1998.
7. L. Qiao, K. Nahrstedt. Watermarking methods for MPEG encoded video: Towards resolving rightful ownership. In: Proc. of IEEE International Conference on Multimedia Computing and Systems, 276-285, Jun. 1998.
8. A. Adelsbach, S. Katzenbeisser, A. Sadeghi. On the insecurity of non-invertible watermarking schemes for dispute resolving. In: Proc. of IWDW 2003, Lecture Notes in Computer Science, Vol.2939: 355-369. Springer-Verlag, Berlin, Germany, 2003.
9. I. J. Cox, M. I. Miller. A review of watermarking and the importance of perceptual modeling. In: SPIE Proc. of Human Vision and Elec. Imaging, Vol.3016: 92-99, Feb. 1997.

10. M. D. Swanson, B. Zhu, A. H. Tewfik, L. Boney. Robust audio watermarking using perceptual masking. Signal Processing, 66(1998): 337-355, 1998.

11. A. Kirsch. An Introduction to the Mathematical Theory of Inverse Problems. Springer-Verlag, Berlin, Germany, 1996.

12. I. J. Cox, J. Kilian, T. Leighton, T. Shamoon. Secure spread spectrum watermarking for images, audio and video. In: Proc. of IEEE International Conference On Image Processing (ICIP'96), Vol.3: 243-246, Sept. 1996.

13. K. R. Castleman. Digital Image Processing, 2nd ed.. Prentice Hall, Inc., Englewood Cliffs, New Jersey, 1997.

14. P. Lancaster, M. Tismenetsky. The Theory of Matrix, 2nd ed.. Academic Press, Inc., Orlando, Florida, 1985.

15. M. Barni, F. Bartolini, V. Capellini, A. Piva. A DCT-domain system for robust image watermarking. Signal Processing, 66(1998): 357-372, 1998.

16. R. L. Burden, J. D. Faires. Numerical Analysis, 7th ed.. Thomson Learning, Inc., Stamford, Connecticut, 2001.

A Generalization of an Anonymous Buyer-Seller Watermarking Protocol and Its Application to Mobile Communications*

JaeGwi Choi and JiHwan Park

Dept. of Information Security, Pukyong National Univ.,
599-1 Daeyeon-dong Nam-ku Busan, 608-810, Korea
jae@mail1.pknu.ac.kr, jpark@pknu.ac.kr

Abstract. Buyer-seller watermarking schemes enable sellers to identify the buyer of illegally distributed contents by providing each buyer with a slightly different version. To protect the privacy of buyers, buyers' purchase should be done anonymously, and unlinkability of contents purchased should be satisfied. In this paper, our concern is to generalize a buyer-seller watermarking protocol to multi-purchase environments. The problem of most schemes in the literature is that the number of keys held by buyer's devices increases in proportion to that of contents purchased, if we apply it to multi-purchase case. Otherwise, they cannot provide unlinkability. We propose an efficient multi-purchase buyer-seller watermarking protocol satisfying anonymity and unlinkability, where a buyer executes registration step one time and the number of buyer's necessary key is also one regardless of that of contents. Our second concern is to extend this scheme to the mobile communications. Our scheme reduces amount of buyers' computations to the minimum by introducing a concept of mobile agents.

Keywords: Copyright protection, buyer-seller watermarking, mobile communications, unlinkability.

1 Introduction

Protection of intellectual property in digital contents has been a subject of research for many years and led to the development of various techniques. Copyright marking schemes have been proposed as the important class of these techniques. They are the embedding of marks into digital contents that can later be detected to identify owners (watermarking) or recipients (fingerprinting) of the contents. While digital finger-printing schemes enable a seller to identify the buyer of an illegally distributed content by providing each buyer with a slightly different version, digital watermarking schemes enable the seller/content owner to prove the rights of the contents by embedding the seller's information into the content. Buyer-seller watermarking scheme is a combination of traditional watermarking and fingerprinting techniques.

---

* This work is partly supported by grant No. 01-2002-000-00589-0 from the Basic Research Program of the Korea Science & Engineering Foundation.

I.J. Cox et al. (Eds.): IWDW 2004, LNCS 3304, pp. 232–243, 2005.

1.1 Related Works

Qian and Nahrstedt first introduced buyer-seller watermarking scheme [1]. They solved the problem of rightful ownership that is usually ignored in most watermarking scheme. It is significant in the sense that their scheme was the first one to provide protection of buyer's rights. But a seller with malicious intentions can falsely implicate an innocent buyer in this scheme, because the seller knows the watermark uniquely linked with the buyer. For example, this could be done by the malicious seller who may want to gain money by wrongly claiming that there are illegal copies around.

This problem is overcome by Memon and Wong [2]. Here, a seller cannot create copies of the original content containing the buyer's unique watermark, because he does not know the exact watermark of the buyer. Hence, if an illegal copy is found, the seller can obtain a means to prove to a third party that the buyer redistributed it and he can identify a copyright violator. However the drawback of these solutions [1][2] is that they do not provide a buyer's anonymity.

To protect buyer's privacy, several anonymous schemes have been suggested [3][4][5][6]. The idea is that the seller can know neither the watermarked content nor the buyer's real identify. Nevertheless the seller can identify the copyright violator later. The possibility of identification will only exist for a copyright violator, whereas honest buyers will remain anonymous.

1.2 Our Contributions

On the Case of Multi-purchase: In general, E-commerce system consists of a set of contents such as image, audio, a set of sellers and a set of buyers. Each buyer wants to buy some contents from a set of sellers. Then the sellers encrypt them with buyer's public key and send them to the buyer in a general buyer-seller watermarking protocol. When the buyer receives the encrypted contents, he has to decrypt them with his own secret key to use them. But a typical buyer's device holds a very limited memory and computation power. That is the reason we propose an efficient protocol for multi-purchase environments. Let's apply previous schemes to multi-purchase case. What is important in anonymous schemes is to offer anonymity of buyers and unlinkability of the contents. Anonymity means that a buyer can buy contents anonymously, and unlinkability means that anyone cannot determine whether the contents were purchased by the same buyer. Consider the case that the anonymity holds and the unlinkability does not hold. Then, if a party can trace the buyer from a transcript by any other means, the party can also trace all transcripts of the buyer. In addition to this, it facilitates de-anonymization [7]. That is, given the history of linkable transcripts of an anonymous buyer, a party may compare the history with the seller's information about when, what, and how many contents each person purchase, and thus may trace the buyer. Thus each content must be bought with different pseudonyms, because the same anonymous key implies that the buyer's purchases are linkable. In order to obtain several different pseudonyms, a buyer must go through the registration or watermark generation step several times in the previous schemes [3][4][5][6]. Besides the buyer must store secret keys as many as the number of contents to be purchased, because each content must be encrypted with different key separately [6]. It is very inefficient. Table 1 shows the comparison with our scheme and extended [6] scheme that uses the original [6] scheme repeatedly in order to provide unlinkability of contents in multi-purchase environments.

Table 1. Comparison our extended one with extended [6] scheme

	Extended [6]	Our Scheme
The number of Execution of W.G. Step[*1]	n[*2]	1
The number of Encryption Key	n	n
The number of Decryption Key	n	1

*1: Watermark Generation Step.
*2: The number of digital contents that buyers want to buy.

The results show that the number of the decryption key and execution of the watermark generation step of our scheme is very smaller than that of [6] scheme. Our scheme is significant in the sense that

1. The number of keys held by a buyer is constant regardless of that of contents purchased. The buyers can decrypt all encrypted contents with just one decryption key even if each content was encrypted with different key separately.
2. It provides unlinkability even if all contents are decrypted with one key. That is, sellers and other buyers cannot determine whether any contents were bought by the same buyer.

On the Case of Mobile Communication: In general, the watermarked content to be used for the seller's ownership can be made in off-line, because every sold copy is the same. But the content with the unique buyer's information can be made in on-line, because every sold copy is slightly different from the original contents and unique to its buyer. But most of schemes to trace a copyright violator are based on computationally unspecified black boxes. These protocols are embodied by difficult problems with much computation such as discrete logarithm problem or graph isomorphic problem. Their complexity is much too high to be materialized even in wire communication. Still less, buyer's memory and computation power in mobile communications is smaller than wire one. Thus a buyer-seller watermarking protocol with high complexity cannot be implemented in mobile communications.

In this paper, we propose an anonymous buyer-seller watermarking scheme considering buyer's device with a small memory and power for mobile communications. Our scheme is practical and secure from the following points.

1. It reduces amount of buyers' computations to the minimum because a mobile agent executes most of steps instead of the buyers.
2. Even if the buyer delegated his information to the mobile agent, only the buyer can obtain the watermarked contents.
3. The honest buyers cannot be identified as a copyright violator if the watermarking algorithm used securely, even if the mobile agent does dishonest things such as collusion with the seller.

We compare our proposal with the previous schemes [3][4][5][6] (we especially compare our proposal with [6] scheme so-called "an anonymous buyer-seller watermarking" of our scheme's basis). Table 2 and 3 show the comparison with participators of each step and computational cost of the buyer.

Table 2. Comparison between our proposal and the previous schems

	[3][4]	[6]	Our Proposal
Registration	**Buyer–RC**[*1]	**Buyer**	**Buyer–RC**
Watermark Generation	.	**Buyer–WCC**[*2]	Mobile agent-WCC
Watermark Insertion	**Buyer-Seller**	**Buyer-Seller**	Mobile agent-Seller
Identification	**Buyer, Seller, RC**	Seller, WCC, Arbiter[*3]	Seller, WCC, RC

*1: Registration Center, *2: Watermark Certification Center.
*3: The arbiter should be fixed party in the [6].

Table 3. Comparison between our proposal and [6] under a single-purchase

		[6]	Our Proposal
Watermark generation (Delegation)	Communications pass	2-pass	1-pass
	Encryption algorithm execution number	1	0
	Signature algorithm execution number	1	1
Watermark insertion	Communications pass	2-pass	1-pass
	Encryption algorithm execution number	1	0
	Decryption algorithm execution number	1	1
	Signature algorithm execution number	1	0

The paper is organized as follows. Section 2, where cryptographic primitives and building block are shown. Then, our protocol for multi-purchase is described in Section 3, and we extend it to a protocol for mobile communications in Section 4. Security and efficiency of the proposed scheme are discussed in Section 5. Finally, we conclude in Section 6.

2 Preliminaries

2.1 Building Blocks

Our scheme is based on a private watermarking scheme and a public key encryption scheme with homomorphic property defined as follows. A cryptosystems $E : G \rightarrow R$ defined on a group $(G, \cdot)$ is said to be homomorphic if f forms a (group) homomorphism. That is, given $E(x)$ and $E(y)$ for some unknown $x, y \in G$, anyone can compute $E(x, y)$ without any need for the private key. For instance, RSA cryptosystems has the property that $E(x) \cdot E(y) = E(x \cdot y)$. Besides RSA, several other homomorphic cryptosystems such as El-Gamal and Paillier cryptosystems are currently known.

Any robust watermarking scheme against various image processing operations, printing, rescanning and multiple-document (collusion) attack can be used in our scheme. For example, we can use a spread-spectrum watermarking techniques for collusion resistance. Here, a set of independent real numbers $W = \{w_1, w_2, \cdots, w_n\}$ drawn from a zero mean, variance 1, Gaussian distribution is embedded into the n largest DCT AC coefficients of an image. Results reported using the largest 1000 AC coefficients show the technique to be remarkably robust against various attack.

2.2 Notations

For ease of exposition we assume that the content being sold is a still image, though in general the protocol is also applicable to audio and video data like [2]. We also assume that all of the underlying primitives are secure.

Let $p(\leq n\ bits)$ be a large prime such that $q = (p-1)/2$ is also prime. Let G be a group of order $p-1$, and let g be a generator of G such that computing discrete logarithms to the base g is difficult.

The watermarking insertion step can be represented as $Image' = Image \oplus W$, where

- $Image$: Original image to be a vector of "features", $Image = \{ima_1, \cdots, ima_m\}$.
- W : Watermarks as a vector of "watermark elements", $W = \{w_1, \cdots, w_n\}$, $m \geq n$.
- $\oplus$: Watermarks insertion operation.
- E/D : Encryption/Decryption algorithm with homomorphic property.
- $Sign(\cdot)$: Signature algorithm.

Registration center, Watermark certification center, and buyer have a pair of a secret and a public key $(x, y) : [(x_R, y_R), (x_W, y_W), (x_B, y_B)]$ such that $y = g^x \bmod p$.

3 A Buyer-Seller Watermarking for Multi-purchase

In this section, we describe our buyer-seller watermarking protocol for multi-purchase environment.

STEP 1. Registration

1. The buyer chooses secret random x_{B1} and x_{B2} in Z_p such that $x_{B1} \cdot x_{B2} = x_B \in Z_p$.
   He sends $y_1 = g^{x_{B1}}$ and $E_{y_R}(x_{B2})$ to the Registration center (RC). The buyer convinces the RC of zero-knowledge of possession of x_{B1} . The proof given in [8] for showing possession of discrete logarithms may be used here.
2. The RC first decrypts $E_{y_R}(x_{B2})$ with his own secret key x_R and then checks that $(y_1)^{x_{B2}} = y_B \pmod{p}$. If it is verified, RC returns to the buyer certificates $Cert(y_1)$ that state the correctness of y_1 . RC keeps y_B, y_2 , and $Cert(y_1)$ secretly.

STEP 2. Watermark Generation
This protocol is performed between Watermark certification center (WCC) and the buyer.

1. The buyer sends $Cert(y_1)$ and *total* to the WCC. Here *total* means the number of contents to be purchased.

2. WCC first verifies $Cert(y_1)$ and if it holds, he generates t watermarks $(W_1, W_2, \cdots, W_t)$ randomly $(total = t)$. Note that each $W_i = \{w_{i1}, w_{i2}, \cdots, w_{in}\}$ $1 \le i \le t$ and W mentioned in the section 2.1 has the same property.

3. WCC chooses t keys $k_1, k_2, \cdots, k_t, (k_i \in Z_p)$ randomly and computes $y_1^*, y_2^*, \cdots, y_t^*$ where $y_i^* = (y_1^{k_i}, g^{k_i})$. Next, WCC encrypts each watermarks W_i with y_i^* and k_i such that $Enc\_W_i = E_{y_i^*}(W_i) = (W_i \cdot y_1^{k_i} \parallel g^{k_i})$. Then he computes signature $Sign\_W_i = Sign_{x_W}(Enc\_W_i \parallel y_i^*)$, which certifies the validity of the watermark and also ensure that y_i^* was used to encrypt W_i as a public key. Here $\parallel$ denotes a concatenation and the encryption algorithm is homomorphic mentioned in the section 2.1.

4. The WCC stores $W_i, Enc\_W_i, Sign\_W_i, Cert(y_1)$ secretly in the buyer's fields of his DataBase W_DB. Then he sends $Enc\_W_i, Sign\_W_i, y_i^*$ to the buyer.

5. The buyer verifies $Sign\_W_i$ using the WCC's public key. If it holds, he obtains the valid watermarks that can decrypt with his own secret key x_{B1}.

As mentioned before, the buyer can use the same $Cert(y_1)$, even if he wants to obtain valid watermarks from the WCC continuously.

STEP 3. Watermark Insertion
This is an interactive protocol between a seller and the buyer.

1. The buyer sends $Enc\_W_i, Sign\_W_i, y_i^*$, $text_i$, and $Sign\_B_i = Sign_{x_{B1}}(text_i)$ to the seller (It does not matter the sellers are different persons or not).

2. The seller verifies $Sign\_W_i, y_i^*$ using the WCC's public key and $Sign\_B_i$ using y_i^*. If the two aforementioned checks succeed, the next step proceeds.

3. Let $Image_i$ denote the original images which the buyer wants to purchase. The seller generates unique V_i randomly and embeds a unique watermark into contents $Image_i$. Let $Image_i'$ be the watermarked image with V_i. When an unauthorized copy $Image_i'$ is generated, this unique watermark V_i is used for identifying the original buyer of $Image_i'$. To embed the second fingerprint W_i generated by the WCC into $Image_i'$ without decrypting $E_{y_i^*}(W_i)$, the seller encrypts the watermarked content $Image_i'$ with y_i^* and finds the permutation σ_i satisfying $\sigma_i(E_{y_i^*}(W_i)) = E_{y_i^*}(\sigma_i(W_i))$. Because of the homomorphic property of the encryption algorithm E used by the WCC, the seller can compute watermarked content $E_{y_i^*}(Image_i'')$ by the following process.

$$E_{y_i^*}(Image_i'') = E_{y_i^*}(Image_i') \oplus \sigma_i(E_{y_i^*}(W_i)) = E_{y_i^*}(Image_i') \oplus E_{y_i^*}(\sigma_i(W_i))$$

$$= \{E_{y_i^*}(ima_{i1}'), \cdots, E_{y_i^*}(ima_{im}')\} \oplus \{E_{y_i^*}(w_{i\sigma_i(1)}), \cdots, E_{y_i^*}(w_{i\sigma_i(n)})\}$$

$$= \{E_{y_i^*}(ima_{i1}' \oplus w_{i\sigma_i(1)}), \cdots, E_{y_i^*}(ima_{in}' \oplus w_{i\sigma_i(n)}), \cdots, E_{y_i^*}(ima_{im}')\}$$

$$= E_{y_i^*}((Image_i \oplus V_i \oplus \sigma_i(W_i)) = [(Image_i \oplus V_i \oplus \sigma_i(W_i)) \cdot y_i^* \parallel g^{k_i}]$$

4. The seller transmits $E_{y_i^*}(Image_i'')$ to the buyer and stores $Enc\_W_i, Sign\_W_i, Sign\_B_i, y_i^*, V_i, \sigma_i$ in his DataBase $Seller\_DB$. $Seller\_DB$ is a table of records maintained by seller for image $Image$ containing one entry for each copy of $Image$ that she sells.

5. The buyer decrypts the encrypted image $E_{y_i^*}(Image_i'')$ and obtains the watermarked image $Image_i''$. Note that, buyers can decrypt the watermarked image encrypted with her owns private key x_{B1} such that

$$D_{x_{B1}}[E_{y*}(Image_i'')] = \frac{(Image_i \oplus V_i \oplus \sigma_i(W_i)) \cdot (y_i^*)}{(g^{k_i})^{x_{B1}}} = Image_i \oplus V_i \oplus \sigma_i(W_i).$$

STEP 4. Copyright Violator Identification

When an illegal copy Y of an original image $Image$ is discovered,

1. The seller extracts the unique watermark U in Y using detection algorithm. Then, he finds V_j $(1 \le j)$ with the highest correlation and obtains the transaction information involving V_j from the table by computing correlations of extracted watermark V_j and every watermark stored in $Seller\_DB$. The information consists of $Enc\_W_i, Sign\_W_i, Sign\_B_i, y_i^*, V_i, \sigma_i$. And the seller sends them with $Image, Y$ to an arbiter.

2. The arbiter verifies $Sign\_W_i$ with the WCC's public key y_W. If the verification holds, the arbiter sends y_i^* to WCC. Then the WCC sends W_i back to the arbiter.

3. The arbiter computes $\sigma_i(W_i)$ and checks the existence of $\sigma_i(W_i)$ in Y by extracting the watermark from Y and estimating its correlations with $\sigma_i(W_i)$. If there exists $\sigma_i(W_i)$, he asks the real identity of the violator to RC and reveals the buyer's ID to the seller. Otherwise, the buyer is innocent.

4   A Buyer-Seller Watermarking for Mobile Communications

In this section, we describe an anonymous buyer-seller watermarking for mobile communications. We use a mobile agent in order to reduce buyers' computation amount. This scheme consists of the 5 steps as follows: Registration, delegation, watermark generation, watermark insertion, and copyright violator identification step. Because the registration step is the same as our first scheme mentioned before, we omit it in this section. And it also can be generalized to multi-purchase protocol, but we describe a single-purchase case for simplicity.

STEP 2. Delegation

An anonymous buyer with $Cert(y_1)$ and a mobile agent execute delegation step. Here, an anonymous buyer delegates the power of signing to the mobile agent. After this step, the mobile agent is able to perform the rest steps on behalf of the buyer.

1. A buyer issues the proxy certificates, $Cert(y_p)$ to the agent. The certificates contains his own identity y_1, signature to be signed with x_{B1} on a mobile agent's public key, and *text* (see Figure 1). Where *text* is a string indicating the valid operations that the agent is allowed to perform while using the certificates.
2. The buyer sends $Cert(y_p)$ and $Cert(y_1)$ to a mobile agent.

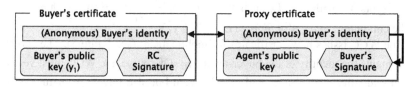

Fig. 1. Buyer binding with a proxy certificate

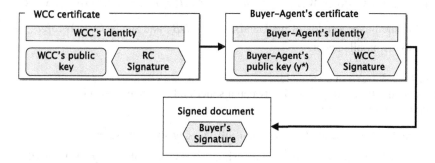

Fig. 2. Issuing new buyer-agent certificates and signature verification

Utilization of mobile agents to facilitate E-commerce is an appealing concept, especially when those operations are tedious or very difficult to perform by human users. But it is very difficult to assume the trust of mobile agent and the delegation key issuing protocol. The delegation to others can be risky because it has to carry the buyer's private information to the mobile agent. This exposes the information to attacks because it is copies outside a protected environment. To solve this problem, we use a concept of proxy certificates, which avoid the need for the mobile agent to have access to the buyer's private information, but still bind the owner to the contents of an order sheet.

The concept of proxy certificates was first introduced in [9]. Here, we modify it like fi gure 1. In our scheme, a proxy certificate is issued and signed by the owner of an agen t. It contains the identity of the agent's owner, and a set of constraints indicating the v alid operations that the agent is allowed to perform while using that certificate. The bu yer is bound to the actions performed by the agent through the owner's identity and si gnature in the proxy certificate. For this purpose, the identity in the proxy certificates must be the same as the identity in the buyer's certificate.

STEP 3. Watermark Generation

1. The mobile agent sends $Cert(y_P)$ and $Cert(y_1)$ to the WCC. If proxy certificate and buyer's certificate are correct (see figure 1), WCC generates a watermark W. In the multi-purchase case, he generates watermarks $(W_1, W_2, \cdots, W_K)$ randomly as many as the number of contents. Note that $W_i = \{w_{i1}, w_{i2}, \cdots, w_{in}\}$.

2. WCC chooses $k_0 (k_0 \in Z_p)$ randomly and computes $y_1^* = (y_1^{k_0}, g^{k_0})$. Next, he encrypts W with y_1^*, k_0 such that $Enc\_W = E_{y_1^*}(W) = (W \cdot y_1^{k_0} \parallel g^{k_0})$. Then he computes $Sign\_W = Sign_{x_W}(Enc\_W \parallel y_1^*)$.

3. The WCC issues new certificates for mobile agent (see figure 2). The certificate contains the identity of the buyer-agent y_1^*. Of course, the WCC must verify not only identity of the buyer and mobile agent but also buyer's signature on *text*. The *text* in the buyer-agent certificates must be the same as that in the proxy's certificate issued by a buyer.

4. The WCC stores $W, Enc\_W, Sign\_W, Cert(y_1^*), Cert(y_1), Cert(y_p), y_1^*$ secretly in the buyer's fields of his DataBase W_DB, and sends $Enc\_W, Sign\_W, y_1^*$ to the mobile agent.

STEP 4. Watermark Insertion

This is an interactive protocol between a seller and the mobile agent who must buy di gital image instead of the buyer.

1. A mobile agent sends $Enc\_W, Sign\_W, y_1^*, Cert(y_1^*)$ the seller.

2. The seller verifies the certificates using the WCC's public key. If the verification holds, the seller generates unique V randomly and embeds it into contents *Image*. To embed the second fingerprint W generated by the WCC into *Image′* without decrypting $E_{y_1^*}(W)$, the seller encrypts the watermarked content *Image′* with y_1^* and finds the permutation σ satisfying $\sigma(E_{y_1^*}(W)) = E_{y_1^*}(\sigma(W))$. The process is the same as the one mentioned in the section 3 (STEP.3).

$$E_{y_1^*}(Image_i'') = E_{y_1^*}(Image \oplus V \oplus \sigma(W)), m \geq n$$

3. The seller transmits $E_{y_1^*}(Image'')$ to the mobile agent and stores $Enc\_W, Sign\_W,$ $y_1^*, Cert(y_1^*), V, \sigma$ in his DataBase *Seller_DB*.

4. The mobile agent sends $E_{y_1^*}(Image'')$ to the buyer. The buyer decrypts $E_{y_1^*}(Image'')$ and obtains the watermarked image $Image''$ as follows.

$$D_{x_{B1}}[E_{y_1^*}(Image'')] = \frac{(Image \oplus V \oplus \sigma(W)) \cdot (y_1^*)}{(g^{k_0})^{x_{B1}}} = Image \oplus V \oplus \sigma(W).$$

STEP 5. Copyright Violator Identification
When an illegal copy Y of an original image $Image$ is discovered,

1. The seller finds V as the same way in the section 3 (STEP5). The information that she obtains consists of $Enc\_W, Sign\_W$, $y_1^*, Cert(y_1^*)$, V, σ. And the seller sends them with $Image, Y$ to an arbiter.
2. The arbiter verifies $Sign\_W$ with the WCC's public key y_W. If the verification holds, he sends $Cert(y_1^*)$ to WCC. Then the WCC sends W back to the arbiter.
3. The arbiter computes $\sigma(W)$ and checks the existence of $\sigma(W)$ in Y by extracting the watermark from Y and estimating its correlations with $\sigma(W)$. If there exists $\sigma(W)$, he reveal the real identity of the violator with the help of RC and WCC.

5 Features and Security Analysis

1. **Anonymity:** We assumed that the registration center does not reveal the buyer's real identity if she is honest. Even if the seller and the mobile agent know a pseudonym y_1 they cannot know y_B. Because finding y_B would require knowledge of x_{B2}. It is know to only the buyer (except RC). Thus buyer's anonymity is provided if the seller and the mobile agent cannot compute discrete logarithms.
2. **Unlinkability:** In multi-purchase, not y_1 but t different keys $(y_1^*, \cdots, y_t^*)$ are transmitted to the sellers. And each watermarked image sold to a buyer must be encrypted with each different key for unlinkability of digital contents. Thus given two digital contents, nobody can decide whether these two contents were purchased by the same buyer or not.
3. **Traceability:** Due to the properties of the underlying encryption and digital signature techniques, we can assume that a malicious buyer cannot change or substitute watermarks generated by the watermark certificate center. The security of traceability is the same as that of [2][6]. Sellers should insert a watermark V_i and $\sigma_i(W_i)$ in the right manner for his own interest. If she does not correctly insert V_i or $\sigma_i(W_i)$, she would not be able to identify the original buyer of an illegal copy. Further a detecting function in the watermark detection must guarantees that the seller can extract the unique watermark V_i that belongs to a copyright violator. Besides, buyers cannot remove $\sigma_i(W_i)$ from $Image_i''$ even though he and his mobile agent know W_i. Because they do not know permutation function σ_i. Thus the copyright violator can be traced in our scheme.

4. **No Framing:** Since, to forge Y with the special watermark W_i, the seller must know either the buyer's private key x_{B1} or the buyer's unique watermark W_i. In our proposal, only the buyer knows his private key x_{B1} and his unique watermark if computing discrete logarithm is hard and used encryption algorithm (underlying primitives) is secure. Because mobile agents can obtain only watermark encrypted with buyer's public key, the seller cannot recreate the buyer copy with specific watermark even if he colludes with the mobile agent. Thus an honest buyer should not be wrongly identified as a copyright violator.

5. **No Repudiation:** Since only the buyer can decrypt encrypted watermarked contents, the others (except WCC) cannot recreate the buyer's copy. Only the buyer can obtain the watermarked contents even though the mobile agent executes its computations instead of him. Since the watermarked contents encrypted with buyer's public key are transmitted. Thus the buyer accused of reselling an unauthorized copy should not be able to claim that the copy was created by the seller or other buyers.

6. **Collusion tolerance:** As mentioned in section 2.1, our scheme has used robust watermarking algorithms against collusion attacks. We assumed that used algorithms are secure. And these algorithms are estimated to be highly resistant at collusion attacks. Our protocol is secure only as much as the underlying watermarking techniques are secure and robust.

7. **Practical Possibility:** In previous scheme [3][5][6], the buyer has to carry out the registration and watermark insertion step. On the contrary, the buyer executes the one-time registration step and delegation step in our scheme. Our scheme reduces buyers' necessary key and computations amounts to minimum. Thus our scheme can be practically realized in real applications. We showed the proof in Table 1,2.

8. **Efficient extension:** In our scheme, the buyer executes the registration step just one time regardless of a number of contents purchased. Besides, buyers can decrypt contents with one decryption key even if each content (watermarked image) is encrypted with each different key. If the previous schemes are applied to multi-purchase protocol, the number of registration step execution and decryption keys increase in proportion to that of contents to be purchased in order to keep unlinkability. But the number of secret key stored in the buyer's device is constant independent of the number of contents purchased in our proposal.

6   Concluding Remarks

We generalized an anonymous buyer-seller watermarking protocol to multi-purchase environment. Then we extend it to system be applicable to mobile communications. Our proposal reduced the number of buyer's necessary key and the amount of buyers' computations to the minimum. We introduced a concept of mobile agent with proxy certificates, which removes risk about exposure of the buyer's private information. In result, we showed buyer-seller watermarking possible to actual practice. We expect that our scheme will be applicable to the customer-centered commercial transaction and mobile communications that buyers have a small memory and computation power.

References

[1] L.Qian and K.Nahrstedt, "Watermarking Schemes and Protocols for Protecting Rightful Ownership and Customer's Rights", J.Visual Commun. Image Represent, vol.9, pp.194-210., 1998.

[2] N.Memon and P.W.Wong, "A Buyer-Seller Watermarking Protocol", IEEE Transactions on image processing, vol.10, no. 4, pp.643-649, April 2001.

[3] B. Pfitzmann and M. Waidner, "Anonymous Fingerprinting", EUROCRYPT'97, LNCS 1233, Springer-Verlag, pp88-102, 1997.

[4] Josep Domingo-Ferrer, "Anonymous Fingerprinting Based on Committed Oblivious Transfer", Second International Workshop on Practice and Theory in Public-Key Cryptography (PKC'99), LNCS 1560, Springer-Verlag, pp43-52, 1999.

[5] B.Pfitzman and Ahmad-Reza Sadeghi, "Coin-Based Anonymous Fingerprinting", Eurocrypt'99, LNCS 1592. Springer-Verlag , pp.150-164. 2000.

[6] Hak-Soo Ju, Hyung-Jeong Kim, Dong-Hoon Lee and Jong-In Lim, "An Anonymous Buyer-Seller Watermarking Protocol with Anonymity Control", ICISC2002, LNCS 2587, Springer-Verlag, pp.421-432, 2002

[7] Tour Nakanish, Nobuaki Haruna, and Yuji Sugiyama, "Unlinkable Electronic Coupon Protocol with Anonymity Control", ISW99, LNCS 1729, Springer-Verlag, pp.37-46, 1999.

[8] Chaum, D., Evertse, J.H, and Van De Graaf. J., "An Improved Protocol for Demonstrating Possession of Discrete Logarithms and Some Generalization", EUROCRYPT'87, LNCS 304, Springer-Verlag, pp.87-119, 1987.

[9] Artur Romao and Miguel Mira da Silva, "Secure Mobile Agent Digital Signatures with Proxy Certificates", E-Commerce Agents, LNAI 2033, Springer-Verlag, pp.206-220, 2001.

Robust Frequency Domain Audio Watermarking: A Tuning Analysis

David Megías, Jordi Herrera-Joancomartí, and Julià Minguillón

Estudis d'Informàtica i Multimèdia,
Universitat Oberta de Catalunya - Av. Tibidabo 39–43, 08035 Barcelona, Spain
Tel. (+34) 93 253 7523 - Fax (+34) 93 417 6495
{dmegias, jordiherrera, jminguillona}@uoc.edu

Abstract. In this paper, a tuning analysis of a robust audio watermarking scheme is performed. The watermarking system analysed here uses a lossy compression (MPEG 1 Layer 3) method to identify the frequencies at which the marking bits will be embedded. Several tuning parameters affect the mark embedding and the mark reconstruction processes. In previous papers, these parameters have been tuned without any systematic methodology and, thus, the capacity, imperceptibility and robustness results of the watermarking scheme could be enhanced. As a final result of the tuning analysis, some tuning guidelines are suggested for the different parameters. In addition, the conclusions of this study can be extended to other spread spectrum watermarking schemes for audio. In particular, the robustness of this watermarking scheme can be enhanced whilst improving imperceptibility and reducing capacity, which is a somewhat counterintuitive result.

Keywords: Copyright protection, Audio watermarking, Frequency domain methods.

1 Introduction

Watermarking is a copy detection technique whereby a digital information (*e.g.* an audio file) is marked prior to its distribution. The embedded *mark* can be retrieved later to find out whether the information is illegally distributed. From a construction point of view, any watermarking scheme can be described in two stages: mark embedding and mark reconstruction. Since the former determines the mark reconstruction process, the real problem is *where* and *how* the mark should be embedded into the audio file.

The three basic properties a watermarking scheme should provide [1, 2, 3, 4] are *imperceptibility*, *capacity* and *robustness*. Imperceptibility measures the distortion produced by the mark embedding process. Ideally, the mark embedded into the audio file should be imperceptible for the listener, in such a way that the marked version of the audio file is indistinguishable from the original one. Capacity is the amount of information that can be embedded into the audio file, normally measured in bits per second. Finally, robustness determines the resistance to accidental removal of the embedded mark. All three properties are mutual dependent, for instance, increasing imperceptibility typically reduces capacity and, also, decreasing capacity decreases robustness. Hence, a trade-off between them must be achieved.

I.J. Cox et al. (Eds.): IWDW 2004, LNCS 3304, pp. 244–258, 2005.

Audio files allow multiple manipulations without affecting its perceptual quality. For that reason, the mark embedding process of an audio watermarking algorithm can be performed in many different ways. However, a convenient strategy to determine where and how to embed the mark is to maximize robustness, since this is the most important property of a watermarking scheme. On the other hand, imperceptibility can be obtained exploiting the spectral characteristics of the audio signal to determine the place where the mark should be embedded [5, 6, 7]. Other proposals [8] use echo coding techniques which encode the mark by using different delays between the original signal and the echo. Such a technique increases robustness against MPEG 1 Layer 3 audio compression and digital-analog conversion, but is not suitable for speech signals with frequent silence intervals. Robustness against various signal processing operations is also increased in [9] by dividing the set of the original samples in embedding segments. A more detailed state of the art in audio watermarking can be found in [3].

In this paper, we present a tuning analysis of the audio watermarking scheme for Pulse Code Modulation (PCM) file formats suggested in [10]. The audio scheme suggested here, following the ideas of [11], uses a lossy compression (MPEG 1 Layer 3) method to identify the frequencies at which the marking bits will be embedded. Several tuning parameters affect the mark embedding and the mark reconstruction processes but, in previous papers, these parameters have been tuned without any systematic methodology. To improve the main watermarking properties: capacity, imperceptibility and robustness, a systematic tuning method has been applied. The ideal goal of the tuning adjustment is to obtain a optimal trade-off between a maximum capacity, a high imperceptibility degree and a maximum robustness against the major number of attacks of the StirMark benchmark for audio (SMBA) [12].

This paper is organized as follows. Section 2 describes the audio watermarking scheme. In Section 3, we define the parameters used to measure the performance of the proposed scheme in terms of imperceptibility, capacity and robustness. Section 4 presents the tuning analysis of the variable parameters used in the embedding algorithm in order to determine the best configuration. Finally, Section 5 summarizes the conclusions and suggests some guidelines for future research.

2   Audio Watermarking Scheme

The audio watermarking scheme presented in [13, 10] is described in the next sections.

2.1   Mark Embedding

Let the (mono) signal S to be marked be a collection of PCM samples (for example a RIFF-WAVE[1] file) and let S_F be the spectrum of S computed with a Fast Fourier Transform (FFT). The signal S is compressed using a MPEG 1 Layer 3 algorithm with a rate of R Kbps (tuning parameter) and decompressed again to PCM format. The result of this compression/decompression operation is a new signal S', and its spectrum S'_F is obtained[2].

---

[1] RIFF-WAVE stands for Resource Interchange File Format-WAVEform audio file format.
[2] Throughout this paper, the Blade codec [14] (**cod**er/**dec**oder) for the MPEG 1 Layer 3 algorithm has been chosen and, thus, the psychoacoustic model of this codec is implicitly used.

Now, the set of marking frequencies F_{mark} is chosen as follows:

1. All $f_i \in F_{\text{mark}}$ must belong to the relevant frequencies F_{rel} of the original signal S_F:

$$F_{\text{rel}} = \left\{ f \in \left[0, \frac{f_{\text{max}}}{2} \right] : |S_F(f)| \geq \frac{p}{100} |S_F|_{\text{max}} \right\},$$

where $f_{\text{max}} = 1/T_s$ is the maximum frequency of the spectrum, T_s is the sampling time, $p \in [0, 100]$ is a percentage and $|S_F|_{\text{max}}$ is the maximum magnitude of the spectrum[3] S_F. This means that the magnitude $|S_F(f_i)|$ must be no lower than a given percentage p (tuning parameter) of the maximum magnitude of S_F.

2. Now, the frequencies to be marked are those for which the magnitude remains "unchanged" after compression and decompression, *i.e.* when the relative error in the magnitude is below some given threshold ε (tuning parameter):

$$F_{\text{mark}} = \{f_1, f_2, \ldots, f_n\} = \left\{ f \in F_{\text{rel}} : \left| \frac{S_F(f) - S_F'(f)}{S_F(f)} \right| < \varepsilon \right\}.$$

Similarly, as done in the image watermarking scheme of [11], a 70-bit stream mark, W ($|W| = 70$), is firstly extended to a 434-bit stream W_{ECC} ($|W_{\text{ECC}}| = 434$) using a dual Hamming Error Correcting Code (ECC). This coding makes it possible to apply the watermarking scheme as a fingerprinting scheme robust against collusion of two buyers [15]. Finally, a pseudo-random binary stream (PRBS), generated with a cryptographic key k, is added to the extended mark as it is embedded into the original signal.

Once the frequencies in F_{mark} have been chosen, the mark embedding process modifies the magnitude of the spectrum at the chosen frequencies as follows:

$$\hat{S}_F(f) = \begin{cases} S_F(f), & f \notin F_{\text{mark}}, \\ S_F(f) \cdot 10^{d/20} & f \in F_{\text{mark}}, \text{ to embed '1'}, \\ S_F(f) \cdot 10^{-d/20} & f \in F_{\text{mark}}, \text{ to embed '0'}. \end{cases}$$

i.e. the magnitude of $S_F(f_i)$ is increased or decreased d dB (tuning parameter) in order to embed a '1' or a '0', respectively[4]. The parameter d must be small to make the mark imperceptible, but large enough to allow the reconstruction of the mark from an attacked signal. Notice, also, that n (the number of frequencies to be marked) should be greater than or equal to the length $|W_{\text{ECC}}|$ of the extended mark (434 in our example). In a typical situation, the mark is embedded tens or hundreds of times all over the spectrum $\hat{S}_F$. Finally, the marked audio signal is converted to the time domain $\hat{S}$ applying an inverse FFT (IFFT) algorithm. The whole mark embedding process is depicted in the block diagram of Fig. 1 and can be denoted in terms of the following expression:

$$\text{Embed}\, (S, W, \text{par.} = \{R, p, \varepsilon, d, k\}) \rightarrow \left\{ \hat{S}, F_{\text{mark}} \right\}.$$

---

[3] Note that the spectrum values in the interval $[f_{\text{max}}/2, f_{\text{max}}]$ are the complex-conjugate of those in $[0, f_{\text{max}}/2]$.

[4] Since the spectrum components in S_F are paired (pairs of complex-conjugate values), the same transformation must be performed to $S_F(f_i)$ and to its conjugate.

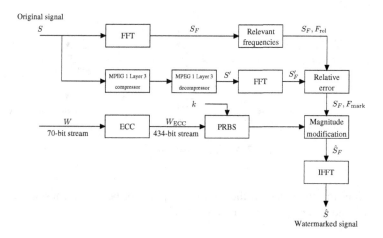

Fig. 1. Mark embedding process

2.2   Mark Reconstruction

The objective of the mark reconstruction algorithm is to detect whether an audio test signal T is a (possibly attacked) version of the marked signal $\hat{S}$. It is assumed that T is in PCM format. If it were not the case, a format conversion step (*e.g.* decompression) should be performed prior to the application of the reconstruction process.

First of all, the spectrum T_F is obtained applying the FFT algorithm and, then, the magnitude at the marking frequencies $|T_F(f_i)|$, for all $f_i \in F_{\text{mark}}$, is computed. Note that this method is strictly positional and, because of this, it is required that the number of samples in $\hat{S}$ and T be the same. If there is only a little difference in the number of samples, it is possible to complete the sequences with zeroes. When the magnitudes $|T_F(f_i)|$ are available, a scaling (Least Squares) step is undertaken in order to minimise the distance between the sequences $\{|T_F(f_i)|, f_i \in F_{\text{mark}}\}$ and $\left\{\left|\hat{S}_F(f_i)\right|, f_i \in F_{\text{mark}}\right\}$. This standard LS step provides with a scaling factor λ which multiplies the sequence $\{T_F\}$ (see [13] for details). Now, the $r_i = \lambda|T_F(f_i)|/|S_F(f_i)|$ ratios are computed and compared with $10^{d/20}$ to decide wether a '0', a '1' or a '*' (not identified) might be embedded at the i-th position:

$$r_i \in \left[10^{\frac{d}{20}}\left(\frac{100-q}{100}\right), 10^{\frac{d}{20}}\left(\frac{100+q}{100}\right)\right] \Rightarrow \hat{b}_i := \text{'1'},$$

$$\frac{1}{r_i} \in \left[10^{\frac{d}{20}}\left(\frac{100-q}{100}\right), 10^{\frac{d}{20}}\left(\frac{100+q}{100}\right)\right] \Rightarrow \hat{b}_i := \text{'0'}.$$

If none of these two conditions are satisfied, then $\hat{b}_i := \text{'*'}$. Here, $q \in [0, 100]$ (tuning parameter) is a percentage and $\hat{b}_i$ is the i-th component of the vector $\hat{b}$ which contains a sequence of "detected bits". Finally, the PRBS signal is removed from $\hat{b}$ to recover the true embedded bits b. This operation must preserve the '*' marks.

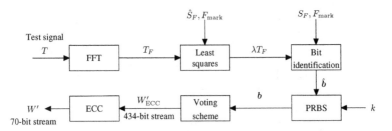

Fig. 2. Mark reconstruction process

According to this equation, the parameter q cannot be freely chosen. In order to recover '1's and '0's properly it is required that[5].

$$10^{\frac{d}{20}} \left(\frac{100 - q}{100} \right) > 1 \Leftrightarrow q < 100 \left(1 - 10^{-d/20} \right), \tag{1}$$

Once b has been obtained, its length n will be greater than the length of the extended mark (434 bits in this paper). Hence, each bit of the mark appears at different positions in b: the i-th bit should appear at b_{i+434j} for $j = 0, 1, 2, \dots$ A *voting* scheme (see [13] for details) is applied to choose wether the i-th bit of the mark is '1', '0' or unidentified ('*'). Let n_0, n_1 and n_*, be the number of '0's, '1's and '*'s identified for *the same* mark bit. The voting scheme used in this method ignores the '*' if n_* is not more than twice the difference $|n_1 - n_0|$:

$$\text{bit} := \begin{cases} \text{'*' if } n_* > 2\,|n_1 - n_0| \text{ or } n_1 = n_0, \\ \text{'1' if } n_* \le 2\,|n_1 - n_0| \text{ and } n_1 > n_0, \\ \text{'0' if } n_* \le 2\,|n_1 - n_0| \text{ and } n_0 > n_1. \end{cases}$$

A more sophisticated method using weighted voting or a statistical analysis of the ratios r_i might be applied instead of this voting scheme. As a result of this voting scheme, an identified extended mark W'_{ECC} is obtained and the error correcting algorithm is used to recover an identified 70-bit stream mark, W', which will be compared with the true mark W. The whole reconstruction process is depicted in Fig. 2 and can be described in terms of the following expression:

$$\text{Reconstruct}\left(T, S, \hat{S}, F_{\text{mark}}, \text{par.} = \{q, d, k\} \right) \to \{W', b\}.$$

The proposed scheme is not blind, in the sense that the original signal is needed by the mark reconstruction process. On the other hand, the bit sequence which forms the embedded mark is not needed for reconstruction, which makes this method suitable also for fingerprinting [16].

---

[5] For $d = 1$, $q < 10.8749$, which is compatible with $q = 10$ chosen for the experiments (see Section 4).

2.3 Modification for Stereo Files

This section summarises a modification to the watermarking scheme, described in [10]. In the stereo case, the original signal $S_{\text{stereo}} = [S_{\text{left}}, S_{\text{right}}]$ consists of two separate mono signals, one for the left channel (S_{left}) and the other for the right channel (S_{right}). In order to work with stereo signals, let us define a new signal $S = S_{\text{left}} + S_{\text{right}}$ and apply the mark embedding process described in Section 2.1 (Fig. 1) to S. In this case, the modified signal S' is obtained by summing S'_{left} and S'_{right} which result after compression/decompression. When the marking frequencies F_{mark} are available, the magnitude modification step is applied to both S_{left} and S_{right} independently **at the same frequencies**. Since magnitude modification is a linear transformation, this is completely equivalent to modify the magnitude of the signal $S = S_{\text{left}} + S_{\text{right}}$. Once both channels have been marked, the marked signal is denoted as $\hat{S}_{\text{stereo}} = \left[\hat{S}_{\text{left}}, \hat{S}_{\text{right}}\right]$.

The modification of the mark reconstruction method for the stereo case is straightforward. Given the test signal $T_{\text{stereo}} = [T_{\text{left}}, T_{\text{right}}]$, the mark reconstruction process depicted in Section 2.2 can be directly applied using: $S = S_{\text{left}} + S_{\text{right}}$, $\hat{S} = \hat{S}_{\text{left}} + \hat{S}_{\text{right}}$, $T = T_{\text{left}} + T_{\text{right}}$, and their corresponding spectra (S_F, $\hat{S}_F$ and T_F).

3 Performance Measures

As pointed out in Section 1, three main measures are commonly used to assess the performance of the watermarking schemes: capacity, imperceptibility and robustness.

3.1 Capacity

Capacity (C) is the amount of information that may be embedded and recovered. In order to measure C (often given in bps) for the scheme described in this paper, it must be taken into account that the extended watermark is highly redundant: 70 bits of information plus 364 bits of redundancy. Hence, only $70/434$ of the marked bits n (the size of F_{mark}) are the true capacity, *i.e.* $C = 70n/(434l)$, where l is the length (in seconds) of the marked signal. Nevertheless, note that this redundancy is useful to the robustness of the method, as it allows to correct errors once the extended mark W'_{ECC} is recovered.

3.2 Imperceptibility

Imperceptibility is the extent to which the embedding process leaves undamaged the perceptual quality of the marked object. In other words, it is concerned with the audio quality of the marked signal $\hat{S}_{\text{stereo}}$ with respect to S_{stereo}. In this paper, the signal-to-noise ratio (SNR) is used to assess imperceptibility. Given a signal σ and a disturbed version $\hat{\sigma}$, the SNR measure determines the power of the original signal relative to the noise:

$$\text{SNR} = \frac{\sum_{i=1}^{N} \sigma_i^2}{\sum_{i=1}^{N} (\sigma_i - \hat{\sigma}_i)^2},$$

where N is the number of samples and σ_i ($\hat{\sigma}_i$) denotes the i-th sample of σ ($\hat{\sigma}$). Usually, SNR values are given in dB by performing the operation $10 \log_{10}(\text{SNR})$. Both the left and right channels are considered in the stereo case: $\sigma = [S_{\text{left}}; S_{\text{right}}]$, where ";" stands for the append operator. Although SNR is a simple way to measure the noise introduced by the embedded mark and can give a general idea of imperceptibility, it does not take into account the specific characteristics of the Human Auditory System (HAS) and, thus, better measures should be used in the future research. In particular, the use of HAS models should be investigated [17] or auditive perceptual tests might be performed.

3.3   Robustness

Robustness is the resistance to accidental removal of the embedded bits. The robustness of the suggested scheme has been tested for 43 different attacks of the SMBA [12], version 0.2, using **default** values for the parameters of the attacks. The attacks which modify the number of samples in a significant way (CutSamples, ZeroLength, ZeroRemove, CopySample and Resampling) cannot be tested with the current version of the scheme. In addition, the attack AddFFTNoise destroys the audio file (it produces no sound) and has not been included in the results.

Robustness has been assessed using a correlation measure between the embedded mark W and the identified mark W'. Let W_i and W'_i be, respectively, the i-th bit of W and W', and let

$$\beta_i = \begin{cases} 1, & \text{if } W_i = W'_i, \\ -1, & \text{if } W_i \neq W'_i. \end{cases}$$

Now, the correlation is computed, taking into account β_i for all $|W|$ bits (70 in our case) of the mark, as follows: Correlation $= \frac{1}{|W|} \sum_{i=1}^{|W|} \beta_i$. This measure is 1 when all $|W|$ bits are correctly recovered ($W = W'$) and -1 when all $|W|$ bits are misidentified. A value of about 0 is expected when 50% of the bits are correctly recovered, as it would occur if the mark bits were reconstructed randomly. In this paper, we consider that the watermarking scheme survives an attack **if the correlation is greater than or equal to 0.8**, *i.e.* if at least 90% of the mark bits are correctly recovered. The results for robustness are shown as an integer number (denoted by **Rob**) in the range $[0, 43]$, which means how many attacks have been survived by the scheme out of the 43 attacks performed. Thus, values approaching 43 mean that the method is robust.

4   Tuning Analysis

In this section, a tuning analysis of the parameters R, p, ε, d and q of the watermarking scheme described in Section 2 is performed. The watermarking scheme has been implemented using a dual binary Hamming code $DH(31, 5)$ as ECC and the pseudo-random generator is a DES cryptosystem implemented in an Output Feedback (OFB) mode. A 70-bit mark W (resulting in an encoded W_{ECC} with $|W_{\text{ECC}}| = 434$) was embedded.

To test the performance of the suggested audio watermarking scheme (the modification of Section 2.3), different files provided in the Sound Quality Assessment Material (SQAM) page [18] have been used. In order to synthesise the results as much as possible, only the experiments performed for the (stereo) violoncello (melodious phase) file[6]

---

[6] In fact, only the first ten seconds (441000×2 samples) of the file have been taken into account.

are shown. Completely analogous results have been obtained for the other files in this corpus set (including instrumental music, voice music and speech). The reason for this choice is that the violoncello file is an average case as capacity is concerned (three times the minimum capacity and one fourth the maximum capacity obtained for the SQAM corpus). Therefore, the results should not be biased in either direction.

The experiments performed in this section start from a "nominal" tuning of the different parameters: $R = 128$ Kbps (the most commonly used bit rate), $p = 2$ (only the frequencies for which the magnitude of S_F is, at least, a 2% of the maximum magnitude are considered relevant), $\varepsilon = 0.05$ (a magnitude is considered unchanged after compression/decompression if it varies less than a 5%), $d = 1$ dB (the disturbance of the spectrum at each marking frequency) and, finally, $q = 10$ (a $\pm 10\%$ band is defined about d in order to reconstruct '1's and '0's). In each experiment, one of these parameters will vary whilst keeping the rest unaltered in order to analyse the effect of that parameter. In this nominal case, the results obtained with the watermarking scheme are: $\{C = 61.08 \text{ bps}, \text{SNR} = 18.95 \text{ dB}, \text{Rob} = 35\}$ *i.e.*, the mark is embedded more than 8 times ($8 \cdot 70 = 560 < 610 \approx 61.08 \cdot 10 < 630 = 9 \cdot 70$) within the file (10 seconds), the power of the noise introduced by watermarking is roughly 0.01 the power of the original signal and the scheme survives 35 attacks out of 43.

The influence of the tuning parameters on these three properties can be told *a priori*. The parameters R, p and ε determine how many frequencies are chosen for watermarking and, thus, they affect both the imperceptibility of the mark and the capacity of the watermarking scheme. Since the marking frequencies are chosen according to the difference between S and S', the rate R is a key parameter in this process. The percentage p determines which frequencies are significant enough to be taken into account and, thus, this is a relevant parameter as capacity is concerned. Finally, the relative error ε is used to measure wether two spectral values of S and S' are taken to be equal, which also affects the number of marking frequencies. The larger the number of marking frequencies is, the more perceptible the mark becomes. This establishes a link between the imperceptibility and the capacity of the watermarking scheme. Hence, a trade-off between imperceptibility and capacity must be achieved. Note, also, that capacity is related to robustness, since it is expected that the scheme becomes more robust as the mark is replicated more times in the mark embedding process. The parameter d does not affect the number of marking frequencies, but it is directly related to imperceptibility. The greater d is chosen, the more distortion is introduced in the mark embedding process. On the other hand, low values of d would affect robustness negatively, since the mark would be more easily removed. Thus, a trade-off value must be chosen. Finally, q is used only in the mark reconstruction process. Therefore, it does not have any influence on capacity or imperceptibility, but it affects the way that the mark bits are recovered from an attacked signal. The effect of this parameter on robustness must be analysed. In the next sections, the effect of the different tuning parameters is examined.

4.1   Bit Rate R

Here, the tuning parameters (p, ε, d, q) are fixed to the nominal values: $(1, 0.05, 1, 10)$, whereas R takes the values:

$$R \in \{32, 40, 48, 56, 64, 80, 96, 112, 128, 160, 192, 224, 256, 320\} \text{ Kbps.}$$

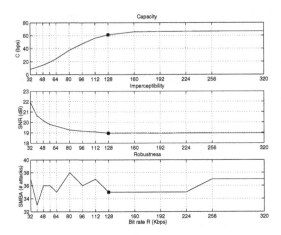

Fig. 3. Tuning results for the bit rate R

The results are displayed in Fig. 3, where a square mark shows the nominal value $R = 128$ Kbps. It can be observed that capacity increases with the bit rate R, as expected, since the larger R is, the more similar S and S' become. In addition, as capacity increases, the imperceptibility of the mark decreases, since the magnitude of the spectrum is modified at more frequencies. Finally, we can see that there is not a clear link between this parameter and robustness. The number of survived attacks varies from 33 to 38 for different values of R, but there is not a monotonic pattern for this variation.

4.2   Magnitude Modification d

The parameter d describes how many dB the magnitude of the original signal is modified at the marking frequencies. Therefore, it only affects imperceptibility and robustness but not capacity (the number of marking frequencies) which is constant and equal to the nominal value $C = 61.08$ bps. In this section, the parameters (R, p, ε) are fixed to the nominal values $(128, 2, 0.05)$ whereas d varies. In this case, the parameter q must vary accordingly, as shown in Equation 1. Taking into account that the nominal tuning is $(d, q) = (1, 10)$, whereas the the maximum q obtained for $d = 1$ is 10.8749, we have chosen a $10/10.8749$ factor applied to Equation 1 to determine the value of q associated with each value of d, giving the pairs[7]:

$$(d, q) \in \{(0.1, 1), (0.2, 2), (0.5, 5), (1, 10), (2, 19), (5, 40)\}.$$

The results obtained with these values are shown in Fig. 4 where, again, the square mark is used for the nominal value $(d, q) = (1, 10)$. Note that imperceptibility clearly increases as d decreases, as expected. SNR values of about 20 dB are obtained with the nominal value $d = 1$ dB, which means that the noise introduced by the mark is about 0.01 times the power of the original signal. With the value $d = 0.2$ dB, the SNR

---

[7] Since q is a percentage, we have used rounded values.

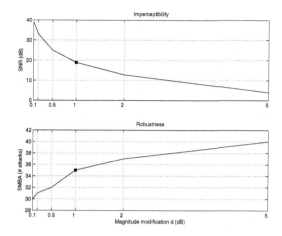

Fig. 4. Tuning results for the magnitude modification d

increases to over 30 dB, meaning that the noise introduced is **less than 0.001 times** the power of the original signal. As a result of an increased imperceptibility, the scheme is less robust for lower values of d (for example, the number of survived attacks reduces to 31 for $d = 0.2$ dB, compared with the 35 attacks survived for $d = 1$ dB). However, when imperceptibility is the priority, d should be chosen for tuning. This experiment is a good example of the link between imperceptibility and robustness. Usually, an increase in the former produces a decrease in the latter and conversely.

4.3   Percentage p

In this section, the nominal parameters are $(R, \varepsilon, d, q) = (128, 0.05, 1, 10)$, whereas p takes the values $\{0.2, 0.5, 1, 2, 5, 10, 20\}$. The results are displayed in Fig. 5 where, as usual, the square mark indicates the nominal value $p = 2$. Note that the horizontal axis in the robustness (bottom) graph is different from the rest. The reason for this is that $p = 20$ has a very low capacity $C = 4.29$ bps and, thus, there is no room for even a single copy of the mark. Hence, the last result for robustness has been obtained for $p = 10$. The figure shows that the larger p is, the lower the capacity becomes. This was absolutely expectable since p limits the amount of candidate marking frequencies. A value near 0 means that all frequencies for which the magnitude does not vary between S and S' would be marked. As p approaches to 100, only the frequencies with a large magnitude can be chosen. At the same time, any increase in capacity leads to a decrease in imperceptibility and conversely. But, the more surprising thing about this experiment is the robustness results. Intuitively, one may think that a greater capacity (more marked frequencies) should improve robustness, but the results are the opposite. The number of survived SMBA attacks increases when capacity decreases. The reason for this pattern of behaviour is that it is better to mark fewer frequencies, if they are significant, than to mark many frequencies which are more easily disturbed by the attacks in the SMBA. Notice that this result makes it possible to improve robustness and imperceptibility at the same time by increasing p.

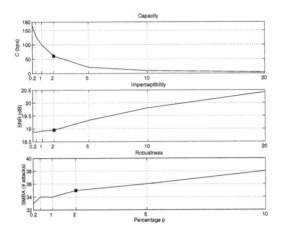

Fig. 5. Tuning results for the percentage p

4.4 Relative Error ε

Here, the fixed parameters are $(R, p, d, q) = (128, 2, 1, 10)$ and ε takes the values $\{0.01, 0.02, 0.05, 0.1, 0.2\}$. The results, shown in Fig. 7 (with a square mark for the nominal value), are analogous to those obtained by tuning p. As ε is larger, more frequencies are candidate for marking, since the relative error between the spectra of S and S' can be greater. Consequently, imperceptibility behaves in the opposite direction. Similarly as obtained for p, the tuning of ε makes it possible to improve both imperceptibility and robustness (choosing low values of ε). The conclusion of this experiment is that it is better to choose those frequencies for which the magnitude is *really* unaltered (note that "exactly unaltered" means $\varepsilon = 0$) after compression/decompression. Again, the results obtained improve when the chosen frequencies are really significant, but when the tuning parameter is ε instead of p, the sense of "significant" is "unaltered by the compression algorithm" rather than "with a large magnitude".

4.5 Tuning the Percentage q

The last parameter to study is the percentage q used to recover the embedded bits. The fixed parameters are $(R, p, \varepsilon, d) = (128, 2, 0.05, 2)$, where d has been increased from 1 to 2 with respect to the nominal case. The reason for this increase in d is that it allows a greater variation in the percentage q as shown in Equation 1. The values chosen for q are $\{0.5, 1, 2, 5, 10, 15, 19\}$. The only property modified by this parameter is robustness, since it does not affect the mark embedding process at all. The results are shown in Fig. 6, where it can be observed that robustness increases monotonically with q. Thus, the conclusion is that it is better to choose q as large as possible (always satisfying the bound given in Equation 1).

Note that this result can lead to a simplified mark reconstruction process. If the percentage q is set as large as possible, there is no need to check the intervals for

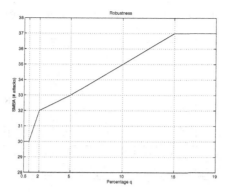

Fig. 6. Tuning results for the percentage q

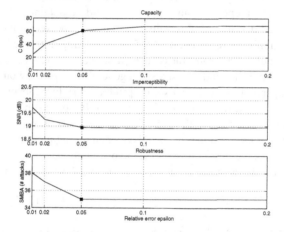

Fig. 7. Tuning results for the relative error ε

the ratios r_i (see Section 2.2). A simpler procedure[8] would assign $b_i := $ '1' when $\lambda |T_F(f_i)| > |S_F(f_i)|$ and $b_i := $ '0' when $\lambda |T_F(f_i)| < |S_F(f_i)|$. In addition, this would also simplify the voting scheme, since n_* would always be 0.

4.6 Tuning Guidelines

In the light of the experimental tuning results presented above, some tuning guidelines for the different parameters are suggested and tested in this section.

The parameter R can be tuned for capacity and imperceptibility. The increase in capacity is low for rates $R > 128$ Kbps, thus, this may seem a good choice. If im-

---

[8] This simpler procedure is not exactly equivalent to choosing the largest possible values for q, since r_i values greater than the upper limit of the interval for '1's result in $b_i := $ '0' instead of $b_i := $ '*'. The same occurs for r_i values lower than the lower limit of the interval for '0's.

Table 1. Performance results for 9 tuning settings

	$p = 2, \varepsilon = 0.01$	$p = 5, \varepsilon = 0.02$	$p = 5, \varepsilon = 0.01$
Capacity	$C = 18.15$ bps	$C = 24.74$ bps	$C = 12.74$ bps
$d = 1, q = 10$	SNR $= 19.49$ dB	SNR $= 19.70$ dB	SNR $= 19.89$ dB
	Rob $= 38$	Rob $= 38$	Rob $= 38$
$d = 0.5, q = 5$	SNR $= 25.52$ dB	SNR $= 25.75$ dB	SNR $= 25.87$ dB
	Rob $= 36$	Rob $= 36$	Rob $= 36$
$d = 0.2, q = 2$	SNR $= 33.48$ dB	SNR $= 33.72$ dB	SNR $= 33.85$ dB
	Rob $= 36$	Rob $= 36$	Rob $= 36$

perceptibility is the priority, lower values of R can be chosen. As d is concerned, a trade-off between imperceptibility and capacity should be obtained. A value of $d = 1$ yields SNR about 20 dB, though this value, of course, depends on the particular file. If better imperceptibility is required, $d = 0.5$ or lower might be used, but taking into account that this would affect robustness. The parameters p and ε have a similar effect on capacity, imperceptibility and robustness. In general, $1 \leq p \leq 5$ would provide good robustness and imperceptibility (larger values produce very low capacity). On the other hand, low values of ε are advisable, for example $\varepsilon = 0.01$. It must be taken into account that reducing ε and increasing p at the same time will have a double effect on imperceptibility and capacity, thus, caution must be taken when tuning these parameters. Finally, the best choice for q is the largest possible value of Equation 1.

Taking these guidelines into account, we have tested 9 different tuning settings:

$$(p, \varepsilon, d, q) \in \{(2, 0.01), (5, 0.02), (5, 0.01)\} \times \{(1, 10), (0.5, 5), (0.2, 2)\},$$

all of them using $R = 128$ Kbps. The performance results are displayed in Table 1. Capacity does not depend on (d, q), and, as expected, the minimum capacity is obtained for $(p, \varepsilon) = (5, 0.01)$. Surprisingly enough, although capacity is really low (not even enough for embedding the mark twice in the last column), the robustness results for $(d, q) = (1, 10)$ are the best (38 survived attacks) among all the experiments performed with this file. The rows for $(d, q) = (0.5, 5)$ and $(d, q) = (0.2, 2)$ show that it is possible to improve imperceptibility, even above 30 dB, at the price of decreasing robustness.

5 Conclusions and Future Research

In this paper, a tuning analysis on a frequency domain audio watermarking scheme is performed. The watermarking system uses MPEG 1 Layer 3 compression (and decompression) in the mark embedding process in order to determine which frequencies should be chosen for watermarking. In this process, several parameters are used: the bit rate of the compressed file (R Kbps), the percentage of the maximum magnitude to choose candidate frequencies (p), the relative error between the magnitudes of the original and the compressed files at a given frequency (ε), and the amount (d dB) that a magnitude is disturbed in order to embed a mark bit. An additional parameter is required for the mark reconstruction process, a tolerance percentage (q) about $\pm d$ dB in order to recover '1's and '0's.

The experiments show that R affects capacity and imperceptibility. Large values of R (about 128 Kbps) produce large capacity at the price of decreasing imperceptibility. The parameter d affects imperceptibility and robustness only, making it possible to enhance imperceptibility (even to over 30 dB in SNR) by loosing some robustness. The most interesting result has been provided by the tuning analysis of the parameters p and ε. These parameters can be tuned in such a way that both imperceptibility and robustness are enhanced at the same time. Some examples show that it is possible to reduce capacity and increase robustness, a possibility which is quite counterintuitive. As q is concerned, the experiments show that it is better to choose the tolerance bands about $\pm d$ dB as large as possible to recover the mark bits. The tuning experiments have led to tuning guidelines which have been also proven successful.

There are several directions to further the research presented in this paper. The first one, is to use alternative measures for imperceptibility. SNR values do not take into account the properties of the Human Auditory System and other methods should be applied. As robustness is concerned, some modification of the scheme is required to cope with attacks which change the number of samples in the attacked signal in a significant way. In addition, the scheme suggested here requires the whole file both for mark embedding and for mark reconstruction. The possibility of working only with pieces should be addressed. Finally, *security* should be the aim of all watermarking schemes. Of course, this scheme is still far from being secure. A secure scheme should be able to survive attacks designed by someone who knows the watermarking algorithm except from a (secret) key.

Acknowledgements and Disclaimer

This work is partially supported by the Spanish MCYT and the FEDER funds under grant TIC2003-08604-C04-04 MULTIMARK and also by the European Commission through the IST Programme under Contract IST-2002-507932 ECRYPT.

The information in this document reflects only the author's views, is provided as is and no guarantee or warranty is given that the information is fit for any particular purpose. The user thereof uses the information at its sole risk and liability.

References

1. Swanson, M., Kobayashi, M., Tewfik, A.: Multimedia data-embedding and watermarking technologies. In: Proceedings of the IEEE. Volume 86(6)., IEEE Computer Society (1998) 1064–1087
2. Petitcolas, F., Anderson, R.: Evaluation of copyright marking systems. In: Proceedings of IEEE Multimedia Systems'99. (1999) 574–579
3. Swanson, M.D.; Bin Zhu; Tewfik, A.: Current state of the art, challenges and future directions for audio watermarking. In: Proceedings of IEEE International Conference on Multimedia Computing and Systems. Volume 1., IEEE Computer Society (1999) 19–24

4. Voyatzis, G.; Pitas, I.: Protecting digital image copyrights: a framework. IEEE Computer Graphics and Applications **19** (1999) 18–24

5. Cox, I.J., Kilian, J., Leighton, T., Shamoon, T.: Secure spread spectrum watermarking for multimedia. IEEE Transactions on Image Processing **6** (1997) 1673–1687

6. M.D. Swanson, B. Zhu, A.T., Boney, L.: Robust audio watermarking using perceptual masking. Elsevier Signal Processing, Special Issue on Copyright Protection And Access Control **66** (1998) 337–335

7. W. Kim, J.L., Lee, W.: An audio watermarking scheme robust to MPEG audio compression. In: Proc. NSIP. Volume 1., Antalya, Turkey (1999) 326–330

8. D. Gruhl, A.L., Bender, W.: Echo hiding. In: Proceedings of the 1st Workshop on Information Hiding. Number 1174 in Lecture Notes in Computer Science, Cambridge, England, Springer Verlag (1996) 295–316

9. Bassia, P., Pitas, I., Nikolaidis, N.: Robust audio watermarking in the time domain. IEEE Transactions on Multimedia **3** (2001) 232–241

10. Megías, D., Herrera-Joancomartí, J., Minguillón, J.: A robust frequency domain audio watermarking scheme for monophonic and stereophonic PCM formats. In: 30th Euromicro Conference, Rennes (France) (2004)

11. Domingo-Ferrer, J., Herrera-Joancomartí, J.: Simple collusion-secure fingerprinting schemes for images. In: Proceedings of the Information Technology: Coding and Computing ITCC'2000, IEEE Computer Society (2000) 128–132

12. Dittman, J., Steinebach, M., Lang, A., Zmudzinski, S.: Advanced audio watermarking benchmarking. In: Proceedings of the IS&T/SPIE's 16th Annual Symposium on Electronic Imaging. Volume 5306 - Security, Steganography, and Watermarking of Multimedia Contents VI., Sant Jose, CA, US (2004)

13. Megías, D., Herrera-Joancomartí, J., Minguillón, J.: A robust audio watermarking scheme based on MPEG 1 layer 3 compression. In: Communications and Multimedia Security - CMS 2003. LNCS 963, Springer-Verlag (2003) 226–238

14. Jansson, T.: Homepage for BladeEnc (2001) `http://bladeenc.mp3.no/`.

15. Domingo-Ferrer, J., Herrera-Joancomartí, J.: Short collusion-secure fingerprinting based on dual binary hamming codes. Electronics Letters **36** (2000) 1697–1699

16. Boneh, D., Shaw, J.: Collusion-secure fingerprinting for digital data. In: Advances in Cryptology-CRYPTO'95. LNCS 963, Springer-Verlag (1995) 452–465

17. Özer, H., Avcıbaş, I., Sankur, B., Memon, N.: Steganalysis of audio based on audio quality metrics. In: Proceedings of the IS&T/SPIE's 15th Annual Symposium on Electronic Imaging. Volume 5020 - Security and Watermarking of Multimedia Contents V., Santa Clara, CA, US (2003)

18. Purnhagen, H.: SQAM - Sound Quality Assessment Material (2001) `http://www.tnt.uni-hannover.de/project/mpeg/audio/sqam/`.

Watermarking Technique for Authentication of 3-D Polygonal Meshes[1]

Wan-Hyun Cho[1], Myung-Eun Lee[2], Hyun Lim[3], and Soon-Young Park[2]

[1] Department of Statistics, Chonnam National University, S. Korea
whcho@chonnam.ac.kr
[2] Department of Electronics Engineering, Mokpo National University, S. Korea
{melee, sypark}@mokpo.ac.kr
[3] DVMM Lab., Dept. of Electrical Engineering, Columbia University, USA
hlim@ee.columbia.edu

Abstract. In this paper, we present a watermarking technique for authentication of 3-D polygonal meshes. The proposed technique is based on a wavelet-based multiresolution analysis to convert an original polygonal mesh model into a simplified mesh model and wavelet coefficient vectors. The embedding procedure is to modify the vertex of a simplified mesh model at a low resolution according to the order of norms of the wavelet coefficient vectors using a look-up table. The watermark extraction process is to restore the binary logo pattern by extracting a binary watermark bit from a look-up table corresponding to the watermarked simple mesh. The experimental results show that the proposed method is invariant to the location, scale and rotation transformation while detecting unauthorized modifications.

1 Introduction

Digital watermarking provides an embedding technology for copyright protection or authentication of digital contents by hiding information in the original data. Until now, many researches have been intensively done on the watermarking technique for digital text, image, video, and sound signals. On the contrary, there are no effective ways to protect the copyright of 3D geometric models and to detect the unauthorized tampering on them. But recently, several researchers have begun to have an interest about watermarking of 3D models and presented their research results.

Theoretically, the principle of watermarking for multimedia data can be grouped into two categories; spatial domain methods and frequency domain methods. The spatial domain method embeds the watermark by directly modifying a digital representation structure of the original data. The frequency domain method, however, embeds the watermark by modifying the coefficients resulted from applying a various transformation to given data.

In the spatial domain watermarking for 3D polygonal model, the pioneer work has been conducted by Ohbuchi et al.[1]. They proposed several watermarking algorithms for polygonal models including Triangle similarity quadratic (TSQ), Tetrahedral

---

[1] This study was financially supported by Chonnam National University in his/her sabbatical year of 2003.

I.J. Cox et al. (Eds.): IWDW 2004, LNCS 3304, pp. 259–270, 2005.

volume ratio (TVR) and a visible mesh-watermarking algorithm. Benedens [2] subtly altered surface normals to embed watermark bits, and the watermark could survive simplification attacks. Yeo and Yeung [3] used a hash function to generate the cryptographic watermark signal and embed the watermark by perturbing the coordinates of vertices forming a given polygonal model.

On the other hand, in the frequency domain watermarking method, Praun et al. [4] proposed the most successful robust mesh-watermarking algorithm that generalized the spread spectrum techniques to surfaces. And Yin et al. [5] adopted Guskov's multiresolution signal processing method for meshes and used the 3D non-uniform relaxation operator to construct a Burt-Adelson pyramid for the mesh, and then the watermark was embedded into a suitable coarser mesh. Kanai et al. [6] used the wavelet transformation to obtain multiresolution decomposition of polygonal mesh, and then embedded the watermark into the large wavelet coefficient vectors at various resolution levels of the multiresolution representation. Finally, Ohbuchi et al. [7] employed the mesh spectral analysis to modify mesh shapes in the transformed domain, and also Kohei et al. [8] computed the spectrum of the vertex series using the singular spectrum analysis for the trajectory matrix derived from the vertices of 3D polygonal mesh, and then embedded the watermark into the singular values given from spectrum analysis.

In this paper, we propose a new fragile watermarking algorithm for the authentication of 3D polygonal models using wavelet transformation. Firstly, we employ the multiresolution analysis using the subdivision method proposed by Stollnitz et al. [9] and derive a simple mesh that is topologically equivalent to the given polygonal mesh model and the collection of wavelet coefficient vectors. Next, we compute the norm of all wavelet coefficient vectors to identify the vertex in a simple mesh where a watermark is embedded. The watermark of a logo image is inserted into the coordinate of vertices using the look-up table.

The structure of this paper is organized as follows. In Sec. 2, we briefly review the multiresolution analysis theory for 3D polygonal mesh models using the wavelet transformation. In Sec. 3, the proposed watermark embedding and extracting algorithm are described in detail. Experimental results are given in Sec. 4. Finally, the conclusions are mentioned in Sec. 5.

2 Multiresolution Analysis for 3D Polygonal Mesh Models

In general, the idea behind multiresolution analysis for 3D polygonal mesh models is the same as it has been applied to images or curves. This split repeatedly a high- resolution polygon into a low-resolution polygon and detail parts. Here the detail parts are represented as the wavelet coefficient vectors. Figure 1 shows a process that multiresolution analysis is recursively applied to the Spock's head. Multiresolution analysis in mathematical concept can be presented as a procedure that generates a sequence of nested linear function spaces.

$$\mathbf{V}^0 \subset \mathbf{V}^1 \cdots \subset \mathbf{V}^{J-1} \subset \mathbf{V}^J \tag{1}$$

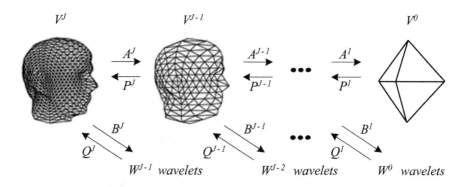

Fig. 1. Multiresolution analysis for Spock's Head

Here the basis functions for the space $\mathbf{V}^j$ are called scaling functions and the resolution of functions in $\mathbf{V}^j$ increases with an index value j.

The next step in multiresolution analysis is to define the wavelet spaces, denoted by $\mathbf{W}^j$. The wavelet space $\mathbf{W}^j$ generated at resolution level j is the complement of low-resolution space $\mathbf{V}^j$ in one level higher resolution space $\mathbf{V}^{j+1}$. These satisfy the following properties;

$$\mathbf{V}^{j+1} = \mathbf{V}^j \cup \mathbf{W}^j, \ \mathbf{V}^j \cap \mathbf{W}^j = \phi. \tag{2}$$

Here the basis function of each wavelet space is called wavelets.

Wavelet transform can be also formulated by using a matrix notation in the filter bank theory as follows;

$$\mathbf{V}^{j-1} = \mathbf{A}^j \mathbf{V}^j \tag{3}$$

$$\mathbf{W}^{j-1} = \mathbf{B}^j \mathbf{V}^j \tag{4}$$

where $\mathbf{V}^j = [\mathbf{v}_1^j \ \mathbf{v}_2^j \cdots \mathbf{v}_{n(j)}^j]^T$ denotes the matrix whose rows correspond to the coordinate of $n(j)$ vertices at resolution level j, and $\mathbf{W}^{j-1} = [\mathbf{w}_1^{j-1} \ \mathbf{w}_2^{j-1} \cdots \mathbf{w}_{m(j-1)}^{j-1}]^T$ denotes the matrix whose rows correspond to $m(j-1)$ wavelet coefficient vectors at resolution level $j-1$. So the number of wavelet coefficient vector, $m(j-1)$ can be calculated from $m(j-1) = n(j) - n(j-1)$.

The matrices $\mathbf{A}^j$ and $\mathbf{B}^j$ are called as analysis filters at resolution level j. For example, Figure 2 illustrates how to decompose the 3D polygon by using lazy wavelet transform [9]. Four triangles at resolution level j are reduced to one triangle at resolution level $j-1$ and three wavelet coefficient vectors are generated to represent the detail parts.

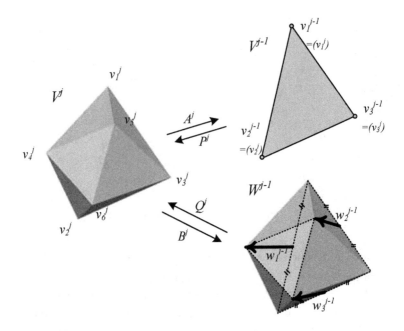

Fig. 2. Geometrical interpretation of the wavelet transform for 3D polygonal Mesh

Hence, the multiresolution analysis means that the coarser representation of the polygonal meshes $\mathbf{V}^{J-1}$, $\mathbf{V}^{J-2}$, $\cdots$, $\mathbf{V}^0$ are obtained by applying the matrix $\mathbf{A}^j$ to the lower resolution part recursively and the wavelet coefficients vectors $\mathbf{W}^{J-1}$, $\mathbf{W}^{J-2}$, $\cdots$, $\mathbf{W}^0$ at each resolution level are also obtained by applying similarly the matrix $\mathbf{B}^j$ to lower resolution part recursively. The relation between matrices, the polygonal mesh and wavelet coefficient vectors can be arranged as;

$$\mathbf{V}^0 = \mathbf{A}^1\mathbf{A}^2 \cdots \mathbf{A}^{J-1}\mathbf{A}^J\mathbf{V}^J \tag{5}$$

$$\mathbf{W}^0 = \mathbf{B}^1\mathbf{A}^2 \cdots \mathbf{A}^{J-1}\mathbf{A}^J\mathbf{V}^J. \tag{6}$$

On the other hand, the high-level resolution polygonal mesh can be recovered by synthesizing both low-level resolution polygonal mesh and wavelet coefficient vector space using inverse wavelet transform. This process is called synthesis or reconstruction, and it can be represented as follows;

$$\mathbf{V}^j = \mathbf{P}^j\mathbf{V}^{j-1} + \mathbf{Q}^j\mathbf{W}^{j-1} \tag{7}$$

where matrices $\mathbf{P}^j$ and $\mathbf{Q}^j$ are called synthesis filters. The synthesis operation employs interpolation that performs splitting and averaging or equivalently multiplying the low-level resolution polygonal mesh by $\mathbf{P}^j$ and multiplying wavelet coefficient vectors by $\mathbf{Q}^j$.

3   Watermarking for 3D Polygonal Mesh Model

We propose a new watermarking technique for authentication of 3D polygonal mesh model. The following block diagram shows the general structure for the proposed watermarking scheme.

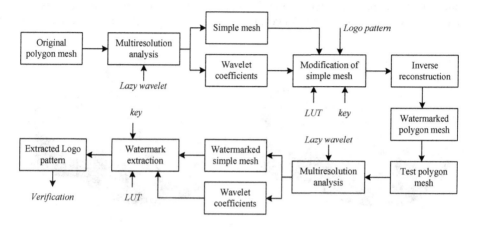

Fig. 3. The block diagram of the proposed watermarking scheme for 3D polygonal meshes

The proposed scheme first conducts the multiresolution analysis for the original polygonal mesh by using lazy wavelet transform and then determines a simple mesh and wavelet coefficient vectors. Next, the scheme extracts the coordinate of the vertices composing the simple mesh and then modifies those coordinates to insert the watermark into vertices using logo pattern and look-up table. After that, the inverse wavelet transform is applied to the modified simple mesh and the unchanged wavelet coefficients vectors in order to produce the watermarked polygonal mesh.

On the other hand, the order of extracting the watermark is processed as a reverse manner with the embedding process. First, we conduct multiresolution analysis for watermarked polygonal mesh by applying lazy wavelets transform and then generate the watermarked simple mesh. Next, we select the coordinates of vertices of simple mesh to extract the embedded logo image using look-up table. Finally, by comparing between the embedded and extracted logo image, we insist the authentication of the original polygonal mesh.

So far, we have considered the outline of watermarking scheme for 3D polygonal mesh. Subsequently, we will think about how to embed the watermark into polygonal mesh in detail.

3.1   Watermark Embedding Procedure

We will propose the algorithm how to embed the watermark into certain vertices selected from the simple mesh model to insist the authentication of original mesh. Our watermark embedding process consists of the four steps.

(1) By applying wavelet transform to an original polygonal mesh, we derive both a simple mesh model and wavelet coefficients vectors.

First, if we conduct the multiresolution analysis for arbitrary 3D polygonal meshes at several times, we can obtain a coarse mesh that is topologically equivalent to the given polygonal mesh and a collection of wavelet coefficients. Here this model is called a simple mesh or a base mesh. Figure 4(b) shows the base mesh that was produced by applying Eck et al.[10] algorithm for the Venus model in Figure 4(a).

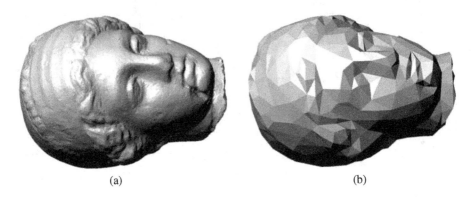

(a)   (b)

Fig. 4. Multiresolution analysis about Venus model, (a) original Venus model, (b) simple mesh constructed by multiresolution analysis

(2) We identify the vertices that are suitable for embedding the watermark and compute the location indices by using wavelet coefficient vector.

Here, we suggest a geometrical criterion for selecting the vertex that will be embedded with the watermark. First, if we conduct the final multiresolution decomposition for original polygonal mesh, then we obtain the simple mesh as well as a collection of the wavelet coefficient vectors given at last stage. In this case, we define the three-wavelet coefficient vectors originated from edges of an arbitrary triangle t_i^j in the simple mesh at multiresolution level j by w_{i1}^j , w_{i2}^j , w_{i3}^j as shown in Figure 5. Next, we compute the sum of norms of three wavelet coefficient vectors corresponding to the selected triangle as being denoted by

$$D_i = \sum_{k=1}^{3} \| \mathbf{w}_{ik}^j \| . \tag{8}$$

We order all these sums according to their magnitudes to insert the watermark into the vertices that compose the triangle with large wavelet coefficient vectors. Triangles of the same number as watermark bits for embedding are sorted from the largest sum in the simple mesh model. Then at the selected triangle we choose a vertex to be opposite to the edge that the wavelet coefficient vector has a biggest norm. Finally, we modify the coordinate of selected vertex to insert the watermark. The fundamental idea in this embedding procedure is to modify the vertex in the rugged region with large wavelet coefficient vectors in order to avoid the perceptual visibility.

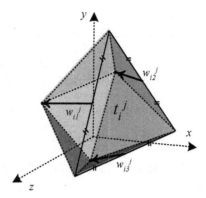

Fig. 5. A typical triangle selected from a simple mesh and its related three wavelet vectors

In general, after embedding the watermark into some vertices, we can exactly identify the watermarked vertex without the original polygonal model even if we modify the coordinate of vertices to insert the watermark into them. The reason is that the wavelet coefficient vectors are invariant to the affine transformation and the selection of the embedded vertex is carried out according to the ordering of the norm of three related wavelet vectors.

Next, we describe the mapping rule to allocate the binary bits in 2D logo image to the selected vertex of a simplified polygonal mesh in 3D space. The procedure to generate a 2D index for the vertex V_i is summarized as follows;

① $R_\alpha = \dfrac{L_2}{L_1}$ and $R_\beta = \dfrac{L_3}{L_2}$.

② $N_\alpha = \text{ToInteger}(R_\alpha)$ and $N_\beta = \text{ToInteger}(R_\beta)$.

③ Location index $(L_x, L_y) = \begin{cases} L_x = f_x(N_\alpha, N_\beta) \\ L_y = f_y(N_\alpha, N_\beta) \end{cases}$.

Here, L_1, L_2, and L_3 is the minimum, medium, and maximum norm value for three-wavelet coefficient vectors originated from the triangle including the vertex V_i. Therefore, in step 1, we compute two ratios of norms of wavelet coefficient vectors that are invariant to affine transformation. Step 2 converts the floating point outputted in step 1 into integers by employing the Integer function. Lastly the location index is computed by inputting N_α and N_β into index generating function. As an example, modulus operators such as

$$f_x = ((N_\alpha + N_\beta) \bmod \text{Height}) \text{ and } f_y = ((N_\alpha \times N_\beta) \bmod \text{Width})$$

can be used to index the logo pattern of size Height by Width.

(3) We compose the look-up table using ratios computed from two components of triangles selected from the simple mesh model.

Once we choose any triangle from the generated simple mesh model and the edge related with the wavelet coefficient vector having the largest norm. Then we draw the straight line from the middle point of the selected edge to the opposite faced vertex. We also compute the lengths of the selected edge and the new straight line. Finally, we compute the ratio of two lengths of the edge and the straight line.

For example, if the selected triangle is represented as shown in Figure 6, each length of two lines are respectively given in the form

$$\| \mathbf{a} - \mathbf{b} \| \text{ and } \| \mathbf{c} - \tfrac{1}{2}(\mathbf{a} + \mathbf{b}) \|. \tag{9}$$

where the vectors $\mathbf{a}, \mathbf{b}$ and $\mathbf{c}$ consist of each vertex of the triangle. Thus, the ratio of two lengths is defined as

$$Ratio = \frac{\| \mathbf{c} - \tfrac{1}{2}(\mathbf{a} + \mathbf{b}) \|}{\| \mathbf{a} - \mathbf{b} \|}. \tag{10}$$

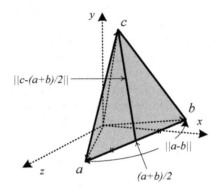

Fig. 6. Geometrical diagram of selected triangle

Finally, we partition a distributed interval of all ratios computed from given triangles into K subintervals (bin) with small and equal size, and we generate a sequence of binary random digits composing with "0" and "1" with use of a secret key. The look-up table is constructed as we allocate each digit to each bin one by one. The following table shows one example of a look-up table made by the Venus simple mesh model.

Table 1. Example of a look-up table made from the arbitrary key

ratio	0.0	...	1.0	1.1	1.2	1.3	...
digit	0	...	1	1	0	0	...

(4) We embed the watermark into the coordinate of vertices using the logo image and the look-up table.

Here, we will show how to insert the watermark into the coordinate of a vertex using a logo image and a look-up table.

Step1: we choose triangles of the same number as watermark bits in the logo image by ordering the sums of norms from a simple mesh model and decide a vertex in the selected triangle to embed a watermark.

Step2: we compute a ratio from a selected triangle and take a binary digit corresponding to this ratio using look-up table. In addition, we take a binary digit of a logo image using the computed location index.

Step3: we compare two binary digits and then if two digits are equal, we don't have any change about the vertex coordinate, but if two digits are not equal, we make two digits to be equal by changing the vertex coordinate using a suitable technique.

For example, either the digit of a logo pattern is "0" and the digit of a look-up table corresponding to the ratio is "1" or the digit of a logo pattern is "1" and the digit of a look-up table is "0," then the nearest neighboring subinterval is selected so that the digit of the look-up table equals to the digit of the logo pattern. The new ratio coming from the selected subinterval is then used to move a vertex c up and down so that the ratio of lengths of two lines computed from new triangle equals to the selected ratio. The following figure explains graphically how to insert the watermark into a vertex.

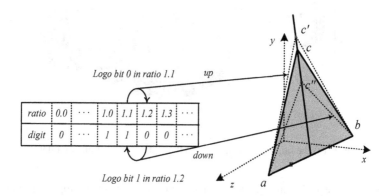

Fig. 7. Graphical displays for watermark embedding method

3.2 Watermark Extraction Procedure

To extract the logo image from a watermarked 3D polygonal mesh, we first apply the wavelet transform to the observed mesh and then generate the watermarked simple mesh and a collection of wavelet coefficients vectors. Second, we choose an arbitrary triangle from simple mesh model, and then compute the sum of norm of three wavelet coefficient vectors related with the triangle. After ordering the sums of norms according to their magnitudes we select the triangle with the embedded vertex and compute a ratio of lengths of a bottom edge and a height of the selected triangle. Now we can restore the logo pattern by displaying a binary digit of a look-up table corresponding to the computed ratio into the location index on the grid. Finally, comparing between the original logo image and the restored logo image, we insist the authentication of 3D polygon meshes.

4 Experimental Results

We have applied our algorithm to the 3D Venus model as shown in Figure 4(a). This model consists of 33,537 vertices and 67,072 faces. Then this model is decomposed into both a simple mesh and wavelet coefficient vectors for a multiresolution analysis by using the lazy wavelet 4-to-1 subdivision scheme. That is, the polygon mesh has the mesh topology fit to 4-to-1 subdivision scheme. The two levels decomposition yields the simple mesh model with the vertices of 2,097 approximately. After ordering the sums of the norms of wavelet coefficients vectors, 1,600 vertices are embedded with binary digits from the logo image of size 40×40 shown in Figure 8(a). Figure 8(b) shows the watermarked polygon mesh.

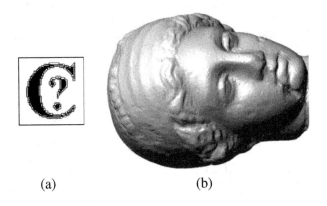

(a)   (b)

Fig. 8. (a) the binary logo pattern, (b) the watermarked Venus model

It can be observed that the watermarked polygon mesh is imperceptible after embedding the binary logo image into the vertices in the rugged region. The extracted logo image from the watermarked Venus model is quite similar to the original logo image. To investigate the effect of affine transformation on the watermarked model, translation, scaling, and rotation operations have been applied to the watermarked polygon. The extracted watermarks were not changed because of the invariant properties of both the norm of wavelet coefficient vectors and a ratio of two lengths as shown in Figure 9(a). However, the unwatermarked polygonal mesh yields the watermark to be exact noise pattern such as Figure 9(b).

Fig. 9. (a) The extracted logo image from the watermarked Venus model, (b) The extracted logo image from the unwatermarked model

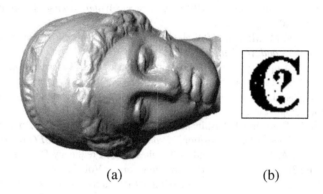

(a)   (b)

Fig. 10. (a) The watermarked polygon mesh modified with 45vertices, (b) The extracted logo image from the modified model

In order to investigate the localization property of the authentication algorithm, we modified 95 vertices on left cheekbone position from the watermarked polygonal model such as Figure 10(a). Figure 10(b) shows that the algorithm can detect the modification of the polygonal mesh by extracting the logo pattern that is partly destructed at some regions.

5 Conclusion

In this paper, we have proposed a fragile watermarking technique to authenticate 3D polygonal mesh model. The proposed algorithm employs a wavelet-based multiresolution analysis to convert the original polygonal mesh model into a simplified mesh model and wavelet coefficient vectors. We select vertices from the simplified mesh model according to the order of sums of wavelet coefficient norms and insert watermarks into them using a look-up table and a logo image. The perceptual invisibility of the proposed technique is provided by embedding the watermark into the rugged region with large wavelet coefficient vectors and the invariance to the affine transformation is provided by employing the invariant properties of both the norm of wavelet coefficient vectors and a ratio of two lengths between the selected vertices.

The experimental results have showed that the proposed technique can be a powerful authentication method of 3-D polygonal meshes by surviving to the innocuous attacks while providing localization of modifications.

References

1. R. Ohbuchi, H. Masuda, and M. Aono, "Watermarking Three Dimensional Polygonal Models," *Proc. ACM Multimedia 97*, (1997) 261-272
2. O. Benedens, "Watermarking of 3D polygonal based models with robustness against mesh simplication," *Proceedings of SPIE: Security and Watermarking of Multimedia Contents, (1999)* 329-340
3. B. L. Yeo and M. M. Yeung, "Watermarking 3-D Objects for Verification," *IEEE Computer Graphics and Application*, Vol. 19, (1999) 36-45
4. E. Praun, H. Hoppe, and A. Frankelstein, "Robust Mesh Watermarking," Proceedings *of SIGGRAPH 99*, (1999) 49-56
5. K. Yin, Z. Pan, J. Shi, and D. Zhang, "Robust Mesh Watermarking Based on Multiresolution Processing," *Computer and Graphics*, Vol. 25, (2001) 409-420
6. S. Kanai, H. Date, and T. Kishinami, "Digital Watermarking for 3D polygons using Multiresolution Wavelet Decomposition," *Proc. Sixth IFIP WG 5.2 GEO-6*, (1998) 296-307
7. R. Ohbuchi, A. Mukaiyama, and S. Takahashi, "A Frequency Domain approach to Watermarking 3D Shapes," *Computer Graphics Forum*, Vol. 21, (2002)
8. M. Kohei, and S. Kokichi, "Watermarking 3D Polygonal Meshes Using the Singular Spectrum Analysis," *ISM Symposium on Statistics, Combinatorics and Geometry*, Mar. (2003)
9. E. J. Stollnitz, T. D. DeRose, and D. H. Salesin, *Wavelets for Computer Graphics,* Morgan Kaufmann Publishers, (1996)
10. M. Eck, T. DeRose, T. Duchmap, H. Hoppe, M. Lounsbery, and W. Stuetzle, "Multiresolution analysis of arbitrary meshes," *In Proceedings of SIGGRAPH '95*, ACM, New York (1995) 173-82

Fidelity-Controlled Robustness Enhancement of Blind Watermarking Schemes Using Evolutionary Computational Techniques

Chun-Hsiang Huang, Chih-Hao Shen, and Ja-Ling Wu

Communication and Multimedia Laboratory,
Department of Computer Science and Information Engineering,
National Taiwan University,
Taipei, Taiwan, R. O. C.
{bh, shen, wjl}@cmlab.csie.ntu.edu.tw

Abstract. Designing optimal watermarking schemes is inherently an interesting and difficult problem since the three most important performance requirements of digital watermarking – fidelity, robustness and watermark capacity – are conflicting with each other. Nowadays, most watermarking schemes hide the watermark information in a heuristic manner, that is, watermarks are often embedded according to predefined rules and empirical parameter settings. Therefore, the performance of digital watermarking can only be passively decided and evaluated, rather than being actively adopted as additional clues helpful to achieve better performance in embedding modules. In this paper, watermark embedding is simulated as an optimization procedure in which optimal embedded results are obtained by using important evolutionary computation techniques – the genetic algorithms. Under the condition that fixed amount of watermark bits are hidden, in this work, the minimal fidelity requirement of embedded content can be specified by users in advance and guaranteed throughout the embedding procedure. Furthermore, concrete measures of the robustness against certain attacks are treated as the objective functions that guide the optimizing procedure. In other words, a blind watermarking scheme with application-specific data capacity, guaranteed fidelity, and theoretically optimal robustness against certain types of attacks is proposed. Experimental results clearly show that the proposed scheme possesses great performance improvements over the original one. More importantly, the proposed enhancing approach has many desired architectural characteristics, such as blind detection, asymmetric embedding/detection overheads, as well as embedding and detection in different domains.

1 Problem Formulation: Optimal Watermarking

In the past decade, various watermarking schemes have been proposed, and many important advances in the field of digital watermarking have been made. A comprehensive introduction to current watermarking technologies and theoretic foundations can be found in [1]. However, designing optimal watermarking schemes is still an open problem to which satisfying solutions are not yet found [2]. The

I.J. Cox et al. (Eds.): IWDW 2004, LNCS 3304, pp. 271–282, 2005.
© Springer-Verlag Berlin Heidelberg 2005

difficulties one might face while designing optimal watermarking schemes is a natural result due to the three conflicting requirements of most watermarking systems: fidelity of embedded content, robustness of the hidden information against common processes or malicious attacks, and the data capacity of hidden information. Among these requirements, capacity is often decided in advance according to the purpose of watermarking application. Therefore, as long as the predefined amount of embedded data is large enough to carry necessary information, such as identifications of content authors for owner proving or usage rules that shall be parsed by DRM-enabled consumer-electronic devices, data capacity can be simply regarded as a fixed parameter. However, even under this assumption, obtaining a reasonable trade-off between fidelity and robustness is still not as simple as one might think.

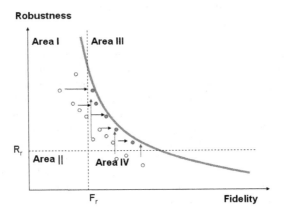

Fig. 1. The performance-space view of watermark embedding is illustrated. The curve represents the inherent performance limit of some watermarking algorithm. The watermark-embedded outcomes of a specific scheme, represented by empty circles, are determined according to predefined rules or models. Assume that if there is an application that its desired embedded results must possess robustness stronger than R_r and fidelity better than F_r, only circles locate within Area III under the curve can be of use. In fact, better embedded results, such as those shown in solid circles, may be available, but conventional watermarking schemes lack the ability to obtain them. The vertically and horizontally arrows indicate possible robustness and fidelity performance enhancements, respectively

In existing watermarking schemes, perceptually acceptable embedded outcomes are often produced according to predefined embedding rules based on complicated perceptual models or assumptions, and then the robustness of that scheme is empirically experimented and evaluated by performing various attacks on the embedded media. In order to clearly illustrate the relationship between traditional watermarking schemes and their performance indexes, the performance-space view of digital watermarking schemes shall be introduced and examined in the beginning. As shown in Fig. 1, any embedded result created using a certain watermarking scheme can be expressed by a point located somewhere within the space spanned by two axes representing fidelity and robustness, respectively. Roughly speaking, it is generally agreed that the higher the required fidelity is, the lower the robustness of hidden signals against attacks will be. In fact, the region that possible embedded outcomes may locate within is consequently determined after the watermarking scheme and the original/watermark pairs are chosen. Although potentially better performance of the chosen watermarking scheme may exist, traditional watermarking schemes lack the ability to exploit better embedded outcomes.

2 Genetic-Algorithms and Watermarking

To solve the watermarking performance optimization problem within reasonable computation time, the genetic-algorithms (GAs) based optimization techniques are used in this paper. GAs are important optimization techniques belonging to the area of evolutionary computation [3]. During GA-based optimization processes, solutions to the problem can be evaluated according to objective function values representing the degree of fitness. A population of candidate solutions will be initialized as finite-length strings - the so-called chromosomes - over finite alphabet. Different from conventional single-point search methods, GAs work with a population of points in a parameter space simultaneously. In practical GA-based optimizations, three GA operators - reproduction, crossover, and mutation - are often applied to the chromosomes repeatedly. After iteratively adopting these GA operations, near-optimal solutions of desired parameters for the original problem can be obtained. A detail explanation of GAs can be found in [4].

The authors first introduced the idea of GA-based watermarking enhancement in [5]. In that paper, the performance of a DCT-domain watermarking scheme, being proposed in [6], is enhanced by applying GA operators, and the best watermark embedding positions for each DCT block can be found. [5] is the earliest publication that connects GAs together with digital watermarking. However, this enhancing scheme was criticized due to several factors that seriously limit its usage. For blind watermarking schemes, the optimal embedding positions must be delivered to the watermark detector as secret keys since the decoder cannot figure out the optimized embedding positions without the original content. However, this is usually not feasible in many important real-world applications, thus seriously limiting its applicability. As for non-blind watermarking schemes, the optimization procedure will be a time-consuming process in both embedding and detection sides. Although the authors proposed a lightweight genetic search algorithm in [7] to shorten the computation time, large amounts of computation overheads in both watermark embedding and detection are still unacceptable. In [8], a similar DCT-domain watermarking scheme is proposed, where optimization for robustness is considered. Furthermore, a GA-based spatial-domain watermarking algorithm is also proposed in [8]. However, the usage of the latter scheme is limited due to the weak robustness of its spatial domain embedding nature, and both schemes suffer from the aforementioned secret key delivery problem.

In this paper, a watermarking-performance enhancement architecture possessing theoretically optimal robustness against certain types of attacks, guaranteed fidelity and application-specific data capacity will be proposed. The proposed architecture is inherently suitable for blind watermarking, and the asymmetric embedding and detection design can effectively reduce the penalty of long computation time. Furthermore, the proposed watermarking scheme has the desirable characteristic that embedding and detection can be performed in different domain, thus both direct control of fidelity in spatial domain while embedding and strong robustness against attacks in frequency domain while detecting can be realized in a single framework.

The paper is organized as follows. Section III describes the proposed watermarking enhancement scheme and related implementation details. Experimental results, including the performance comparisons against original watermarking scheme under the assumption of equal data capacity, will be listed and explained in Section IV. Section V gives a brief discussion about the pros and cons of the proposed performance enhancing architecture, and section VI concludes this write-up.

3   The Proposed Architecture and Implementation Details

The proposed performance enhancement architecture is general and can be used to enhance the performance of various existing blind watermarking schemes. However, in order to save the implementation time and consider that frequency-domain watermarking schemes are well known for their better robustness and fidelity, a blind version of the block-DCT based image watermarking scheme originally introduced by [6] is used to evaluate the power of this enhancing approach. [9] illustrates the details about turning the originally non-blind watermarking approach into a blind one. In this scheme, embedded watermarks are meaningful binary patterns and are randomly permuted before embedding. Watermark bits are embedded into predefined positions within the middle-band coefficients of each DCT block. The polarity between AC coefficients at selected positions and scaled DC coefficient of each block, after considering the effects of JPEG compression, is adjusted to insert the watermarking bits. Due to the blind nature of the adopted scheme in [9], the original perceptual model introduced by [6] cannot be applied directly, thus the degree of coefficient adjustment is empirically and uniformly determined. The definition of polarity for the m-th watermarking bit that will be embedded into one coefficient block is given by:

$$P_m = \begin{cases} 1, & if\ \dfrac{|AC_m|}{Q_m} \times Q_m > \dfrac{|DC|}{Scale\_Factor \times Q_{DC}} \times Q_{DC} \\ -1, & otherwised, \end{cases} \tag{1}$$

where AC_m is the AC coefficient at the position that the m-th watermark bit within each 8x8 DCT block will be embedded. DC denotes the DC value of that block. Q_m is the value in the JPEG quantization table corresponding to the position of AC_m, and Q_{DC} is the value for DC in the JPEG quantization table.

Fig. 2 depicts the flowchart of our scheme. The required fidelity of embedded content is specified by users according to different application scenarios and guaranteed throughout the embedding process. To concretely express the fidelity, the commonly used PSNR (Peak Signal to Noise Ratio) of the embedded image is adopted as the index of fidelity. In addition, the robustness becomes the performance index that we would like to enhance.

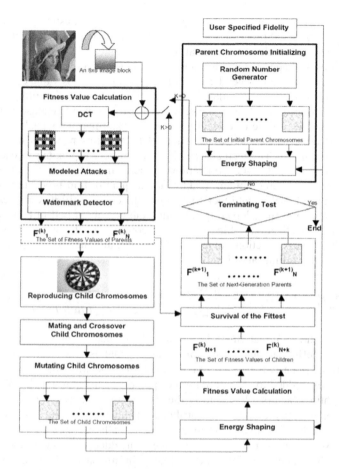

Fig. 2. The flowchart of the proposed enhancing scheme is depicted. The blocks with dotted outlines are intermediated data sets; other blocks are required functions. This optimization process terminates after a predefined number of generations is performed

The optimization process is done in a block-by-block manner. For each 8x8 image block, a set of N initial parent chromosomes will be generated. Each initial parent chromosome is a randomly generated 8x8 block where the value of each pixel uniformly distributes over a range taking equal positive and negative extent. In fact, a parent chromosome represents a possible distortion block that stands for the difference between the original image block and the embedded one in spatial domain. Next, the energy-shaping module is applied to all initial parent chromosomes so that they can satisfy the minimum fidelity requirement specified in advance. For example, according to the definition of PSNR, if the user asks for a required PSNR value higher than 40, the maximal allowable block energy (that is, the sum of the squared value of each distortion pixel) of an 8x8 chromosome block shall be less than 416. If the energy of a randomly generated chromosome block is higher than the maximal allowable energy, the chromosome block will be uniformly scaled down to satisfy the fidelity limit. The difference between the energy of the obtained chromosome and the maximal energy limit can be further reduced by slightly adjusting randomly selected pixels. In this way, all processed parent chromosomes will result in embedded results that user-specified fidelity requirement will be guaranteed.

Each energy-shaped parent chromosome will be respectively added to the original image block to form an embedded candidate. Then the fitness value corresponding to each candidate shall be calculated. As mentioned before, the fitness value must describe the robustness of the adopted watermarking scheme against certain attacks. Therefore, the percentage of correctly extracted watermarking signals against certain attacks, named as correctly extracted rate (CER) in this paper, is undoubtedly the most intuitive index. To calculate the fitness value corresponding to each candidate chromosome, a block DCT operation is performed for each candidate block. Furthermore, a JPEG-compliant quantization/dequantization procedure is performed to each produced coefficient block to simulate the effect of JPEG compression. Every quantization step of the adopted quantization table is about half of that of the default JPEG luma quantization table. Finally, according to the adopted watermarking scheme, the fitness function value of the n-th initial candidate block is figured out according to the definition of Eq. (2):

$$F_n^1 = \sum_m P_m \cdot w_m \cdot (W_1 + W_2 \cdot \left| \frac{\|AC_m\|}{Q_m} \times Q_m - \frac{|DC|}{Scale\_Factor \times Q_{DC}} \times Q_{DC} \right|) \quad (2)$$

where w_m is the m-th watermark bit going to be embedded into a predefined position of current coefficient block, and this binary signal is represented as 1 or -1. P_m represents the polarity extracted from the predefined position that the m-th watermark bit shall be embedded to. The definition of polarity is listed in Eq. (1). W_1 and W_2 are both weighting factors. W_1 controls the degree that the case "a watermark bit is correctly or wrongly extracted" contributes to the fitness value, i.e., W_1 stands for each embedded coefficient's contribution to a visually recognizing detector.   On the contrary, W_2 controls the degree that the embedded coefficient contributes to a correlation-based detector. For all experiments in this paper, W_1 is set to 100 and W_2 is 1. Other symbol definitions are the same as those given in Eq. (1).

Next, a set of N child chromosomes will be reproduced and processed according to GA-based rules. The reproduction is done by the famous roulette-wheel-method [4]. The parent chromosomes have higher fitness values are more possible to generate more offspring. As for the crossover operation, reproduced child chromosomes are randomly mated into pairs and exchange arbitrary portions of chromosomes to the other. In other words, parts of two child chromosomes are combined to form a new 8x8 distortion block. After performing the crossover operation, each pixel component of the child chromosomes has a small possibility to change from positive to negative or from negative to positive. This is the mutation operation adopted to help generating new candidates.

Now although these child chromosomes are generated based on their parent chromosomes, the adopted GA operations may result in child chromosomes violating the fidelity requirement specified in the beginning. Thus the energy-shaping procedure shall also be performed on these generated children chromosomes.

Finally, a survival-of-the-fittest policy is used to select N next-generation parent chromosomes from the set consisting of N parent chromosomes and no-more-than N child chromosomes. Since the whole set of original parent chromosomes is included in this survival competition, the fitness values of next-generation parent chromosomes will never get lower than those of previous-generation ones. These aforementioned GA optimization processes will be done repeatedly until a specified number of iterations (named as the generation number in a GA-based approach) have been performed. Finally, the chromosome with the highest fitness value will be added to the original image block, and this added block is regarded as the embedded block of best robustness.

It is worth noting that the watermark is never explicitly "embedded" to the original. On the contrary, we search for the best candidate subject to the fidelity constraint directly according to the simulated robustness performance. On the other hand, the watermark extraction process is exactly the same as the watermark detector in the original watermarking algorithm. This asymmetric behavior of the embedding and detecting modules is quite different from that of the traditional watermarking schemes. To be more specific, the proposed embedding module can be regarded as a generalized performance enhancement module depending on the given watermark detection algorithm and performance indexes. Similar optimization can be applied to various blind watermarking algorithms as long as the watermark detector is given. The involved performance indexes and attack models can be reasonably replaced, e.g. using subjective perceptual index to substitute the objective PSNR or changing the JPEG compression attack to the most probable operations that your application might encounter. In other words, more flexibility and better performance to the actual application can be obtained.

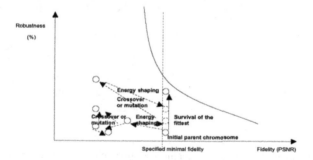

Fig. 3. From the viewpoints of performance-based watermarking model, different effects of components used in the proposed enhancing scheme are depicted

Viewing the proposed enhancement scheme by the aforementioned performance-based model, the roles played by each operation within the proposed scheme can be clearly identified. As shown in Fig. 3, crossover and mutation operators discover new embedding candidates, the energy-shaping module modifies over-distorted candidates so that the required fidelity constraint can be observed, and the survival-of-the-fittest operation guarantees that the newly generated parent chromosomes never locates at lower positions than their parents in the performance space.

4   Experimental Results

Experiments are performed to evaluate the effectiveness of the proposed scheme. The 512x512 gray-level Lena image and a 128x128 binary watermark pattern are adopted, as shown in Figure 4. According to the dimension ratios of the original and the watermark images, 4 watermark bits will be embedded into each 8x8 block. In other words, a fixed data capacity of 16,384 bits is determined in advance.

Fig. 4. The 512x512 original Lena image and the 128x128 watermark image are shown. Actual size ratio between the two images is not preserved due to layout considerations

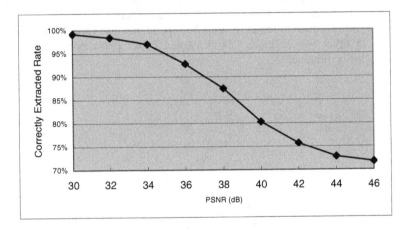

Fig. 5. The relationship between different specified minimal fidelity requirement and the corresponding robustness of embedded results, given the same number of optimizing iterations, is depicted. It clearly shows that: the higher fidelity the user demands, the worse robustness the embedded result will possess

Fig. 5 reveals some important characteristics of our enhancement schemes. According to the performance curve of the GA-based enhancement scheme, it obviously proves the assumption that the lower the specified fidelity constraint is, the higher the optimized robustness will be. In this experiment, the generation number of optimization process is set to 1000, and the mutation rate is set to 0.1. It is worth noting that even for embedded images of excellent visual quality, e.g. PSNR larger than 40, the percentage of correctly extracted watermark bits is still high enough to identify the existence of a watermark.

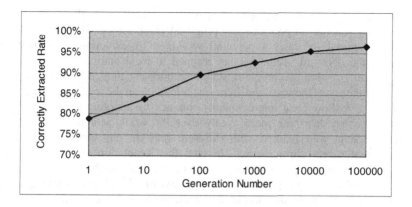

Fig. 6. The relationship between the number of optimizing iterations and the corresponding robustness performance, given that the pre-specified fidelity requirement is 36dB, is depicted. The more optimization computation we performed, the more-robust embedded results we can obtain

Fig. 6 shows the quality improvements after performing different generations of iterations. As we expected, the more the iterative operations we performed, the stronger robustness the obtained embedded results may possess. Fig. 7 lists the corresponding extracted patterns of the embedded watermark for visual evaluation.

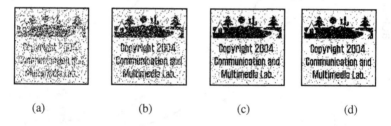

(a)   (b)   (c)   (d)

Fig. 7. Extracted watermark patterns after performing (a) 1 generations, (b) 100 generations, (c) 10,000 generations and (d) 1,000,000 generations of optimization computations, given that the pre-specified PSNR requirement is 36dB, are listed for visual evaluation

In Fig. 8, to show that the results obtained by the proposed enhancing scheme have better performance than those created by using the original watermarking scheme, the performance curve of the non-optimized algorithm introduced in [9] is also listed for comparison. The coefficients to be embedded by the non-optimized approach are uniformly adjusted in order to create embedded results of different PSNR values. And then, JPEG compression attacks are performed on these embedded images for further evaluation of the correctly extracted rate. According to the comparison results, the proposed enhancement scheme outperforms when high fidelity is required. More importantly, for cases where embedded results the original algorithm cannot produce, such as embedded results of PSNR values higher than 42 dB, the proposed scheme can still successfully generate the needed output.

However, the seemingly-counterintuitive phenomenon that the original watermarking scheme outperforms the proposed enhancement algorithm when low fidelity is required indicates a potential weakness of evolutionary computational techniques: the obtained results may be trapped in local optimum when the search space is large. To solve this problem, simple solutions such as adopting better initial search candidates or increase the iteration number can be of help. Experimental results in Fig. 8 show great improvements obtained by adopting better initial parent chromosomes that distribute more evenly over the whole search space, e.g. using embedded results watermarked with different uniform adjustment magnitudes to produce initial parent chromosomes. In fact, this simulation also implies a more general watermarking performance enhancement philosophy – producing the embedded results based on predefined rules of existing blind watermarking schemes first and fed them in to the proposed enhancement architecture as initial search candidates. Then, the proposed GA-based enhancement architecture can effectively improve the performance of any adopted blind watermarking scheme.

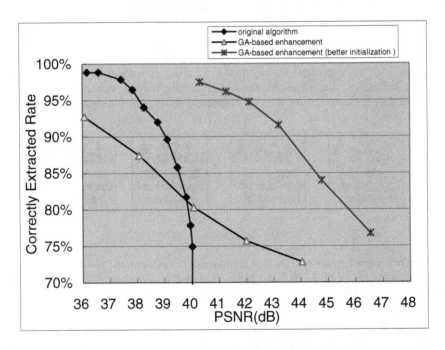

Fig. 8. The results obtained by using the proposed scheme with better initial parent chromosomes show great improvements over the original watermarking algorithm and the proposed scheme with randomly generated parent chromosome

It is also intuitive to assume that, the larger the iterative generation number is, the more the number of searched candidates are, and thus better embedding results can be found. According to our simulation, the increase of iteration number also results in better embedding results. However, the improvements are not as obvious as those contributed by adopting better initialization. In addition, for real-world applications, the generation number used for performance optimization is often limited by the actual computation power of embedding devices and the time constraint of the application scenarios, thus only adequate iteration numbers can be adopted.

In spite of the JPEG compression attack that has been incorporated into the design of embedding module, robustness against other attacks shall be examined too. According to our experiments, the results obtained by the proposed enhancement scheme successfully survive various other processing/attacks, such as cropping, blurring, adding noise, and scribbling.

5 Discussions

The proposed GA-based watermarking-performance enhancing architecture has a lot of advantages. First, system users can specify the required watermarking fidelity that must be guaranteed according to different application needs. Next, the asymmetric embedding/detection structure not only suits most kinds of blind watermarking schemes but also greatly alleviates the problem that evolutionary computation techniques are most often criticized – long computation time. Since the watermark detector is exactly the one used in the original watermarking scheme, many common applications of watermarking will not be affected by the required computation in the embedding process. Furthermore, the proposed watermarking scheme has the desirable characteristic that embedding and detection can be performed in different domain, thus both direct control of fidelity in spatial domain for embedding and strong robustness against attacks in frequency domain while detecting can be realized in a single framework.

An obvious problem that shall be taken into consideration is the modeling of more than two attacks while calculating the fitness value. Though the experimental results have shown robustness against other attacks, modeling multiple types of attacks and trying to optimize the performance against them are still important issues that worth further exploitation. This will be an important topic of our future research.

6 Conclusion

In this paper, a novel watermarking performance enhancement architecture based on existing watermarking schemes and evolutionary computation techniques is proposed. The proposed scheme optimizes the robustness against certain attacks and guarantees minimum fidelity, under the condition of fixed data capacity. The proposed embedding procedures in our architecture is quite different from current watermarking schemes in concepts, and the architecture can be easily adopted to improve the performance of existing blind watermarking schemes. Experimental results show its superiority in real image watermarking applications against certain attacks, such as the JPEG compression attack.

References

1. I. J. Cox, J. Bloom and M. L. Miller, *Digital Watermarking*, Morgan Kaufmann Publishers, 1st Edition, 2001
2. I. J. Cox and M. L. Miller, "The First 50 Years of Electronic Watermarking," Journal of Applied Signal Processing, 2002, 2, pp126-132, April 2002
3. D. B. Fogel, *Evolutionary Computation toward a New Philosophy of Machine Intelligence*, IEEE Press, 1995
4. D. E. Goldberg, *Genetic Algorithm in Search, Optimization & Machine Learning*, Addison-Wesley, 1989
5. C. H, Huang and J. L. Wu, "A Watermark Optimization Technique Based on Genetic Algorithms," SPIE Electronic Imaging 2000, San Jose, January, 2000
6. C. T. Hsu and J. L. Wu, "Hidden Digital Watermarks in Images," IEEE Transactions on Image Processing, vol. 8, No. 1, January 1999
7. J. L. Wu, C. H. Lin and C. H. Huang, "An Efficient Genetic Algorithm for Small Range Search Problem", *Intelligent Multimedia Processing with Soft Computing*, Springer-Verlag, pp253-280, 2005
8. J. S. Pan, H. C. and F. H. Wang, "Genetic Watermarking Techniques," The 5th Int'l Conference on Knowledge-based Intelligent Information Engineering System & Allied Technologies.
9. C. H. Huang and J. L. Wu, "A Blind Watermarking Algorithm with Semantic Meaningful Watermarks," 34th Asilomar Conference on Signals. Systems, and Computers, Pacific Grove, October, 2000.

Robust Watermarking on Polygonal Meshes Using Distribution of Vertex Norms

Jae-Won Cho[1, 2], Min-Su Kim[1, 2], R. Prost[2],
Hyun-Yeol Chung[1], and Ho-Youl Jung[1,*]

[1] Dept. of Info. and Comm. Eng., University of Yeungnam, Korea
ram56@yumail.ac.kr, hoyoul@yu.ac.kr
[2] CREATIS, INSA de Lyon, France

Abstract. Most watermarking techniques for 3-D mesh models have mainly focused on robustness against various attacks, such as adding noise, smoothing, simplification, re-meshing, clipping, and so on. These attacks perceptually damage the stego model itself. Unlike watermarking of other multimedia data, serious attacks for 3-D meshes includes similarity transform and vertex re-ordering. They can fatally destroy the watermark without any perceptual degradation of the stego model. In this paper, we propose a new watermarking technique for 3-D polygonal mesh model, which modifies the distribution of vertex norms according to watermark bit to be embedded. In particular, the proposed employs blind watermark detection technique, which extracts the watermark without referring to cover meshes. The simulation results show that the proposed is remarkably robust against similarity transform and vertex re-ordering.

1 Introduction

With remarkable growth of network technology such as WWW (World Wide Web), digital media enables us to copy, modify, store, and distribute digital data without effort. As a result, it has become a new issue to research schemes for copyright protection. Traditional data protection techniques such as encryption are not adequate for copyright enforcement, because the protection cannot be ensured after the data is decrypted. Unlike encryption, digital watermarking does not restrict access to the host data, but ensures the hidden data remain inviolate and recoverable. Watermarking is a copy right protection technique to embed information, so-called watermark, into cover data.

Most of the previous researches have focused on general types of multimedia data, including text data, audio, still image, and video stream [1-3]. Recently, with the interest and requirement of 3-D models such as VRML (Virtual Reality Modeling Language) data, CAD (Computer Aided Design) data, polygonal mesh models, and medical objects, several watermarking techniques for 3-D models have been introduced [4-12].

"This work was supported both by Korea Science and Engineering Foundation (KOSEF, 000–B–105-898) and Centre National de la Recherche Scientifique, France (CNRS, 14894)."
* Corresponding author. Tel.: +82-53-810-3545, Fax: +82-53-810-4742 (Ho-Youl Jung).

I.J. Cox et al. (Eds.): IWDW 2004, LNCS 3304, pp. 283 – 293, 2005.
© Springer-Verlag Berlin Heidelberg 2005

There are several challenges to develop robust watermarking technique in 3-D polygonal mesh models. Unlike image data represented by brightness (or color) at pixel uniformly sampled over regular grid in dimension two, polygonal mesh model has no unique representation, i.e., no implicit order and connectivity of vertices [5][6]. For such a reason, most techniques developed for other types of multimedia are not effective for 3-D meshes [7]. Besides it is hard to decide embedding primitives for robust watermark. And a variety of complex geometrical and topological operations are available to disturb the watermark extraction for assertion of ownership [9]. In particular, some distortionless attacks such as vertex re-ordering and similarity transform (including rotation, translation, and uniform scaling) are possible. They can fatally destroy the watermark without any perceptual change of the stego model.

Since 3-D mesh watermarking technique was introduced in [8], there have been several trials to improve the performance in terms of transparency and robustness. R. Ohbuchi et al. [8] proposed three watermarking schemes, so-called, TSQ (Triangle Similarity Quadruple), TVR (Tetrahedral Volume Ratio), and a visible mesh watermarking method. These schemes provide many useful insights into mesh watermarking, but they are not sufficiently robust to various attacks [5]. For example, TVR method is very vulnerable to synchronization attacks such as re-meshing, simplification, and vertex randomization [9]. Beneden [9] introduces a blind watermark embedding technique, which modifies local distribution of vertex direction from center point of model. The method is robust to synchronization attacks, since the distribution is not sensitive to such operations. An extended method was also introduced in [12], which supplements a week-point of Beneden's algorithm against cropping attack. However, both methods require a heavy pre-processing for re-orientation in the process of watermark detection, as the local distribution depends essentially on the rotation of the object. Z. Yu [5][6] proposed a vertex norm modification method, which perturbs the distance between the vertices to the center of model according to watermark bit to be embedded. It employs, before the modification, scrambling the vertices for the purpose of preserving the visual quality. It should be noted that it is not only non-blind technique, but also requires pre-processing such as registration and re-sampling. Several trials using multi-resolution scheme also have been introduced [4][7][10]. S. Kanai [7] proposed watermarking algorithms based on wavelet transform. Similar methods, using Burt-Adelson style pyramid and mesh spectral analysis, were also published [4][10], respectively. These multi-resolution techniques could achieve good transparency of watermark, but have not yet concrete solution for various synchronization attacks such as vertex re-ordering, re-meshing, and simplification.

In this paper, we propose a new watermarking technique for 3-D polygonal mesh model, which modifies the distribution of vertex norms so as to shift mean value of vertex norms according to watermark bit to be inserted. Distribution of vertex norms is divided into several sections, called these bins later, so as to improve capacity and transparency of watermark. Clearly, the distribution of vertex norms is invariant to similarity transform and vertex re-ordering. In addition, the proposed employs blind scheme, which can extract the watermark without reference of cover mesh model.

This paper is organized as follows. In section 2, the proposed watermarking method is introduced. Here, we first describe main idea using the distribution of vertex norms. General embedding and extracting procedures of the proposed are described. After that, we introduce a robust technique which improves the efficiency of the proposed via modification of a part of vertex norms. Section 3 shows the simulation results of the proposed against adding noise and clipping, as well as similarity transform and vertex re-ordering. Finally, we conclude this paper.

2 The Proposed Watermarking Scheme

The watermarking scheme proposed in this paper embeds watermark information into 3-D polygonal mesh model by modifying the distribution of vertex norms. Fig. 1 shows main idea of the proposed watermarking scheme. Assume that the vertex norms of cover meshes have uniform distribution as shown in Fig.1-(a) for the sake of simplicity. The distribution is modified according to watermark bit to be embedded. For embedding watermark bit of +1, vertex norms are modified to make their distribution concentrate on the right-side as shown in Fig.1-(b). In this case, the mean value of vertex norms grows bigger. For embedding watermark bit of −1, the distribution concentrates to left-side shown in Fig.1-(c). Watermark detection process is quite simple, as the hidden watermark bit can be easily extracted by comparing the mean value of vertex norms and a reference value.

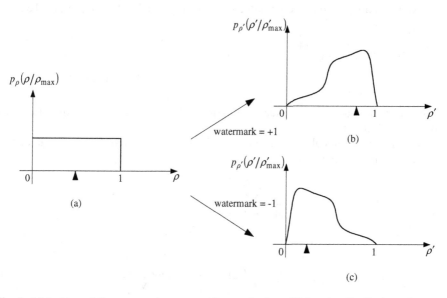

Fig. 1. Main idea of the proposed watermarking method modifying the distribution of vertex norm. Here, the mean value is denoted by ▲

2.1 Watermark Embedding

General embedding process of the proposed method is shown in Fig. 2. To begin with, Cartesian coordinates (x_i, y_i, z_i) of a vertex on cover mesh model **V** are converted to spherical coordinates $(\rho_i, \theta_i, \phi_i)$ by means of

$$\rho_i = \sqrt{(x_i - x_g)^2 + (y_i - y_g)^2 + (z_i - z_g)^2},$$

$$\theta_i = \tan^{-1}\frac{(y_i - y_g)}{(x_i - x_g)}, \qquad\qquad for\ 0 \le i \le L-1\ \ and\ \ v_i = (x_i, y_i, z_i) \in \mathbf{V}. \quad (1)$$

$$\phi_i = \cos^{-1}\frac{(z_i - z_g)}{\sqrt{(x_i - x_g)^2 + (y_i - y_g)^2 + (z_i - z_g)^2}},$$

Where, L is the number of vertex, $(x_g,\ y_g,\ z_g)$ is the center of gravity of mesh model, and ρ_i is i-th vertex norm. Vertex norm is the distance between each vertex and center of the model.

The proposed uses only the vertex norm to embed watermark information, with keeping other components intact. We modify the distribution of vertex norm, which is invariant to similarity transform and vertex re-ordering.

In the second step, the interval of the distribution is divided into N small sections. Here, each section is employed as watermark embedding unit, so-called *bin*. That is, vertices are classified into N bins according to their norm, and each bin is independently processed for watermark embedding. This allows enhancing both capacity and transparency of the watermark. For such purpose, maximum and minimum vertex norms, ρ_{max} and ρ_{min}, should be found in advance. The n-th bin $\mathbf{B}_n$ is represented as

$$\mathbf{B}_n = \left\{ \rho_{n,j} \middle| \rho_{min} + \frac{\rho_{max} - \rho_{min}}{N} \cdot n < \rho_{n,j} < \rho_{min} + \frac{\rho_{max} - \rho_{min}}{N} \cdot (n+1) \right\},$$

$$for\ 0 \le n \le N-1\ and\ 0 \le j \le M_n - 1. \tag{2}$$

Where M_n is the number of vertices belonging to the n-th bin and $\rho_{n,j}$ is the j-th vertex norm of the n-th bin.

The third step is to calculate mean and reference values of vertex norms, μ_n and r_n, respectively in each bin.

$$\mu_n = \frac{1}{M_n}\sum_{j=0}^{M_n-1}\rho_{n,j}\ ,\ \ for\ \rho_{n,j} \in \mathbf{B}_n, \tag{3}$$

$$r_n = \rho_{min} + \left(\frac{\rho_{max} - \rho_{min}}{N}\right) \cdot n + \frac{1}{2} \cdot \left(\frac{\rho_{max} - \rho_{min}}{N}\right), \tag{4}$$

Where, middle value of the corresponding section is used as the reference to estimate the distribution by comparing with the mean. For the case of $\mu_n > r_n$, it can be estimated that the distribution is centralized into right-side, and vice-versa.

Next step is to alter the distribution of vertex norms, so that the mean and the reference values are changed according to watermark bit $\omega_n \in \{-1, +1\}$ to be embedded in each bin. For embedding watermark bit of +1, vertex norms are modified in order that the mean and the reference values satisfy $\mu'_n > r'_n$. Here, the superscript prime means

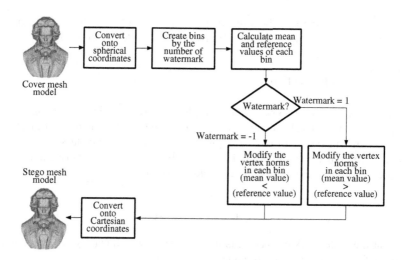

Fig. 2. Block diagram of the proposed watermark embedding process

the value obtained from the modified vertex norm, $\rho'_{n,j}$, and $r_n \equiv r'_n$ is preserved since we do not modify both minimum and maximum norms, ρ_{max} and ρ_{min} . For embedding $\omega_n = -1$, vertex norms are modified in order to be $\mu'_n < r'_n$. In our proposed, the modified vertex norm is obtained by

$$\rho'_{n,j} = \rho_{n,j} + \alpha_n \omega_n \,, \tag{5}$$

where strength factor of the n-th bin, α_n, is determined so as to guarantee such that $\mu'_n > r'_n$ for $\omega_n = +1$ and $\mu'_n < r'_n$ for $\omega_n = -1$, respectively.

$$
\begin{aligned}
\alpha_n &> |r_n - \mu_n| && if \ (\omega_n = 1 \ and \ \mu_n < r_n) \ or \ (\omega_n = -1 \ and \ \mu_n > r_n) \\
\alpha_n &= 0 && otherwise.
\end{aligned} \tag{6}
$$

This means that the whole vertex norms in each bin are added by $+\alpha_n$ or $-\alpha_n$. The relation between mean and reference values is retained, when the processing is performed in separate bin. Unfortunately, it leads to serious impact on robustness of watermark when the processing is performed in every each bin, because some modified vertices belong to certain bin can invade into other neighbor bins. A robust technique is introduced in Section 2-3.

The final step is inverse transformation of vertex from spherical coordinates onto Cartesian coordinates. The Cartesian coordinates (x'_i, y'_i, z'_i) of vertex v' on stego mesh model $\mathbf{V}'$ is given by

$$
\begin{aligned}
x'_i &= \rho'_i \cos\theta_l \sin\phi_l + x_g, \\
y'_i &= \rho'_i \sin\theta_l \sin\phi_l + y_g, && for \ 0 \le i \le L-1 \\
z'_i &= \rho'_i \cos\phi_l + z_g,
\end{aligned} \tag{7}
$$

Note that the watermark embedding method utilizes only the distribution of vertex norms, which is invariant to similarity transform and vertex re-ordering.

2.2 Watermark Extraction

Watermark extraction process is quite simple as shown in Fig. 3. Similar to embedding process, stego mesh model is first represented on spherical coordinates. After finding maximum and minimum vertex norms, vertex norms are classified into N bins. Mean and reference values, μ'_n and r'_n, in each bin are respectively calculated, and compared in order to extract the hidden watermark ω'_n.

$$\omega'_n = \begin{cases} 1, & if \ r'_n - \mu'_n < 0 \\ -1, & if \ r'_n - \mu'_n > 0. \end{cases} \tag{8}$$

Note that the watermark extraction is blind scheme, which can extract the watermark without reference of cover mesh model.

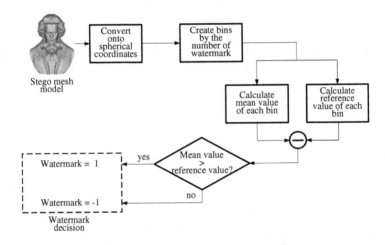

Fig. 3. Block diagram of the proposed watermark extraction process

2.3 Robust Watermarking Technique

The watermark embedding method proposed in Section 2-1 modifies vertex norms by adding (or subtracting) with strength factor. The objective of the process is to shift the mean value in each bin according to its watermark bit. However, the method is not efficient in terms of watermark transparency, since every vertex norms in bin are modified. Moreover, some modified vertices belong to certain bin can invade into other neighbor bins. It might lead to a serious impact for robust watermark detection. To cope with the disadvantages, a robust technique is introduced in this section.

Mean value can be shifted by modifying only some part of vertex norms. In our approach, vertex norms that are smaller/greater than reference value are modified. For embedding watermark bit of +1, vertex norms being smaller than the reference is modified so as to move its mean, μ^L_n, to the reference value.

$$\rho'_{n,j} = \rho_{n,j} + \beta \cdot \alpha^L_n \omega_n, \quad for \quad \rho_{n,j} < r_n$$
$$= \rho_{n,j} \qquad\qquad otherwise \tag{9}$$

For embedding watermark bit of −1, vertex norms being greater than the reference is modified so as to decrease its mean μ^R_n.

$$\rho'_{n,j} = \rho_{n,j} + \beta \cdot \alpha^R_n \omega_n, \quad for \quad \rho_{n,j} > r_n$$
$$= \rho_{n,j} \qquad\qquad otherwise \tag{10}$$

where β is a weighting factor, and α^L_n (or α^R_n) is a distance between reference value r_n and μ^L_n (or μ^R_n).

$$\alpha^L_n = \left| r_n - \mu^L_n \right|$$
$$\alpha^R_n = \left| r_n - \mu^R_n \right| \tag{11}$$

Although only part of vertex norms are modified, this technique guarantees always the relation between mean and reference values, such that $\mu'_n > r'_n$ for $\omega_n = +1$ and $\mu'_n < r'_n$ for $\omega_n = -1$, whenever β is greater than one. Moreover, the strength of watermark can be adjusted by weighting factor β within appropriate range, which prevents the modified vertex norms from getting over boundary of the bin. Watermark extraction is processed by the same method as Section 2-2.

3 Simulation Results

The simulations are carried out on triangular mesh model of *beethoven* with 2655 vertices and 5028 cells. The quality of mesh model is measured by *Metro* [11], which is error-measuring software for polygonal mesh models. In the simulation, maximum between forward and backward *Hausdorff distances* is measured.

$$D_{forward}(\mathbf{V},\mathbf{V'}) = \max_{v \in \mathbf{V}} \{ \min_{v' \in \mathbf{V'}} \| v - v' \| \}$$
$$D_{backward}(\mathbf{V'},\mathbf{V}) = \max_{v' \in \mathbf{V'}} \{ \min_{v \in \mathbf{V}} \| v' - v \| \} \tag{12}$$
$$H(\mathbf{V},\mathbf{V'}) = \max \{ D_{forward}(\mathbf{V},\mathbf{V'}), D_{backward}(\mathbf{V'},\mathbf{V}) \}$$

where $v \in \mathbf{V}$ and $v' \in \mathbf{V'}$ are respectively vertices of cover mesh model and stego mesh model. The performance of watermark detection is evaluated using *DR* (Detection Ratio).

$$DR = \frac{\text{\# of watermark bits correctly extracted}}{\text{\# of watermark bits placed}} \tag{13}$$

To consider transparency of watermark, we embed watermark sequence of 55 bits.

Fig. 4 shows the efficiency of the proposed watermarking methods, in terms of Hausdorff distances and *DR*, in the case of no attacks. Dashed curve indicates the method described in Section 2-1, and solid curve indicates the robust watermarking technique mentioned in Section 2-3. Both are obtained with varying α_n and β ($0.4 \leq \beta \leq 1.0$).

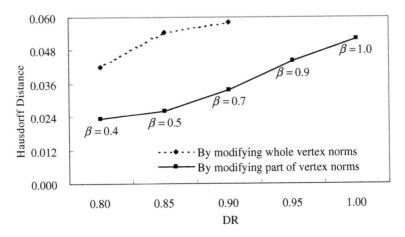

Fig. 4. Efficiency of transparency and robustness after controlling the strength factor

(a)   (b)

Fig. 5. (a) cover mesh model (b) stego mesh model : $H(\mathbf{V}, \mathbf{V}') = 0.004415$, $DR = 1.0$

The method modifying every vertex norms does not achieve to high detection rate, even when strong watermark is embedded with higher distortion. This is caused by that the modified vertex norms could invade into other neighbor bins, as mentioned in Section 2-3. Dashed curve shows that the proposed robust technique guarantees always the relation between mean and reference values for β being greater than one.

Table 1. Evaluation of the proposed, in terms of Hausdorff distance and *DR*, after various attacks

Attacks	Conditions				$H(\mathbf{V},\mathbf{V}')$	DR
Adding random noise	0.25%				0.005125	1.00
	0.50%				0.005836	0.95
	0.75%				0.006538	0.89
	1.00%				0.007234	0.82
Clipping	5%				0.099973	1.00
	20%				0.099999	1.00
	50%				0.099976	0.98
Similarity transform	x-axis	1°	×0.8	+0.001		
	y-axis	1°	×0.8	+0.001	0.076339	1.00
	z-axis	1°	×0.8	+0.001		
	x-axis	1°	×1.2	+0.010		
	y-axis	3°	×1.2	+0.030	0.068946	1.00
	z-axis	5°	×1.2	+0.050		
	x-axis	15°	×1.5	+0.010		
	y-axis	30°	×1.5	−0.030	0.099996	1.00
	z-axis	45°	×1.5	+0.080		
Vertex re-ordering	Average of 100 times trials				0.004415	1.00

Hereafter, we analyze only the robust watermarking technique through simulations against various attacks. Weighting factor is experimentally selected as $\beta = 1.5$ and used over simulations. Cover mesh model and stego mesh model are showed in Fig. 5.

To evaluate the robustness of the proposed, stego meshes suffer from several attacks such as adding random noise, clipping, similarity transform and vertex re-ordering. Fig. 6 shows stego models after three attacks. And the simulation results are given in table 1. In case of adding random noise, *DR* decreases proportionally to error rate. Here, the error rate represent the relative variation of vertex norm, and the random noise is added to whole vertex norms. The proposed has good watermark detection performance up to 1.00% of error rate.

For the case of clipping attacks, we assumed that the center of gravity is known in watermark detection side. The proposed can extract correctly most watermark bits from some part of stego model, as it uses statistical approach. Vertex re-ordering attack is carried out repetitively 100 times, changing the seed value of random order generator. Similarity transform is carried out with various rotation, translation, and uniform scaling parameters. Simulation results demonstrate that the proposed is remarkably robust against both similarity transform and vertex re-ordering.

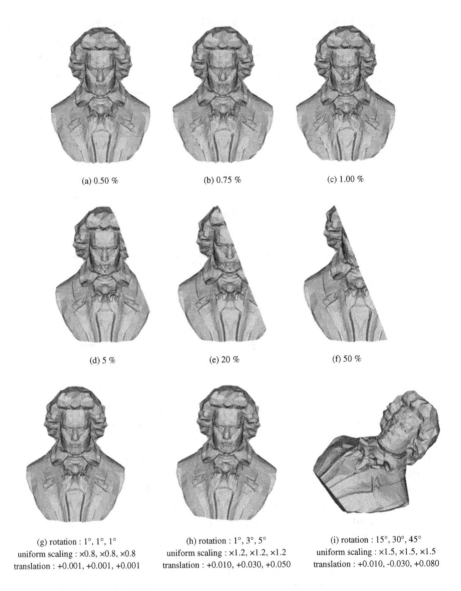

(a) 0.50 %   (b) 0.75 %   (c) 1.00 %

(d) 5 %   (e) 20 %   (f) 50 %

(g) rotation : 1°, 1°, 1°
uniform scaling : ×0.8, ×0.8, ×0.8
translation : +0.001, +0.001, +0.001

(h) rotation : 1°, 3°, 5°
uniform scaling : ×1.2, ×1.2, ×1.2
translation : +0.010, +0.030, +0.050

(i) rotation : 15°, 30°, 45°
uniform scaling : ×1.5, ×1.5, ×1.5
translation : +0.010, -0.030, +0.080

Fig. 6. Stego mesh models after attacks: such as adding random noise (a) –(c), clipping (d) –(f), and similarity transform (g) –(i)

4   Conclusions

In this paper, we proposed a new blind watermarking technique for 3-D polygonal mesh model. The proposed embeds watermark by using distribution of vertex norms. Through the simulations, we proved that the proposed is remarkably robust against similarity transform and vertex re-ordering, which are serious attacks on 3-D watermarking field. In addition, the proposed has good watermark detection performance against adding random noise and clipping attacks. Moreover, the method is very simple in both embedding and detection processes. As results, the proposed presents a new possibility to solve the fundamental problem of 3-D watermarking.

References

1. J.W Cho, H.J Park, Y. Huh, H.Y Chung, H.Y Jung : Echo Watermarking in Sub-band Domain. IWDW 2003, LNCS2939 (2004) 447–455
2. I.Cox, J.Kilian, F.Leighton, and T.Shamoon : Secure spread spectrum watermarking for multimedia. IEEE Transaction on Image Processing, Vol.6 No.12, (1997) 1673–1687
3. F.Hartung and B.Girod : Watermarking of uncompressed and compressed video. Signal Processing, (1998) 283–301
4. Ryutarou Ohbuchi, ShigeoTakahashi, Takahiko Miyazawa, and Akio Mukaiyama : Watermarking 3D Polygonal Meshes in the Mesh Spectral Domain. Proceedings of Graphics Interface, (2001) 9–18
5. Zhiqiang Yu, Horace H.S.Ip, and L.F.Kwok : A robust watermarking scheme for 3D triangular mesh models. Pattern Recognition, Vol.36, Issue.11, (2003) 2603–2614
6. Zhiqiang Yu, Horace H.S.Ip, and L.F.Kwok : Robust Watermarking of 3D Polygonal Models Based on Vertice Scrambling. Computer Graphics International 2003, (2003) 254–257
7. Satoshi Kanai, Hiroaki Date, and Takeshi Kishinami : Digital Watermarking for 3D Polygons using Multiresolution Wavelet Decomposition, Proceedings Sixth IFIP WG 5.2 GEO-6, (1998) 296–307
8. Ryutarou Ohbuchi, Hiroshi Masuda, and Masaki Aono : Watermarking 3-D Polygonal Models Through Geometric and Topological Modifications. IEEE Journal on Selected Areas in Communications, Vol.16, No.4, (1998) 551–560
9. Oliver Benedens : Geometry-based watermarking of 3D models. IEEE Journal on Computer Graphics and Applications, Vol.19, Issue.1, (1999) 46–55
10. Kangkang Yin, Zhigeng Pan, Jiaoying Shi, and David Zhang : Robust mesh watermarking based on multiresolution processing. Computers and Graphics, Vol.25, (2001) 409–420
11. P.Cignoni, C.Rocchini and R.Scopigno : Metro: measuring error on simplified surfaces. Computer Graphics Forum, Vol.17, No.2, (1998) 167–174
12. S.H Lee, T.S Kim, B.J Kim, S.G. Kwon, K.R Kwon, and K.I Lee : 3D Polygonal Meshes Watermarking Using Normal Vector Distributions. IEEE International Conference on Multimedia & Expo, Vol.3, (2003) 105–108

A Video Watermarking Using the 3-D Wavelet Transform and Two Perceptual Watermarks

Seung-Jin Kim[1], Suk-Hwan Lee[1], Tae-Su Kim[1],
Ki-Ryong Kwon[2], and Kuhn-Il Lee[1]

[1] School of Electronic Engineering and Computer Science,
Kyungpook National University
1370, Sankyug-Dong, Buk-Gu, Daegu, 702-701, Korea
{starksjin, skylee, kts1101}@m80.knu.ac.kr, kilee@knu.ac.kr
[2] Department of Electronic Engineering, Pusan University of Foreign Studies,
55-1, Uam-Dong, Nam-Gu, Pusan, 608-738, Korea
krkwon@pufs.ac.kr

Abstract. An effective video watermarking algorithm is proposed to protect the copyright. Two perceptual binary images are used as the watermark and the watermarking procedure is based on a three-dimensional discrete wavelet transform (3-D DWT) and two spread spectrum sequences. Two perceptual watermarks are preprocessed using mixing and pseudorandom permutation. After dividing the video sequence into video shots, the 3-D DWT is performed, then the preprocessed watermarks are embedded into the 3-D DWT coefficients, while considering robustness and invisibility, using two spread spectrum sequences defined as the user key. Experimental results show that the watermarked frames are subjectively indistinguishable from the original frames, plus the proposed video watermarking algorithm is sufficiently robust against such attacks as low pass filtering, frame dropping, frame average, and MPEG coding.

1   Introduction

With the rapid growth of networks and multimedia systems, digital media, such as images, audio, and video are distributed and manipulated much faster and readily. As a result, creators and distributors of digital media have become increasingly interested in protecting their copyright and ownership.

Digital watermarking involves embedding copyright information into digital data, and its basic requirements include that the watermark must be perceptually invisible in the original digital media and robust to incidental and intended attacks on the digital media. As such, digital watermarking has been attracting attention as an effective method for protecting the copyright, resulting in the development of a variety of watermarking algorithms.

Hsu et al. [2] use a discrete cosine transform (DCT) and the relationship between neighboring blocks to embed a watermark. Thus, a preprocessed visible watermark is embedded into middle frequency coefficients based on modifying the polarity between the corresponding pixels in a neighboring block. However,

I.J. Cox et al. (Eds.): IWDW 2004, LNCS 3304, pp. 294–303, 2005.
© Springer-Verlag Berlin Heidelberg 2005

since the DCT coefficients are changed to maintain the polarity, an error is accumulated during the change process of the DCT coefficients.

Niu et al. [3] use a 3-D DWT and gray level digital watermark image, where the 3-D DWT is performed as a unit of 64 frames and the embedded watermark is made using a multi-resolution hierarchical structure and hamming code. However, since this method uses the error correction coding to correct error bits, the side information is large. Thus, to embed the bit planes of the gray watermark and error correction bits, this method requires a complex structure. The bit error of the most significant pixel also affects the extracted gray watermark image.

Accordingly, the current study proposes an effective video watermarking algorithm using a 3-D DWT and two spread spectrum sequences. Two visible binary watermark images are preprocessed using mixing and permutation. Thereafter, the video sequence is divided into video shots, and a 3-D DWT is performed about video shots. Subbands selected for embedding the watermark are determined based on robustness and invisibility, then the watermark is embedded using two spread spectrum sequences define as the user key. As regards the watermark extraction, the watermark is finally extracted by comparing the similarity between the user key and the extracted spread spectrum sequence. Although visible binary images are used as the watermark, the use of two spread spectrum sequences allows different watermarks to be embedded into each video frame, making it robust against noise and increasing the precision of watermark extraction.

As such, the proposed algorithm produces watermarked frames that are subjectively no different from the original frames and robust against such attacks as low pass filtering, frame dropping, frame average, and MPEG coding.

2   The Video Watermarking Procedure

The proposed video watermarking procedure roughly consists of three steps: the preprocessing of the binary watermark image, watermark embedding, and watermark extraction. A block diagram of the proposed video watermarking algorithm is shown in Fig. 1.

2.1   Watermark Preprocessing

A binary image with visually recognizable binary patterns is used as the watermark. As using a stamp or signature to prove identity, the viewer can subjectively compare the original watermark with the extracted watermark. Therefore, a binary image is more visually effective than a sequence of random numbers.

Two binary watermark images are embedded into the middle frequency range in the wavelet transform domain. If one is broken, the other will identity the ownership. They can be also used as the ownership watermark to identify the owner and the recipient respectively. Before the embedding step, two watermark images are mixed and a two-dimensional (2-D) pseudorandom permutation is performed about two mixed watermark images [4], as without the appropriate

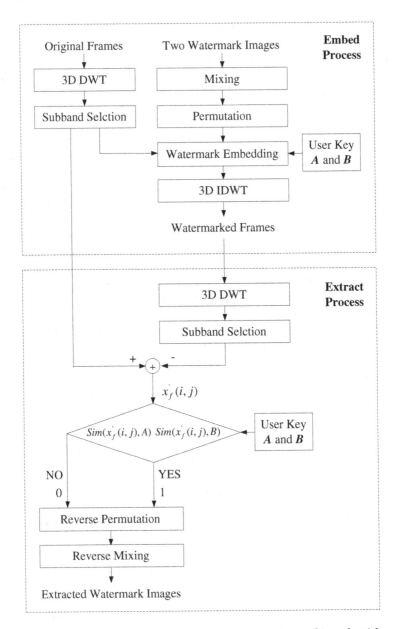

Fig. 1. A block diagram of the proposed video watermarking algorithm

adjustment for the spatial relationship of the watermark, a common picture cropping operation could eliminate the watermark.

Two mixed watermarks $w_{m1}(i,j)$ and $w_{m2}(i,j)$ are

$$w_{m1}(i,j) = \begin{cases} w_1(i,j) & \text{if } i = 2k \\ w_2(i,j) & \text{otherwise} \end{cases} \tag{1}$$

$$w_{m2}(i,j) = \begin{cases} w_1(i,j) & \text{if } i = 2(k+1) \\ w_2(i,j) & \text{otherwise} \end{cases} \tag{2}$$

where $w_1(i,j)$ and $w_2(i,j)$ are the watermark image A and B respectively, $k = 1, 2, \cdots, N/2$, and N is the horizontal size of the watermark image.

The 2-D pseudorandom number traversing method is also used to permute two mixed watermarks respectively, namely,

$$\begin{aligned} W_p &= Permute(W) \\ w_{p1}(i,j) &= w_{m1}(i',j'), & 0 \le i, i' \le M \text{ and } 0 \le j, j' \le N \\ w_{p2}(i,j) &= w_{m2}(i',j'), & 0 \le i, i' \le M \text{ and } 0 \le j, j' \le N \end{aligned} \tag{3}$$

where pixel (i',j') is permuted to pixel (i,j) in pseudorandom order and $M \times N$ is the size of the watermark image.

2.2 Watermark Embedding

The proposed method uses a 3-D DWT that is computed by applying separate one-dimensional (1-D) transform along the temporal axis of the video frames transformed by a 2-D DWT [5], [6].

Considering a video watermarking scheme as a direct extension of an image watermarking by treating each frame as an individual still image is ineffective for two reasons. First, a pirate can easily extract the watermark by statistically comparing or averaging successive video frames. Second, if different watermarks are embedded into each frame, the watermark amount is large. Thus, to prevent pirate attacks on the watermark and reduce the watermark amount, a 3-D DWT is used that decomposes frames along both the spatial and temporal axis.

In the proposed watermark embedding procedure, the video sequence is first divided into video shots using a spatial different metric (SDM) [7] to determine the dissimilarity between an adjoining frame pair. Although the efficiency of this method is low, the algorithm is simple. Then, a spatial 2-D DWT and temporal 1-D DWT are both performed about the selected video shot.

In the resulting 3-D DWT coefficients, two preprocessed watermark images are embedded into the HL subband and the LH subband of the three levels (HL_3, LH_3) about the spatial axis and the lowpass frames about the temporal axis. The LL subband of the three levels (LL_3) is excluded to satisfy invisibility, while highpass frames consisting of dynamic components are excluded to satisfy robustness.

Two preprocessed watermark image A and B are embedded in HL_3 and LH_3 of the lowpass frames respectively. The watermark $x_f(i,j)$ is embedded using the following relationship [1].

$$v'_f(i,j) = v_f(i,j) \times (1 + \alpha \times x_f(i,j)) \tag{4}$$

where $v'_f(i,j)$ and $v_f(i,j)$ denote the 3-D DWT coefficient of (HL_3) and (LH_3) in the watermarked frame and the original frame respectively, f is the frame number, and α is the scaling parameter. The binary images are used as the watermark. But when the watermark is embedded, it is not a binary watermark anymore but one of two independent spread spectrum sequences [8], which can be defined as the user key for the visible binary watermark. Two independent spread spectrum sequences $\mathbf{A}$ and $\mathbf{B}$ with a low cross correlation are

$$
\begin{aligned}
\mathbf{A} &= \{a_1, a_1, \cdots, a_f, \cdots, a_n\} \\
\mathbf{B} &= \{b_1, b_1, \cdots, b_f, \cdots, b_n\}
\end{aligned}
\tag{5}
$$

where n is half of the number of the frame shot. Two spread spectrum sequences are repetitively used as the user key according to each video shot. This method is sufficiently robust against various attacks such as frame dropping, frame average, and MPEG coding. But different two spread spectrum sequences can be used every frame shots for robust scheme against the estimation attacks. The spread spectrum sequence $\mathbf{A}$ or $\mathbf{B}$ is used according to bit 1 or 0 of the binary watermark image.

The watermark $x_f(i,j)$ really embedded in HL_3 is

$$
x_f(i,j) = \begin{cases} a_f & \text{if } w_{\mathrm{p}1}(i,j) = 1 \text{ in } \mathrm{HL}_3 \\ b_f & \text{if } w_{\mathrm{p}1}(i,j) = 0 \text{ in } \mathrm{HL}_3 \end{cases}
\tag{6}
$$

where $w_{\mathrm{p}1}(i,j)$ is the preprocessed watermark image A. The watermark embedded in LH_3 is also determined by equation (6).

2.3   Watermark Extracting

The watermark extraction process is the inverse procedure of the watermark embedding process, and the similarity is used to extract the final watermark image. The proposed algorithm requires the original video sequence and the user key. Although difference values between wavelet coefficients of the original frame and the watermarked frame are calculated, difference values are not the extracted binary watermark image but the extracted spread spectrum sequence modified by attacks. Accordingly, the similarity between the user key and the extracted spread spectrum sequence is calculated to extract the binary watermark image. The extracted watermark image $w'(i,j)$ is

$$
w'(i,j) = \begin{cases} 1 & \text{if } Sim(x'_f(i,j), \mathbf{A}) \geq Sim(x'_f(i,j), \mathbf{B}) \\ 0 & \text{otherwise} \end{cases}
\tag{7}
$$

where $x'_f(i,j)$ is the extracted spread spectrum sequence. The similarity is

$$
Sim(x'_f(i,j), \mathbf{A}) = \frac{\sum_{f=0}^{n} x'_f(i,j) \cdot a_f}{\sum_{f=0}^{n} a_f^2}
\tag{8}
$$

As a 2-D reverse pseudorandom permutation and reverse mixing have been performed, two binary watermark images are extracted.

Since the resulting watermark is a binary image, the viewer can subjectively compare the extracted watermark with the original watermark. However, as the subjective measurement depends on the ability of the viewer, a normalized correlation (NC) is also used as an objective measurement. The NC is

$$NC = \frac{\sum_i \sum_j w(i,j) \cdot w'(i,j)}{\sum_i \sum_j w^2(i,j)} \tag{9}$$

where $w(i,j)$ is the original watermark image and $w'(i,j)$ is the extracted watermark image.

3 Experimental Results

Computer simulations were carried out to demonstrate the performance of the proposed algorithm. A football and a flower garden video sequence were used as the test video sequence. Each frame was 352×240. The watermark was a binary image sized 44×30, as shown in Fig. 2. The video sequence was divided into video shots by the SDM. However, the video shots consisted of a double number of 16 or 24 frames to carry out the 3-D DWT with three levels. The peak signal to noise ratio (PSNR) was used as an objective measure of invisibility, while the NC denoted by (9) was used to measure robustness.

The first original frame and first watermarked frame of the football and the flower garden video sequence are shown in Fig. 3 and Fig. 4. The proposed algorithm produced an almost invisible subjective difference between the original frame and the watermarked frame.

(a)   (b)

Fig. 2. (a) The watermark image A and (b) The watermark image B

(a)   (b)

Fig. 3. The first frame from (a) original football video sequence and (b) watermarked football video sequence

(a)   (b)

Fig. 4. The first frame from (a) original flower garden video sequence and (b) watermarked flower garden video sequence

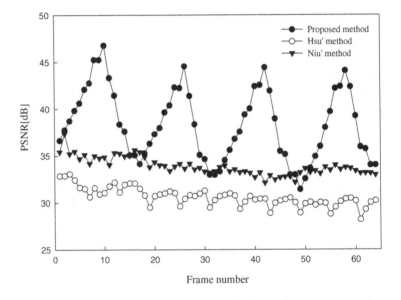

Fig. 5. The PSNR for football 64 frames watermarked using proposed method and conventional methods

The PSNR for football 64 frames and flower garden 64 frames watermarked using the proposed algorithm and conventional algorithms is shown in Fig. 5 and Fig. 6 respectively. The proposed algorithm produced a higher PSNR than conventional methods.

To measure the robustness, various attacks were used, such as spatial low pass filtering (LPF), frame dropping, frame average, and MPEG coding. For frame dropping and interpolation, the odd index frames were dropped and the missing frames replaced with the average of the two neighboring frames. The

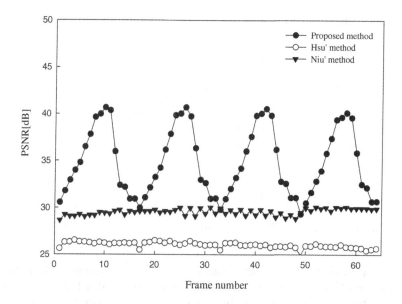

Fig. 6. The PSNR for flower garden 64 frames watermarked using proposed method and conventional methods

(a)   (b)

Fig. 7. (a) The watermark image A and (b) The watermark image B extracted after frame dropping for the football video sequence.

(a)   (b)

Fig. 8. (a) The watermark image A and (b) The watermark image B extracted after MPEG coding for the football video sequence.

extracted watermarks are shown in Fig. 7, and the NC for the two watermarks was 0.819 and 0.793 respectively. For MPEG coding, watermarked video frames coded at 1.5 Mbps were used. The watermark images extracted after MPEG coding are shown in Fig. 8, and the NC for the two watermarks was 0.844 and 0.846 respectively. The quality of the extracted watermark images was good enough to claim copyright and ownership of the digital media.

Table I. The average NC of the watermarks extracted in football 64 frames after the various attacks

Methods / Attacks	Hsu's method	Niu's method	Proposed method	
			Watermark Image A	Watermark Image B
Spatial LPF	0.510	0.652	0.743	0.751
Frame Dropping	0.614	0.685	0.798	0.796
Frame Average	0.482	0.661	0.692	0.718
MPEG Coding	0.510	0.812	0.851	0.850

The experimental results after various attacks are summarized at Table I. The watermark extracted by the proposed algorithm had a higher the average NC than those extracted by conventional methods. As shown by the results, the proposed algorithm was robust against all the above attacks.

4   Conclusions

A video watermarking algorithm was proposed using a 3-D DWT and two perceptual watermarks. Two binary image are used as the watermark. Two watermarks are preprocessed using mixing and permutation. The video sequence is then divided into video shots and the 3-D DWT is performed about video shots. Two preprocessed watermarks are embedded into specific subbands in the 3-D DWT domain, based on considering robustness and invisibility, using two spread spectrum sequences defined as the user key. The watermark is finally extracted by comparing the similarity between the user key and the extracted spread spectrum sequence. Although two binary images are used as the watermark, Because of the use of two spread spectrum sequences, the different watermark value are embedded into each frame and the amount of the watermark is not also large. Therefore, the proposed algorithm produces watermarked frames that are subjectively no different from the original frames and sufficiently robust against various attacks.

Acknowledgements. This work was supported by grant No. (R01-2002-000-00589-0) from the Basic Research Program of the Korea Science & Engineering Foundation.

References

1. I. J. Cox, I. Kilian, T. Leighton, and T. Shamoon: Secure spread spectrum watermarking for multimedia. IEEE Trans. Image Processing, Vol. 6, No. 12, (1997) 1673-1687

2. C. T. Hsu and J. L. Wu: Dct-Based Watermarking for video. IEEE Trans. Consumer Electronics, Vol. 44, No. 1, (1998) 206-216

3. X. Niu, S. Sun, and W. Xiang: Multiresolution Watermarking For Video Based On Gray-Level Digital Watermark. IEEE Trans. Consumer Electronics, Vol. 46, No. 2, (2000) 375-384

4. C. T. Hsu and J. L. Wu: Hidden Digital Watermarks in Images. IEEE Trans. Image Processing, Vol. 8, No. 1, (1999) 58-68

5. M. D. Swanson, B. Zhu, and A. H. Tewfik: Multiresolution Scene-Based Video Watermarking Using Perceptual Models. IEEE Journal Selected Areas in Communication, Vol. 16, No. 4, (1998) 540-550

6. C. I. Podilchuk, N. S. Jayant, and N. Farvardin: Three-Dimensional Subband Coding of Video. IEEE Trans. Image Processing, Vol. 4, No. 2, (1995) 125-139

7. X. Gao and X. Tang: Unsupervised Video-Shot Segmentation and Model-Free Anchorperson Detection for News Video Story Parsing. IEEE Trans. Circuits and Systems for Video Tech., Vol. 12, No. 9, (2002) 765-776

8. J. J. K. O. Ruanaidh and G. Csurka: A Bayesian Approach To Spread Spectrum Watermark Detection and Secure Copyright Protection of Digital Image Libraries. IEEE Conf. Computer Vision and Pattern Recognition, Vol. 1, (1999) 23-25

Author Index

Lecture Notes in Computer Science

For information about Vols. 1–3306

please contact your bookseller or Springer

Vol. 3353: J. Hromkovič, M. Nagl, B. Westfechtel (Eds.), Graph-Theoretic Concepts in Computer Science. XI, 404 pages. 2004.

Vol. 3352: C. Blundo, S. Cimato (Eds.), Security in Communication Networks. XI, 381 pages. 2005.

Vol. 3350: M. Hermenegildo, D. Cabeza (Eds.), Practical Aspects of Declarative Languages. VIII, 269 pages. 2005.

Vol. 3349: B.M. Chapman (Ed.), Shared Memory Parallel Programming with Open MP. X, 149 pages. 2005.

Vol. 3348: A. Canteaut, K. Viswanathan (Eds.), Progress in Cryptology - INDOCRYPT 2004. XIV, 431 pages. 2004.

Vol. 3347: R.K. Ghosh, H. Mohanty (Eds.), Distributed Computing and Internet Technology. XX, 472 pages. 2004.

Vol. 3346: R.H. Bordini, M. Dastani, J. Dix, A.E.F. Seghrouchni (Eds.), Programming Multi-Agent Systems. XIV, 249 pages. 2005. (Subseries LNAI).

Vol. 3345: Y. Cai (Ed.), Ambient Intelligence for Scientific Discovery. XII, 311 pages. 2005. (Subseries LNAI).

Vol. 3344: J. Malenfant, B.M. Østvold (Eds.), Object-Oriented Technology. ECOOP 2004 Workshop Reader. VIII, 215 pages. 2005.

Vol. 3342: E. Şahin, W.M. Spears (Eds.), Swarm Robotics. IX, 175 pages. 2005.

Vol. 3341: R. Fleischer, G. Trippen (Eds.), Algorithms and Computation. XVII, 935 pages. 2004.

Vol. 3340: C.S. Calude, E. Calude, M.J. Dinneen (Eds.), Developments in Language Theory. XI, 431 pages. 2004.

Vol. 3339: G.I. Webb, X. Yu (Eds.), AI 2004: Advances in Artificial Intelligence. XXII, 1272 pages. 2004. (Subseries LNAI).

Vol. 3338: S.Z. Li, J. Lai, T. Tan, G. Feng, Y. Wang (Eds.), Advances in Biometric Person Authentication. XVIII, 699 pages. 2004.

Vol. 3337: J.M. Barreiro, F. Martin-Sanchez, V. Maojo, F. Sanz (Eds.), Biological and Medical Data Analysis. XI, 508 pages. 2004.

Vol. 3336: D. Karagiannis, U. Reimer (Eds.), Practical Aspects of Knowledge Management. X, 523 pages. 2004. (Subseries LNAI).

Vol. 3335: M. Malek, M. Reitenspieß, J. Kaiser (Eds.), Service Availability. X, 213 pages. 2005.

Vol. 3334: Z. Chen, H. Chen, Q. Miao, Y. Fu, E. Fox, E.-p. Lim (Eds.), Digital Libraries: International Collaboration and Cross-Fertilization. XX, 690 pages. 2004.

Vol. 3333: K. Aizawa, Y. Nakamura, S. Satoh (Eds.), Advances in Multimedia Information Processing - PCM 2004, Part III. XXXV, 785 pages. 2004.

Vol. 3332: K. Aizawa, Y. Nakamura, S. Satoh (Eds.), Advances in Multimedia Information Processing - PCM 2004, Part II. XXXVI, 1051 pages. 2004.

Vol. 3331: K. Aizawa, Y. Nakamura, S. Satoh (Eds.), Advances in Multimedia Information Processing - PCM 2004, Part I. XXXVI, 667 pages. 2004.

Vol. 3330: J. Akiyama, E.T. Baskoro, M. Kano (Eds.), Combinatorial Geometry and Graph Theory. VIII, 227 pages. 2005.

Vol. 3329: P.J. Lee (Ed.), Advances in Cryptology - ASIACRYPT 2004. XVI, 546 pages. 2004.

Vol. 3328: K. Lodaya, M. Mahajan (Eds.), FSTTCS 2004: Foundations of Software Technology and Theoretical Computer Science. XVI, 532 pages. 2004.

Vol. 3327: Y. Shi, W. Xu, Z. Chen (Eds.), Data Mining and Knowledge Management. XIII, 263 pages. 2005. (Subseries LNAI).

Vol. 3326: A. Sen, N. Das, S.K. Das, B.P. Sinha (Eds.), Distributed Computing - IWDC 2004. XIX, 546 pages. 2004.

Vol. 3325: C.H. Lim, M. Yung (Eds.), Information Security Applications. XI, 472 pages. 2005.

Vol. 3323: G. Antoniou, H. Boley (Eds.), Rules and Rule Markup Languages for the Semantic Web. X, 215 pages. 2004.

Vol. 3322: R. Klette, J. Žunić (Eds.), Combinatorial Image Analysis. XII, 760 pages. 2004.

Vol. 3321: M.J. Maher (Ed.), Advances in Computer Science - ASIAN 2004. Higher-Level Decision Making. XII, 510 pages. 2004.

Vol. 3320: K.-M. Liew, H. Shen, S. See, W. Cai (Eds.), Parallel and Distributed Computing: Applications and Technologies. XXIV, 891 pages. 2004.

Vol. 3319: D. Amyot, A.W. Williams (Eds.), System Analysis and Modeling. XII, 301 pages. 2005.

Vol. 3318: E. Eskin, C. Workman (Eds.), Regulatory Genomics. VIII, 115 pages. 2005. (Subseries LNBI).

Vol. 3317: M. Domaratzki, A. Okhotin, K. Salomaa, S. Yu (Eds.), Implementation and Application of Automata. XII, 336 pages. 2005.

Vol. 3316: N.R. Pal, N.K. Kasabov, R.K. Mudi, S. Pal, S.K. Parui (Eds.), Neural Information Processing. XXX, 1368 pages. 2004.

Vol. 3315: C. Lemaître, C.A. Reyes, J.A. González (Eds.), Advances in Artificial Intelligence – IBERAMIA 2004. XX, 987 pages. 2004. (Subseries LNAI).

Vol. 3314: J. Zhang, J.-H. He, Y. Fu (Eds.), Computational and Information Science. XXIV, 1259 pages. 2004.

Vol. 3313: C. Castelluccia, H. Hartenstein, C. Paar, D. Westhoff (Eds.), Security in Ad-hoc and Sensor Networks. VIII, 231 pages. 2005.

Vol. 3312: A.J. Hu, A.K. Martin (Eds.), Formal Methods in Computer-Aided Design. XI, 445 pages. 2004.

Vol. 3311: V. Roca, F. Rousseau (Eds.), Interactive Multimedia and Next Generation Networks. XIII, 287 pages. 2004.

Vol. 3310: U.K. Wiil (Ed.), Computer Music Modeling and Retrieval. XI, 371 pages. 2005.

Vol. 3309: C.-H. Chi, K.-Y. Lam (Eds.), Content Computing. XII, 510 pages. 2004.

Vol. 3308: J. Davies, W. Schulte, M. Barnett (Eds.), Formal Methods and Software Engineering. XIII, 500 pages. 2004.

Vol. 3307: C. Bussler, S.-k. Hong, W. Jun, R. Kaschek, D.. Kinshuk, S. Krishnaswamy, S.W. Loke, D. Oberle, D. Richards, A. Sharma, Y. Sure, B. Thalheim (Eds.), Web Information Systems – WISE 2004 Workshops. XV, 277 pages. 2004.